SAN JOSÉ DE GRACIA

Mexican Village in Transition

THE TEXAS PAN AMERICAN SERIES

UNIVERSITY OF TEXAS PRESS, AUSTIN

San José de Gracia

MEXICAN VILLAGE IN TRANSITION

By LUIS GONZALEZ

Translated by John Upton

Copyright © 1974 by El Colegio de México
All rights reserved
Printed in the United States of America
Fifth Paperback Printing, 1998

Translated from *Pueblo en vilo: Microhistoria de San José de Gracia* by
  Luis González
© 1972 by El Colegio de México

Requests for permission to reproduce material from this work should be
sent to Permissions, University of Texas Press, Box 7819, Austin, Texas
78713-7819.

⊗ The paper used in this publication meets the minimum
requirements of American National Standard for Information Sciences—
Permanence of Paper for Printed Library Materials, ANSI Z39.48-1984.

Library of Congress Cataloging in Publication Data
González y González, Luis.
  San José de Gracia: Mexican village in transition.
  (The Texas pan-American series)
  Translation of the 2d ed. of Pueblo en vilo.
  Bibliography: p.
  1. San José de Gracia (Michoacán)   I. Title.
F1391.S1865G613   972'.3   73-11495
ISBN 0-292-77571-7 (paper)

CONTENTS

Part Two. Thirty Years of Suffering

Part Three. Twenty-five Years of Change

PLATES
(*Following page* 244)

The Plaza of San José de Gracia
Don Andrés González Pulido
Don Gregorio González Pulido
A Group of *Cristeros*
Don Juan Gudiño
Don David Sánchez
Don Guadalupe González Buenrostro
Don Honorato González Buenrostro
Don José Martínez and His Wife
The Kitchen of Doña Inés Betancourt
Traditional House
Modern House
Animal Transport
Farmers at the Entrance to the Village Offices
The Parish Church
Doña Rosa González Cárdenas
General Lázaro Cárdenas
The Primary School

Contents

Padre Federico González Cárdenas
Don Agustín Arriaga Rivera
Street Scene

M A P S

Abbreviations Appearing in Text and Footnotes

AC	Acción Católica
ACJM	Acción Católica de la Juventud Mexicana
ACNC	Archivo de la Confederación Nacional Campesina (Mexico City)
ADAAC	Archivo del Departamento de Asuntos Agrarios y Colonización (Mexico City)
AGNM	Archivo General de la Nación (Mexico City)
AJJ	*See* ANJ
AJTO	Archivo de la Jefatura de la Tenencia de Ornelas (San José de Gracia, Michoacán)
AMS	Archivo Histórico del Municipio de Sahuayo (Sahuayo, Michoacán)
ANJ	Archivo de Notarías del Distrito de Jiquilpan (Jiquilpan, Michoacán)
APC	Archivo Parroquial de Cojumatlán (Cojumatlán, Michoacán)
APM	Archivo Parroquial de Mazamitla (Mazamitla, Jalisco)
APS	Archivo Parroquial de Sahuayo (Sahuayo, Michoacán)
APSJ	Archivo Parroquial de San José de Gracia (San José de Gracia, Michoacán)
ASRO	Archivo de la Subreceptoría de Rentas de Ornelas (San José de Gracia, Michoacán)
DAAC	Departamento de Asuntos Agrarios y Colonización
INPI	Instituto Nacional de Protección a la Infancia
PAN	Partido de Acción Nacional

PNE	Papeles de la Nueva España
PPS	Partido Popular Socialista
PRI	Partido Revolucionario Institucional
UCM	Unión Católica Mexicana
UFCM	Unión Femenina Católica Mexicana

PROLOGUE

A Delimitation and Justification of the Subject

The parish, or *municipio*, of San José de Gracia, the subject of this study, is not mentioned in any history of Mexico, nor is it even referred to in any of the annals of the state of Michoacán. It is not to be found at all on most maps, and nearly none show its correct location: at the intersection of the 20th parallel and the 103d meridian. It is an unknown point in space, in time, and in the consciousness of the Mexican republic.

This history concerns a very small area, comprising 231 square kilometers. It is slightly larger than the combined territories of two principalities (Liechtenstein and Monaco), a republic (San Marino), and the Vatican City State. The choice of such a small area may at first glance seem whimsical, and it is certainly unjustifiable from a geographical standpoint. The fragment selected is only the fourth or fifth part of a plateau lying two thousand meters above sea level. Viewed historically, however, it can claim to be a separate entity. On the same plateau, there are five other communities similar to San José, but they are, after all, not identical. Together they make up what is very nearly a separate region—although it may not appear so in any of the attempts at regional classification that have been made to date by the republic.

The geographical limitations of the theme are in obvious contrast to its chronological amplitude. It is a history covering four centuries: from the sixteenth to the present. It ignores pre-Hispanic history, which lies beyond its compass and is nearly nonexistent. It is interested

only slightly in the three colonial centuries. Life before 1800 is regarded only as an antecedent. The community we have to deal with
here came into being just before and during the War for Independence. In other words, the span of this work is a little more than a
century and a half.

There are not many people in it, either. Before the revolution
there were more than three thousand inhabitants, but during that
struggle there were considerable losses. Since then the plant has shot
up wildly; there are now more than eight thousand people, not counting those who have emigrated. In a word, a small amount of humanity
in a little space and a short time.

Furthermore: no event has ever taken place on the San Joséan
stage that was important enough to raise dust anywhere but in the
immediate neighborhood. No important battle was ever fought there;
no "convention" of belligerent forces or "revolutionary plan" bears
its name. The community has produced no figure of stature in state
or national circles, no personage in politics, letters, or the military.
It has borne no gaudy fruit and has been the scene of no memorable
incident. It would seem to represent historical insignificance at its
purest, to be an area absolutely unworthy of attention, an immaculate
nullity: unproductive land, plodding lives, undistinguished inhabitants. Smallness, but typical smallness.

In its typicalness lies its strength. The selected historical area is
neither influential nor transcendent, but it is certainly typical. Everything it is and has been can also be said of many tiny, orphaned mestizo communities in the mountainous regions of central Mexico. Life
in San José, in not being unique, in being a conglomerate of others,
in presenting a broad section of the national subconscious, may perhaps be of interest in academic circles, thus justifying the present
study.

The community chosen is not, of course, the most typical in the
entire Mexican republic. In fact, it was selected not because it was
considered typical, but because it was felt to be out of the ordinary.
Any village seems ordinary until it is examined closely and deliberately, with love. When—as in the present case—one moves in closer,
filled with sympathy, he discovers that each village has its originality,

its individuality, its peculiar mission and destiny, and he forgets what it has in common with other communities.

The subject of this study is interesting for another reason: it remained isolated from the nation's mainstream until quite recently, when it took an unforeseen course and joined the central river that is Mexico. In short, the choice of San José de Gracia as the subject for a historical study does not seem to have been an unlucky one.

The career of a community, no matter how tiny, suggests themes for research, even though they may not be as numerous or as valuable as those relating to urban life; but precisely because they are few and simple and modest, they are more manageable. This study is an attempt to tell the history of the world of San José de Gracia. It leaves out very little; what it has had to exclude or consider only superficially are those things that have left no trace in the form of documents, monuments, or memories. On the other hand, it includes matters that apparently lie outside the central theme. It was not always within the writer's power to decide what should be embraced and what should be ignored in this history. The superabundance, scarcity, or nonexistence of various sources of information forced him at times to write more or less than he would have liked on one subject or another.

One aspect that was deliberately treated rather fully was the geographical one. The idea here was that there exists an intimate relationship between natural surroundings and rural life. In view of this preconception—which was borne out by the facts—there will be found frequent references to geographical constants and weather cycles. We shall mention the soil, flora and fauna, floods, droughts, earthquakes, comets, epidemics, and endemics. We shall not ignore the yearly change of seasons, or the ten- and thirty-year cycles—so vitally important in cereal-producing areas, but much less so in regions devoted to cattle raising, such as San José.

Neither weather cycles nor figures have much meaning here. The latter are unimportant, probably, because, as Paul Leuilliot says, "local history is qualitative, not quantitative,"[1] because it is a field in which

[1] "Défense et illustration de l'histoire locale," *Annales* (*Economies, sociétés, civilisations*), 22nd year, no. 1 (January–February), p. 157.

statistics count for very little. However, in order not to disregard the current mania, an unreasonable amount of quantification has been done, and here and there long, terrible rows of numbers have crept in.

These people's lives have often been subject to pressures from without, for they do not live at all in the same way as those who govern them. Their existence has a different essence and rhythm. In order to gauge the distance that separates them from those in the vanguard of state and national affairs and to see how disturbing the pressure has been, it has seemed necessary to say something concerning those political elements. For this reason, before reviewing the lower-case events of local life within each period, I have sketched the capital events of national life, as well as some incidents, set in medium-sized type, in the career of the state of Michoacán.

With these limitations and excursions, I have attempted to write the history of the world of San José. In it we shall turn our eyes in every direction: toward what is lasting and what is ephemeral, everyday and unusual, material and spiritual. There is a little of everything: retrospective demography, economics, and various aspects of social life (the family, groups, classes, work and leisure, bullying, the wild masculine pride known as *machismo*, alcoholism, and folklore). There will be found a complete account of the vicissitudes connected with the ownership of land. Although political life has not been really very vigorous, it has not been excluded; the antipolitical attitude has been fully treated, and there is an occasional flirtation with public officials. Military comings and goings are described, too. We have not missed the chance to tell of battles that took place in the area or in which men from San José took part.

The religious phenomenon is central, although it has undergone little change. From the beginning until today, everyone in San José and its jurisdiction has been a faithful Catholic. No cases of heterodoxy or apostasy have ever been recorded. We are in the presence of a faith so firm that it does not permit even tolerance of any other. Although there have been only superficial changes in religious life, the leaders of the community have nearly always been men of the cloth, and, to defend them and the institution they represent, the men of San José have been willing to kill and be killed.

It was not possible to consider the ideas, beliefs, and attitudes concerning the outside world, nature, history, life, death, money, comfort, modernity, and tradition for every period. Nor was it feasible to undertake a complete history of collective woes. It is unquestionably easier to trace physical vicissitudes than psychological ones.

Most microhistories written by the old guard end with a list of the famous people who came from the area in question. Those of the New Wave, however, dispense with names, in the belief that individuals in small communities are of no importance. Here we have gone to neither extreme. There seemed to be no point in mentioning the very few persons who made names for themselves in the outside world, such as soldiers, politicians, or writers. However, many people are referred to by name, and there are lists and biographical sketches of the founding fathers and of those individuals who made notable contributions to the progress or regress of San José.

Since this history does not pretend to subscribe to the tenets of "historical materialism," here the mass does not replace the individual. Nor has it fallen into the opposite extreme of hero worship. This is neither an anonymous history nor a collection of biographies. About the same amount of attention has been directed toward the individual as toward the multitude. No great effort has been made to eliminate anecdotes—which can at least be amusing. I have, however, tried to include only those that seemed most meaningful, even when they were not the most entertaining.

Every history is necessarily incomplete. The chosen social unit, which comprehends all those individuals who are not called "outsiders," offers an inexhaustible fund of material. Its story is, to some extent, the story of rural life anywhere, in any age; to a lesser degree it is peculiar to the world of the peasant all through Mexico's history; and perhaps in some ways it can be said to be true only of San José.

Some Remarks on Method

It seems that in the process of writing a history limited to a small area one must utilize every recourse of historical methodology—and several others as well. In this kind of research, one encounters a great many obstacles at every stage—some of them peculiar to the discipline. Two problems come up at the very beginning. One cannot simply set to work, as in other fields of history, with the prescribed accouterment of set patterns, prepared questionnaires, working hypotheses, and models. In the present case, I set out with no model in mind; I did not even draw up a list of subjects, or of questions that ought to be answered. I entered the field with a minimum of preconceptions and prejudices, with a great deal of sympathy, and with some antipathies.

It has been asserted that the history of no small community can be written, because the essential documents are missing. As everyone knows, the events of country and village life usually leave few traces; moreover, the evidence tends to get lost, misplaced, and dispersed. In the case of San José, the losses, mislaying, and scattering have been considerable. In the first place, there are no newspaper sources. With a few rare and unrewarding exceptions, happenings in San José have never made the national or provincial dailies. No kind of periodical has ever been published in the village, not even a parish bulletin.

Whatever information could be extracted from national and regional chronicles was used in the historical sketches that appear at the beginning of this work and accompany each of its chapters. For factual matter, two books were very useful: *Bosquejo estadístico e histórico del distrito de Jiquilpan de Juárez* [A statistical and historical sketch of the District of Jiquilpan], written by Don Ramón Sánchez in 1896, and *Quitupan*, a recent work by Don Esteban Chávez. Much more was learned from nonhistorical writings, although the footnotes may not give that impression. A debt must be acknowledged to Agustín Yáñez for his *Al filo del agua* [The edge of the storm] and *Las tierras flacas* [The lean lands], to Juan José Arreola for *La feria* [The fair], and to Juan Rulfo for *El llano en llamas* [The burning plain] and *Pedro Páramo*.

Documentation through manuscripts was not extensive; for the most part, they were hard to find. I rummaged with some success through the National General Archives and the files of the Department of Agrarian Affairs and the National Farm Confederation; through court and notary documents in Jiquilpan, town records in Sahuayo and San José de Gracia, and church registers in Sahuayo, Cojumatlán, Mazamitla, and San José, and half a dozen private collections. It would be pointless to list the places where a search turned up nothing, or to mention the files that were closed to me. Perhaps this observation is worth making: the number of documents that have been lost seems to be much greater than the number of those that are still available. It is no exaggeration when people deplore the disgraceful condition of local and regional archives.

The lands division of the National General Archives supplied records concerning land grants conceded to the first usufructuaries in the area, the setting up of a vast latifundium incorporating those grants, and successive changes in ownership of the property during colonial times. In the historical division of the same archives, some notes of a statistical nature from the last third of the eighteenth century showed up.

Some extremely interesting items in the files of the Department of Agrarian Affairs served as the basis for the chapter on agrarian reform in the thirties. It may be added that consulting these and the National General Archives was greatly facilitated by the proper classification and cataloguing of their contents, the expert staffs, and the cooperation of their directors.

The chaotic Notarial Archives in Jiquilpan would have remained inaccessible without the assistance of the Judge of First Instance, Licenciado Julián Luviano. He put a couple of boys to work removing the huge masses of paper that had been piled in a damp room overrun with scorpions, spiders, tarantulas, and a thousand other bugs. Then he did everything he could to help bring some order to that mountain of records. Thanks to his efforts, it was possible to reconstruct, on the basis of notaries' books of registry and other documents, the history of landownership in the jurisdiction of San José from the point where the lode ran out in the National General Archives, at the end of the eighteenth century, up to the present time.

There was no luck to be had with municipal records. Sahuayo's are crammed into a latrine in the jail. By mere chance, I found in that compact mass a few volumes recording transactions among people from the last third of the nineteenth century. In Cojumatlán they keep files only from the previous year. Jiquilpan's city records were destroyed by the *cristeros* in 1927, and none have been kept since. The oldest documents to be found in San José de Gracia's Jefatura de Tenencia date from 1933. Thanks to the kindness of Elías Elizondo and Jorge Partida, respectively chief and secretary of the *tenencia*, I was able to examine all of these.

Parish registers turned out to be the principal written source for the history of San José. For the period 1718–1822, the records in Sahuayo were consulted; for the years 1823–1888, the registry in Cojumatlán was useful; from 1888 on, data were taken from the volumes of baptisms, deaths, and marriages in San José de Gracia. Other information was obtained in Mazamitla. I am grateful for the assistance of three parish priests: Antonio Méndez of Cojumatlán, José Santana García of Mazamitla, and Carlos Moreno of San José.

As for private collections: the late Don José Dolores Pulido's account books, papers of various kinds accumulated by my mother, the *cristero* diary kept by Don Bernardo González Cárdenas, photograph albums belonging to Arcelia Sánchez and Honorato González, the many documents saved by Doña Rosa González Cárdenas, and the magnificent library and archives of Professor José Ramírez Flores were all extremely useful. Licenciado Bernardo González Godínez provided me with some most important papers and made useful observations of many kinds. The private records belonging to my mother, Doña Josefiría González Cárdenas, were particularly fruitful. They included documents concerning local religious organizations, as well as an abundant correspondence. Among all these papers was one thing I found very valuable: her notebooks containing records of household expenses. She has kept them without interruption for sixty years.

The techniques of formal interrogation were not used in recording oral tradition and the life of today. We conversed without questionnaires; our interviews had no agenda. This kind of informal discussion with country people turned out to be extremely productive. Of my hundred or so informants, none gave me more information than my father, Don Luis González Cárdenas, who has an excellent memory and has always been fascinated by recollection of the past.

Much of what I have to relate concerning events since 1932 or 1933 I did not read or hear; I saw it with my own eyes. Generally speaking, the introduction of this book is based on written sources, the first four chapters on oral tradition, and the remainder on my own experience.

I shall comment very briefly on my remaining historiographic procedures. I did not fall into those traps anticipated by so many researchers in the field: fabrication and duplicity. It was not very difficult to recognize and discount lies and pranks. I was able to evaluate broad sections of oral tradition by means of collation with documents. When there were no reliable written records to substantiate a given oral account, I accepted the verdict of collective memory. But what took more time than any of this detective work was the process of understanding: trying to rethink and refeel what the protagonists in San José's history had thought and felt. My fondness for my subject— or, if you will, my sympathy—was enormously helpful in this.

This book is not free from my own interpretation. Although its point of departure was George Trevelyan's thesis ("In history we are interested not only in causal relationships between events, but also in the events themselves," or words to that effect),[2] the writer has not neglected explication: the "necessary explanation by means of final causes," as it has been called, and, to a greater extent, explanation by efficient causes.

Among possible architectures for regional history, two of the most popular are the chronological and the sectorial. Village scholars prefer the first. Thus, they are able to take in ephemeral events, but those with more lasting effects escape them. They give their readers a sense of change, but no picture of the community that lives through or sets in motion those changes. Professional historians take the opposite tack. They distribute their material according to duration and cultural sectors. They offer a great deal in the way of separate expositions of demographic, economic, social, political, and psychological structures;

[2] Cf. Bertrand Russell, *Retratos de memoria y otros ensayos*, p. 171.

but they give little space to the conjunctive aspect, and none, or almost none, to the isolated event.

I have tried to find a structure into which can be fitted, without too much forcing, the slow and the rapid, the tiny and the huge, the chronological and the sectorial. This architecture may not be harmonious or even symmetrical, but it is quite functional. Besides, it is very simple. It makes use of the two time-honored frameworks: the temporal and the systematic. The first is the basic one. To begin with, the material has been divided into periods of unequal size: three hundred, fifty, thirty, and twenty-five years. Subdivisions within the three-hundred-year period are not very sharply defined; the others have been broken up in accordance with Ortega y Gasset's theory of generations. Each period has been sliced twice: longitudinally and transversely. Along the first cross section lies the narration of events, while in the second is presented the description of structure. At any given moment four planes are being considered (socioeconomic, political, psychological, and that of external relationships), but they do not always appear in that order, nor are they examined with the same degree of attention. It seemed desirable to keep the architecture in tune with the landscape, and not to allow it to disturb the actual interrelationships.

Local history, like biography, seems nearer to literature than do the other branches of historiography; this may be because concrete existence demands a literary treatment, or perhaps because the local historian's reading public is allergic to the dry style of most contemporary historians. The compiler of parochial history should be a man of letters. I should have liked to employ the kind of speech used in the community I was studying. I tried to do this, but when I reread the manuscript I realized that in San José people do not talk that way.

Self-Defense, Self-Criticism, and Aims

According to Professor Finberg, the parochial historian needs maturity, wide reading, a great deal of sympathy, and good legs.[3] By maturity, Finberg means a long and varied experience with men,

---

[3] Herbert P. R. Finberg, *Approaches to History*, pp. 124–125.

an acquaintance with many different modes of existence. As for reading, he recommends, among other things, books on national and international history. He calls for sympathy because only like can know
like, and because one can learn a great deal about something only if he
loves it. Sturdy legs are needed because the village historian must walk
back and forth, over and over again, covering his study site and calling in person on the greatest possible number of local inhabitants.

I was lucky enough to have put Finberg's principles into practice,
to some extent, before I had heard of them. Without really trying,
I have attained the age of forty-two, and I have spent considerable
time, willingly or otherwise, in various surroundings and occupations.
For five years I taught a course in the history of culture, and, in order
to do it even passably well, I had to read several histories of the human
race. In addition, I have been asked on several occasions to teach Mexican history and thus have read quite a bit in the field.

Before undertaking the present investigation, I knew only a handful of writers of local history, and all of them were of the old school.
In the process of my research I became acquainted with some others—
but not (I regret to say) with the great contemporary authors from
France, England, and the United States. Deep in my hole, far from
libraries and bookstores, I had no chance to learn of the new currents
in microhistoriography; these could have helped me in my handling
of panoramic views, and, besides, they would have brought me up to
date as far as parochial history is concerned.

My natural myopia made up, to some extent, for this lack of previous erudition. I love tiny facts; I rejoice in the details despised by
great minds; I enjoy examining small things that are invisible to
those who are endowed with wings and the eyes of eagles. I suppose
Professor Finberg will approve of the fact that I am nearsighted and
pedestrian by nature.

I made excursions on foot and on horseback; I traveled in all directions across the land from which springs the history I shall tell here;
and, as I have said, I talked with villagers and people in the country.

The idea of writing this book came to me during a sabbatical leave
granted by the Colegio de México in 1967. I had seven months to explore the archives mentioned above; to read works that would be of

immediate use to me; to visit, one by one, the settlements within the
tenencia of San José; to talk with people; to keep my eyes open and
see as much as I could; and to listen to sounds and echoes.

My center of operations was a large old house in the village. One
entered the house through a short, broad corridor that opened onto an
interior porch surrounding a garden. In the center of the patio was a
well with a stone rim, and, at one side, a fountain of glazed tiles. The
most luxuriant plant in the garden was a *granada de china*, in whose
shade many rose bushes, begonias, and *belenes* had died. Some other
plants, not under that canopy, had survived. The porch, with its slant-
ing roof, enclosed three sides of the patio. The floors were of tile. The
bedrooms, the living room, and the dining room—all large—opened
onto the porch. Behind the house lay the *ecuaro*, where there were
growing a couple of each of the following trees and plants: peach,
avocado, loquat, lime, piñon pine, apricot, maguey, prickly pear, fig,
pomegranate, and palm. At the back of the property stood the store-
house and stable, housing two horses, two cows with their calves,
half a dozen pigs, and a dozen chickens.

From the room where I worked I could look out on a panorama of
red tile roofs, the church towers, the town square, Larios Mountain,
and the blue sky. I assembled my material and wrote in the quiet hours
of the early morning: from four until nine. In the afternoon, Armida
took what had been written that morning, corrected mistakes, suggested improvements, made any changes she deemed necessary, and
began to type. Because of Armida I cannot assume sole responsibility
for these notes.

In another sense, too, I was not entirely the author of the book. In
the introduction, put together with material from other places and
other times, I think of myself more as an amanuensis, putting written
statements into some kind of order, assembling old attestations with
scissors and paste. As for the first and second parts, my function has
been that of an interpreter of my fellow townsmen's views of their
own past; I feel like the village's official chronicler, compiling and
reconstructing a collective memory. In the last part I abandon the roles
of laborer and intermediary; I put in my oar and begin giving opinions. This is, of course, the part of the book that is most subjective,

most exclusively mine—although perhaps not the most attractive to my readers.

These notes were not intended—in the beginning, at least—for an academic public. During the research and writing I kept my neighbors in mind more than I did my colleagues. I see no reason to regret having made that choice, if only because, as Azorín said, "the admiration of modest people is just as much worth having as that of celebrities."

As things stand today, local history can be sure of only a local reading public. People in villages and on farms do not buy books to build libraries or adorn their elegant living rooms; and they do not read them, or merely begin them, or only leaf through them in order to give the impression of being cultured, as many city people do.

If a farmer buys a book, he reads it from cover to cover, and lends it to his friends. Often several neighbors will gather to hear it read aloud. The present work will not sell as well as some others with academic prestige, but it will undoubtedly have more readers. I believe that my book will be read and listened to by thousands of people, for I am sure of the local patriotism in my native region and of the curiosity among the inhabitants of the surrounding parishes.

The local historian's rustic and limited reading public is attractive in another way: it is steadfast. Among city dwellers, most authors (except for the classic writers who are read by certain select souls because they love them, and by students because they must) are soon forgotten; their books go out of style overnight. But when someone publishes a few mediocre or badly written pages about a village, in that village they are read and reread; they are apt to become local classics. One can be sure that they will be a subject of passionate study for generations, or as long as the village endures.

But it would be misleading on my part to declare that I hope for the approval only of those to whom this book is directly addressed. I should be pleased if it proved to be useful beyond the borders of the plateau known as La Meseta del Tigre, beyond the limits of San José and the other towns that are its friends and rivals. Moved by this desire for recognition, I submitted my manuscript to the Seminario de Profesores e Investigadores del Centro de Estudios Históricos at the Colegio de México. Several teachers, friends, and students read it and gave me their comments. Many of their suggestions have been followed. My debt to teachers Daniel Cosío Villegas, José Gaos, and Víctor L. Urquidi is a very great one. I have many reasons to be grateful also to my colleagues María del Carmen Velázquez, Jan Bazant, Romeo Flores, Enrique Florescano, Bernardo García, Moisés González Navarro, Roque González Salazar, Jorge Alberto Manrique, Jean Meyer, Alejandro Moreno Toscano, Luis Muro, Rafael Segovia, Berta Ulloa, and Josefina Vázquez de Knauth.

NOTE CONCERNING THE SECOND EDITION

The kind reception accorded the 1968 edition, as well as my discovery of additional private records and individuals with good memories, has prompted this second edition of *Pueblo en vilo*, with its amplifications, deletions, and corrections. At the suggestion of the critic Fernando Díaz, the French translator Anny Meyer, and other friends, Part One has been considerably abridged and retitled "Three Beginnings." The original Part Two (now Part One) contains two new paragraphs; the present Part Two, seven new paragraphs; and Part Three, eleven. The "Small Epilogue," now much more substantial, has been rechristened as "Three Conclusions." Errors in events and dates have been rectified, and certain equivocal statements have been amended so as to leave no room for doubt. For the new photographs I am indebted to the kindness and skill of Israel Katzman.

SAN JOSÉ DE GRACIA

Mexican Village in Transition

Three Beginnings

The Mountain Landscape

The plateau lying at the intersection of the 20th parallel and the 103d meridian, where the states of Jalisco and Michoacán now meet along the western section of the Volcanic Axis, rose from the sea in the dawn of the Cenozoic. It took on its present configuration as the result of two spectacular episodes. The first was "a vigorous volcanism covering the original fold with enormous cones and great streams of lava." The second consisted of "a series of four floods" that produced a "sculpturing of the land, interrupted only by dry periods occurring between the stormy glacial epochs." Water shifted masses of loose rock and filled the valleys; the cones were planed off; and the rivers cut fissures and vast gorges from which hot springs still gush today.[1]

According to a "Relación de Xiquilpa y su partido" [Report on the township of Jiquilpan], written in 1579, "west of Jiquilpan stand some high, rolling hills, covered with sparse vegetation."[2] The area measures fifteen leagues from east to west, and five from north to south: that is, a little less than 580 square miles. It is a rolling table-

---

[1] Severo Díaz, "La desecación del lago de Chapala," *Boletín de la Junta Auxiliar Jalisciense de la Sociedad Mexicana de Geografía y Estadística*, 10 (September–October 1956): 13–18.

[2] *Relaciones geográficas de la diócesis de Michoacán*, I, 9.

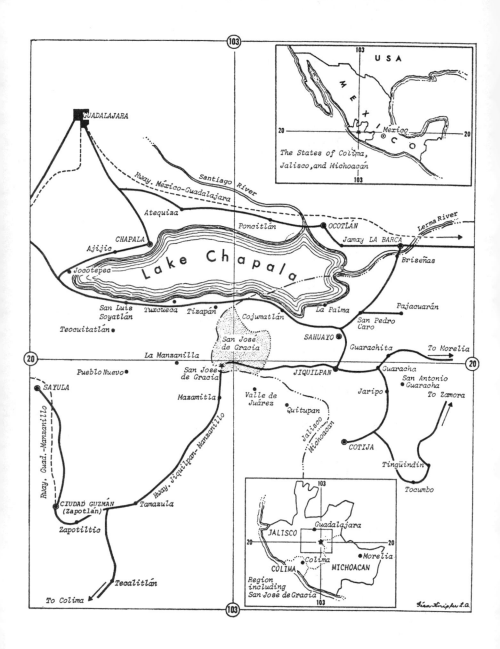

The States of Colima, Jalisco, and Michoacán

Region including San José de Gracia

land 6,500 feet above sea level and 1,650 feet above the waters of Lake Chapala, to which it descends on the north. To the south it rises to "the steep and rugged" mountain range where the village of Maza-mitla lies.[3] On the west, after dropping 2,300 feet, it meets the Sayula basin; and on the east it slopes down to the valley of Jiquilpan.

In short, this high, undulating expanse lies between a mountain range and a crescent of lacustrine lowlands. Lake Chapala is "fifteen leagues long, with fresh, clean water; it is like a sea, even in its storms."[4] The "Chapalic Sea" stretches out to the southeast in a train of swamps, lakes, and valleys. On the southwest it overlooks a "vast basin that in the rainy season is largely covered with briny water, and in the dry season exposes extensive saltpeter flats."[5] Both horns of the crescent contain areas that are "very fertile and grassy, with abun-dant crops of corn, chili, and beans," and every kind of "the unusual fruits of this country," such as *guamúchil*, guava, avocado, plums, and white and dark sapodilla.[6] Throughout the entire silver-and-bronze crescent the climate is "more hot than cold."[7] The Tigre Range, where "it is very cold," is covered with vast pine forests; there are found "a very good clear honey" and "some little creatures resembling martens."[8]

The plateau has no large hills or extensive areas of level terrain; it is neither the austere sierra nor the gentle plain. A swift and capri-cious river has cut a deep gash in it from north to south. Several creeks, also at the bottom of ravines, flow into the river. Thus, it is a rolling landscape marked with fissures. In the dry season, mere trick-les of water follow the gullies; but after the heavy summer storms the river and its creeks become wild, deafening torrents. Much of the water in the lakes and swamps of the surrounding crescent originates on the geographic stage where this story takes place.

[3] Ibid., II, 101.

[4] Alonso de la Mota y Escobar, *Descripción geográfica de los reinos de Nueva Galicia, Nueva Vizcaya y Nuevo León*, pp. 57–60.

[5] *Relación breve y verdadera de algunas de las cosas que sucedieron al padre fray Alonso Ponce . . .*, II, 21.

[6] *Relaciones geográficas de la diócesis de Michoacán*, II, 90.

[7] Ibid., I, 8.

[8] *Relación breve y verdadera*, II, 22.

In this country there are two seasons: the dry one, from October to May, and four months of the rains. The wet season is all water and thunder. About thirty-one inches of rain fall in a normal year. Nearly "every day when the sun passes the meridian, dark clouds gather, there is a great deal of thunder and lightning, and it begins to rain ... which continues until nightfall" in brief, successive showers.[9] Yet it is not a damp region, much less a tropical one; all the water runs off into Lake Chapala. Toward the end of October the winds from Colima begin to blow; the clouds dissipate; the green of the earth turns to grayish yellow; and the overcast sky changes to blue. Gold at your feet and blue above are the colors of the dry season.

It is never very hot, or terribly cold. The climate is a little short of temperate. According to the system proposed by Wilhelm Koeppen, it could be described by the formula CWb: rainy temperate, with rainfall in summer; mean temperature during the hottest month below 71.5° F., and that of the coldest month slightly above 50°. December and January are the coldest months, May and June the warmest. At three o'clock on the hottest afternoon the thermometer seldom reaches 86°. On some winter nights the temperature drops below freezing. Frosts are not unusual, and some years there are icy rains, known as *aguasnieves* or *cabañuelas*. In short, it is a cool, windy land, with a brief, stormy rainy season, a long dry season, and "a glistening light that makes the face of heaven gleam." Many places have aspired to be called "the most transparent region of the air," but very few have merited the designation as richly as this plateau.

From a farmer's point of view, it is not desirable land; wind and water erode it easily; it is poor in organic matter and phosphates, poorer still in nitrogen; and, to make matters worse, it is rocky. Far from being the ideal cattle-raising country with grass three feet high, its brown earth is barely concealed by a carpet of scrub vegetation. It is neither farming land nor forest. A gravelly, mediocre soil, with no fields to invite the plow: only prairies suitable for shepherds and cowboys.

This dry, windy, rolling, glistening tableland wears a sober vege-

---

[9] Domingo Lázaro de Arregui, *Descripción de la Nueva Galicia*, pp. 23–25.

table cloak. No flashy verdure. A good number of knotty trees and bushes protected by thorns; a large quantity of grass and creeping, aromatic plants; these are the green patrimony of that landscape, "not without a certain aristocratic sterility."[10] During the dry months, it is the hostile aspect of the vegetation one notices most: maguey, nopal, thornbushes, *tepame*, cat's claw, white oak, and live oak. During the rainy season, the nutritive aspect appears: pasture grass. Then, when the rains are over, one is aware of the gay aspect: poppies, sunflowers, and a thousand bright colors and aromas.

Prominent among the abundant fauna are the destructive mammals: mountain lions or *huindoros*, wildcats, raccoons, wild pigs, foxes, squirrels, rats, armadillos, deer, wolves, and coyotes; the high-flying ovipara: eagles, hawks, swifts, larks, quail, thrushes, and hummingbirds; venomous reptiles (rattlesnakes, hognoses, coral snakes) and harmless ones (*alicantes* and lizards); the amphibians (frogs, toads, and turtles); and uncountable stink bugs, fireflies, ants, crickets, spiders, grasshoppers, mites, bees, wasps, flies, mosquitoes, worms, beetles, and earwigs. Until the second half of the sixteenth century, there were no domestic animals and very few human beings.

The high, undulating terrain, the seasonal and torrential rains, the flood of light, the semiarid-semifrigid climate, the sober and thorny vegetation, and the hostile and destructive fauna were not to the liking of the agricultural peoples of Middle America. Nor was the landscape mountainous enough to attract the hunters. Perhaps this explains why neither the Tarascans, who were being pushed to the east in the valleys and mountains of Michoacán, nor the Tecos, who were so numerous in the Sayula and Zapotlán basins, nor the fishing people of Lake Chapala, nor the savage Chichimecas, who used to raid the villages along the lake shore, had ever made any use of the rolling mesa. Half a dozen toponyms (Churintzio, Ahuanato, Achuen, Cuspio, Bembérecua, and Juruneo), a trio of tombs in the vicinity of San José, traces of dwellings scattered along the slopes of Larios Mountain and on Colongo Hill, some earthenware pots here and there, an occasional piece of sculpture, and a great many arrowheads everywhere,

[10] Alfonso Reyes, *Visión de Anáhuac.*

suggest the proximity of pre-Hispanic villages, if not any permanent and massive Indian occupation of the area. These phenomena tell us that, while the mesa may not have been the site of any permanent settlement, it was traveled and used as a battleground. Although no archaeologist has given his opinion as to the artifacts unearthed here, one may venture the hypothesis that there were very few inhabitants in the area at the time of the early arrival of the Purépechas and the later advent of the Spaniards.

At the beginning of the fifteenth century four western domains surrounded the nameless, unoccupied plateau. To the south lay that of Tamazula, inhabited by Xilotlatzincas or Pinomes, whose northern frontier was the Tigre Range. On the north there was probably a political entity made up of the people who lived in the villages along the shore of Lake Chapala. To the west was the dominion of Sayula, with its famous salt flats. The lord of Coynan dominated the region lying to the east, until the arrival of the Purépechas in the last half of the sixteenth century.

About 1401, "Hiripan called Tangáxoan and Huiquíngare to him, and said: 'Brothers, our uncle Tariácuri is dead. . . . Brothers, let us make new conquests.' " The triple alliance of the Purépecha lords from Lake Pátzcuaro began taking villages—not only neighboring ones, but also others farther off, whose people spoke a different tongue. In 1450 the triple alliance came under the leadership of a single chief, or *irecha*, and imperialistic aims were consolidated. The Tarascan wars of expansion spread toward the western dominions, and the anonymous plateau became a battlefield.

In the "Relación de Michoacán" [Account concerning Michoacán] we find that in the second half of the fifteenth century Tzitzipandácu-are and Zuangua "conquered Tamazula and Zapotlán and the [Sayul-teca] villages of Ávalos and the rest."[11] It was not a lasting victory, for the struggle between the Sayultecas and the Tarascans continued for many years. At the beginning of the sixteenth century the Purépe-chas established fortified towns to defend the western end of their

---

[11] *Relación de las ceremonias y ritos y población y gobierno de los indios de la provincia de Michoacán*, p. 155; José Bravo Ugarte, *Historia sucinta de Michoacán*, I, 75.

empire. Among these were Jiquilpan and Mazamitla, both manned by warriors who made periodical expeditions to harass the Sayultecas and Pinomes "with bows and arrows and clubs." Some historians have used the term "The Saltpeter War" when referring to this carnage, which took place, in part, at least, on the rolling hills that lay between the lands ruled by the Empire and the people of the nitrate country, who were not resigned to the Purépecha domination. It may have been this dissatisfaction that led them to welcome the Spanish conquest as a kind of salvation.

An Early History of Construction and Destruction

From the ruins of Tenochtitlán, which had fallen to the Spaniards on August 13, 1521, the steel-clad soldiers of Hernán Cortés's army set out to conquer the states bordering the Aztec Empire. Cristóbal de Olid led the expedition to Michoacán, with seventy bearded men on horseback, two hundred more on foot, and thousands of Indians. Don Cristóbal crossed the border of the Tarascan Empire on July 17, 1522. It was an opportune moment. A year earlier a smallpox epidemic had carried off the emperor Zuangua; "two huge comets had just been seen in the sky," which were believed to be omens of great upheavals in the world; and the bad news had just arrived: "The people of the city of Mexico have been overthrown. . . . The entire city is filled with the stench of corpses."[12]

From Tajimaroa, Olid sent a message offering peace and friendship to the young Tangaxoan, Zuangua's successor. The messenger ran to Tzintzuntzan, telling the warriors he met along the way, "Go back. . . . The Spaniards do not come in anger. . . . They come in good cheer." When the emperor received the message, he was torn between throwing himself into Lake Pátzcuaro and running away; finally, he crept into a hiding place and refused to come out and meet the white men. The conquerors, who were to remain in the Tarascan capital for nine months, proceeded to sack the absent emperor's palaces with great care. In one of these, where they found twenty chests of gold and twenty of silver, many jewels, and a crowd of women, they met

---

[12] Cf. Bravo Ugarte, *Historia sucinta*, II, 16.

their first armed resistance. The imperial concubines advanced on them "with heavy canes, and began to beat them." After finding Tangaxoan in another palace, the Spaniards put him under guard "so he could not run away and hide again," and demanded gold. Tangaxoan went in person to Coyoacán to present Cortés with three hundred loads of both yellow and white metal. He remained for four days of music and feasting, at the end of which Cortés ordered: "Go back to your country. . . . Do not harm the Spaniards. . . . Give them food, and do not collect any more tribute from your villages, for I must put my own men over them."[13]

With the emperor subdued and the source of his wealth located, expeditions were organized to explore the dominions to the west and southwest, whence came the precious stones and metals in the imperial treasury. The group led by Alonso de Ávalos, Cortés's cousin, was the luckiest. Alonso took Sayula, Tamazula, and Zapotlán without a struggle and made them part of "The Province of Ávalos," at the northeastern end of which lay the plateau with which this history is concerned.

Men driven by gold fever passed through the area like whirlwinds. According to Fray Toribio de Motolinía, in 1525 a man named Morcillo discovered in Tamazula "an exceedingly rich silver mine"— so rich, in fact, that, when the inhabitants of the city of Mexico heard of the strike, "in their greed for silver" they rushed to the mine and "left the city depopulated." At that point the mine disappeared. "Some say that a mountain fell on the mine and blocked it up completely; others that the Indians covered it over . . . and others that it was an act of God, because people had stolen it from the man who had discovered it" and because the capital was being drained of its population. Never before had the city been in such danger of being abandoned.[14]

Some Spaniards were sent racing across the mesa by rumors of a town on the Southern Sea that was peopled by wanton single women, naked amazons armed with bow and arrow. Alonso de Ávalos and his men set out to find them. For the same purpose (and for gold, too)

13 *Relación de Michoacán*, pp. 248–261.
14 Toribio de Motolinía, *Memoriales*, p. 218.

Nuño de Guzmán organized the army of 150 horse, 150 foot soldiers, 8,000 Indians, and a few Negroes that with blood and fire was to forge New Galicia.[15] Entranced by the triple attraction of gold, amazons, and the Far East, Hernán Cortés arrived in Jiquilpan with a sizable retinue, crossed the plateau, and passed through Mazamitla on his way to the Southern Sea. He spent a year searching for the amazons of California, and probably would have stayed longer if his new wife had not engaged Francisco de Ulloa to bring him home. Fray Juan de Padilla and other men of the cowl were seen on the mesa from 1533 on; in the populated areas of the Province of Ávalos they smashed idols, built churches and chapels, and preached the Gospel. Officials and attorneys came, too, some to fix the boundaries between the dioceses of Michoacán and Guadalajara, and some to curb the excesses of the Spaniards.[16]

Our tableland was a thoroughfare and nothing more, until cattle and sheep discovered it. After 1545, the cattle introduced by the Spaniards took over the northern plains, the coastal lowlands, and the western foothills. During the dry season "more than 80,000 sheep" appeared in the swampy areas near Jiquilpan every year, and along the border between Michoacán and Jalisco 200,000 head of cattle and sheep were grazing. These would have continued their invasion of our no man's land if the viceroys Mendoza and Velasco had not obliged their owners to confine them within the land grants, far from populated areas, that they conceded to cattlemen. Some of the relatives and followers of Alonso de Ávalos obtained such grants of "virgin soil with good pasture."[17]

When the gold and amazon fevers passed, Alonso de Ávalos with-

---

[15] José López Portillo y Weber, *La conquista de la Nueva Galicia.*

[16] For the spiritual conquest of the region, see Nicolás Antonio de Ornelas, *Crónica de la provincia de Santiago de Xalisco*; Francisco Mariano de Torres, *Crónica de la santa provincia de Xalisco*; Diego Muñoz, *Crónica de la provincia de San Pedro y San Pablo de Michoacán*; and Bravo Ugarte, *Historia sucinta de Michoacán*, II.

[17] For the occupation of western New Spain by cattlemen, see François Chevalier, "La formación de los grandes latifundios en México"; José Miranda, *España y Nueva España en la época de Felipe II*; Luis Chávez Orozco, *Breve historia agrícola de México en la época colonial*; and José Matesanz, "Introducción de la ganadería en Nueva España," in *Historia Mexicana*, XIV, no. 4.

drew into his province to become an encomendero; he waxed rich on tribute paid by thousands of Indians, and surrounded himself with servants and relatives. The old conquistador was the third of half a dozen brothers. The first-born was drowned on the expedition to Las Hibueras [Honduras]; the second left a good impression in Honduras and an illegitimate daughter in Mexico City; the fourth and fifth followed Alonso to Sayula in 1536 and 1540. The youngest never reached Mexico, but his four sons did. Three of them came to flourish under the protection of their powerful uncle: Alonso de Ávalos Saavedra, Juan de Ávalos Saavedra, and Francisco de Saavedra Sandoval.[18] Two were attracted by the cattle business. For them, and for some of his followers as well, Don Alonso obtained fat land grants on the high, unproductive section of his province: the plateau.

In 1564 the viceroy, Don Luis de Velasco, granted to Francisco de Saavedra land for a cattle ranch measuring two thousand paces on a side, in the Juruneo area.[19] Soon afterward Toribio de Alcaraz took possession of a ranch in the Juruneo foothills, "where there is a spring."[20] The following year Hernando de Ávalos was given two parcels for cattle raising "on the downs" and two caballerías of land "near a creek along the road leading from Mexico City to the towns of Ávalos"; he sold the lot at once to Francisco de Saavedra.[21] In 1575 Francisco Rodríguez sold Saavedra half of another ranch, so that the latter became the owner of some seven thousand hectares and a great many cattle, goats, and sheep.[22]

In 1568 Pedro Larios received a ranch grant and a caballería of pasture land along the road to Colima, east of the peak of Juruneo.[23] That these were in use by 1587 is attested by Father Ponce: "On Friday, November 28, he left Vanimba or Jiquilpan so early in the morning that by seven o'clock he had covered five leagues of rather bad road," all uphill, and was crossing what was known as "The Larios

---

[18] Jesús Amaya, Los conquistadores Fernández de Híjar, pp. 77–78.

[19] Archivo General de la Nación (National Archives), Mexico City (hereafter AGNM), Tierras, vol. 1193, fol. 311.

[20] Ibid., fols. 89–91.

[21] Ibid., fols. 95–96.

[22] Jesús Amaya, Ameca, protofundación mexicana, pp. 149–150.

[23] AGNM, Tierras, vol. 1193, fol. 94.

Place" near a pond "where there were a lot of gray geese," a creek, and some cornfields.[24] In 1591 Larios obtained a second ranch adjoining the first, and in 1595 still another on the western slope of Juruneo. He now owned a latifundium of about six thousand hectares.[25]

In the memorable year of 1567, shortly before the great earthquake on Holy Innocents' Day that knocked down houses, blocked up springs, "split open many mountains with cracks and deep chasms, and [made] a terrible noise for nine days on end,"[26] Alonso de Ávalos Saavedra, who had owned a ranch in Jocotepec since 1547, was granted two parcels for cattle raising and two *caballerías* of pasture land in Puerto de la Pasión, on the road to Sayula.[27] He was given another section on a hill between the Larios and Saavedra properties in 1590; and in 1594 he received a grant of land for raising goats and sheep, with an additional four *caballerías*, in Tizapán.[28] As if this were not enough, he married his niece María Delgadillo, who was as ambitious and businesslike as he.[29] After the death of Alonso de Ávalos the elder in 1570 or thereabouts, young Alonso found himself the richest and most powerful landowner in the province.

This Eve (María Delgadillo) and these three Adams (Pedro Larios, Francisco de Saavedra, and Alonso de Ávalos) who had been put "into the garden of Eden to dress it and keep it," cleared the land of wild animals and populated it with horses and "chickens and pigeons and ducks and cows and sheep and pigs and dogs and cats," and all these creatures grew and multiplied in great degree. Virgin pastures nourished the domestic animals that flourished along with "creeping things and beasts of the earth." The men from Extremadura built huts with pitched roofs and around them planted trees native to both Spain and the New World. "And a river went out of Eden," fed by several small streams where the cattle drank. They named the river, with its cascades and boulders, "Río de la Pasión," "because on some of the stone cliffs overlooking the water they had found drawings

[24] *Relación breve y verdadera*, I, 42–50, 51, and II, 14.
[25] AGNM, *Tierras*, vol. 1193, fol. 309.
[26] Muñoz, *Crónica*, p. 42.
[27] AGNM, *Tierras*, vol. 1189, fol. 186.
[28] Ibid., fols. 194, 198.
[29] Amaya, *Ameca*, p. 37.

representing the Passion of Christ . . . very clear and skillfully done," in places that were totally inaccessible. As they took possession of these rolling highlands drained by the Pasión River, they assigned names to various features of the landscape.[30] One ranch took the name of the river; another was called Del Monte; and the peak overlooking the broad pastures belonging to Larios, which had been known as Juruneo, became Larios Mountain. The panorama of hills rising beyond the mesa came to be called the Tigre Range.

Shortly before the 1603 eruption of the Colima volcano, so vigorous that it blotted out the sun at noon, María Delgadillo bought two ranches and two *caballerías* adjoining her property from her brother-in-law Francisco's widow. Then she took over Pedro Larios's holdings and became the owner of the entire plateau. She named the eastern part of the mesa the Hacienda del Monte and established its boundaries as the Pasión River and the towns of Mazamitla, Tizapán, Cojumatlán, and Quitupan. She peopled it with cowboys to handle her "hundreds and even thousands of cattle." These were men who knew how to break horses, repair arquebuses, castrate, concoct and administer medicines, "make and mend a saddle, cut a suit of clothes, build a house, cook a meal, load a mule, keep a careful eye on a bull, file a complaint, and complicate a lawsuit."[31]

María Delgadillo, who owned several other haciendas in addition to Del Monte, bore five children: Alonso, Pedro, Micaela, María, and Diego. Alonso entered the church and was the parish priest in Sayula when he fell heir to the Del Monte hacienda. He had not inherited a taste for ranching, however.[32] Ávalos the priest had no intention of going to live among cows, pigs, and chickens; in 1625 he got rid of the estate. On April 6 of that year he executed a bill of sale transferring to Don Pedro de Salceda Andrade "all cattle ranches and pasture lands held in grant by his family between the Pasión River and the watershed of Jiquilpan, together with the existing buildings and corrals."[33] Aside from changing its name to the Cojumatlán

[30] Ornelas, *Crónica*, p. 97.
[31] Arregui, *Descripción*, p. 38.
[32] Amaya, *Los conquistadores*, pp. 80–81.
[33] AGNM, *Tierras*, vol. 1193, fol. 93.

hacienda, the new owner seems not to have paid any more attention to the estate than had Father Ávalos. Perhaps times were bad for stock raising. The property that lay on the eastern part of the plateau remained unemployed, on vacation, idle, possibly because of a high mortality rate in the herds, a shortage of ranch hands, or a poor market. The same was true of the estate bordering it on the west: the Toluquilla hacienda, Cojumatlán's twin.

For 170 years a succession of owners ignored the property; it remained almost uninhabited, with its cattle gone wild. It was an idle latifundium, retained out of mere pride of possession rather than because it profited its distant proprietors in any way.

After 1791 things were different, however. Don Victorino Jasu, a prosperous merchant from Tangancícuaro, opened the estate to tenant farmers.[34] The mere six families living on the 190 square miles of the hacienda were joined by thirty more. The great majority were *criollos*, although there was a sprinkling of mestizos and mulattoes. Three families settled in Los Corrales, where the Cárdenas clan already had their homes. José de Cárdenas founded the settlement at Sabino, where the land was level and there was a good rainfall. The shepherd Antonio Eulloque built his hut on wild, thorny, sloping terrain, near a spring. On an equally rugged site nearby, at the foot of Larios Mountain, thirteen families established the *ranchería* of Jarrero. Two more from Sahuayo settled at La Rosa and three from the village of Cojumatlán moved into the ancient Estancia del Monte.

The first to build homes in Llano de la Cruz were two men from Tangancícuaro (Juan Francisco Chávez and Antonio Valencia) and a little woman named Simona, who was Valencia's daughter and Chávez's wife.[35] It was the grass that gave Llano de la Cruz its name, because of a marvelous event that occurred on the western slope of Larios Mountain. At the end of the rainy season, when the grass normally turns yellow, a patch in the form of a cross remained dark green. One arm of the cross pointed toward El Durazno, the other in the direction of the settlement at Jarrero. At the left end of the

---

[34] Ibid., *Historia*, vol. 73, file 13, fol. 29.
[35] Archivo Parroquial de Sahuayo (Sahuayo Parish Records, hereafter APS), register of baptisms and marriages.

crosspiece stood Juan Francisco's hut, at the right end, Antonio's house; Simona spent most of her days on the way from one to the other.[36]

It was the duty of these settlers to bring civilization to the old Del Monte hacienda, in return for the use of all the wild cattle they could round up and redomesticate, the right to plant and harvest crops on all the land they cleared, and the privilege of making liquor and keeping bees. It was another of their obligations to take care of Don Victorino's herds, which were driven in on St. John's Day and taken away on All Saints' Day; the animals had to be protected from wolves and rustlers. The cattle were raised for their hides and tallow; the milk and meat were for local consumption.[37]

These were unruly people, who lived by the sling and the machete. The men, dressed in trousers of sheepskin or deerskin and coarse cotton shirts, rode as though they and their mounts were one. Some of the newcomers became bandits, preying on the salt and nitrate caravans. Their leader was Martín Toscano, a grandson of Cristóbal de Cárdenas. According to Don Ramón Sánchez, the classic annalist from Jiquilpan, around 1800 "a notorious gang of bandits led by Martín Toscano and Francisco Gil was roaming the highways, reportedly robbing people of great sums of money. . . . Sometime between 1803 and 1805 they were ambushed and captured by Don Serafín Ceja, the overseer of the Guaracha hacienda. Toscano was executed in Mexico City, and Gil in Guadalajara."[38] The old people of today have stripped Martín of his glory as a highwayman and instead have awarded him that of the first hero in the Wars of Independence.

The second hero, José Antonio Torres, was the administrator of a hacienda in the Bajío when he decided to take up the priest Hidalgo's cause. He rode into Don Victorino's domain at the end of the rainy season, and people flocked about him. In Guadalajara the story was circulated that Torres was no more than a foolish hayseed, leading

[36] From conversations with Luis González Cárdenas.

[37] Archivo de Notarías del Distrito de Jiquilpan (Notarial Records of the District of Jiquilpan, hereafter ANJ). These files are in such a state of disorder that no precise reference can be made.

[38] Ramón Sánchez, Bosquejo estadístico e histórico del distrito de Jiquilpan de Juárez, p. 106.

an army of clodhoppers. The "flower of Guadalajara's youth" believed it and sallied forth to put down the rebel. The battle took place on the outskirts of Zacoalco. Torres's forces showered such a rain of stones from slings upon the dandies from the city that 257 were laid low.[39] A week later they entered Guadalajara, only to suffer defeat at Puente de Calderón. After many reverses, Torres retreated to the Cojumatlán hacienda, where his army was wiped out at a village called Palo Alto, on the shore of Lake Chapala. A royalist officer named Merino reported on April 4, 1812: "My satisfaction is complete. . . . I took old Torres by surprise as he was gathering a new gang of cutthroats, and made him prisoner. . . . The rabble with him amounted to about 400 men. Those who did not die on our bayonets were roasted to death when I set fire to the barns where they had taken refuge." Torres was taken to Guadalajara and quartered.[40]

By that time other regional leaders had appeared. Don Luis Macías, owner of the La Palma hacienda, which adjoined Cojumatlán, and Padre Marcos Castellanos, the ex-priest from Sahuayo, set up a base of operations on a small island in Lake Chapala with six hundred men from the lakeside villages. They engaged in several skirmishes, most of them against the Cojumatlán hacienda. The battle at El Divisadero was an extremely bloody one. Santa Ana and Chávez, two of Padre Castellanos's lieutenants, with five hundred men, took on Don José Vallano and his large army. The insurgents drove back the enemy and killed the captain. Overjoyed with their victory, Santa Ana and Chávez rode off to carry the news to Padre Castellanos, as their exhausted troops lay down to sleep. General Correa fell upon the slumbering rebels and had the pleasure of wiping out three hundred of them. The spot would later come to be known as El Potrero de los Muertos [Dead Man's Pasture].[41]

The thirty families installed by Jaso on his Cojumatlán hacienda were swept up by the winds of revolution, and not many rebels from Los Corrales, Jarrero, Llano de la Cruz, and Estancia del Monte came

[39] Luis Pérez Verdía, *Apuntes históricos sobre la guerra de independencia en Jalisco*, pp. 18–22.

[40] Ibid., pp. 33–34.

[41] Niceto de Zamacois, *Historia de México*, VII, 236, 237.

out of the struggle alive. The domestic animals that were not slaughtered or stolen took to the hills and ran wild. The settlements were
reduced to ashes. With disease raging among his men, Padre Castellanos was no longer able to hold the little island of Mezcala; he surrendered November 25, 1816.[42]

That year the third wave of settlers arrived. Many people, terrified
by the royalist order calling for the burning of villages and crops
along the shores of Lake Chapala, took refuge on the neighboring
mesa, the highlands where the Cojumatlán and Toluquilla haciendas
lay. Some of the defenders of Mezcala ended up there, too. Both
groups founded new *rancherías*: Auchén, Cerrito de la Leña, Palo
Dulce, San Miguel, Ojo de Rana, along the Leona ravine; San Pedro,
on one of the promontories overlooking Lake Chapala; Colongo and
La Tinaja, on the little hill called La Española in memory of the
Spanish woman who resisted the rebels so fiercely there; and La Breña,
in the deep canyon of the Pasión River. New *rancherías* were established and old ones revived. Lino Partida settled in Los Corrales.
Three couples refounded Sabino, seven moved into Jarrero, and two
set up housekeeping in Ojo de Agua del Pastor. La Venta and Durazno were rebuilt, with some houses in Jalisco and others in Michoacán.
Llano de la Cruz came back to life with vigor. Its new inhabitants were Mariano and María Guadalupe Arteaga, José María Barajas, and Juan Arteaga (the Arteaga girls were remarkable for being
mulattoes and very well built); Basilio Cárdenas and María Toscano,
Antonio González Horta and Lugarda Toscano (people say the Toscano women were striking blondes); Julián Barajas and Marcela
Chávez, Teodoro Valencia and Juana Chávez, and the young José
Vicente Pulido and María Eduarda Chávez.

Antonio González Horta and José Vicente Pulido were typical of
the ex-combatants who had come to live in the highland *rancherías*
of Cojumatlán. Antonio was the son of Juan Antonio and Salomé
Horta; before the War for Independence the parents had leased farming land in Rincón de María, in the La Palma area. Juan Antonio's
father and mother were Toribio and María Díaz of Cotija, of Sephar-

---

[42] Pérez Verdía, *Apuntes históricos*, pp. 123–125.

dic origin. The two Antonios, father and son, were predestined to be insurgents, since they were related to the priest Marcos Castellanos and had been in the employ of Luis Miguel Macías, both of whom were revolutionary leaders. Antonio the younger was born in 1799 and built his hut in Llano de la Cruz about 1818. He had already fathered a child before he married Lugarda Toscano, the unwed mother of Ignacio Buenrostro. To Antonio and Lugarda were born José Guadalupe, Vicente, Luis, José María, and Jesús. Antonio planted corn every year and sometimes made mescal; but he never had a cent. He was poor, cheerful, and almost a drunk. He could outrun a yearling calf in full flight, and he excelled at the knife dance, or *morisca*.

Less disorderly, if not edifying, was José Vicente Pulido's career. In 1788 his father had been living in Cotija. After the independence, father and son took up residence on the Cojumatlán hacienda, quite near Llano de la Cruz, where the elder José Vicente planted the ash tree that still stands today. The Pulidos owned cows, which they milked from St. John's until All Saints' Day. They made cheese and, like most people who had cattle, sold hides. During the long dry season José Vicente Pulido kept bees for wax and honey. The sale of clarified beeswax and hides brought him a modest fortune. He married María Eduarda Chávez, a daughter of Antonio Chávez, the hero and villain of the battle at El Divisadero, and had numerous children by her. He was a good horseman and a hard drinker all his life.[43]

A hundred heads of families like Antonio González Horta and José Vicente Pulido Arteaga were living on the highlands of the Cojumatlán hacienda when independence was won. During the peaceful parenthesis between 1821 and 1832, there was little change in the population. In 1833 it dropped because of cholera, which carried off nearly a hundred people between September and December.[44] After 1834 the civil war that had broken out in the center of the republic began to drive citizens into the more sparsely populated areas. The highlands of the Cojumatlán and Toluquilla haciendas took in fugitives from a nation in flames. Some took up residence on the hacienda

---

[43] APS, ANJ, and conversations with Luis González Cárdenas.
[44] Archivos Parroquiales de Cojumatlán y Mazamitla (Parish Records in Cojumatlán and Mazamitla, hereafter APC and APM, respectively).

properties, and others built homes on land belonging to the village of Mazamitla. In Durazno, seven *criollo* families erected a huge house with a tile roof and found good land. In 1835 a group of 177 Mazamitleco Indians charged that they had been robbed of property "they had held as descendants of the original inhabitants."[45] Since no one paid any attention, in 1857 they attacked the squatters with rocks, clubs, and machetes. Pablo and Jesús Rojas, Rafael and Dolores Reyes, Miguel, Manuel, and Juan Martínez, Manuel Calleja, and Vicente Chávez complained that they had been driven "by armed force" from their homes at El Carrizo, Pie de Puerco, Zapatero, and Milpillas.[46]

But even the Indian uprising in Mazamitla was not enough to stem the influx; neither were the activities of some of the local bandits— such as the one who disguised himself by blackening his face with soot and operated in the neighborhood of a hill that would come to be known as El Tiznado. In less than thirty years the population of the plateau tripled. In a fifth of the area alone, in what would in time become the parish of San José de Gracia and the *municipio* of Marcos Castellanos, the number of inhabitants rose from four hundred to a thousand.[47]

A Society of Cowboys

By 1860 the upper third of the Cojumatlán hacienda, lying along the Pasión River, had had five lives. Between 1523 and 1563 it had been examined and found wanting by Spanish adventurers in search of gold and amazons. From 1564 to 1615 it had provided homes for a dozen inhabitants and pasture for thousands of cattle. After 1616 it had become an economic and demographic vacuum, a hacienda without a master, a lifeless corpse. In 1791 it had begun to undergo a repopulation; the guerrilla Martín Toscano had lent it distinction; it had served as a battlefield and had provided fighting men during the struggle for independence; and it had died for a couple of years.

---

[45] ANJ, Alcaldes' Records in Jiquilpan, 1835.

[46] Ibid., Records of Licenciado Alejandro Abarca, 1866.

[47] These figures are based on the number of births recorded in what was then the vicariate of Cojumatlán, assuming one thousand inhabitants for every fifty children baptized.

About 1818 it had been reborn. During the forty years of its fifth existence, as a place of refuge during the civil war, it had accumulated a population with rather diverse backgrounds but with similar customs.[48]

In 1860 there were about a thousand people occupying the third of the Cojumatlán hacienda that a century later would become the *municipio* of Marcos Castellanos. They were scattered among sixteen *rancherías*, each of which comprised from five to thirty little houses. The largest, Llano de la Cruz, housed less than two thousand individuals. These people did not live together; the huts in each settlement stood at some distance from each other and were almost totally removed from the rest of the nation. The *criollos* in each of these hamlets associated with their counterparts in other settlements on the mesa, but not with the mountain people in Mazamitla, who were still largely Indian. After the Independence these *rancherías* were taken into the vicariate of Cojumatlán, a town that they visited three times in their lives. The first time was in a basket, to be baptized; the second was on horseback, to be married; the final trip was made wrapped in a *petate* and strapped on the back of the mule known as "The Gravedigger." Once a year these families usually went to the nearest village to attend the celebration of its name day: San Francisco Tizapán, Santiago Sahuayo, or Quitupan de la Candelaria. There were very few occasions when a man felt that it was necessary to discuss his problems with the authorities in Sahuayo, the seat of the *municipio*, or in Jiquilpan, the capital of the district. Once in a while someone ventured out of the area to sell his products—but only as far as Cotija, or some other neighboring village; it was never farther than he could ride or walk in one day.

A couple of times a year a mule train from some nearby settlement would call at the clusters of huts and carry away cheese, beeswax, and mescal brandy in exchange for salt, saltpeter, tools, or a little money. Traveling salesmen were not seen very often. A few fugitives from justice and deserters from the army showed up; but whether they were there because they had killed, or because they did not want to,

---

[48] The following reconstruction of social life is based on oral tradition, personal interviews, and papers in the judicial archives of Jiquilpan.

they had never come from very far away. Squads of soldiers came by to impress men for the army, too. In any case, contacts between the outside world and the highlands of the Cojumatlán hacienda were minimal, and nobody wanted it any other way.

A thousand human beings, each planted for life on his scrap of land, existing on the fringe of a nation in which the citizens were at each other's throats, they reproduced, worked, ate, slept, oblivious of the passing days. From 1850 to 1860 they brought into the world an average of fifty-three children every year. The population began to increase by leaps and bounds. There occurred no major epidemic during that decade. Of course many infants and adults died, as always. According to the register of deaths in the parish of Cojumatlán, people succumbed to pneumonia, diarrhea, dysentery, smallpox, measles, snake bites and scorpion stings, machete and knife wounds, and pains of one kind or another. No one was ever killed by a wild animal.

In spite of fifty years of bloody persecution, wolves still howled at night, and people were still making traps for them. Over a pit six or eight feet in diameter they would suspend some small animal from a crossbar as bait; the opening below was concealed by interwoven twigs and grass. In this way they caught wolves, various other carnivores, and an occasional human being—as Pascuala's story attests. She was up before dawn one morning, and before starting to grind corn for tortillas decided to retrieve the rooster she had left as bait in the wolf trap the night before. When her husband came in from milking, wanting his breakfast, he found the house empty. Since his wife was young and attractive, he concluded that she had run off with some other man; he left the house in a fury to look for her. Happening to pass near the wolf trap, he looked in; to his astonishment he saw Pascuala down there, in the company of a wolf and a coyote.

The ranchers made their living by raising cattle, bees, and maguey. In the dry season the cows provided hides, and in the rainy season, cheese; the bees gave them wax, which they bleached; and from the maguey plant they made *aguamiel* and *aguardiente*. The small amounts of cheese, clarified beeswax, and liquor they sold brought in enough money to buy a few things and add to their tiny savings. Actually, they bought and sold very little. They made and repaired nearly everything with their own hands; almost everyone was skilled in some agrarian or domestic art.

Every man planning to marry built his own hut, single-handed, with walls of poles plastered with mud and a grass roof; it had a bedroom, a kitchen, and a porch to sit on. In the bedroom were the *petates* to sleep on, the little chest for clothing, the saddles, and a picture of some saint. Hats, lariats, machetes, and ox goads hung from pegs on the wall. The kitchen was furnished with a counter with two openings for cooking fires, a water jar, an earthenware griddle, pots, pitchers, a *metate*, a clay casserole, a large wooden bowl and spoon, a *molcajete*, and its stone pestle. Meat hung from a hook. A platform of woven reeds hung from the ceiling on maguey-fiber ropes attached to its four corners, on which cheeses were stored for aging. Corn and beans were heaped in one corner, dry firewood in another. Outside on the little porch a piece of wooden beam served as a bench, and farming tools were scattered about: the plow, the mattock, and the leather straps for the ox yoke.

The house was surrounded by a yard containing trees, chickens, beehives, pigs, burros, and the horse. Adjoining the yard there was nearly always an *ecuaro*, where corn for eating on the cob was cultivated with the mattock. Corn for tortillas was raised in the *milpa*, which was worked with the plow. In both the *ecuaro* and the *milpa*, beans, squash, and tomatoes were planted among the corn. The rest of the land was used for pasture. Corn, beans, cattle, and bees provided an abundant, simple diet. Women not only cooked, but also spun, wove, and sewed the family's everyday clothing; they helped the men with the milking and in the cornfield.

Women's work was unending and onerous. Men could do their chores at any hour of the day, or not at all. It was labor punctuated by the seasonal cycles, but not rigidly ruled by them. It was possible for a man to live with very little effort, in the open air under the trees, or riding and dreaming on a good horse. Salaried jobs did not exist. The hacienda's fifty thousand hectares were leased to a rich man from Cojumatlán, who retained control of the best half of the estate as pasture for his cattle; he employed a few tenant farmers as cowhands. The other half was subleased to individual ranchers. In the section that looked toward the setting sun there were no hired hands—only free men who, in exchange for a small yearly payment, had the use of fifty or more hectares, which they would have preferred to own.

This handful of people made up a small patriarchal society. The social unit was the family itself, comprising the man, his wife, and the unmarried children. When the sons took wives of their own, they settled near the paternal home and continued working with and for their father. It then became a kind of larger family, ruled by the grandfather, with his long, white beard. At the middle of the nineteenth century, twenty larger families, ruled by the men and especially by the elders, lived on the plateau. Even so, the wife's role was an important one, not only in regard to her everyday contribution to a self-sustaining economy, but also whenever family decisions had to be made. In the husband's absence, it was she who gave the orders. Most of these women were fearless and strong, approaching the ideal represented by Jesusa Santillán.

Jesusa, daughter of the Indian José Santillán and the *criolla* María Guadalupe Pulido, was so muscular that she could lift a load weighing 175 pounds, and so skillful in farm chores that she could plow an absolutely straight furrow two hundred yards long. At a wedding one day a fellow named Cayetano, who was always spoiling for a fight, challenged the other men who had come to the celebration. When they ignored him, Jesusa changed into men's clothing, donned a sombrero, saddled a roan, seized her machete, and confronted the troublemaker. He dropped his knife and fled. On another occasion she quarreled with one of the women in her husband's family and gave her a drubbing. When the husbands—Jesusa's and the injured party's—came to the woman's defense, Jesusa thrashed both of them. Once, when some young unmarried nieces were visiting her, she decided to entertain them by taking them to a wedding dance; the girls got drunk and out of hand and began making a spectacle of themselves. When Jesusa announced that it was time to go home, the nieces armed themselves with knives and refused. Then there was a real battle. She seized a club, beat them until they dropped their weapons, and carried them home.

Children, too, had an important role in that small society. Their parents, always aware of the responsibility of making their offspring into "real men" and "real women," taught them to take care of themselves at a very early age. At ten they already knew how to provide themselves with the necessities of life and assist their father and mother in every farm chore. They attained complete maturity at fifteen and then were free to marry—which they did without much delay, to the music of the *papaqui*. While the bride and groom went to Cojumatlán to confess, hear mass, and receive the priest's blessing, the young man's parents prepared the bower and the wedding feast. Beneath the bower they arranged the table, the dais, and the dance floor. While the musicians were tuning up their guitars, *guitarrón*, and harp, the guests went out to meet the bridal couple. When the newlyweds were seated on the dais, the men launched into a few lines of a satirical song, to which the women retorted in chorus. This picaresque musical exchange continued until at last the men attacked the women with a bombardment of eggshells filled with colored confetti. The rest of the *papaqui* (a Náhuatl word meaning "great joy") consisted of music, an inordinate consumption of punch and mescal, and dancing. One couple after another executed the *jarabe* on the dance floor.[49]

Sponsors and godparents were indispensable at weddings and christenings. The bonds of affection between sponsors and sponsored and between parents and godparents helped to maintain friendly relations among the families of the mesa. Fights and killings were not infrequent, however. There was no authority higher than the head of each larger family, except for the rare occasions when the priest from Cojumatlán or the town fathers of Sahuayo stepped in. It was a society of free people, where every man was as good as any other, where only the patriarch and the dictates of tradition called for blind obedience.

The dead usually continued interfering in the affairs of the living. When the souls of the departed returned on moonlit nights, these ranchers, so fearless when dealing with the natural world or with other men, turned to cowards. They feared the dead more than they did God. They were particularly terrified by the devil who showed up either in the shape of a black dog with eyes like glowing embers, or in

<hr />

[49] For a modern description of this type of wedding, see José Ramírez Flores, *Matrimonio*, pp. 49–58.

his traditional form (a small, red, beardless man with a long tail), or as a woman, or even as a bat—as in the case of the sinner of Devil's Ravine. As he was coming home just before dawn, after a night of carousing, an enormous bat with flashing eyes snatched him up and carried him off through the air. Sure that the monster was Satan inhabiting the body of a bat, the poor fellow called on Jesus, Mary, and Joseph, and made the sign of the cross. This was enough to make the beast release him, and he fell into the branches of a tree, where some shepherds found him in the morning, unconscious. When his neighbors heard the tale, they got together and marked the spot with an oak cross nine feet high. From that day on, the ravine was known as La Barranca del Diablo.

Needless to say, the ranchers on the Cojumatlán hacienda were Catholics. On rising in the morning, they crossed themselves. They went to confession and received Communion at least once in their lives. Every year they went to one of the religious festivals in a neighboring village. They observed the days of fasting and abstinence and paid their tithes. They were married by the priest and took their children to be baptized within a week after they were born. In some homes the family recited the Rosary together every evening at nightfall. No household was without the picture of some saint. They memorized the Pater Noster, the Credo, the Ten Commandments, and the five precepts of the church. A knowledge of the breviary was indispensable for permission to marry. Being "a good Christian" was of less importance. Instincts were often stronger than the Commandments, and out of fear they sometimes engaged in superstitious practices instead of those recommended by the church. The absence of a priest allowed a wide margin of extrareligious behavior. Even so, serious moral and liturgical derelictions were not very common.

Since one or two exceptions do not disprove the rule, these people could not read. They did know hundreds of sayings and proverbs, handed down by word of mouth. Their memories were rich in family history, sometimes reaching back as far as a century and a half. The local skirmishes that had taken place during the struggle for independence, some of whose protagonists were still living, were in the public domain. But there is no reason to believe that they thought of themselves as part of the Mexican nation; their feeling of race was stronger than any sense of patriotism. Although their way of life differed very little from that of the Indians of Mazamitla, they took pride in their Spanish blood. Marriages with individuals of Negro or Indian descent were not rare, however.

In summation, the history that is about to be related here springs from three beginnings, three points of departure: a quasi-mountainous landscape; an early stage of upheaval and subsidence; and a small cultural backwater made up of rude cattle farmers.

Part One

Half a Century in Search of Communion

1. THE *RANCHOS* (1861–1882)

As EVERYONE knows, General Antonio López de Santa Anna, the one-legged president who insisted on being addressed as "Your Most Serene Highness," was enjoying the spectacle of a grand ball when he learned that Colonel Florencio Villareal, at the head of an army of peasants in the hamlet of Ayutla, had launched a plan calling for the overthrow of the government and the setting up of a Constitutional Congress to create a republican, representative, and popular state. Support for the Plan of Ayutla came from all sides. The revolution spread. Santa Anna fled. The all-out or "hurry-up" liberals seized power; they passed anticlerical laws that turned the church solidly against them. The Constitutional Congress tried to go even further. "In order that humanity may progress from the present system of property rights, which is invalid because it invests only a minority with those rights, to a valid system which will grant the fruits of its labor to the hitherto exploited majority," Ponciano Arriaga demanded that "our fertile but untilled lands" be distributed "among the working people of our country."[1] The congress

[1] Francisco Zarco, *Historia del Congreso Constituyente, 1856–1857*, pp. 363–365, 387–404, 690–697.

took no notice of this suggestion, or of similar ones made by Olvera and Castillo Velasco. The delegates turned out a constitution very much like that of 1824, but with a larger dose of liberty for the individual and less for institutions—among which the church figured prominently.

The reforms agreed upon by these legislators aggravated the dissension among the citizens. Liberals and conservatives fell upon each other in a war that was to endure without a break for three years. The first year was one of victories for the counterrevolutionaries; the second was characterized by a balance of power, highway robbery, theft, famine, epidemics, political oratory, and war literature; and the third saw major triumphs for the liberal party and the shaping of the second set of Reform Laws. In Justo Sierra's opinion, the struggle stirred up "consciences, homes, farms, and cities." There was hardly a state that did not take part in it.

The fighting was especially savage in Michoacán, but not even there did it reach into every corner. Don Ramón Sánchez states that there were no armed encounters in the district of Jiquilpan—"merely frequent demands for money and some brutality." The people of Sahuayo came out in favor of the reaction, but the citizens of Jiquilpan sent them home with no great difficulty. Only the tail of the storm touched the Cojumatlán hacienda.

By 1860 the conservatives had no army; but they did have generals, political leaders, and sponsors. The defeated generals launched into a "synthetic war," consisting of cowardly assassinations of the best men in the victorious faction. The deposed politicos appealed to their sponsors: some of the crowned heads of Europe. France's imperial couple came to their assistance because, it was said, they were eager to raise a monarchical Latin wall against the expanding United States; it was a propitious time for erecting such a barrier, for one-half of the American republic was engaged in battle with the other half. In 1862 a French army, reinforced by Mexican royalists, reopened hostilities against the ruling liberals. They lost the battle of the Fifth of May and won many others—enough to take the helm, send for an emperor, and set him on the throne, but not enough to wipe out the opposition. There was bitter fighting in nearly every part of the nation from 1862 to 1867; but it never really concerned the country people. On the Cojumatlán hacienda the ranchers had other things to do and worry about, even though they did not remain completely on the margin of the squabble.

The six years between 1861 and 1866 were remarkable on the Cojumatlán tableland for half a dozen events of major importance to its denizens. These were the things that left indelible memories: the aurora borealis, the dissolution of the hacienda, the visit of the French soldiers, the founding of the diocese of Zamora, the appearance of the teacher Jesús Gómez, and the advent of Tiburcio Torres. Other events, such as Maximillian's arrival and subsequent execution by firing squad, Don Epitacio Huerta's anticlerical attacks, the rise of Benito Juárez, Bishop Clemente de Jesús Munguía's litigations and banishments, and, in general, anything else that happened more than a hundred kilometers away were not heard of here. The ranchers never saw a newspaper; the parties of belligerents who visited the area did not bother to explain to the country people what they were doing; and the peasants went to the neighboring cities and towns as seldom as possible, for fear of the levy and of bandits. The few who were unlucky enough to be conscripted and lucky enough to return from the scuffle with their lives never learned why they had been in the theater of war. While the French were landing at Veracruz, the ranchers on the hacienda were concerned with nothing more serious than the subdivision and the aurora borealis.

For these fifteen hundred Mexicans living on the edge of national existence, immersed only in the natural world about them, the aurora borealis was the greatest spectacle the world had ever seen. They knew that there had been an earlier one in the fall of 1789, but none of them had seen it. When compared with the reports of its predecessor, this one, in 1861, seemed no less marvelous and fearsome. It appeared in the early mornings, toward the end of the year, in the north. It was nothing at all like the rosy glow that comes in the sky just before sunrise. The dancing lights were like those that hovered over places where treasure was buried, but they were so enormous that people were terrified. It was as if all the flames in the world had joined in a dance. It was like a battle in which Saint Michael and his angels were hurling thunderbolts, sparks, and balls of fire down upon an army of demons.

It is said that the northern lights terrified the city people, too— but never as much as the peasants. And yet, for the ranchers of Cojumatlán they marked the beginning of a new life. They needed land and freedom. The latter they already had, and the former was to come to some of them in the year of the aurora, when the Cojumatlán hacienda was subdivided. If there were others who did not get as much as a single square foot of earth, it was in part because they were mistrustful. They could not believe that a hacienda could fall into ruin. What they were seeing with their own eyes was probably not true. Perhaps these sales were faked; perhaps it was a trick on the part of the *licenciados* to get hold of the modest savings the ranchers kept buried in earthenware pots. It was hard to believe that the powerful owners of Guaracha, San Antonio, and Cojumatlán had to dispose of one of their estates, and even more incredible that they should be willing to do so. The normal procedure was to increase their holdings, not divide them up into *ranchos*.[2]

Some had no money to buy land: they had not saved any. Some had enough to buy a small parcel but did not hear about the sale in time. And some, of course, were cheated. In any case, it is certain that every holder of a sublease on Cojumatlán hacienda, without exception, aspired to own his land outright. The reasons are easy to see: they wanted to improve their condition, gain social prestige, and command greater respect. Having money was a mark of prestige, but not the basic one. In the eyes of these ranchers, what made a man important was, more than anything else, owning land. It brought esteem and, in addition, security. Pots of gold could be dug up and stolen. Cattle could be wiped out by blackleg in one season. The earth remained; no one could carry it off, and no calamity could destroy it. For all these reasons, the idea of buying a section of the old Cojumatlán latifundium was extremely tempting. At the same time, it was a risky operation. The offer seemed too good to be true.

---

[2] Information concerning the aurora borealis and the beginnings of the subdivision was provided by oral tradition. Also see Mariano de Jesús Torres, *Historia civil y eclesiástica de Michoacán*.

The fact is that the powerful owners of the Guaracha haciendas, pressed by their creditors, were ready to dispose of their least productive holdings. Perhaps the rumor going around—that Doña Antonia Moreno was losing enormous sums at cards—was true. Perhaps these losses were the immediate cause of the decision to sell Cojumatlán. Perhaps, as some said, it was because the civil wars had ruined some of the large landowners. The breaking up of Cojumatlán hacienda was not an isolated case. If we are to believe General Pérez Hernández, several estates that had been "excessively large in the past" were divided up.[3] Cojumatlán's financial troubles dated from the 1830's. The governor, Diego Moreno, had been short of money. His properties were already weighed down by several mortgages, and he had added to the load. In 1836 he leased the Cojumatlán hacienda to Don Luis Arceo for 4,700 pesos a year. The tenant agreed to allow the cattle from Guaracha to graze on the property during the rainy season, as had been the custom.[4] Don Luis Arceo died in 1837, and it was not easy to find another tenant. Finally, Don José Dolores Acuña came along. It must not have gone badly for him, for he renewed the lease in 1846.[5] And then Diego Moreno died. The heirs agreed that the late owner's third wife should take over the management of the property. Señora Sánchez Leñero died during the three years' war. Acuña fell farther and farther behind in his rent, and the owners went on loading themselves with debts. Doña Antonia Moreno de Depeyre, Don Diego's eldest daughter, whose favorite pastime was games of chance, took charge of the vast property.[6]

Doña Antonia appeared before Don Ramón de la Cueva, a notary, in Mexico City; there, on behalf of herself and her brothers and sisters, by whom she had been fully authorized, she granted a power of attorney to Don Tirso Arregui, a respected citizen of Sahuayo, to repossess the Cojumatlán hacienda from the tenant, José Dolores Acuña. Once this had been done, he was to "proceed to the subdivision and sale of the property." She gave another special power of attorney to

---

[3] José María Pérez Hernández, *Compendio geográfico del estado de Michoacán de Ocampo*, p. 27.

[4] ANJ, Judicial Records of Licenciado Alejandro Abarca.

[5] Ibid., Book of the Alcaldía of Jiquilpan.

[6] Ibid., Judicial Records of Licenciado Miguel E. Cázares, 1861–1864.

Don Felipe Villaseñor, also from one of the good families of Sahuayo, to establish the hacienda's boundaries and to exact from Don José Dolores Acuña "payment of whatever amounts he may be owing."[7]

Don Tirso Arregui carried out Señora Moreno's instructions to the letter. In 1861–1862 he extracted fifty-odd parcels of unequal sizes from an area of nearly fifty thousand hectares, which land was "excellent for raising cattle, sheep, horses, and pigs," and parts of which "produced corn, wheat, beans, and maguey." On the northern plain, people could "fish in the great lake of Chapala."[8] The estate was limited on the east (with Sahuayo and Jiquilpan in between) by the haciendas of Guaracha and La Palma; on the west by the hills of Toluquilla beyond the Pasión River, belonging to Don José Guadalupe Barragán; on the north by Lake Chapala; and on the south by land belonging to "the Indians of Mazamitla, the joint owners or partners of the Pie de Puerco hacienda," and Quitupan. Its successive owners had held the property quietly and peacefully for "two hundred and twenty-six years."[9] In 1837 it had been assessed at 55,000 pesos; Don Tirso Arregui sold it in parcels for 110,000 pesos.[10]

Two classes of people bought land from the hacienda. Those who took the largest and best pieces were not former tenants; they were rich citizens of Jiquilpan, Cotija, and Sahuayo, as well as members of some rather well-to-do families in the Pajacuarán valley, Cojumatlán, and Mazamitla. The subleaseholders were able to buy only small *ranchos*, without good farming land or first-class pasture. The man who got the best piece (the hacienda residence and property along the lake) was Don José Dolores Acuña, who paid 25,000 pesos for it. Manuel Arias, the merchant from Sahuayo who lived in Guadalajara, took over four thousand hectares at Sabino for 8,000 pesos. Other Sahuayans who bought large sections were Pedro Zepeda (El Nogal, 5,000 pesos), his brother Bartolo (La Raya, 4,700 pesos), Ignacio Sánchez (Govea and the surrounding area, 7,877 pesos), Manuel Sánchez (Los Ortices, 4,000 pesos), José Guadalupe Sandoval (Ojo

7 Ibid.
8 Pérez Hernández, *Compendio geográfico*, pp. 107 and 109.
9 ANJ, Judicial Records of Licenciado Miguel E. Cázares, 1861–1864.
10 The sum of the prices stated in the individual bills of sale.

de Rana, San Miguel, and La Rosa, 4,575 pesos), Vicente Arregui (Tinaja de los Arceos, 4,500 pesos), and Antonio Méndez (Buenos Aires, 8,000 pesos). Those who bought smaller parcels, from a thousand to two thousand hectares, were Francisco and Rafael Arias of Mazamitla (Palo Dulce and Guayabo), Ramón Contreras (Arena), Fructuoso Chávez of Valle de Mazamitla (Cerrito de la Leña), Francisco Gutiérrez of Sahuayo (another Tinaja), Manuel Macías or Cárdenas of Cojumatlán (San Pedro), Ignacia Pamplona, also of Cojumatlán (Tinaja de los Ruiz), Rafael Quiroz of Jiquilpan (another Ojo de Rana), José María Ruiz of Cotija (El Izote), and Antonio Barrios, also of Cotija (Estancia del Monte). Of those who had lived on the hacienda, José Guadalupe Cárdenas bought Los Corrales for 2,200 pesos, Antonio Martínez gave 3,000 for El Saucito, and Rafael Rodríguez, a ranch foreman from Pajacuarán, bought San Pedro for 3,725 pesos. The rest, almost all tenants, were able to acquire only parcels of a hundred to a thousand hectares, from 200 to 2,000 pesos: Trinidad, Ramón, and Vicente Chávez bought El Espino, Sauces, and Tiznado; Eusebio and Víctor Fonseca took China; Ramón and Solano Plancarte bought La Venta; Isabel, Teodoro, and Vicente Pulido bought Llano de la Cruz; José Guadalupe, José María, and Luis González acquired Llano de la Cruz and the western slope of Larios Mountain; Lino Partida took a part of Los Corrales; Andrés Vega and Miguel Valdovinos bought other sections of the same *rancho*; Dolores and Encarnación Zepeda bought Llano and Durazno; José María Toscano got part of La Venta; Antonio and José María Contreras bought Tábanos and Puerto de las Milpillas; and José María Olivo took Ojo de Agua Seco. Other purchasers included Don José Dolores Ortega (Panzacola and Colongo) and Mateo Barriga of Mazamitla, who died in 1862 after buying Cuspio.[11]

Taking possession of the *ranchos* was a solemn affair. One example will suffice. On July 27, 1862, Amadeo Betancourt, Judge of the First Instance for the district of Jiquilpan, having given Manuel Arias formal title to the Sabino hacienda the day before, and having spent the night in the best house in the *ranchería* of the same name, rose at

---

[11] ANJ (some of these documents are listed in the records of Licenciado Cázares and others in the records of Licenciado Abarca).

seven in the morning. With his secretary and Don Tirso Arregui, as well as Don Ignacio Sánchez Higareda, the attorney Villaseñor, Don Ramón Contreras, the interested party (Don Fructuoso Chávez), and others, he proceeded to the confluence of the San Miguel and La Estancia creeks. There the buyer made formal application for the first deed of ownership; the judge asked if anyone present had any objections to the sale. Don Ramón Martínez, who lived nearby, spoke up. He said that when "Don Frutos decided to buy El Cerrito, he had promised to sell part of it to him . . . and when he [Don Ramón] got the agreed amount of money together—with great sacrifice on his part—and took it to Chávez, the new owner told him that he did not feel like keeping his promise." The judge set aside Martínez's claim, without prejudice, and ordered the ceremony to proceed. Since there was no other objection, Don Frutos took the seller, Tirso Arregui, by the hand and led him along a section of the boundary line; then he picked up a few stones and threw them; he pulled up clumps of grass, cut some branches, and performed other acts symbolic of legal possession. The party then mounted and rode along San Miguel Creek and the Leona ravine until they reached the Pasión River, where the ceremony of pulling up grass was repeated. This was done again in two other places; finally, the judge took Don Fruto's hand and, "in the name of the National Sovereignty," gave him title to all the land on Cerrito de la Leña.[12] When the tiresome jaunt was over, the secretary, Don Ignacio Bravo, made out the deed; then everyone went to have a few glasses of mescal and a feast. Similar parties were held on fifty other *ranchos* at different times.

Once in possession of their properties, the new owners set to work improving them: building fences, corrals, houses, thatched huts, and anything else they could in view of the times they lived in, their poverty, and their ignorance. The wealthier ones began enclosing their land with double stone fences. Most built simple fences about five feet high, a little less than the height of a man, which were enough to keep out their neighbors' cows and bulls. The first fences to go up were those marking property lines; then others were built to divide planted fields from pasture. Some of these ranchers began

12 Ibid., Judicial Records of Licenciado Alejandro Abarca.

using fences to subdivide their grazing land into several pastures, into which they would turn the cattle successively. The richest erected houses of adobe with tile roofs; those with less money put up thatched huts. Near his house or hut everyone had a milking yard and corrals for branding, and around the house or hut they planted fruit trees. On *ranchos* where there was no river or creek, those who could afford it had the fun of making reservoirs for rain water.

The number and variety of livestock increased considerably. The new settlers brought in both cattle and sheep. Greater areas were devoted to crops and pasture; land was cleared; groves of ancient oaks were felled; the leafy cloak on mountains, hillsides, and ravines was thinned. It was the beginning of an era of transformation and depredation. If the changes were not very rapid at first, it was largely because of the civil war.

Pedro Ávila, famous for his cruelty, fought on the side of the royalist *güeros.* Antonio Rojas, the captain who wore a devil painted on his body, who had helped the Indians of Mazamitla recover their lands from the "colonists" from Durazno, and who had shot (among others) the administrator and two employees of the Tizapán hacienda, was fighting the *güeros* in the west. One afternoon, the royalists rode into Llano de la Cruz. (Colonel Clinchat was among them, at the head of four hundred Zouaves.) The women began making tortillas for them. (That same afternoon a republican army of four hundred men under General José María Arteaga entered Jiquilpan.) The ranchers of Llano de la Cruz and the neighboring settlements were astounded at the Zouaves' uniforms: loose blue jackets and baggy red trousers. When night fell, the French galloped out of Llano de la Cruz and headed east. At four o'clock in the morning Clinchat's forces fell upon the sleeping republican army in Jiquilpan. In the battle that followed, General Ornelas died of a ball in the neck, and General Pedro Rioseco was killed by a blow with a club. The defending army was routed.[13] The *güeros* marched back again; and once more the

---

[13] Ramón Sánchez, *Bosquejo estadístico e histórico del distrito de Jiquilpan de Juárez,* pp. 128–129; some of this information was also obtained from Apolonia Oceguera, who was a girl of thirteen when the French troops arrived.

women of the *ranchos* on the former hacienda of Cojumatlán began grinding corn and making tortillas for them.

From then on the "Frenchies," advancing or retreating, appeared in one hamlet after another. It was then that Tiburcio Torres came along: short, fat, red-faced, bearded, a native of Zapotlanejo. It was said that he had brought down many French and Mexican monarchists in Los Altos de Jalisco while a member of the famous gang headed by Brígido Torres, who was defeated at Pénjamo. He was on the run, for all of Los Altos was now in the hands of his enemies. He would settle down to live and go on recounting his exploits here on the former hacienda. Later his brothers would follow, and together they would found the Torres family.[14]

The establishment of the diocese of Zamora created less stir among the local country people than had the aurora borealis, the subdivision of the hacienda, or the advent of the Zouaves. In any case, the news reached them, had its effect on their lives, and made them feel honored to be living near a real personage: the bishop, who seemed as remote as the inhabitants of heaven. During their exile in Rome, Pelagio Antonio de Labastida and Clemente de Jesús Munguía had engaged in negotiations before Pius IX for setting up the sees of Chilapa, Tulancingo, León, Querétaro, Zacatecas, and Zamora. In accordance with the papal bull (*In Celsissima Militantis Ecclesiae Specula*) dated January 26, 1862, the diocese of Zamora was founded.[15] Señor Don José Antonio de la Peña, its first bishop, occupied the seat of his diocese in December, 1865. He was ill at the time. One of his first acts was to found a seminary, and another was to make his pastoral visit. He was in Jiquilpan and Sahuayo in 1866, although his illness did not permit him to make frequent journeys.[16] From his residence in Zamora he undertook the reform of the clergy, bearing out his reputation as "a severe, zealous man, with little or no tolerance. . . ." "His soft voice thundered from the pulpit . . . damning impiety and denouncing vice." In his actions, however, he was merciful.[17]

[14] According to Ángel Torres, Don Tiburcio's nephew.

[15] José Bravo Ugarte, *Diócesis y obispos de la Iglesia Mexicana*, pp. 96–97.

[16] Sánchez, *Bosquejo estadístico e histórico*, p. 164.

[17] Arturo Rodríguez Zetina, *Zamora: Ensayo histórico y repertorio documental*, p. 422.

Economics of the Ranchos

The republic headed by President Juárez (1857–1872) and his successor, President Sebastián Lerdo (1872–1876), went to work reforming agriculture by introducing new crops and farming techniques; stimulating industry; encouraging immigration of foreign colonists; building railroads, canals, and highways; making every peasant a small landowner; instituting freedom of employment; establishing democracy; and lifting people out of "their moral prostration—superstition; their mental degradation—ignorance; and their physiological abjection—alcoholism—toward a better life, no matter how slowly."[18] None of these good intentions had the slightest effect upon the lives of the two thousand people living on the uplands of the former hacienda in 1870. This tiny, isolated society, made up of descendants of families who had settled there before the Independence, as well as those who had moved in at the time of the hacienda's subdivision, was showing signs of growth. In the fifteen-year period from 1867 to 1882, this small, lone community was beginning to consolidate its livestock economy; to settle upon the foursquare diet whose corners were milk, meat, corn, and beans; to set up a solid system of small rural properties; to apportion labor according to specialties; to form groups based on property and wealth; to be brought together by bonds of kinship and *compradazgo*; to be alienated because of money or honor; to create its own standards of virtue and vice; to rise from a purely oral culture to a written one; to enact its own epic; and to bring to maturity its Christian faith and customs.

In 1866, the year the bishop came to visit, "there happened to be heavy rains in December";[19] the following year was a very wet one, too. The fifteen hundred milch cows grew fat, and in each of those years gave about 250,000 liters of milk, or a little more than a liter a day per animal. Cattle prices rose to the sky. Don José Guadalupe González sold one lot of heifers at thirteen pesos a head. Among

[18] Justo Sierra, *Evolución política del pueblo mexicano*, p. 423. The broadest and most complete picture of the period is found in the first three volumes of Daniel Cosío Villegas's *Historia moderna de México: La república restaurada*.
[19] M. Torres, *Historia civil y eclesiástica*, p. 169.

all the settlements in what would be the jurisdiction of San José, a thousand large cheeses were turned out annually. The cattle were handled in about the same way as always. People still milked only from St. John's to All Saints' Day, and calves still were not branded until after the rains, so that the wound would not fill with maggots.[20]

Sheep raising came into fashion, and by 1870 there were as many sheep as cattle. They were kept in flocks of from twenty-five to one hundred. It was the children's job to take the sheep to the best pasture, defend them from the coyotes, lock them up at night, and give them their weekly saltpeter. Adults did the shearing in April and November and took a kilo of wool from each animal. When a sheep reached the age of ten years, it was sacrificed without hesitation and made into *birria* or barbecued. At the time of the death of Juárez the local sheep ranchers were selling some 2,500 kilos of wool every year to the sarape makers in Jiquilpan.

The processing of beeswax was also a booming business. In those days every hut had its apiary, set on a wooden frame a yard from the ground. The bees lived in boxes with tile or shingle roofs. Honey and wax were removed in May and November. The honey was consumed at home, while the clarified wax was made into cakes and sold. There came a day when local hives could no longer supply raw material for the wax-bleaching industry, and people began traveling in search of untreated wax. They brought the round cakes from Pihuamo; some were yellow, some orange, some brown. They all contained a sediment of dead bees. The cakes, weighing an arroba or more, were melted over a slow fire; the liquid wax was poured out in thin sheets, which were laid on the green grass and left to bleach in the sun for a week. Then they were sprinkled with maguey juice and remelted; the beeswax was then poured into round molds. Clarified wax was taken to be sold in Cotija, where it was made into candles and widely distributed. In Llano de la Cruz and its neighboring ranches alone, some six hundred arrobas of the commodity were produced every year, at a profit of a peso per arroba. If to this we add the price paid

[20] From private records of José Dolores Pulido (1828–1913), owned by the author.

for the local raw beeswax, we can conclude that beekeeping brought in 16,000 pesos annually.[21]

Making cheese, shearing sheep, purifying wax, and distilling mescal brandy took the ranchers out of their extreme poverty and into a market economy. When Porfirio Díaz was serving his first term as president of the republic, there were still many maguey plants on the hills and rolling plains surrounding Llano de la Cruz. From the heart of the maguey was extracted *aguamiel*; from the panache of thorny, pulpy leaves, ropes and sacks were made; and the entire plant was chopped up to make *aguardiente*, or mescal. Mexicans say: "Whether you're feeling bad, or in the pink—mescal's the drink." Not pulque, which is fermented *aguamiel*, but only *aguardiente*. Here is the recipe. Mash the plant with wooden hammers, strain it through a leather sieve, and let it stand until it ferments, when it is called *tuba*. Boil the *tuba* over a slow fire in an earthenware pot and let the alcoholic vapor condense on the lower surface of a copper vessel filled with cold water. Let the condensate drip into the channel of a maguey leaf and run off into a barrel. By 1880 the area with which we are concerned here was producing two hundred barrels of mescal brandy a year, which were snatched up at fifteen pesos each.[22]

Raising corn and beans had never been profitable, for the soil on the mesa is not suitable for these crops. But since tortillas and beans were absolute necessities, people planted just enough of both so that they did not have to buy them. Cornfields, of course, were still tended in the traditional way, with plow and oxen. Orchards of fruit trees became popular. Near every little house there grew from two to a dozen trees: peaches, limes, sweet limes or *limas*, prickly pears, avocados, and the like. Meat (including the flesh of the cattle that died of starvation during severe dry seasons), milk, corn, and beans, supplemented by purslane, cactus leaves, prickly pear, the heart and flowering stalk of the maguey, and small and large game, kept these people in good condition. In fact, they often fell into the capital sin of

21 Information supplied by Luis González Cárdenas.

22 *Aguardiente* was usually not exported. A detailed description of its manufacture can be found in Esteban Chávez Cisneros, *Quitupan: Ensayo histórico y estadístico*, pp. 219–221.

gluttony—in food as well as drink. The fact that victuals were adequate and even abundant does not necessarily mean that they were healthful. The water they drank, for example, cannot have been very good, for water-borne diseases were common.[23]

The relative comfort of their stomachs was not matched by that of their clothing, houses, and furniture. It is a cold region, and their garments were light. The sarape, which the men wore over a cotton shirt and trousers, was not warm enough. Women wore nothing under their cotton dresses. Pneumonia claimed more victims than any other disease: one out of every three deaths involved great pain in the chest. Both men and women had but one change of clothing: while they were wearing one, the other was in the wash. They protected themselves from the rain and sun with sombreros made of palm fiber and capes of palm leaves. Everyone but the wealthiest wore huaraches. That they had not yet developed a taste for comfort could be seen in their dwellings, too.

The houses, not to say hovels, did not provide adequate shelter. Except for a few "big houses" with adobe walls and tile roofs, erected by the larger landowners, they were the most modest structures, thatched with grass, with a room for sleeping and another for cooking, and a porch to sit on—just as they had been before the subdivision. Pictures of saints and a few utensils still hung on the walls of mud and sticks. The floor was dirt. In the yard around the house, under a sheltering tree, lived the chickens, pigs, cats, and the pack of dogs.

Furnishings were meager. People slept on grass mats, *petates,* which during the day were rolled up and stacked in one corner of the bedroom. They ate sitting on the floor or, in the best houses, on low wooden stools. There were few kitchen utensils: some pottery cups and bowls, the *metate,* the earthenware griddle for making tortillas, the bean pot, the wooden spoon, the *molcajete,* the water jar, and the wooden bowl. Clothing was stored in a chest or a small leather trunk. Hats and lariats hung from nails, along with weapons: machetes, a spear, occasionally a rifle.

---

[23] According to the APC, the principal causes of death were measles, whooping cough, smallpox, pneumonia, dysentery, and diarrhea.

Small landowners and ordinary day laborers, those who had property and those who did not, were alike in that they lived without conveniences. They did not make money in order to live comfortably. Money was good for three things: you were treated with greater respect, you could buy land, and you could bury it. These ranchers loved to show up at weddings and roundups with their pockets full of silver coins, so that they jingled when they walked or danced. Another of their ambitions was to build a large estate and ride from one end to the other on a good horse. Their strangest whim, however, was collecting gold coins and burying them in a clay pot near the house. The urge to save, the worship of land, and the status value of money were the three essential elements in their economic thinking.

Labor did not pay much and was only in a limited sense a source of wealth. Livestock increased spontaneously, requiring the hand of man only from July to October, and even then for little more than milking. Chores were more important morally than economically. Idleness was a vice and work was a virtue. To work and to be good were almost synonymous. Besides, those who did not work were bored. Work also meant amusement, for fun and labor were not mutually exclusive. To these ranchers living on their own land, the life of an absentee landlord was incomprehensible. And so man's toil had two principal dimensions—moral and recreative—and one secondary one—lucrative.[24]

Ranching Society

Before the Cojumatlán hacienda was subdivided, the differences between a man and his neighbors were almost entirely natural ones. People were distinguished according to skin color, sex, age, height, physical strength, degree of bravery, intelligence, and the like. A highly important social distinction lay in one's surname. Within a patriarchal and patrilineal order, belonging to a certain clan or large family counted for a great deal. Otherwise, nearly everybody did the same things and shared the same poverty. From 1861 on, however,

[24] Most of the assertions in the last four paragraphs were taken from conversations with old people, especially Don Luis González Cárdenas. Other facts were gleaned from Don José Dolores Pulido's letters.

new marks of distinction began to be noticeable. Specialization increased: there were those who tilled the soil and those who did not; cattle raisers and farmers; artisans and an occasional merchant. Some worked their own land; others—sharecroppers or even hired hands—worked other people's land. By this time, too, there were distinctions among the rich, the poor, and those in between. Specialists and social classes were beginning to appear. Labor, property, and capital created differences that until then had been unknown. Thus, there was a marked upheaval in the social structure.

In order not to deviate from the usual practice, we shall say that three groups took shape: the aristocracy, the middle class, and the proletariat. Let us consider as aristocrats the dozen men who enjoyed the profits from their land without ever leaving their homes in town. They lived comfortably on the income from their ranches, which were worked by others; they made money for their amusements and business ventures from the efforts of their cowhands, sharecroppers, and laborers. Among these aristocrats were Don Manuel Arias, who ultimately took up residence in Guadalajara; Don Francisco and Don Rafael Arias, who lived in Mazamitla; Don Vicente Arregui, Don Bartolo and Don Pedro Zepeda, Don Nestor and Don Antonio Ramírez, all of Sahuayo; Don Miguel Mora, who bought El Nogal from Pedro Zepeda in 1867 and managed it from his residence in Pajacuarán; and Don Rafael Quiroz and Don José Guadalupe Sandoval, of Jiquilpan and Sahuayo, respectively.[25]

Let us place in the middle class another fifty heads of families, some of them merchants, but for the most part owners of smaller properties, a sitio or less in area. They lived on their ranches, at least during the rainy season; they personally supervised the raising of their cattle and crops, even if they did not milk or sow, themselves; and they saved money at the cost of their families' comfort.

In the third group let us put the three hundred remaining heads of families. In 1870 most of them were working as sharecroppers, artisans, cowhands, and field laborers in Sabino, Auchen, Palo Dulce, Guayabo, Cerrito de la Leña, Nogal, Ojo de Rana, and La Rosa, as

---

[25] Some meager data concerning absentee landlords were provided by notarial archives in Jiquilpan; the anecdotal information is from family tradition.

employees of absentee landlords. In appearance, and in the lives they led, there was little to distinguish the middle-class rancher from the poor man.

Guadalupe González Toscano, a prominent resident of Llano de la Cruz, was the archetype of the rural middle class. He was born there in 1821, the eldest child of Antonio González Horta and Lugarda Toscano. His father taught him how to raise corn, handle a horse and lasso, and keep cattle, as well as other rural occupations. He went to a teacher in Durazno to learn to read, write, and calculate. No one knows where he learned to pray, but he prayed often all his life. When it was time to marry, his eye fell on one of Vicente Pulido Arteaga's daughters. The girl's father was the "rich man" of the *ranchería*, while the boy was penniless. In his favor was the fact that he was good-looking, well-thought-of, and could turn his hand to anything. Gertrudis, the girl he wanted, aspired to a husband with these qualities, but not such a poor one. Guadalupe left the traditional load of firewood at Gertrudis's door; her eldest sister took it in and burned it, simply to get rid of Gertrudis. All unaware, Gertrudis had said yes. The load had been left for her; it had been burned; therefore she had to marry the lad. The couple had six sons (Ciriaco, Fermín, Gregorio, Andrés, Bernardo, and Patricio) and four daughters (Andrea, Salomé, Lucía, and Genoveva). Guadalupe subleased land on the hacienda; Gertrudis saved money and bleached beeswax. He was sober and hard-working; he took good care of his family and gave to the poor. At the end of fifteen years he and his wife had saved 750 pesos, with which they bought the 350 hectares with the oak grove and the maguey field that descends the western slope of Larios Mountain. Guadalupe González began buying land and cattle in 1861; in 1867 he bought grazing land and some fields for summer planting in Espino; finally, he was able to get hold of the hill called Pitahayas. Thus, he had enough property for two hundred head of cattle. He had the noblest heart in the region and was like a father to many people. Don Antonio Carranza, a rich man from Cotija, was a good friend to him. Guadalupe was up before sunrise and went to bed two or three hours after sunset. He ate very moderately, and he never wore anything but a cotton shirt and trousers, huaraches, and a palm-fiber sombrero. His house was a hut consisting of a kitchen and a bedroom. He worked hard every day of his life and shared everything he made with the poor. He was a virtuous man—the kind people call a giant. Don Guadalupe González died in 1872, of a tumor on his middle finger.

The ranchers lived a poor life, but not an unpleasant one. Their notion of the ideal man was a simple one: the things that counted were hard work, strength, courage, and cunning. Above all else, they admired physical endurance, good horsemanship, and daring: in other words, the concomitants of the primitive life. They did not look down on a man because of vices of the flesh: drunkenness, extramarital intercourse, dozing in the shade of a tree, using tobacco. In addition to the corporeal vices and virtues, the ideal man must have land, a woman, cattle, and money of his own. Because the possession of these things was such a serious matter, there was never any shortage of quarrels, fights, and killings. There were ferocious duels over a few feet of land, a glance at someone else's wife, the "grass in my pasture that so-and-so's damned cow ate," the "money I lent what's-his-name that he never paid back." All in all, honor and reputation were the most common and the most dangerous virtues. Treating each other with respect was the norm, for the slightest show of discourtesy could be costly.

The man who knew how to read, write, and do sums was highly respected. The heads of families in the various *rancherías* got together to hire teachers. Two of the teachers in Llano de la Cruz were Don Jesús Gómez, from Sahuayo, and Pedro Torres, who came from Los Altos. The latter had to give up his job because of a woman. He and a bullying rancher were courting the same girl. She accepted both of them—one of her own free will, the other under duress. The girl went to Cojumatlán to arrange her wedding with the rancher. The two rivals followed, each by a different route. The bully was made to agree to be married at the High Mass; but the priest married the girl and the teacher at the first mass, and by sunup the newlyweds were crossing the lake. The betrayed man's gifts for horsemanship and homicide were of no avail on the water.

School caught up with very few of them, and it did not take the place of training at home. The ultimate shaping of the rancher was the result of contact with the natural environment and rural life. Children learned to eat sitting on the floor, as their mother tossed them their cornmeal *sopes* hot from the griddle. They taught themselves to walk, run, and climb in oak trees and over horses and bulls. It was the animals who showed them the customary methods of perpetuating the species. From infancy they were trained in all kinds of chores: the boys as future cowboys, *alzadores*, shepherds, and beeswax bleachers, and the girls as mother's helpers at home and in the field. The female ideal continued to be the biblical strong woman.

Most of the hard work fell to the women: grinding corn on the *metate*, making tortillas, cooking meals for the men, keeping the fire going, cleaning, washing clothes, sewing, darning, carrying water, scolding their husbands and children, taking care of the pigs and chickens, bleaching wax, making cheese, weaving—in short, keeping so busy with household chores and home industries that they got no rest. It was only the men who could allow themselves the vice of idleness; and those of the generation following that of José Guadalupe González—those born between 1834 and 1847—indulged in it to a greater degree than did their fathers and older brothers. This was especially true of the landowning class. It never exceeded the limits set by the ruling elders, however. Respect for the old men remained intact.[26]

The national, state, and *municipio* governments remembered the ranchers in the western part of the district of Jiquilpan only when one of them committed some misdeed, or when it was time to pay taxes. As soon as the war was over, the court in Jiquilpan and the rural police once more assumed their customary severity toward poor people. The jail was filled with prisoners, "mostly because of fights and killings."[27] Then, too, in 1866 the office of the state tax collector reopened in Jiquilpan, as well as a subordinate one for tax stamps. They were equally efficient in collecting revenue. And, as if this were not enough,

[26] Almost everything I have written here concerning social life is based upon what I was told by Mariano González Vázquez, Apolonia Oceguera, and Luis, Josefina, and Agustina González Cárdenas.

[27] Sánchez, *Bosquejo estadístico e histórico*, p. 197.

the vigor of the *municipio*'s treasurer in Sahuayo was worthy of note. Thus, the behavior of public officials did nothing to inspire respect and love for authority in the minds of the ranchers.

Religion, Games, and Insecurity

The refusal to submit to civil law and authority contrasted with the obedience accorded to ecclesiastical government and to the commandments of religion. With little instruction, no public worship, and not a little superstition, religious life retained its exuberance. A prominent part of it consisted of the direct, physical contact with beings from the beyond. No one doubted that the devil and souls in purgatory could appear on earth. In order not to clash with regional customs, Satan usually showed up on horseback. One day, when he had swept up a sinner and was carrying him off through the air, he saw his victim drawing a rosary from his shirt pocket. This was enough to make the devil loosen his grasp. The poor sinner would have been dashed to pieces if he had not fallen miraculously into the branches of a wild olive tree in the ravine that is still known as the "Devil's Barranca."[28]

Religious practices were widespread. It was a common, everyday thing to say one's rosary at dawn and at nightfall. On Sundays many people traveled from ten to twenty kilometers to hear mass in one of the neighboring villages. The most popular holy figures were those of the Virgin of Guadalupe, St. John, St. Isidore the Farmer, and St. James the Greater. It was not unusual for parents to examine their children on Father Ripalda's catechism, and it was common for anyone who could to read aloud from religious books. Nearly everyone went to confession once a year and paid his tithes. All this, however, did not keep them from breaking the fifth and sixth commandments (proscribing killing and adultery) without a second thought. Most people could recite the following from beginning to end: the Pater Noster, the Credo, the Ave Maria, the Ten Commandments, the "Todo fiel," the "Yo, pecador," the "Señor mío Jesucristo," the Mag-

---

[28] Old people still love to tell this story.

nificat, and the short prayers and litanies. No one questioned a single article of faith. For these country people, heaven, hell, and purgatory were as real as night and day.

Besides praying, the ranchers had three other favorite occupations: playing games, horseback riding, and talking. They especially liked games of chance, and cards most of all. But the event they greeted with wild transports of joy was the annual roundup and its rodeo. Here they could show off all the skills acquired in the never-ending battle with the animal world; here the best of them could exhibit their dexterity in handling horses and roping; here they could practice bullfighting and breaking horses in "the old-fashioned way." All this was embellished with mariachi music, with its songs filled with malice, erotic allusions, and encapsulated desires: a music that prompted them to roar, howl, scream, and get falling-down drunk on *aguardiente*.

Conversation around the fire, by the red light of pitch-pine torches, was a very popular pastime. Exchanging anecdotes and fables was the favorite amusement from sundown until nine at night. And there can be no doubt that there were excellent storytellers within the limitations of a rudimentary art and an extremely meager repertoire of themes: feats of horses and horsemen, the cultivation of crops, "the crimes of men," feuds and violent deaths, natural phenomena, rainstorms, lightning, rising rivers, signs regarded as portents of the day of judgment—the comet, or the aurora borealis. There were tales of famous bandits, reminiscences about the *tincas*, stories about those who had died in the two cholera epidemics, the doings of ghosts, the wild tricks of the devil and other scoundrels, tales with erotic themes, "reports" of buried treasure, and a few biblical stories: Samson and Delilah, Tobit and the angel Gabriel, Joseph and his brothers, Adam and Eve, Moses rescued from the river. They recited other people's poetry and composed their own, both descriptive and satirical. José Dolores Toscano (1834–1903) was the most popular rhymester. He left behind him folk ballads, epigrams, and comic verses. The other branches of the art were less popular. Needless to say, they sang *valonas* and the *Alabado*, this last at dawn. Verses were exchanged during the *papaquis*, and the tunes from José León's harp were indispensable at any fandango, whether for a baptism, a wedding, the harvest, or a rodeo.

This free, semibarbaric, gay, egalitarian life would have been idyllic had it not been for feelings of anxiety about evil spirits, the yearly dry spell that wiped out the cattle, decennial droughts, frosts that came early or too late, plagues, pains in the chest, smallpox, "the disease of Lazarus," venomous snakes, meteors, sudden death, being poisoned by eating pork and drinking milk on the same day, bad luck, backbiting, unrequited love, other people's dirty tricks, being made to look like a fool, the presence of the dead, feeling the icy fingers of ghosts on one's face, coming across the flaming figures of the damned, the devil and his temptations, and, especially, the fear of the disruption of peace and of a return to the anarchic days of banditry, rape, and impressment.

But only six things came along to break the calm in the fifteen-year period between 1867 and 1882: Ochoa's rebellion, the atrocities committed by "El Nopal," the great famine, the bishop's visit, the snow-storm, and the comet.

The Ochoa affair was an episode in the *cristero* uprising, which involved the states of Michoacán, Querétaro, Guanajuato, and Jalisco during the presidency of Lerdo de Tejada. The *cristeros* rose in rebellion because of political interference in religious matters, and particularly because the Reform Laws had been incorporated into the constitution. The local ringleaders, Ignacio Ochoa and Eulogio Cárdenas, with 150 mounted men, suddenly fell on Sahuayo on January 9, 1874. From then on, they subjected the ranchers of the former Cojumatlán hacienda to every kind of robbery and harassment. At last the people of the region lost patience, and, with the help of a local peace officer named Martínez, they succeeded in overpowering Ochoa in the hamlet of Sabino. The rebel leader and his men had hemmed in General Luna, who had taken refuge in the main house of the hacienda; there was a cordon of besiegers all around the building, except on the side facing the reservoir. During the night, Colonel Gutiérrez's forces, together with Martínez and local reinforcements, swam across the pond and reached the besieged house. The next morning every door flew open at once, and the occupants came out shooting;

they killed a hundred of Ochoa's men, and the rest took to their heels. Finishing off the scattered remnants was child's play.[29]

In the wake of the "old *cristeros*," Francisco Gutiérrez, nicknamed "El Nopal" (the Cactus), came along. Toward the middle of 1874 he and twenty fellow-prisoners broke out of the Jiquilpan jail. As leader of this band of convicts-turned-highwaymen, "he spread terror and dread among the people of this region because of his many robberies and horrible murders."[30] As in the case of Ochoa, battalions and regiments were ineffective against Gutiérrez and his men. Once again it was the ranchers, themselves, who took justice into their own hands.

Partly because of Ochoa's and Gutiérrez's depredations, and partly because of the frosts and drought of 1876 and 1877, there was hunger in western Michoacán. The lack of corn was not as disastrous on the cattle ranches as in the flatland, for the ranchers were able to supplement their diet with meat. But, in any case, that year without corn or beans was put down on the unforgettable list.

In August, 1881, people flocked to Jiquilpan and Sahuayo to see the new bishop of Zamora, the majestic Don José María Cázares y Martínez. Episcopal visits were rare. A few could still remember when Don Clemente de Jesús Munguía had appeared in Sahuayo in 1854. Another visit, by Don José Antonio de la Peña in 1866, also in Sahuayo, had not been as heavily attended. Only the residents of Llano de la Cruz and Durazno had been able to enjoy the brief appearance of Pedro Espinosa, the bishop of Guadalajara, in Mazamitla. Cázares's visit presented additional attractions: aside from the prescribed confirmations, there were sermons preached by the "holy fathers." To these country people, anyone who delivered a sermon was a holy father. Some of the older residents had heard the preaching in Mazamitla, and they were still living by those sermons when Cázares's homilists arrived.[31]

A frightening thing occurred in February, 1881. After many days of drizzling rain and frosts, "a wind like a hurricane came up, so that

29 Chávez, *Quitupan*, p. 40.
30 Sánchez, *Bosquejo estadístico e histórico*, p. 131.
31 Ibid., pp. 164–165.

people could hardly get about." The wind brought "a snowstorm that began at dusk and ended at dawn." More than three inches of snow fell. The sun came up more bright and radiant than ever before. No one had ever seen anything like it. The snowstorm stole some of the comet's thunder. Comets, like pastoral visits, were showy and unusual; but they had happened before. The white, glistening snow, like little feathers of cotton and glass, left a lasting impression. It was all so fantastic, like an enormous Nativity scene. The snowstorm marked the end of the era that had opened with the aurora borealis.[32]

[32] Information provided by Luis González Cárdenas.

2. THE TOWN (1883–1900)

The Generation of the Snowstorm

It is customary to characterize Porfirio Díaz's regime as an epoch of peace, prosperity, national consolidation, and dictatorship. Daniel Cosío Villegas has shown that the Porfirian peace was not as widespread or as stable as has been supposed.[1] Still, it seems to have been more solid than that of any preceding period since the Independence. Don Pedro Henríquez Ureña assures us that Díaz's prosperity reached only the upper levels of society.[2] And yet, it was dazzling, with its railroads, machines, and palaces. National consolidation by means of public education, legislation, and nationalistic propaganda did not penetrate to any great depth, either, but, even so, one cannot ignore the resplendent schools of positivism, the great variety of legal codes, and the general feeling of "a splendid, multimillion-dollar nation, with an honorable present and a heroic past."[3] The dictatorship and the political bossism, too, were not unqualified. The dictator proved to be a paternal opportunist, and not every cacique in his retinue was unscrupulous. In any case, the virtues and vices of the Díaz regime, already so well known in the cities, made themselves felt over vast areas of rural Mexico; but there were some corners of

[1] Daniel Cosío Villegas, "El Porfiriato: Era de consolidación," *Historia Mexicana* 13, no. 1 (July–September 1963): 76–87.
[2] Pedro Henríquez Ureña, *Historia de la cultura en la América Hispánica*, p. 111.
[3] Ramón López Velarde, *El león y la virgen*.

the country, including even those that were culturally accessible, where they did not penetrate.[4]

Of all the ingredients of Porfirio's reign, only one was felt in the vicariate of San José de Gracia: peace. None of the modern methods of communication and transport fostered by the regime reached that far. There were no technical innovations and there was no foreign capital. Not one of the national products for export was produced there. The area had been forgotten by the government of the republic, the administrators of Michoacán, the prefects of Jiquilpan, and, to a great extent, the *municipio* of Sahuayo and the *tenencia* of Cojumatlán. It remained on the margin of the nation's political life, as usual. Nobody there noticed that what Porfirio Díaz and his coryphaei detested more than all else was freedom of speech and of labor. No political bosses committed abuses there; no one reverted to the institution of latifundia, or serfdom. They merely lived in peace; and under the aegis of that peace appeared a new generation of ranchers who were luckier than their fathers. They made their little world grow and prosper with hardly any outside help and with none at all from the governments.

Since 1818 four generations of men had appeared on the highlands of the vicariate of Cojumatlán: the revolutionaries, those of the great cholera plague, those of the little cholera epidemic, and those of the northern lights. The first of these were vigorous in fulfilling their double task of repopulating the hilly sections of the Cojumatlán hacienda and fighting zoological savagery with savage methods. It was that generation of patriarchs who redomesticated the wild cattle and horses, dug pits for trapping wild animals, and cleared the land of weeds and brush. Its members were lighthearted jacks-of-all-trades.[5] On the other hand, the men of the time of the great cholera epidemic, those born between 1803 and 1817, had a bad time of it. While they were still youngsters their world was shaken by anarchy, bandits, and impressment. They came along at a terrible time, and they were unable

---

[4] For further information on society under Díaz, see the detailed account by Moisés González Navarro: "El Porfiriato: La vida social," in Daniel Cosío Villegas, *Historia moderna de México*, vol. IV.

[5] See "Three Beginnings," above.

to extract any benefit from their toil. They did little more than help their fathers with the chores and try to protect their heads from the hailstorm of civil war. The generation of the little cholera plague, born between 1818 and 1833, forsook the purely defensive and conservative attitude of its elders. The atmosphere these men had been born into was not an easy one to breathe. One very important thing, however, was in their favor: the subdivision and sale of the Cojumatlán hacienda in 1861. Another lucky circumstance was the injection of new blood. The generation was enlivened by some enterprising people: the five Antonio Martínezes, the Chávezes from Espino and Tiznado, the Pulidos and the Gonzálezes from Llano de la Cruz—especially José Guadalupe González. The members of this generation introduced, once and for all, the more or less complete utilization of beef cattle—above all, the industrialization of milk products. It was they who made the first chink in the wall of the self-sufficient and natural economy, and became, as a result, the first rich generation. They were the only ones, aside from Martín Toscano, who amassed considerable amounts of gold and silver—either to buy more land or to hide in the earth. It was the following generation that inherited and spent that buried treasure; it included a great many drunkards, men with itchy trigger fingers and silver-bedecked *charros*, men who lent passion and flavor to ranch life, but no economic stimulus. It was the hundred families of the snowstorm generation who would return to the occupation of serious ranchers; they would take over in the 1880's, in the first years of the Porfirian peace.

Among the snowstorm generation—born between 1848 and 1862 —were grandchildren of the insurgents and elder children of those who had bought land at the time of the breaking up of the Cojumatlán hacienda. As children and adolescents they knew the terror and anguish of the struggles of the Reform, the Intervention, the Second Empire, and the *cristero* revolution. This, coupled with the fact that most of them were landowners, tended to inspire in them a love of peace and order and a certain tinge of cupidity. It was a generation that did not resist the general movement of the country but swam with the current. It was not, however, a homogeneous one. The insurgent generation had not been homogeneous, either, but its members had

nonetheless been very active. Guadalupe González Toscano's con-
temporaries had been heterogeneous and yet most enterprising. Members of the snowstorm generation, too, even though they were not
united, would be builders—at times out of sheer competition. There
were differences in class and habitat. It was not only ranchers and
townspeople who did not get along well, but also, at times, the ranchers, themselves. There were even sometimes differences of opinion
among the large families, but these were not as obvious as those between the rich and the poor.

The wealthiest members of the generation of peace and progress
did not live on their ranches, as a general rule. Thus, the Arias family,
who since 1888 had owned more than ten thousand hectares, or half
of all the land within the vicariate of San José, lived in Mazamitla
and Guadalajara. The Moras, who had owned the vast area of El
Nogal since 1887, made their homes in Pajacuarán. The Zepedas were
residents of Sahuayo, El Valle, and Mazamitla; the Ramírez and
Arregui families lived in Sahuayo; the Sandoval and Quiroz clans had
homes in Jiquilpan. Seven families owned a fourth of the land. And
this absentee-landlord aristocracy, who all together held three-quarters
of the entire region, possessed other properties as well. It was said
that Don Manuel Arias, owner of Sabino, had six other haciendas; the
other large landholders were not nearly as rich and pretentious. Most
of them lived well, some in large city houses with many servants.
They sent their children to good schools. The Mora family saw one of
their offspring become the archbishop of Mexico. Many of them engaged in the sport of impregnating their employees' daughters; others
spent their time at the gaming table and taking promenades. Still, we
must grant them some constructive zeal; they were interested in
making the most of their properties—putting in stock ponds, increasing milk production, and attempting a few daring industrial innovations, such as the flour mill that Don Manuel Arias set up at Aguacaliente.[6]

Those of the "peace," or snowstorm, generation who could be considered middle class lived—unlike the rich—the year round on their

[6] The date, 1893, can still be seen on one of the stones of the ruined aqueduct
that led to the mill. The mill operated for about five years.

ranches or in neighboring *rancherías*. These included groups of small landowners in Llano de la Cruz (the sons and brothers of Don Guadalupe González Toscano, and the children of Don Vicente and Isabel Pulido), Saucito (Don Antonio Martínez's children), San Miguel (Abraham and Filemón Aguilar, Simón Contreras, Antonio Cárdenas, and the Ortega brothers, Felipe and Ramón), La Estancia (Don Antonio Barrios's children—except for the musician who gave up his inheritance and went to live in Cotija), San Pedro (the children of the foreman named Rodríguez, José María Higareda, and Luis García), Izote, Breña, and Tinaja (the Ruiz and Ruiz Pamplona families), and Espino and China (Trinidad and Vicente Chávez, Valeriano Cárdenas, and the Fonsecas). All these small landholders, alone or with the help of a few cowboys and farmhands, dedicated themselves body and soul to working their land, raising cattle, and in general improving the area. Their ambition was to provide ease and comfort for their descendants, rather than to secure these things for themselves. On the whole, they worked so hard that they had no leisure. Unlike the rich property owners, they had a great love for the earth.[7]

The third group within the snowstorm generation were those who owned no land: cowboys, sharecroppers, the simplest kind of artisans, and laborers. The greater part of this proletariat worked for the large proprietors and lived (without much freedom, although not in such servitude as the peasants on the huge estates under Porfirio Díaz) on the employers' land. Only the dispossessed of Llano de la Cruz (two dozen families) got along without an employer, hiring themselves out here and there, driving mules, refining wax, making lariats from maguey fiber, or turning out mescal. All of them—the free and the not so free—were able to make a meager living, but it was impossible for them to save any money. They were as devoted to the land as the small property owners, and later they would collaborate in the development of the region in a generous and cheerful way.[8]

The four most distinguished bearers of the standard of progress were, in order of age, Gregorio, Andrés, and Bernardo González from

[7] See chap. 1.
[8] These data were supplied by notarial files in Jiquilpan, parish records in Cojumatlán, and word of mouth.

Llano, and Juan Chávez of China. The first three were the sons of Don Guadalupe González and Gertrudis Pulido; the last was the child of Vicente Chávez and Ana María Tejada. Gregorio was born in 1850, Andrés in 1852, Bernardo in 1857, and Juan in 1859. Don Jesús Gómez taught them to read, write, and do sums. From their fathers they learned farm work and the recipe for a blameless life. Gregorio and Juan were full of fun, Bernardo was serious, and Andrés solemn. It was said that Andrés had picked up his solemnity and sedateness in Cojumatlán, where he had been sent as a boy to complete his education. There he learned penmanship and how to draw up "papers" (contracts of sale, wills, deeds, and receipts). His bent was for letters, Juan's for science, Bernardo's for business, and Gregorio's for religion.

Juan was a man of diversified talents, and he tried various professions: ironworking, soapmaking, medicine, surgery, and other mechanical arts. It was vital for country people to be able to predict the rains—when the season would begin, how often it would rain, and how much. Juan invented a system for forecasting this. Women were demanding to be freed from the slavery of the *metate*; he conceived the idea of a small, household-size mill for grinding corn. No one in the area had a knowledge of remedies for aches and pains; Don Juan applied himself to the art of medicine, and he came to be an expert in the use of a multitude of mixtures, syrups, and unguents.

Don Gregorio, too, tried many roads: he took up business, raised cattle and sheep, tended bees, and refined beeswax. In 1882 he took possession of his first ranch, La Tinaja, where he used to go with his family during the milking season. When the people of Pachuca stopped coming to buy the products of the region, Don Gregorio began his long trips to the capital with cheese, pigs, and whatever else he had on hand. He had kept milch cows, sheep, and hogs since he was a boy, but rural economy was not his calling. He was unique in one thing: his piety. The Bible and Father Ripalda's catechism were the sources of his inspiration. No one knew as many prayers as Don Gregorio—prayers to be recited, and prayers to be sung.

All four were devout men. All four, too, were businessmen, although it was Bernardo whom no one ever beat in a deal; he came to be a wealthy cattleman and landowner. All making friends easily, each with his specialty, they worked for themselves and for others. Their greatest achievement was leading their neighbors from a rural to an urban way of life.[9]

There came a day when people—the middle-class ranchers, principally—felt the need for living in a town. The rich were already doing so in Mazamitla, Jiquilpan, Sahuayo, and El Valle. Being part of a community had all kinds of advantages. Buying and selling were easier; one's money, honor, and life were safer. It was the best defense against rebel bands, bandits, and even against the devil and ghosts. In every village there was a priest and a church. One was never far from his dead, for there was a cemetery at the edge of town. If the dead and the quick were to live together, a village community was essential. Girls would have a chance to show off their beauty, their clothes, and their virtues. Educating one's children was easier, too. In town were merchants, stores, a market, a plaza, pretty girls, a school, teachers, craftsmen, law and order, the proper kind of authority, a church, a priest, and a cemetery.

The middle-class ranchers, who were eager to make a change, had two choices: they could move to one of the neighboring villages, or they could start a village of their own. People in the other three zones on the mesa had already made their choice; they had recently set up the villages of El Valle, Manzanilla, and Concepción de Buenos Aires, better known as Pueblo Nuevo. The ranchers on the quondam Cojumatlán hacienda would take the same path. There were enough of them now to get together; by 1885 they numbered 3,000. Some of them lived in the three large *rancherías*: Ojo de Rana, with 100 people, Sabino with 125, and Llano de la Cruz with 217.[10] Auchen had about 75 inhabitants, and San Miguel was growing by leaps and bounds. Any one of these settlements could be made into a village. Three of them presented difficulties because of some of the rich

[9] Biographical information on the patriarchs is from parish records in Cojumatlán, Mazamitla, and San José, and, in particular, from recollections on the part of their children and relatives.
[10] Antonio García Cubas, *Diccionario geográfico, histórico y biográfico de los Estados Unidos Mexicanos*, and APC, Baptismal Records.

ranchers, who did not want a town and could not be convinced that
it was a good idea. People in San Miguel were in favor of becoming a
town, but the will of the large landowners prevailed. Only in Llano
de la Cruz, the largest of the *rancherías*, were there no rich residents
to scotch the idea. Llano was not ideally situated as far as natural surroundings were concerned, but it was the best choice under the circumstances. Like so many other small towns, San José would lie at
the foot of a mountain.

The Founding of San José de Gracia

Once, when the priest from Cojumatlán came to Llano de la Cruz
to hear a dying man's confession, he was accompanied by his deacon,
Esteban Zepeda, the son of a good family in Sahuayo. The deacon suggested to the ranchers that they build a chapel in the center of their
ranchería. Everyone agreed that it would be a good idea, and nobody
did a thing. The deacon became a priest, and he was assigned to his
native town in 1886. By this time, the idea of building a chapel in
Llano de la Cruz had grown. Now Father Zepeda decided to found a
town, with a plaza, a church, and its streets all in a line. The opportunity presented itself at the close of 1887, when Don José María
Cázares y Martínez came to Sahuayo on a pastoral visit. A few people
from Llano de la Cruz took their children to Sahuayo to be confirmed. Father Zepeda took them aside and said, "Let's build a town
up there where you live. Ask His Excellency to give us his permission." Then he gave them instructions as to the proper way to
approach the bishop. They must kneel before him and kiss his *esposa*.
That was the ring he wore on his right hand; they were not to be
confused, like the simpleton who kissed a lady of high rank who happened to be sitting at the bishop's side.

The people from Llano de la Cruz went to see Bishop Cázares. He
was well worth seeing, sitting in all his majesty in the beautiful vestments of his office. All the streets were decorated with crepe paper.
The brass bands never stopped playing. There were rockets, too. The
whole town was shooting off rockets. The bishop looked solemn and
worthy of respect. Gregorio González explained why they had come.

The bishop wanted to know if there was not already another town near the site where they planned to build theirs. Yes, they told him; there was Mazamitla. "That's too bad," he said; but he gave them the authorization. Then they went back to see the priest. "Very well," Father Zepeda told them. "I'll come and lay out the town."

It must have been about the eighteenth of March, 1888, when a lad rode into Llano de la Cruz with the news that the priest and a lot of other people were coming. The men dashed into the house to put on their *charro* trousers and comb their beards. Small children were sent "to tell people working in the fields that the padre is here." Other children ran around collecting tortillas, meat, and whatever else there was at the neighboring houses. At that point the party arrived. It comprised the leading citizens of Sahuayo; besides the padre, there were the president of the *municipio*, Don Tomás Sánchez; the apothecary Don Estanislao Amezcua; Don Melesio Picazo; Don Pedro Zepeda; and some others. Doña Refugio, the priest's sister, and a few other women had come, too. Everybody ate well.

That afternoon the neighbors assembled to discuss ways of raising money to begin building the town. The first to speak was the priest, who was not yet thirty years of age. Then Don Tomás Sánchez suggested taking up a collection and conducting a raffle. Right there at the meeting people pledged over a hundred pesos. Some promised to give cows and steers; others agreed to contribute pigs, chickens, or labor. Don José Dolores Zepeda announced that he would make a donation only if they built no town at all (probably because he was from Mazamitla). There were others who agreed to give something but in the end failed to keep their word.

The following day they considered the question of the best site for the town. Some wanted it at Ojo de Agua, while others were in favor of Ahuanato. They finally chose the slope facing the *ranchería* of Llano de la Cruz, on the west, just on the other side of the creek. The hillside belonged to José María and Luis González Toscano and was covered with cactus, maguey, and thornbushes. The owners agreed to sell lots. The locations of the plaza and the church were precisely marked. With a plow drawn by a team of oxen, straight furrows were made to indicate the perimeter of the town square and the courtyard of the church (here some holy relics were buried). Seven rectangular blocks were laid out in this way, and then everybody went to lunch.

In those days people ate at high noon. During lunch they discussed the matter of a name. They could continue to use Llano de la Cruz, but it would be better to find a new one. Anyway, how could you call it "Llano" (plain) when it was on a hillside? It would be a good idea to name it after a saint, but there were so many in the celestial court! Doña Refugio, the priest's sister, said, "Call it San José; today is March 19, the day of the Patriarch." Everyone agreed; later someone added "de Gracia." When the party returned to Sahuayo, San José de Gracia had its name. (End of Act One.)[11]

Don Gregorio González Pulido agreed to promote and direct construction of the church. Many people took part in the laying of the foundation. A deep trench in the shape of a cross was dug and filled with stones, under the direction of Marcos Pulido, the superintendent of construction. Then a mason came to supervise the raising of the adobe walls; it was Don Atanasio Alonso, who had shown his skill in the craft in another new town, Concepción de Buenos Aires. He was a native of Tepatitlán, in the heart of Los Altos.[12]

While some men were working on the church, others were building their houses within the outlines that had been laid out for the town. These houses were not like those in the *rancherías*. All outside walls were of adobe. Hardly anyone built with wattle-and-daub or used grass roofs.

The system of construction was the same as that used in the larger towns nearby. Stones were laid in a mud mortar for the foundations. On these the adobe walls rose from two to three meters. The adobe bricks were of sun-baked mud, 50 by 40 by 18 centimeters (about 20 by 16 by 7 inches). On them rested the wooden beams and rooftree

[11] These facts were given me by Luis González Cárdenas. His story is based principally on what he was told by his father, one of the founders, but also on some of his own recollections.

[12] Information supplied by Mariano González Vázquez, born in Llano de la Cruz in 1865, the son of Antonio González Horta.

that supported the gable roof. A grillwork of sticks was fastened to the beams to support the overlapping tiles of red terra cotta. Beneath the framework was laid a plank ceiling, or *tapanco*. This was the floor of a loft to be used for storing corn and fodder. Most of the houses were modeled after structures in Jiquilpan, Sahuayo, and Manzanilla.

In those days it occurred to no one to build his house according to the dictates of hygiene. Nobody worried about whether a house was properly ventilated, or well lit, or even whether it was warm. Human excrement would still be deposited, as always, on the ground in the yard, where the pigs would eat it. Some people put shed roofs at the rear of their houses for domestic animals—especially for the horses. Garbage was thrown into the yard for the chickens to pick over.

Everyone knew that the houses in the best towns of the area had no yard or garden around them. So here, too, the front door and the garden were placed inside, hidden from the eyes of passersby· it was the Andalusian patio. The porch disappeared from the outside of the building, to reappear inside, around the patio. Don Andrés González Pulido, who had taken on polish from living in Cojumatlán [There is a pun here, since "Pulido" means "polished."—J. U.], built a house with not only a kitchen and bedrooms, but a living room, as well. Years later others would follow his example.

Another widely imitated practice was that of filling the inside garden with Spanish impatiens; the *belenes* that Doña Lucía Cárdenas brought from Manzanilla and planted in the shade of her fruit trees multiplied rapidly. Finally, there were the windows: now every room facing the street had a window—except for the entrance hall. Inside and out, the houses in San José were better than those in any of the *rancherías*, and better furnished. Chairs, beds, and tables were added to the traditional household equipment. A new town called for a new kind of house.[13]

1888 . . . 1889 . . . 1890. Every year at least two dozen families came to settle down, new house and all, in San José. The *ranchería* of Llano de la Cruz was practically emptied at the end of the first three

---

[13] Information provided by Luis, Josefina, and Rosa González Cárdenas, María Gonzáles Zepeda, María Pulido, and other trustworthy informants.

years, as its residents moved into the village. Durazno, too, made its contribution. From La Venta came the Toscano family; Francisco and Manuel Pérez moved from Valle de Mazamitla; from Mazamitla proper came the carpenter Blas Ramos and the butcher Pascual Barriga. Tizapán collaborated in the settling of San José with the baker Martín "Chapala" López and the mule driver Andrés Gálvez. Los Corrales de Toluquilla sent a couple of worthies called the Ortiz brothers; Paso de Piedra contributed the Lara family and the fine carpenter Vicente Chávez; Pancho "Cotija" Chávez, Ildefonso "Penche" Contreras, and the majestic Don Lorenzo Zepeda opened stores. Among San José's early inhabitants were the especially distinguished Partida family from Palo Dulce and the Chávez clan from Espino and China. Don Juan Chávez and Don Apolinar Partida, Don Lorenzo Zepeda, Don Fermín and Don Patricio González Pulido (both polished gentlemen), Don Tiburcio Torres, the Morenos (Padre Luis and Padre Marcos) were some of the outstanding people who became residents of the newborn village from about 1888 on.[14]

By June of 1888 the vicariate of San José de Gracia was functioning as part of the parish of Sahuayo. Its jurisdiction would grow until it embraced the settlements at Aguacaliente, Arena, Auchen, Breña, Ceja, Cerrito, Colongo, China, Durazno, Española, Espino, Estancia, Guayabo, Izote, Jarrero, El Nogal, Ojo de Rana, Palo Dulce, Paso Real, Sabino, San Miguel, San Pedro, Sauces, Saucito, La Tinaja, and La Venta. There were three thousand parishioners where, twenty-seven years before, in 1861, there had been only half as many inhabitants.[15] Father Luis Martínez, the priest from Cojumatlán, came through several of these settlements in April of 1888 on his way to confess a man who was dying in Llano de la Cruz. As he stood in Llano and contemplated the hillside where the town had just been laid out, his comment was: "Is that where the new village is going to be? Because if it is, the priest who will come to say its first mass has not been born yet." He returned to Cojumatlán. In June of the same year he was back in the town he had thought would never take root

[14] APSJ, Marriage Records, 1888–1900.

[15] Ibid., Baptismal Records, Book I. The number of inhabitants was estimated by multiplying the baptisms that year by twenty-five.

on that hillside, having been appointed to the vicariate of San José de Gracia. Gregorio González Pulido sold a good many cattle in order to buy his vestments. Quite against his will, Father Martínez, who was a native of Sahuayo, remained in the nascent village for a year and a half. Then he went off to serve as companion to the owner of the Guaracha hacienda, a role in which he was happier. He was replaced by Father Marcos Núñez, a native of Ixtlán, who also loved his comforts. He was no good, either; he was too ineffectual even to discourage his flock. The builders of the town put up with him for more than a year.[16]

At the beginning, the new town's political rank was no higher than that of any *ranchería*. Rodrigo Moreno was installed as peace officer and *jefe de acordada*. His deputy was Don Abundio Chávez, and their assistants were Justo Ramírez, Toribio Eulloque, Timoteo Chávez, Crescencio Negrete, Francisco Chávez, Marcos Rojas, Desiderio Ortiz, Cornelio García, José Pérez, and Luis Buenrostro.[17] The town council of Sahuayo appointed all these gentlemen, after examining the proofs of honesty and courage presented by each of them. But on April 19, 1890, the councilmen changed their minds. They ordered that "the citizen Gregorio González be named as peace officer in San José de Gracia, with Lorenzo Zepeda as his deputy, inasmuch as some citizens have alleged that Rodrigo Moreno and Abundio Chávez . . . are unsuitable, although Rodrigo has been satisfactory as *jefe de acordada*."[18]

At the end of 1890 a notable event brought to a close the second act of the town's founding. Bishop Cázares decided to visit San José. He left Cojumatlán with an imposing retinue, ascended the necessary four hundred meters, and was just beginning to ride across the mesa, with its clear air, when the first parties of *charros* came to receive him. As he proceeded, the escort grew in numbers "so that he was acclaimed by those who rode ahead as well as behind him . . ." José María, the bishop of Zamora, rode into San José in the midst of a multitude—and remained for a day and a half. He administered the slap of

16 The dates of the priests' tours of duty are from APSJ. The personalities of the first two were drawn from reports by Luis González Cárdenas.
17 AMS, Resolutions of the Council.
18 Ibid., 1890.

confirmation to nearly a thousand children, and the town set off a small *castillo* in his honor. Soon afterward Father Núñez was replaced by Father Othón Sánchez, who had just been ordained.[19]

Padre Othón was born and raised in Sahuayo, a town that had grown remarkably since the Independence; it had surpassed Jiquilpan, the capital of the district, in population and wealth. The census of 1895 showed 7,199 Sahuayans, who, according to Ramón Sánchez, were notoriously individualistic, irreverent, and aggressive. "Their extreme sensitivity leads them to harbor resentment, thus creating discord . . . The people of the town are even insolent, with pretensions to equality with persons of social position. They have another deplorable habit: giving people nicknames."[20] They were also—which Sánchez does not mention—religious to the point of fanaticism.

Padre Othón was from Sahuayo's middle class. He had just been graduated from the Zamora seminary that had been founded by Señor Cázares in 1864, where, in addition to Latin grammar, they taught scholastic philosophy and theology, a rigid moral code, and contempt and hatred for the form of government that had sprung from the Reform. Padre Othón was tall and strong, a Sahuayan to the hilt, and an old-fashioned Christian. He had been assigned to San José by Bishop Cázares, with the mission of shaping a nascent village society. The envoy set out to create a town in the image and likeness of Sahuayo, with the ideals of the Zamora institute.

The settling of the town was completed between 1891 and 1900. The church was put into service. The schoolteacher Francisco Gama (an ex-colonel of the Second Empire, face pitted by smallpox, ugly, and bad-tempered) hammered literacy and arithmetic into half a hundred children from 1896 until he became totally blind in 1898. Soon the nuns opened their school. There were a great many stores and shops by this time. Gregorio Núñez from Guayabo, and Sabás Flores from Ocotlán had opened meat markets; Julián Godoy of Quitupan ran a bakery; Emigdio Martínez from Jiquilpan had a tailor's shop; Heliodoro Amezcua of Sahuayo had set up a drugstore;

[19] My informant: Luis González Cárdenas. Also, APSJ, Confirmations, Book 1.
[20] Ramón Sánchez, *Bosquejo estadístico e histórico del distrito de Jiquilpan de Juárez*, p. 147.

Pilar Villalobos from Los Altos made and sold leather goods; Bartolo Ortiz from Los Corrales had a shoe store; Braulio Valdovinos from Jarrero sold hats; and Don Lorenzo Zepeda from Sahuayo ran the inn. Including local people and outsiders, more than a dozen carpenters, masons, adobe-brick manufacturers, and roof-tile makers were helping to build San José.

Padre Othón was the leading character in the last act of San José's founding. In the first, the leading personage had been Don Esteban Zepeda, the priest from Sahuayo; in the second, the people of Llano de la Cruz had been the protagonists; and now, in the third, it was the young priest from Sahuayo, Father Zepeda's *paisano*, an equally enthusiastic builder. The bishop of Zamora, Don José María Cázares y Martínez, played his part in all three.

Don Othón took care of the thousand minutiae that have to be thought of when a town is born. He helped lay out the streets; he pushed the construction of the church to its completion; he erected the parish house; he built the school; he brought in teachers; he imported artisans; he made use of pageants and other devices to strengthen Christian doctrine among his flock; he clothed the poor; he had drunkards and gamblers flogged; he helped the country people with contracts dealing with land and cattle; he tried to provide the infant town with a saint of its own, but the saint's brother ruined everything. (After a forty-day fever, Ponciano Toro fell into a trance and began having visions. He saw the whole celestial court and the denizens of hell, and he began to predict which of his neighbors would end up among the winged angels and which would spend the afterlife being tormented by little red devils. Padre Othón urged that the seer be made an object of public veneration; but Ponciano's brother Rosendo woke him from one of his trances by sticking a pack needle into him, and he never had another.)

Padre Othón never preached; he enjoyed reading devotional books and instilled that love of reading in young people. The padre went from house to house doing charitable works, and he persuaded others to follow his example. Everyone in town and in the *rancherías* came to him for advice. He would prescribe medicine for a sick little girl; he would suggest ways to tame a husband given to beating his wife, he would show someone else how to build a privy. He organized gaudy receptions for the bishop and the missionaries who accompanied him on his pastoral visits. (His Excellency and his missionaries came in 1893, 1896, and 1900. On all three occasions they administered confirmations and led retreats. During the retreats everyone wept copiously.) Bishop Cázares was very fond of Padre Othón, and the parishioners loved and respected him even more.[21]

The town prospered so under Don Othón that by 1895 it had become an apple of discord between the states of Michoacán and Jalisco. Jalisco, on the basis of some vague colonial rights, maintained that the southwestern salient of the former hacienda—all lands and hamlets south of a line drawn from Aguacaliente to the peak of Larios Mountain—lay within its boundaries. To resolve this border dispute, as well as some others that had come up between the two states, a commission of experts was appointed. The commission served from 1895 to 1897 and called in several ranchers as consultants—among them Gregorio González Pulido. As a result of the detailed study, the state line was carefully fixed on the west; at the same time, the boundaries of the vicariate of San José were established on the north, south, and west. The commission declared that the northern limits of that vicariate and also of the nose on the face of Michoacán that points toward the sunset, were "the line between Angostura Hill and El Molino"; that is: "a line drawn from the top of that hill to the summit of Portillo Hill, to the upper end of the Azulillos ravine, to the boundary of Cebollas, to La Joya, to the mouth of the Soromutal ravine, to a point halfway up the promontory of San Pedro, to the mouth of the ravine of the same name, to the slope called El Izote, to the middle of the hillside called Organera, and to Molino de Los Coyotes, on the banks of the Pasión River."[22] The commissioners from the two states had no difficulty in agreeing that the western limit should be the Pasión River, from Molino to the place where the river meets Agua-

---

[21] Many people offered information concerning Padre Othón's life and virtues: Agustina González Cárdenas, who is 81; María Pulido, 82; Margarita Orozco, 78; Luis and Josefina González Cárdenas, and others.

[22] *Límites entre Michoacán y Jalisco: Colección de documentos oficiales*, Morelia, 1898, p. 82.

caliente Creek.²³ They argued over San José and its environs. The San Joséans made it clear that they preferred to be Michoacanos. Michoacán claimed that San José and the surrounding area "had never belonged to Jalisco" and declared that it was in its interest to keep the town because it was "a village with a future."²⁴ It was finally agreed that the dividing line would continue to run along the Pasión River as far as Milpillas Pass; from there it would leap to the peak of Larios Mountain, then to Palo de la Labor; and from there it would follow the bed of the Fresnos ravine.²⁵ The agreement was approved by Porfirio Díaz on December 17, 1897, and published February 5, 1898.²⁶

San José did not want to be part of Jalisco for one very simple reason. Like every village in the Spanish American world, San José had a rival town. It was, of course, the nearest one: Mazamitla. If the San Joséans had agreed to belong to Jalisco, they would, temporarily, at least, have become subjects of Mazamitla, which was the head of a *municipio*.

Towns separated by a river, etymology tells us, are *rivals*. Between San José and Mazamitla there is only a creek—for at that point it is not yet the Pasión River—and a distance of two leagues. In any case, from San José's point of view, Mazamitla was the handiest town to regard as an enemy. Manzanilla was too far away; besides, its people were blood relatives of the San Joséans. Anyway, Manzanilla already had a rival in Concepción de Buenos Aires. Valle de Mazamitla (or Valle de Juárez) had a standing feud with Quitupan. For the people of San José and Mazamitla there was no way out: they had to be antagonists. The inhabitants of each town were obliged to hold those of the other in low regard. Also, there had to be rock fights between the boys.

San José had drawn a rival that was older and more powerful than itself. Mazamitla had been in existence for at least four hundred years; it was a pre-Hispanic community. It had suffered some reverses in the

²³ Ibid., p. 83.
²⁴ AMS, Resolutions of the Council, 1896.
²⁵ *Límites entre Michoacán y Jalisco*, p. 83.
²⁶ Ibid., pp. 98 ff.

first centuries of the colonial period, but it had prevailed as the most important town of the mesas and the Tigre Range. There was no place to equal it within a radius of forty kilometers. Its name had been a familiar one during the struggle for independence. At the beginning of its life as part of the new nation, there had been some difficulties with the white settlers. The *criollos* who moved in had no intention of mingling with the ancient inhabitants. The palefaces set themselves up as masters over the aborigines. At the end of the nineteenth century it was not a mestizo town, but a community divided into two castes. It had twice the population of San José de Gracia and controlled a vast territory.

By 1898 the vicariate of San José de Gracia was a well-defined entity: a little over 230 square kilometers,[27] containing a town and twenty-five hamlets, more than three thousand people, and about nine thousand cattle.[28] There were not as many people living in the village as could have been desired. The rich families would not allow their servants to live there. Some people said, "I can't make a living in town." Others left their families in San José while they themselves stayed and worked out in the country.[29] Even so, it already had the unmistakable look of a town.

Straight streets intersecting at right angles; a church that could hold a congregation of five hundred; a cemetery outside town; a plaza planted with large trees; a parish house, a school, three little stores, several shops, and 150 houses—these constituted the town at the end of the nineteenth century. The women no longer dressed in the same old way, for the padre had made them wear underclothes. Women "in blouses that came up to the ear and skirts that came down to the ankle"; women wrapped in *rebozos*, with only one eye and the end of a braid showing; women in kitchens that consumed great quantities of firewood; men who had begun to wear tight trousers and felt hats

[27] This figure was obtained by measuring, with a planimeter, the area indicated on a map of the *municipio* of Jiquilpan. The map was prepared by the Department of Agrarian Affairs, and my copy was furnished by the department's office in Morelia, Michoacán.

[28] The number of cattle was found on a loose sheet of paper in that great heap of documents that constitutes the files of the *municipio* of Sahuayo.

[29] According to Luis González Cárdenas.

with huge brims and crowns like towers, and boots—these signs distinguished them from the poor people, but only on the surface.

Poor people's houses were smaller and less comfortable, although they lived nearly as well as their wealthy neighbors. "The rich, stoical and tight-fisted, and the stoical poor, led the same humdrum lives."[30] The town was the same for everybody: streets of dirt and grass, water in the "miraculous well," where rich and poor women alike went with their water jars at dawn; rich and poor on horseback mingled in the morning bustle. The rich spent little on comforts; the poor could spend nothing at all. They were all living much better than they had before the town existed, but only as one lived in any tiny settlement under Don Porfirio: without urban comforts, better than in a *rancheria*, worse than in any city.

The Great Fright of 1900

According to the national census, in 1900 there were 3,251 inhabitants in the vicariate of San José—twice as many as in 1867. Twenty-eight percent of the total, 894 people, lived in the town itself. The *rancheria* of Sabino, the center of the hacienda, had 239 residents; Paso Real had 258, and San Pedro 251. In other words, three *rancherias* contained another 23 percent of the population. Each of the following hamlets accounted for 100 to 200 persons: Auchen, 168; Colongo and Española, 162; Ojo de Rana, 145; and San Miguel, 173. There were between 50 and 100 people in La Breña; in China, 69; in Durazno, 69; in Espino, 52; in Estancia del Monte, 97; in Laureles, 76; in Milpillas, 100; in Palo Dulce, 93; in Rosa, 92; in Saucito, 73; in Tinaja, 86; and in La Venta, 51. The 1900 census recorded only one place with less than 50 people: Arena, with 38. It did not mention Aguacaliente, Izote, or Cerrito de la Leña, which together contained a little more than 100. The total population within the vicariate can be estimated conservatively at 3,400.[31]

A quarter of the population was concentrated in the town; another quarter lived on small, independent ranches; the rest were spread out over the large estates. This would indicate that the lowest density

---

30 Agustín Yáñez, *Al filo del agua*, Overture.
31 *Censo y división territorial de la República Mexicana*, 1904.

occurred on the latifundia. The Sabino hacienda, for example, had only 275 people living on its forty-two square kilometers: between six and seven persons per square kilometer. It contained the best farming and pasture land in the region, and it was the most intensely worked of all the large holdings. It is significant, too, that a third of the population lived along the Michoacán-Jalisco border; this was partly because the Pasión River ran there, and also because it was possible for those who lived on the state line to escape prosecution in one state by crossing over to the other.[32]

Although the population was not exclusively white, the whites were in the majority. About 30 percent were mestizos, and 10 percent were Indians. Needless to say, these were not Indians by culture: they spoke Spanish and prayed to Jesus Christ. While the whites did not feel themselves to be any different from the mestizos, they did regard the Indians as a people apart: a little because of skin color, a little because of social status, and mostly, perhaps, because the Indians were outsiders, since many of them lived in the jurisdiction of Mazamitla, San José's rival community.

By 1900 the population was, on the whole, homogeneous. For thirty years there had been hardly any immigration. And, as we have seen, the early immigrants of the sixties had come from nearby areas and by 1900 were totally assimilated. From 1891 on, those who came to the newly founded town either lived there for only a time (like Padre Othón's numerous relatives and the artisans he imported), or were people from Manzanilla and neighboring places who were in no way different from the San Joséans. Practically all of Padre Othón's parishioners were on the same cultural level. The fact that only 20 percent could read and write was of no great significance in those days.[33]

To a large extent this homogeneity was due to isolation. Once the squabbles were over, no outsiders to speak of showed up—even on their way to somewhere else. Even the mule drivers from Cotija and

---

[32] *Límites entre Michoacán y Jalisco*, p. 46: "Criminals who cross the line believe that they are under the protection of the other state, and thus not liable to prosecution."

[33] This figure is not taken from the census, but estimated on the basis of oral information and data from San José's parish records.

Sahuayo (who were not considered foreigners, anyway) came along the king's highway from Colima less often. Now things could be brought in and sent out by that modern means of transportation, the railroad. The Mexico City–Guadalajara line had been inaugurated in 1888; in 1899 the Yurécuaro-Zamora section was put into service, and parallel to it, the Guadalajara-Colima line was being built through the Sayula Valley.[34] Steamships were plying Lake Chapala.[35] The telegraph had come to nearly every one of the towns in the crescent north of the mesa.[36] In short, new and efficient means of communication surrounded—but did not touch—the mesa lying between Jiquilpan and Sayula, and between Lake Chapala and the Tigre Range. The vicariate of San José did not even have mail service. By the end of the century, hardly anyone came into or out of San José. Don Gregorio González, with his trips to Mexico City, and the people who occasionally came down from the hills were the exceptions.

The isolated population of the vicariate grew rapidly, although not because of immigration. Between 1890 and 1899, there were 1,187 births and 360 deaths. This shows a credit balance of 827, even in spite of some bad years: the whooping cough epidemic of 1890 carried off a great many children, and in 1894 smallpox killed 18.[37] Adding the 79 who came from the outside to take up residence in the newly founded village, we arrive at the figure 906 as the increase over a decade. So, then, in ten years the population showed almost a 25 percent gain, in spite of endemics and epidemics, against which there was hardly any defense. Sixteen percent of the deaths were due to pneumonia, 5 percent to whooping cough, and 8 percent to smallpox. (Vaccination against smallpox was just being introduced.) In San José one out of every ten children died within its first year; in rural areas infant mortality was 14 percent. A good many mothers were lost through complications of pregnancy and childbirth. After the age of fifteen, one man in a thousand died an accidental or violent death. Between 1891 and 1900 there were only five murders.[38]

---

34 José Bravo Ugarte, *Historia sucinta de Michoacán*, III, 174.
35 Antonio de Alba, *Chapala*, p. 104.
36 Sánchez, *Bosquejo estadístico e histórico*, pp. 201–202.
37 APSJ, Baptismal Records and Death Records.
38 Ibid.

Some other characteristics of this vicariate of 3,400 inhabitants were a preponderance of males on the ranches and of females in the town; numerous children; a considerable number of old people; a high percentage of workers and scarcity of work. The 1900 census records 1,618 men and 1,633 women—0.4 percent more men.[39] Fifty-one percent of the country people were men, while, in the town, 53 percent were women. Forty-three percent of the population consisted of children under fifteen, and 5 percent were over sixty-five.

Everything was going splendidly, when a piece of news came along to strike terror into the hearts of townspeople and *rancheros* alike: "The world will come to an end on the last day of 1900." Someone— nobody knows who—made the prediction toward the end of the rainy season, during the time of thunder and lightning.

The bishop arrived in November. There was preaching, as always. The people scourged themselves and wept. Someone heard one of the priests say that the end would come on the night of December 31. There were others who claimed that the bishop himself had made the prediction. There were sinister omens, too; the principal one was a comet. Padre Othón tried to stem the rising tide of terror, but no human power could have stood up against it. Ranchers began coming down from the hills into San José. The church was filled with despairing people. No one wanted to be caught unshriven, but the priest could not hear everyone's confession at once. He announced that he would begin with mothers who had babes in arms. There was an uproar in the church when it was discovered that one of the women had been holding a pillow in her arms instead of a child. At any rate, nobody's sins remained unconfessed. Don Othón did not rise from the confessional for three days and three nights. At last the dreaded night arrived. Terrified parishioners filled the church and overflowed onto the porch. Midnight came and went, and life went on as before. People began filing back to their homes. The great fright was over. From now on there would be nothing but next year's weather to worry about.

Apparently the widespread fear occasioned by the anticipated end of the world brought on all kinds of calamities. Women's fertility di-

[39] *Censo y división territorial*, México, 1904.

minished remarkably. In 1900 the birthrate dropped off 12 percent, and there were 51 percent more deaths than during the previous year. There were more burials in San José than baptisms. An epidemic of smallpox and the endemic pneumonia claimed many victims. Some people were left penniless; they had decided to enjoy themselves before going to the next world. Marcos Chávez, having just received a legacy, and seeing that everybody was taking this end-of-the-world business seriously, took thought for pleasure; he spent his entire inheritance on some famous drunken sprees.[40]

[40] This is a summary of many individual recollections concerning the great fright.

3. THE *RANCHOS* AND THE TOWN (1901–1910)

The Business World and Social Life

IF HALF a dozen scrupulous observers had visited San José in 1901, they would have gone home with an equal number of conflicting reports. One might have concluded that it was a village of cattle, fiery horses, farmers, and whiskered cowboys; another would have seen a community of small and medium-sized ranch owners, all related by blood and *compadrazgo*; a third would have had the impression of a little town made up of peaceable and cheerful loafers; a Jacobin liberal might have thought of it as a Trappist cloister without walls; a progressive patriot would have seen a hotbed of conservatives, indifferent to their country; the sixth, if he were the chief of an indigenous Indian community, would have found the blonds and brunets of San José grasping, restless, nervous, and fond of change. No one of these facts alone matched the physiognomy of San José; but if all six were taken together, they could be said to make up an accurate picture.

The principal characteristics of economic life were a predominant farming and cattle-raising element, rudimentary manufacturing, a little small-scale trading, widespread self-sufficiency, low-yield activities, small production, and low prices. Farm work (raising the seasonal corn crop and tending dairy cattle) occupied 80 percent of the active population in 1901. Only part of the goods produced on the cattle ranches was marketed. Industrial activities consisted principally of simple processing of some of the livestock products, and minor handicrafts. Economic life centered about the annual cycle of seasons. The working calendar was as follows: In the spring, the principal crops (corn, beans, and squash) were planted, and the wheat and garbanzos harvested. Summer, the season par excellence for ranch chores, was the time for weeding the cornfields, milking, making cheese—and hard work for everybody. Fall was the season for sowing small areas with garbanzos and wheat, cutting cornstalks and leaves for fodder, turning out the cows—and the roundup. Winter was the time for bringing in the corn crop and for the harvest festivals. At the end of winter, beeswax processing, a dying industry, was begun. Mescal was made, too, in the dry season. The greatest activity during this time, however, was salvaging the hides of the cattle that had died from lack of water. In good years a quarter of the herds were lost in this way, and, in bad years, half or more.

Not all years were equally productive. The abundance and distribution of rain, wind, and frost changed from one year to the next. There were three kinds of years: dry, good, and spotty. It was basically a matter of rainfall. In dry years no rain fell in the winter, and that during the wet months was brief and scant, as occurred in 1894–1896. On the other hand, 1898 and 1899 were quite the opposite. But it was not only the amount and duration of the rain that made a good year. Some years were spotty, and it did not rain in the same way in any two places in the entire region. All activities, and cattle raising in particular, were at the mercy of changes in the weather—at the mercy of the weather and of Saint Isidore the Farmer.[1]

Livestock raising was still the leading industry. There were seventy ranchers who owned more than 10 head of cattle each.[2] Large proprietors, like Don Manuel Arias, grazed 2,500 animals—a little less than one-third of the total for the region. In the entire district of Jiquilpan, there were 21,200 cattle;[3] the vicariate of San José, occupying only one-thirteenth of the district, contained one-third of the beef cattle. Thus, it was the cattle-raising zone par excellence. During the

[1] According to Luis González Cárdenas.
[2] AMS, Registry of Marks and Brands, 1897.
[3] Ramón Sánchez, *Bosquejo estadístico e histórico del distrito de Jiquilpan de Juárez*, p. 213.

rainy season, from Saint John's Day to All Saints' Day, about 60 herds of dairy cows, each comprising from 40 to 60 animals, gave for four months and one week 6,000 liters of milk a day; in the entire season they produced 750,000 liters, valued at the time at 15,000 pesos. The calves were worth 9,000 pesos a year. By adding to this the income from the other animals (horses, mules, donkeys, pigs, and sheep), we can estimate that the annual yield from livestock was 30,000 pesos.[4]

The basic industry was making milk into hard cheese; on a much smaller scale, the farmers also made *jocoque, requesón,* butter, sour cream, and other products. About four-fifths of the milk was made into these products in accordance with precise traditional formulas. All the solid cheeses, except for small varieties, such as *panela,* were large and round, with a flavor and odor like cheddar. Most of the cheese went to market. Don Gregorio González Pulido took local products to the capital once a month. Cheese was taken by muleback to Tizapán; from there it went by boat to Ocotlán, where the train picked it up and took it to Mexico City. There it was sold by some Spaniards named Pérez. The other milk products were consumed at home: the *jocoque,* or curd of the raw milk; the *requesón,* or ricotta, made from the whey; and the sour cream and butter. Other products from livestock were not turned to any great commercial use. Defective calves and other unwanted animals that did not die off during the dry season were sold on the hoof to the uplanders (the traders from the Bajío) and, to a lesser extent, were slaughtered for local consumption. Wool from the few flocks of sheep was partially consumed by the small local sarape industry. Half of the pigs were utilized locally, and the other half went to Mexico City along with the cheese. The hides of cows and sheep supplied modest local tanneries and harness makers. The best-known harness maker was Don Eulalio Vargas.

Less than 5 percent of the land within the vicariate was devoted to corn and other cereals. Three hundred *yuntas* plus a few hoe-tilled patches were planted in corn. In either May or June, depending upon the weather and upon whether planting was to be done in dry or wet earth, the sowers began dropping kernels of corn into the furrows,

[4] According to Luis González Cárdenas.

kicking the soil over them as they went. In the following month the dry planting was done, with the help of the *alzadores*; a month later the fields were plowed again, during the rains, almost in mud. Each of the processes of sowing, plowing, and replowing took from two to three weeks. When these were finished the oxen were unyoked, and there was nothing to do until it was time to cut the stalks. The farmer looked over the cornfield once or twice to make sure no destructive animals got in, plugged up the holes in the fences, and did any other necessary housekeeping.

After the cutting of the stalks came the harvest. If it had been a good year, each *yunta* yielded from thirty to fifty *fanegas* of corn, besides the beans and squash. If things went well, the entire area produced some eight hundred tons of corn and fifteen tons of beans, with a value of about twenty thousand pesos. At that time a kilo of corn sold for two and a half centavos, and one of beans for three. Wheat and garbanzos brought higher prices, but very little of either was grown in these parts. The Sabino hacienda was the only property near the lake that raised wheat and, occasionally, garbanzos. Its owners made money on these crops; other people merely raised enough for their own consumption.

All corn and beans were for home use. Every human being ate three fanegas of corn and twelve liters of beans a year. Rotten or defective corn, along with husks and stalks, was given to the horses and cows. The women had charge of turning the products of the harvest into food. Almost all the corn, after being stripped from the cob, was made into tortillas; but some ended up as *atole blanco* (a corn beverage drunk during the dry season), tamales, boiled or roasted corn on the cob, corn soup, and tacos. All three meals of the day ended with boiled or refried beans. Squash was eaten roasted or *en tacha* (boiled with unrefined sugar or honey). Other foods that were prepared by boiling were tender cactus leaves, purslane, mushrooms, and squash blossoms. Prickly pears, peaches, *charagüescas*, and *aguamiel* went to the stomach in their natural state.[5]

From the maguey fields (and there were many in those days) came

[5] Information supplied by Luis and Josefina González Cárdenas.

not only the juice called *aguamiel*, but also mescal brandy. There were a dozen well-known distillers. Don Rafael Córdova carried on the trade in San José. But the making of alcohol was on the decline because of competition from Quitupan. Another craft that was beginning to disappear was beeswax refining. At the beginning of this century, the town alone—without counting the *rancherías*—had seven carpenters, two blacksmiths, three bakers, two sarape weavers, five ropemakers, three harness makers, thirty candlemakers, two saddle makers, a tailor, a painter, six stonemasons, a couple of musicians, an apothecary, a thief, half a dozen mule skinners, two shoemakers, a potter, a lime burner, a cigar maker, a barber, four teachers, the priest, a gardener, a midwife, three butchers, and many tradesmen.[6]

Trade moved ahead faster than other occupations. A merchant class sprang up, particularly in the town itself, where in 1901 there were eighteen citizens engaged in full-time buying and selling. There were traveling tradesmen and storekeepers. Of the former, some operated only within the jurisdiction of San José, while others were importers and exporters. Among the exporters, Gregorio González Pulido was the champion. Two notable storekeepers were Lorenzo Zepeda, a native of Sahuayo, and Ildefonso Contreras from Epenche. Stores stocked all the usual items (except for those things produced locally): the best unbleached muslin at nine centavos a meter, percale at seven centavos, salt from Colima at four centavos a kilo, sugar at ten, soap from Zapotlán at ten, raw sugar at eight, rice at nine, a palm-fiber hat at sixty centavos, and one of German felt at eight pesos. The butcher threw on his table the meat of the animal he had killed personally the day before. A kilo of beef went for one and a quarter reales, and a kilo of pork for ten centavos. Lard for frying cost twenty-five centavos (that is, two reales) a kilo.[7]

The least productive of all economic pursuits was searching for buried treasure. There were four ways to go about this, all equally ineffectual: "communications," fire, wands, and listening to souls in

---

[6] According to the author's retrospective census for 1901. Most of the data come from parish records in San José (APSJ).

[7] These prices, as well as some that will appear later in various sections, were taken from records of household expenses kept by Doña Josefina González Cárdenas.

purgatory. The last of these persecuted women a great deal. Sometimes these spirits appeared to beg them to pay some obligation or other and whispered directions for finding the money. When the ladies awoke, they searched in vain. Magic wands were no better than the voices from beyond the tomb. For this, the usual method was to have each of two people hold a pair of wands a short distance above the ground in places where treasure might be buried. Someone would recite: "Magic wand, by the power God gave you, tell me if there is money here." The wands' way of giving this information was to drive themselves into the earth at the spot. Of course, whenever one set out to find the exact location of some treasure, it was because fire had been seen in the area. This fire appeared as little flames that hovered just above the earth, showing the general direction, but not the precise spot. It was only the "communications" that gave very clear instructions; but it was difficult to receive them and to meet the conditions they demanded for finding the treasure. Some "communications," such as those from Martín Toscano, were held in high esteem. People who had put them into practice told of seeing a herd of phantom horses.

There was a rapid increase in specialization. A man like Don Juan Chávez, who could do anything, came to be regarded as an exceptional and admirable figure. The day of the jack-of-all-trades was over, but the time of the "specialist" was still far in the future. It was not unusual for a man to take care of four jobs of different kinds simultaneously. It was common for a man to switch as many as three times from one group of occupations to another within his lifetime. A couple of examples may be given. Most small landowners raised livestock, made cheese, and refined beeswax; some did all these, and, in addition, they were merchants and peace officers, like the brothers Bernardo and Gregorio González. Among those who held no land, or only very small parcels, it was common to be first of all a field hand, then a cowboy or an adobe brickmaker, and after that a corn farmer, a milker, a bricklayer, a small merchant, an artisan, or anything else. There was no limit to how many times a man might change his trade. Lugardo Gómez, a schoolteacher in 1892, was listed as a milker in 1894.

There were no full-time occupations nor was there any grinding toil. On the Sabino hacienda there were peons who labored from sun to sun; but elsewhere no one worked very hard. In a predominantly autarchic economy it is not easy to determine the rewards of effort. Most workers (the majority of whom were men, although no less than 20 percent of the economically active population engaged in gainful pursuits were women) consumed the larger part of the fruit of their labor, without converting it into money. It is possible, *grosso modo*, to affirm that a small landowner, who milked his own cows, made cheese, and refined beeswax, took in about three hundred pesos a year by selling what he and his family did not use. A sharecropper, a milker, or a worker in the maguey fields might be able to save forty pesos in a year. Hardly anyone worked for wages alone. Day labor paid so little that it was difficult to support a family by that means. "The daily wage of a peon on the hacienda was twelve and a half centavos in cash and a quarter of an arroba of corn . . . and on small ranches it was twenty-five centavos a day, with no corn ration."[8] Peons usually kept one or two cows "costing them a centavo a head per month for pasturage. . . . Those who owned one or more cows were able to feed their families with what the animals produced, and thus devote the income from their personal labor to buying goods."[9]

In 1901 there were about 140 ranches within the vicariate of San José. The average size was 178 hectares. The rest of the *municipio* of Jiquilpan contained 1,171 ranches, each of which comprised, on the average, 265 hectares. In this district and throughout the rest of Michoacán, it was common to find vast estates side by side with tiny parcels. The vicariate of San José, however, was an exception. It contained only one hacienda of moderate proportions, and the rest were small ranches. In addition to the hacienda with its slightly more than 4,000 hectares, 7 owners in the area held from 1,000 to 3,000 hectares each; 16 had from 300 to a thousand hectares; 28 held parcels of from 100 to 300; and there were 88 very small proprietors with less than 100 hectares. In 1896 Don Ramón Sánchez was pleased to see that

---

8 Sánchez, *Bosquejo estadístico e histórico*, p. 205.
9 Ibid., p. 204.

there were "many landowners on the highlands west of Jiquilpan."[10]
The number grew greater every year, as properties were divided up
through legacies or pieces were sold off. In 1892 a ranch at La Tinaja
was divided between Don Francisco Gutiérrez's two sons; in 1893,
Don Vicente Chávez's children sold Los Sauces to many individual
buyers (Secundino Haro, Francisco Orozco, Julián Moreno, and
others); in 1894 Don Jesús Zepeda bought the pasture at San Miguel
from one of Don Francisco Arias's sons; in 1895 Don José Martínez
began assembling his large holdings by buying several sections of La
Arena from his brother-in-law Contreras. In 1897 Valeriano Cárdenas
took possession of a ranch at Espino, made up of three separate parcels
he had bought. On the other hand, the property that had belonged to
Dolores Zepeda at La Venta was split up among her three children.
In the following year Don Antonio Barrios's widow divided La Estancia del Monte among her five children, and Don Manuel Arias, the
rich owner of the Sabino hacienda, acquired several pieces of land
bordering on his property. While some lands were cut to pieces,
others grew larger. It was division that predominated, however. The
62 landowners of 1867 had become 140 in 1900.[11]

At the end of the last century, almost a quarter of the six hundred
families within the vicariate of San José de Gracia owned ranch properties. There were a dozen large landowners, too, who lived elsewhere.
Those who had land and cattle and did live within the vicariate, half
of them in the village itself, made up the region's middle class. They
lived at a respectable level of material comfort. Don Ramón Sánchez
states that in the district of Jiquilpan there were, in the direction of
the setting sun, "great, high plains planted with crops, and forests of
oak and madroña and other trees proper to a cool climate. The many
owners, who bought their land from the Guaracha hacienda, have
comfortable houses on their small ranches, furnished with some
luxury, and it is not unusual to see good collections of chromolitho-
graphs."[12] Some of these people owned a house in the country and

[10] Ibid., p. 30.
[11] ANJ, Records of Licenciados Ignacio Zepeda and Aurelio Gómez.
[12] Sánchez, *Bosquejo estadístico e histórico*, p. 30.

another in town: houses with adobe walls and tile roofs, spacious bedrooms with furniture lined against the wall (leather-covered chests,
beds, chairs with seats of woven maguey fiber), portraits and land-
scapes on the walls, flowerpots along the inside porch, and many
plants and flowers in the interior garden. Houses with dining rooms
and well-supplied kitchens, and, at a distance, three-holed privies in
the back yard, along with pigs and chickens and horses; houses with a
second yard filled with fruit trees; dwellings inhabited by men wearing *charro* outfits or loose white cotton trousers and shirts—well-off,
yet living in almost the same way as the poor: with a minimum of
luxury. These well-to-do residents of San José de Gracia used their
income of three hundred pesos a year to buy land and to educate their
children, to fill buried earthenware pots, and to acquire a few small
comforts and pleasures. Poor people, on the other hand, were just able
to buy a little amusement with their forty pesos a year.

The large landowners, who lived in Sahuayo, Mazamitla, Jiquilpan,
and Tizapán, made up a separate and hostile world. They were always
growling about something. San Joséans complained to the *municipio*
authorities about the selfishness of these hacienda owners. Don
Manuel Arias visited Sabino, true enough; but it was also true that
when he came he made trouble. He forbade anyone to ride across his
property, for it set his teeth on edge to see some traveler's horse
snatch a mouthful of his miserable weeds. Residents of the *municipio*
of Sahuayo took legal action against this old miser and the other rich
landowners whenever it became necessary.[13] These outsiders were the
thorn in the social body.

There were also disagreements within the bosom of San José's society, of course; but they were of little importance. Between 1890 and
1900 there were only five homicides and a few fights without serious
consequences.[14] Stealing and offenses against a man's honor caused
occasional uproar, but relations were usually amicable and restrained.
"Cautious dealings, full of respect and reserve."[15] Each man lived in

13 AMS, Resolution of the Council, 1896–1903.
14 ANJ, Criminal Judgments, 1891–1900.
15 Village life in San José de Gracia was similar in many ways to that described
by Agustín Yáñez in *Al filo del agua*.

his own way, and all lived in the same way: strict separation of men and women, sexual life regarded as shameful, absolute authority of the father. The hacienda owners used "Don" when addressing their tenant farmers; these, in turn, took off their hats in the presence of their masters. The doffing of the hat and the murmured greeting were indispensable when two men met. Everyone kissed the priest's hand. Old people were treated with every courtesy. *Compadres, comadres,* and relatives visited each other. Everyone attended weddings and funerals; neighbors crowded into the dying man's house to help him meet death; bereaved women wept as they prepared the corpse, and the dead were dressed as splendidly as brides; one was expected to pray and weep for both. Padre Othón presided over all social ceremonies; he prescribed them, embellished them, and saw that children and adults alike took part in them.

Padre Othón was the highest authority. The political leaders, who were called "peace officers," and the judges, known as *jefes de acordada,* recognized and bowed to the priest's supremacy; they consulted with him about what was to be done, and they worked closely with him in the few public services required by the village. Don Juan Chávez, Don Gregorio, and Don Bernardo González took turns as peace officer. It was a job nobody wanted: one made enemies, reaped few rewards, and received no salary. Peace officers and judges were proposed by the head of the *tenencia* in Cojumatlán and appointed by the municipal council in Sahuayo. Cojumatlán and Sahuayo asked only two things of them: honesty and courage. These were virtues that abounded in the village; the three men mentioned above shared them, and Don Bernardo González Pulido was beyond reproach in both respects.[16]

Amusements and Religious Duties in Padre Othón's Small World

In San José and its political jurisdiction, there was in those days neither social discord, nor extreme poverty, nor back-breaking toil, nor comfort. Life moved along unhurriedly, far from the world and its temptations. Anxiety and sudden terror and uncontained joy were common. The swing of the emotional pendulum seems to have been

[16] AMS, Resolutions of the Council.

wider than it is today. One passed easily from misery to joy, and vice versa. Strong emotions were often mingled with religious ideas: fear, sharp awareness of sin, erotic pleasure, mass repentance. Neither masters nor servants were idlers, but both had a great deal of leisure and the means to indulge in amusements. If their fathers, who had been poorer than they, had allowed themselves such things, they had even more right to do so. But pleasure was always sporadic and brief. It never took up as much time as the business of spirit. In these parts, people prayed almost as much as a community of cloistered monks. It was a conservative mentality, fed on a cultural tradition that was centuries old; it recognized no motherland beyond that which it could encompass with the eye. Yet, it was a mentality that loved the idea of change, of going beyond the confines of its own corner of the world. A great many currents went to make up life in San José de Gracia at the close of the last century. Amusements headed the list.

There were pleasures that appealed to the senses: intoxicating liquors, cigars, and delicacies. A great deal of mescal was consumed. In the village alone there were ten professional drunkards. We have no information to indicate that there were any teetotalers. Men (but never women) usually got drunk at fiestas. But fiestas did not take place very often: there were 130 baptisms a year, but few parties to celebrate them; of the thirty weddings, many were dry. For most people, hard liquor was not the daily bread; but the cigar was more than that. Both men and women smoked a great deal. Delicacies were made not only to satisfy the whims of pregnant women, of course; they also were served on fiesta days, at baptisms and weddings, during the roundup, and at harvest time, and they might appear any day in the home. Women made them to please their husbands, fathers, and brothers. The men were often regaled with tamales, crullers, *atole*, enchiladas, corn soup, cheese cake, and rice pudding. During Lent they had *capirotada* and *torreznos*.[17]

Sports were the traditional ones. They were for all ages, but exclusively, or nearly so, for the men. Little boys, in addition to being allowed to play with tops and marbles and to fly kites, were trained to be good horsemen. They learned to break a horse and accustom him

---

[17] According to Josefina González Cárdenas. *Boys*

to the bridle, to make him gallop and jump on command, to lasso and fight from the saddle, to ride as straight as a tower or to fall asleep without losing their seat; to ride and throw a calf, brand and castrate him; to bring down doves and other birds; to kill badgers, squirrels, hares, rabbits, coyotes, and snakes with slings, stones, and rifle; to climb trees and cross rivers in flood; and to ride great distances. These everyday amusements brought prestige to anyone who was good at them; they were enjoyable at roundups and gave one access to other kinds of fun—especially fun with the opposite sex.

There were three kinds of amorous amusements: premarital, marital, and extramarital. The first was a bit acrobatic and risky, since it called for getting through fences and scaling walls at all hours of the night. A tryst with the loved one—if her parents found out about it—could easily end in gunfire. Premarital exercises also involved letter writing, arrangements with go-betweens, and often a brief theatrical work presented by the young man who was asking for the girl's hand and the parents, who were not going to give her away just like that. As for marital pleasures, let it suffice to say (for these people were not like those from other towns) that they seldom included the sport of wife beating.

When a girl's parents opposed the marriage, it was not unusual, especially in the *rancherías*, for her to be kidnapped. Padre Othón was unable entirely to stamp out this custom. However, he did succeed in putting an end to the time-honored wedding party with its exchange of verses between the choruses of men and women, its battle with confetti-filled eggshells, and its drinking and dancing. In spite of all he could do, extramarital affairs went on as always; the incontrovertible proof of this was the number of illegitimate children. In the decade from 1890 to 1899, one out of every twelve was born out of wedlock.[18] An innocent and very popular extramarital amusement was spying on the girls as they bathed in the creek in the open air, naked as the day they came into the world, in the buff, in the altogether.

The daily musical treat was provided by the chorus of morning birds, the early-rising cock-a-doodle-dooers, the crickets with their

18 APSJ, Baptismal Records, Books I and II.

interminable tuning of violins, and all the whinnying, bellowing, snorting, barking, grunting, meowing, purring, braying, howling, cackling, peeping, roaring, and cuckooing. The sound of the church bells began in 1895, when Don Camilo Ocaranza cast them. From then on their knelling, pealing, tolling, ringing, clanging, chiming, and clanking told the parishioners what they should be doing at any given time. The ancient music of the horns was meaningful, too. While the bells were like bugles, calling out orders for the entire community, the horns carried messages between individuals or families. They could be heard over great distances. They were closely associated with the night, like the songs people sang in the streets in the darkness, in fluty tones, during the months of tender corn and harvest. These nocturnal choruses, melancholy and sensual, were the antithesis of the women's choir heard at solemn masses and rosaries; nor were they anything like the multitude of voices singing the *Alabado* morning after morning. Instrumental music was something else again; during large fiestas it was blasted out by Don Antonio Vargas's famed mariachi band.[19] Besides the harp, the guitars, and the singers, there were sometimes drums, too, to raise the spirits. One unforgettable occasion was the fiesta at Don Epifanio Arias's country place, when the drums and violins never stopped pounding and squeaking for a whole month. But any music was exceptional, for silence was the rule; music was a window in a habitually soundless life. To that it owed its force and its attraction.

Fiery fun was not to be had very often, either. In the first place, such amusements could take place only at night, or under the aegis of the church. Second, they called for nights of total darkness. In the third place, frequent repetition would have made them less exciting. There were many ways of playing with fire. Among the most spectacular was having a bonfire on a moonless night in the open country, to the accompaniment of music and singing. Another was setting fire to a field of grass, or a thicket, on a silent, windy night. And, last, because they were first in importance, there were fireworks: the strings of exploding rockets set off at Masses and Rosaries in May and June,

[19] As recollected by Luis González Cárdenas.

and the colored star rockets, pinwheels, and *castillos* during the March 19 festivities.[20]

Literary pastimes could never compare with the igneous and philharmonic ones. There was little bookish culture, in spite of Padre Othón's efforts to get people to read. He recommended and lent books and set an example himself by reading a few paragraphs of some devotional work following the Rosary. Women took up the reading habit more readily than men. They would gather to peruse *The Rainbow of Peace* (a commentary on the mysteries of the Rosary), *The Christian Year* (a collection of the lives of the saints), *The Imitation of Christ, Estaurófila,* and *The Story of Genoveva de Bravante.*[21]

When men got together, they discussed all the traditional subjects: the weather, crops, cattle, the doings of criminals, and other age-old topics. They talked about Don Antonio Vargas's visit to hell, and similar lies. Don Dolores Toscano was still turning outstanding events into rhyme. They all learned his verses by heart, along with those of "El Pronunciado." Men found reading difficult; their field was talking. And yet the practice of reading aloud (but not silently) was slowly spreading.

Theatrical amusements were introduced by Padre Othón, in the absence of any tradition in such matters. In order to entertain and instruct his flock, he presented the mysteries of the Passion of Our Lord Jesus Christ in the village streets, with village actors, for a couple of years. The Pharisees wore masks and costumes in screaming colors; Judas carried a whip. At the beginning of this century, Holy Week was quite different from what it is today. It opened on Palm Sunday, with the blessing of the palms. From Wednesday afternoon through the Monday after Easter, nobody worked; the time was devoted to worship. The church bells were mute, their ringing replaced by the clackety-clack of a wooden clapper. On Maundy Thursday the padre washed and kissed the feet of twelve children and then delivered a sermon while the congregation wept softly. That night there was a sermon on the Last Supper, and on Good Friday he gave two more: on the Seven Last Words and the Pésame. Throughout all the Holy

[20] As recalled by Agustina González Cárdenas.
[21] According to Josefina González Cárdenas.

Days, Don Tiburcio Torres went through the streets playing the mournful *chirimía*. Fasting was scrupulously observed. No one spoke. Women in mourning and men in white shirts and cotton trousers filled the church at all hours. The tears, the silence, and the grief ended abruptly when the bells rang out the Gloria on Saturday morning.[22]

With Padre Othón's arrival, the already robust religous life had grown more vigorous than ever. The villagers were more devout than those who lived in the *rancherías*. On awakening in the morning, everyone in San José crossed himself and recited several prayers, or sometimes sang them. This is the "Gracias":

> Great God, I give thee thanks,
> And glorify thy Holy Name;
> For thou hast preserved my soul
> For yet another day.

Then came Mass, celebrated by Padre Othón just as the sun was coming up. Nearly everyone in town attended—and accompanied the service with a chorus of coughs. One cough was the signal for many others to explode. While the pastor murmured in Latin, the congregation alternately knelt and rose with devotion and dignity. A large number received the Sacrament and then went about the day's business, cheerily singing:

> He who goes to Mass
> Can never come to grief;
> An angel walks beside him,
> And ever guides his feet.

When the bells struck twelve, everyone recited the Angelus:

> The Angel of the Lord came unto Mary,
> And she conceived through the Holy Ghost.
> "Behold the handmaid of the Lord;
> Be it unto me according to thy word."
> The Divine Word was made flesh,
> And came to live among us.

Evening prayers were the Rosary and the Litanies of the Virgin,

---

[22] I owe this description to José Chávez Fonseca, who is 82.

followed by a quarter of an hour of meditative reading. At night they prayed again. At any hour the famous *Alabado* could be heard in the fields or from the houses in the village:

> And meeting John the Baptist,
> She said these words to him;
> "Hast thou not seen the Son
> Of my body pass this way?"
> "Yes, Lady, I saw him pass
> Three hours before the dawn;
> His blessed back was marked
> With blood from a thousand whips.
> He wore a purple tunic
> And a rope around his neck."
> The Virgin, hearing this,
> Fell senseless to the ground.
> Saint John, the goodly nephew,
> Then ran to lift her up.

Two groups guided the religious lives of the parishioners: The Daughters of Mary, and the Apostles of Prayer. The first was a strict, preconventual organization, to which all the girls belonged. Its members were required to wear an ankle-length black dress with a high collar, long sleeves, a blue belt, and a silver medallion. The Daughters of Mary were models of virtue. They were remarkable for their devotion in attending Mass and the Rosary, as well as for the number of prayers and canticles (such as the Trisagion) they added to the normal daily quota. It was they who decorated the church for the fiestas of San José, Easter, the Marian month, Saint Isidore, Annunciation Day, the Twelfth of December, and Christmas Eve. They also provided the flowers for High Mass every Sunday—the Mass attended by the entire vicariate, including both ranchers and townspeople. All these duties were in addition to the penances and charitable works performed by these pale, mournful young ladies who assisted Padre Othón in his campaign of indoctrination and inculcation of virtuous habits.[23]

---

[23] As recollected by Agustina and Josefina González Cárdenas.

The Daughters of Mary and (from 1900 on) the teachers in the "nuns' school" taught Father Ripalda's catechism to the children. The adults knew it from cover to cover; they believed every word in it, and for the most part they practiced its precepts. Their faith remained immaculate, like that of their fathers and grandfathers and of those who had come from Spain to settle this land. They firmly believed that one should not expect to be happy or comfortable in this life, since it is merely a bridge leading to another; that ultimately one has to leave it all behind; and that, at the time of judgment, on the day of one's death, it is better to appear with a light load of pleasures. There were small theologians among Padre Othón's parishioners, and they often argued over differences of doctrine. Any debate could be settled by appeal to the padre or by an opportunely adduced text. The great majority, no less Catholic than this informed minority, shared a creed with some vestiges of superstition, a vast repertoire of prayers, and a moral code that was often violated.

Like all conservative communities, San José lived by a set of concrete rules that had been accumulating in the mind since time immemorial, and that were carefully observed. There were precepts for nearly every activity and a ritual for almost every act. Naturally, these villagers and country people had a code of behavior that was less stringent and complex than that of aristocratic city people. While in Indian communities rules of conduct may have been as numerous and strict as in the capital, among the *criollos* and mestizos they were not. Nowhere within the vicariate of San José were there fixed forms to be followed in weeping, laughing, eating, or walking, and there were only a few prescribed modes of address.

The generation who founded San José de Gracia can be described as conservative—although with a few "buts." Between the old, well-traveled road and the new, untried one, its members usually chose the first—but not always. They did not put one foot forward until the other was firmly in place. They "looked for the best way to do things" so as to derive the maximum advantage. Their conformity with the way of life handed down by their ancestors was nearly total; but the worm of ambition still gnawed at them—the wish to be more respected, richer, and wiser than their parents. Above all, they wanted

their children to be better than themselves. At times conformity overcame ambition; on other occasions the outcome of the struggle was
uncertain; but it was not unusual for the spirit of change to emerge
victorious. They were slow in making up their minds, precisely because
they were not unconditionally subject to the rule of tradition; they
were slow, but not obstinate. They moved from one point to the next
deliberately, without impatience. Perhaps because of vague feelings of
inferiority, these villagers and ranchers tended to adopt city ways,
to seek social standing and education for themselves and, especially,
for their children. According to José López Portillo, "since the
peasant, even when rich, is often the victim of trickery and made to
feel ashamed during his lifetime because of his lack of sophistication
and education, he has a powerful urge to see his descendants emerge
from the intellectual and social darkness in which he has moved, hoping to derive help, counsel, and strength from them."[24] Perhaps that
is why the founders of San José were so concerned with their children's education. They hired Lugardo Gómez to teach the village
youngsters, but he didn't last long. He gave up teaching to become
a milker. He was replaced by Don Francisco Balsas, the tippling
schoolmaster, and then by the extremely strict Don Francisco Gama,
who, by dint of breaking switches cut from the quince tree over his
pupils' bottoms, taught them to read, write, and cipher as long as his
failing eyesight permitted.

When Gama went blind, they looked about for another teacher;
they found what they needed in a newly established order. About 1884
Señor Cázares, learning that a secularized nun named Sister Margarita
Gómez was living in Sahuayo, invited her to found a new order in
Zamora, to be dedicated principally to providing primary education
in the villages. The bishop also decreed that each town should have a
school, to be known as "the Haven." All the citizens of San José
collaborated enthusiastically in the construction of their school; even
before it was finished, Sister Juana Garnica arrived to teach reading
and catechism to the smaller children. The next year, 1900, she was
followed by Sister Ángela Gómez and three other colleagues. The

---

[24] José López Portillo y Rojas, *La parcela*, p. 36.

building was still not completed. Even so, the nuns set to work, teaching various subjects to nearly every boy and girl in the village. Their repertoire included reading, writing, elementary grammar, arithmetic, Father Ripalda's catechism, and Fleury's history of religion. The girls were also given supplementary courses in sewing and embroidery. About two hundred pupils attended this first religious school.[25]

Within the vicariate of San José de Gracia, people lived as closely tied to tradition as to the earth—which is to say very closely indeed—but not to the point where they could not break away if they wanted to. The vast majority who lived in the village and its environs had seen no more of the world than the mesa they lived on; some of them had been as far as the saltpeter beds of Teocuitatlán, the shore of Lake Chapala, the towns of Jiquilpan and Sahuayo, the little city of Cotija, and Contla, Tamazula, and Zapotlán, in the lands of beeswax and honey. Some men (but very few) had made trips to Zamora, Guadalajara, and Mexico City. But it was more usual not to travel at all. People planted themselves for life in their little nation, in the narrow homeland that stretched only as far as the eye could see. One generally felt at ease in his own little corner. Very few chose to exchange their land for another that was more generous, such as some nearby, or for one where life was easier, as in the cities. Here one lived poorly, but without toil. And yet the gnawing of curiosity had its effect. There was a growing interest in distant places, in news of what was happening far away. People asked mule skinners what it was like in the jungles of Tabasco. Don Gregorio González Pulido brought back marvelous tales from the capital of the republic. One day Don Gregorio ventured as far as Orizaba and came back with news of the electric light. He was the one people looked to for descriptions of Don Porfirio and the magnificent processions in the capital. He was familiar with the train, but most of his neighbors had never laid eyes on one. People who saw a locomotive for the first time found their legs trembling; some even took to their heels.[26]

Curiosity about distant lands was followed by curiosity about modern inventions. People took trips just to see what the train was like.

[25] As recalled by Luis and Josefina González Cárdenas.
[26] According to Agustina and Josefina González Cárdenas.

The first reports of the phonograph and of photography were arriving. Winds from a new world outside were beginning to be felt.

Winds from the Outside World

The first years of the twentieth century were not good ones. Beginning in 1902, there was a period of drought that killed half the cattle. However, no cattleman even considered giving up his business. During the last years of the previous century many people were selling land; now there were buyers, but they could find hardly anyone who was willing to sell. Rural land values rose. In 1902 people were saying that Don José Martínez had just bought the Auchen ranch for almost nothing, for he had paid only 10,000 pesos. Forty years earlier the same property had brought 2,000 pesos, which at the time was considered to be an extremely high price.[27] Don José Martínez had been fortunate not only in having paid so little, but also in having found a seller. For another thing, with the opening of the century, death seemed to have forgotten about San José. In 1899 there had been twenty-eight deaths in the village; but in the first year of the new century there were only nine, and only five in 1902. Personal relations improved, too. There were fewer fights and robberies. In the five-year period ending in 1905, only two homicides were reported.[28]

New settlers continued to arrive in San José. A very small number moved in from the neighboring *rancherías*; one of this group was Don Isidoro Martínez, co-owner of El Saucito. Most were from elsewhere: the potters Salomé Barriga and Mateo Zavala, with their wives and children, from Zináparo; the shoemaker Don Carmen Berbera and family, from La Manzanilla. In 1902 Don Herculano Zepeda, one of the rich men from El Valle, settled in San José, with numerous children from his first marriage; later he was followed by his brothers.[29]

As some arrived, others went away. Many of the people who had

<hr/>

[27] ANJ, Judicial Records of Licenciado Ignacio Zepeda, 1902, and of Licenciado Miguel E. Cázares.
[28] APSJ, Death Records, Book I.
[29] Ibid., Marriage Records, Book II.

been brought by Padre Othón left with him. On April 5, 1903, the priest handed over his vicariate to Francisco Castillo, a native of Sahuayo like himself. Don Othón said his farewells amid general consternation; he had belonged to San José for twelve years. The new priest was as young as the first and better educated, but he was uncompassionate, unbending, ascetic. He arrived swinging his machete right and left against the enemies of the soul: the world, the devil, and the flesh. He set out to raise even higher the walls that isolated San José, to cast out every sin, to purify the body, and to show no mercy in imposing Christian purity and order.

Padre Castillo made a few changes. He closed the nuns' school and in its place opened another in which he himself taught, assisted by the best students from the former institution: María Pulido, Elena Cárdenas, and María and Agustina González Cárdenas. He reduced the number of secular celebrations. From the popular fiestas, including the one on March 19, he excised the music, rockets, and *castillos*. It was his ambition to convert every member of his flock into an ascetic. The standard-bearers of his purification campaign were the Daughters of Mary. They were forbidden to have boyfriends, to dress in an attractive manner, and to attend parties or public spectacles.[30] His campaign against the yearnings of the flesh was able to boast some modest victories. Several girls from the best families remained spinsters all their lives. He succeeded in reducing the number of marriages. In 1902 Padre Othón had married forty couples; in his first year Padre Castillo officiated at only thirty-two weddings, and in his second, thirty-one. But he suffered some notable defeats, too.[31] During his reign the walls of isolation began to crumble.

Strangers were beginning to arrive at the inn that had belonged to Don Lorenzo Zepeda. It was a modest lodging house with a long, spacious entrance hall. In the center of the cobblestone patio was a well. Around it were tiny rooms with crudely made doors, without furniture, but not without bedbugs and fleas. There were no mice, thanks to the *cincuates*—black snakes, two meters long, that lived on rodents and kept poisonous reptiles away. At the rear of the patio

[30] According to Agustina González Cárdenas.
[31] APSJ, Marriage Records, Book I.

were stables for mules and horses. At all hours there could be heard footsteps, braying, whinnying, singing, and talking. At first the inn had been patronized only by visiting ranchers and mule drivers from Sahuayo and Cotija. Then gypsies began to appear, and mountebanks, sharpers, acrobats who leaped through flaming hoops, fortunetellers, puppeteers, clowns, hucksters selling salves and herbs, and traveling salesmen from well-known business houses. It was then that an agent for the Bayer firm introduced aspirin, the miracle pill, which was for some time regarded as a cure-all.

In 1905 a snappy dresser with a fedora hat showed up. He knocked at the doors of the best houses in town. Some residents, in confusion, kissed his hand. They thought he was a priest. He was, in fact, a traveling salesman for the Singer company, selling treadle sewing machines. He succeeded in interesting several heads of families. A month later five shiny machines arrived, accompanied by a young lady from Jiquilpan to demonstrate how they worked.[32]

Mail began coming to San José de Gracia in 1906, when the post office was opened. Once a week Don Camilo made a leisurely round trip between San José and Tizapán, carrying the mail bags on horseback.[33] Until then it had been difficult and expensive to send a letter: one hired a messenger or entrusted it to a mule driver. Now it was a simple matter. Much more important, however, was the fact that, on the advice of the seminary students, some of the village men—perhaps no more than three or four—subscribed to newspapers. Some San Joséans became aware, for the first time, of the extent of the world and of the things that were happening in it, thanks to the newspapers—or, rather, the newspaper, since there was only one: *El País*, from Mexico City.

El País was the most widely read Catholic newspaper in the provinces. Its editor, Don Trinidad Sánchez Santos, was country-bred himself, having come from the foothills east of La Malinche. He had gone to Mexico City when he was twenty-one, and in 1899 he had founded *El País*, which opposed "political bossism and other vices of the dictatorship . . . There were vain attempts to draw him into the

[32] As recalled by Josefina González Cárdenas.
[33] *Huanimba* no. 1 (1941): 13.

soft comfortableness of conformity. But he chose obduracy and peril . . . His brief, furious editorials reached the common people and raised blisters."[34] However, the San Joséans were astonished, not so much by the political editorials and articles, or by the details of the strikes at Cananea and Río Blanco, or by President Díaz's interview with the American journalist James Creelman, or even by the news of the Third Agricultural Congress at Zamora and the Third Catholic and First Eucharistic congresses at Guadalajara, or by any other coverage of national events, as by the news of seemingly incredible inventions. There were flying machines with wings, the wireless telegraph, the telephone, the automobile, motion pictures, electric streetcars, photographs, the phonograph, the incandescent light, the submarine, aspirin, and other medicaments and artifacts of modern life.

Don Gregorio González Pulido was still going regularly to the capital and returning loaded down with money and news. He confirmed many things that had been reported in the paper. In Mexico City he had beheld streetcars and electric lights, telephones, automobiles, movies, and other mechanisms of the good life, and he told his neighbors about what he had seen. Don Gregorio brought political news, too, but it was vague and sketchy. One had to take into account that Don Gregorio's visits to the capital were brief ones, spent in the Merced market and the neighboring churches, and that he had no way of getting much news beyond that concerning the inventions everyone was talking about.

Seminary students were another source of information to be added to the rich one provided by the newspapers. They came in the first days of November, from the Consolidated Seminary in Zamora. Two or three of them were from San José, and they almost always brought an invited guest. As many as half a dozen students would appear in the village, talking about everything under the sun. They referred contemptuously to the national government, because it was liberal, and they spoke of Madero and Reyes, who were quite the opposite; they predicted Don Porfirio's downfall; and they showed off their political knowledge. But, more than anything, they enjoyed excelling in

---

[34] Alfonso Junco, *Sangre de Hispania*, pp. 56–57.

conversation, settling questions of conscience, giving their opinions as to where virtue left off and sin began, and talking about the new inventions—some of which had reached Zamora, but not San José.[35]

Among those inventions which had appeared in San José was the phonograph, and it had stirred up a whirlwind of excitement. Then came the camera: a few people had seen the device in Tizapán or Sahuayo or Jiquilpan, but they had lacked the courage to have their pictures taken. In 1908 a few families, with solemn, astonished expressions on their faces, sat for their portrait. The oldest woman in town, Doña Gertrudis Pulido, the widow of Don Guadalupe González Toscano, was unwilling to have her picture taken, but her grandchildren overcame her resistance. No power on earth could have made some of the others face the camera.[36]

Padre Castillo tried to hold back the avalanche of news and inventions. He absolutely forbade women to read the newspaper. For those who enjoyed such things he provided religious texts. But both men and women who could read continued, with no diminution of piety, to peruse *El País* and astound themselves with the gramophone, the sewing machine, the "views" of the stereoscope, and the camera. It was probably the newspaper that brought the new styles in dress and ornament to San José. It was undoubtedly because of *El País* that political arguments sprang up among the villagers. Through the windows of the newspaper from the capital, the seminary students, Don Gregorio's trips, the "views," the phonograph records, and the photographs, the winds from the outside world blew in: the nation's troubles, the new machines designed for man's comfort and pleasure, the exotic ideas. These breezes made no great impression on the older generations, but the young people sniffed them eagerly.

The generation of the new century, made up of the younger brothers and sisters and the older children of the men who had founded San José—that is to say, those born between 1862 and 1877—was a rebellious one. Its members rebelled against Padre Castillo's rigidity and narrow-mindedness and his long face, and they rebelled against their elders. Men who were between twenty-five and forty

[35] As recalled by Luis González Cárdenas.
[36] According to Josefina González Cárdenas.

shaved, unlike their bearded fathers and grandfathers. They wore long mustaches they could twist, and the wealthier ones embellished their *charro* suits with silver cord and buttons. New conveniences were introduced into the houses, among them running water. Water from the spring was brought in a terra-cotta pipe to the edge of town, where a reservoir was built. From there it was piped to the largest houses. The streets were paved with cobblestones; house fronts were decorated with red plaster baldachins, carved stone ornaments, and balconies with railings. The children of this new generation were active and enterprising. They retained their fathers' spirit of social initiative. They were nationalistic, politically minded, and interested in new things, and their leaders were aggressive and vigorous.

Padre Juan González was the most important figure of that generation. Born about 1873, he was the grandson of Antonio González, of the poor branch of the González tree. He was mixing mud for mortar when Padre Othón noticed him and arranged to send him to the seminary. At the auxiliary school in Sahuayo they nicknamed him "the Awl." There and in Zamora he was famous for his shrewdness. His great charm, his ability to inspire confidence, his enthusiasm and energy helped him realize his greatest ambition: to become a rich man. He was a superb businessman. Padre Juan was ordained in 1907. The banquet was attended not only by the new priest's relatives, but also by the wealthy families of the area. He returned to Zamora to become a distinguished professor at the seminary. He was a clear-thinking philosopher, and he could have been an intellectual of importance if he had not succumbed to the temptation to make money. Almost overnight he made a respectable fortune and bought ranches and cattle. He believed so strongly in the creative virtues of wealth that he tried to attract other rich men of the region to San José; he set out to fill the town with "successful people." He was also fond of politics.

The merchant Manuel González Cárdenas, the son of Don Gregorio González Pulido, followed in Padre Juan's footsteps. Without education, but just as enterprising as the priest, he made a fortune in trade and farming. He opened a store that was so well stocked with groceries, dry goods, and hardware that he drove the other shops out of business, and storekeepers from neighboring villages came to buy their stock from him. He invested his profits in land and cattle. Like Padre Juan, he aspired to become the rich man's rich man. He, too, favored the policy of attracting wealthy men to San José. He was active in improving the appearance of the village, and he was not averse to new political ideas.

Narcisco Chávez was a revolutionary of a different kind. Like his uncle, Don Juan, he entered the field of the skilled crafts and, again like his uncle, became an expert in these matters more by dint of enthusiasm and intelligence than by education. He was an expert at anything he turned his hand to. Evidence of some of his many and unusual talents may be seen today in the balcony railings on some of the village houses and in the balustrade near the entrance of the church. A thousand wonderful things emerged from his clinking blacksmith shop.

Don Apolinar Partida was to be another central personage in the new century. He grew up with Don Juan Chávez, and he had come from La Villita when San José was founded. Here Don Juan taught him the art of making small household mills for grinding corn to make tortillas. He set up a workshop and traveled far and wide selling his mills. Then he opened a butcher shop, slaughtering steers and selling the meat in the plaza. His true destiny had still not been revealed, for he had been born to be neither an artisan nor a butcher. His sang-froid, and his love of danger and physical exploits inclined him toward the life of a soldier. With the coming of the revolution he found his calling.

Then, too, the longed-for rich people came to join the padre, Don Manuel, Don Narciso, and Don Apolinar. The town was suddenly filled with moneyed visitors. Don Ignacio Sánchez appeared, armed with pistol, rifle, machete, dagger, shotgun, and clasp knife. He was the owner of a couple of fairly large ranches. Another of his merits was that his wife was the daughter of Don José Martínez. The latter owned Auchen and La Arena and was on the point of acquiring Palo Verde. Don José was also a new immigrant, along with three others with the same family name: Don Proto, Don Vicente, and Don Ignacio Martínez, the owners of El Saucito. One of the proprietors of the Del Monte ranch, Don Gumersindo, also took up residence in San José. With the old settlers and these new arrivals, San José now had a round dozen rich men. These new residents certainly gave no sign of love for the town or of any interest in its development. They came out of a desire for comfort, or because of fear. Those who arrived on the eve of the revolution accepted the invitation to build in the village for the first reason; those who followed later, in the midst of the scuffle, were running for safety.

It became fashionable to be rich. Those who already had some wealth in land and cattle tried to get more of these commodities. This was the case with Don José Martínez, Don Juan Arias, Don Gregorio and Don Bernardo González, Don Emiliano Barrios, and others. Men who had nothing tended to go into trade in order to make enough to buy land and herds. "Rich" was still a synonym for "large landowner" and "cattleman." However, it was not easy to get into that class. Ranch owners hardly ever let their property go. Only the Indians, having been made individual landowners by the release of corporation lands, under the liberals, were still selling parcels; buyers were snatching them from their hands. Some people were able to add to their modest holdings by acquiring these sections of land, most of which were in the Mazamitla area.

Padre Castillo left in January, 1909, and for the rest of that year Padre Juan González Zepeda was the priest in charge of the vicariate. This gave him the opportunity to supervise closely the realization of his two ambitions: attracting substantial landowners to San José and transforming the town into an entity of political and economic importance. Politically, it was still a *ranchería*. Its highest authority was a peace officer, whose rank was at the bottom of the list of public officials. Don Gregorio González Pulido was put in charge of a campaign to have the town raised to a higher political category. He visited one government office after another until he reached Don Porfirio himself. He spoke with the dictator.[37]

In 1909 the vicariate of San José was promoted to a *tenencia*. Its official name was Ornelas, in honor of the general who received a

---

[37] As recalled by Don Gregorio's daughter, María González Cárdenas.

bullet in his neck and lost his life while defending Jiquilpan against
the French. The seat of the *tenencia*, the town of San José de Gracia,
would retain its original name. There would be a resident *jefe* and
three *alcaldes de tenencia*. The *jefe*'s duties were "to maintain peace
and order, provide for the safety of the residents within his jurisdiction, enforce the laws and ordinances," and, especially, to carry out
orders issued by the president of the *municipio* and the higher authorities. The alcaldes (an officer and two deputies) were to "discharge the
functions of judicial police; be familiar with those offenses punishable
by jail sentences of less than thirty days . . . carry out elementary
procedures in criminal cases; be acquainted with civil suits involving
sums less than twenty-five pesos . . . keep a record of crimes, summon
witnesses and any other persons required by the judicial authorities."
To assist the *jefe* and the *alcaldes de tenencia*, fourteen peace officers
were to be appointed (one from each *ranchería*), as well as police and
tax collectors.[38] The new *tenencia* (San José and its surrounding *rancherías*) was no longer to be part of the *municipio* of Sahuayo; it was
now included within the *municipio* of Jiquilpan, because Don Gregorio wanted it that way.

With San José's promotion to a *tenencia* came the birth of political
passions. No one was interested in being a peace officer in a village
with no territorial jurisdiction; but, now that it was the seat of a
tenencia, political ambitions awoke. Now there was no shortage of
candidates for the position of *jefe* and alcalde. And yet, when we say
that political passion came into being at this time, we mean something more: the awakening of interest in the nation's political life.
In this new batch of bread it was a rare man who did not comment or
argue—for or against—the doings of Don Porfirio and his cabinet, the
acts of the governor, Aristeo Mercado, and the behavior of the authorities in general. Not everyone was an *antiporfirista*, but everyone
felt hostility toward the functionaries who surrounded the dictator.
This hostility was, for the most part, conservative in origin, forged in
the columns of *El País*. The government was filled with liberals who
were said to be Masons, enemies of the clergy, evil people who
preferred to be married by the civil ceremony, like animals. If

---

[38] Mariano de Jesús Torres, *Historia civil y eclesiástica de Michoacán*, p. 80.

morality was sliding downhill, it was because of impious rulers. If
there were so many taxes . . . if there were no jobs . . . if the courts
were corrupt . . . it was all the fault of the authorities, who had no
fear of God. The young men of San José de Gracia received, as a rule,
neither benefits nor injuries from the government; but they decided
to take on as their own some of the complaints against the regime.
This was undoubtedly an indication of something very important:
the beginnings of San José's identification with the Mexican fatherland, the first budding of nationalism in a remote and nearly isolated
village.

All in All, Half a Century of Peaceful and Orderly Progress

We have seen that the time between 1861 and 1910 may be divided into three periods: (1) That from 1861 to 1881 is clearly set
off by the northern lights and the snowstorm. It contains an event of
great consequence: the breaking up and sale of the Cojumatlán hacienda. The "war of the *güeros*" and the first *cristero* rebellion also
fall within this period. It was, then, a block of time ruled by a dynamic generation, men born between 1818 and 1833—not those of
1834–1847, who were never responsible for anything. (2) The second
wave (1882–1900) was directed by those born between 1848 and
1862. It was then that the town was founded and that the lives of a
quarter of the country people underwent notable changes. (3) From
1900 on, events were determined by the tastes of the generation of
1863–1878, the ranchers and villagers who were anxious not to be
different, who wanted to be like everyone else. The town of San José
grew up. It became a real capital for twenty-odd *rancherías*, a cere-
monial, mercantile, and civilizing center. The last two periods enjoyed
a climate of optimism and expansion. It was a case of a rural *belle
époque*.

From 1861 to 1910 the population of the San José area grew much
faster than that of the country as a whole; while the latter barely
doubled, the former tripled. The 1,300 inhabitants of 1861 had become 3,850 by 1910. In addition to the natural increment, there were
small waves of immigration around 1860, 1890, and 1910. The families who came during those times were from neighboring villages and

rancherías; with five or six exceptions, they were all from the region itself. Some were seeking refuge from the war, but most came looking for work.

There was little change in the demographic structure. The birth rate remained high (forty per thousand), and the death rate was moderate (sixteen per thousand). In spite of the influx of young people and adults, the age pyramid kept its traditional shape. There was a very broad ground floor, then narrower ones occupied by adolescents and young people, and then a quite small one representing adults between forty and sixty, almost as narrow as that for old people. Infant mortality was high, and so were deaths among youngsters; but there were few deaths among adults. Anyone who survived infancy and youth was almost sure to reach old age.

The most important fact, from the demographic point of view, was the tendency toward concentration. In half a century there sprang up only three new settlements, while, on the other hand, the number of inhabitants in those already in existence increased. This was especially true of the town of San José de Gracia, founded in 1888, which grew from zero to 410 in 1890, to 894 by 1900, and to 980 by 1910. The last figure represents 26 percent of the total population within the zone we are studying.

Parallel with the population concentration came the transition from a consumer economy to a market economy and the increase in extension, if not in intensity, of production. There were no appreciable technical advances; no improved systems of growing cereals or raising cattle were introduced, nor did there appear more efficient tools or machinery. And yet the increase in production could be seen a mile away.

Cattle raising was still the predominant industry, but within it the production of milk and the manufacture of cheese became more important. The principal value of cattle no longer lay in their hides. Occupations outside the dairy industry were more or less secondary. Greater areas were planted with the traditional corn, beans, and squash, although these crops were no more important than before. Some other occupations, without tradition or future, became more conspicuous.

Within the short period of fifty years, three economic activities sprang up, reached their apogee, and declined: raising sheep for wool, making mescal from the maguey plant, and, most important, refining beeswax. This last industry was second in importance only to dairy farming during the last third of the nineteenth century, but, with the introduction of electric lights and paraffin candles in the cities, it began to languish as a business, and by 1910 it had been reduced to almost nothing.

From 1861 on, trade became more important. Between 1861 and 1888 there was a tremendous rise in the quantity and value of local products that were delivered to the regional markets—especially to Cotija. The ranchers of the area also bought more goods in neighboring towns, principally Cotija, Teocuitatlán, and Zapotlán. After 1888 the Mexico City–Guadalajara railway, with its station at Ocatlán, only twenty-five kilometers from the San José area, was instrumental in bringing the village into the national market. From then on, two of the principal local products—cheese and pigs—were taken to the capital of the republic, at first by two merchants from Pachuca, and a little later by a dealer from San José. By the first decade of this century the town had become a regional mercantile center of some importance.

Between 1861 and 1910 considerable quantities of money began to flow into the area. At first, very little of this wealth was destined to be spent on comfort. Most of it ended up buried in earthenware pots; the rest went to buying farming land. In short, it was used principally as a means of attaining prestige. After 1888 some people spent their money building fine houses in the town, and after 1906 small amounts went for things to make life easier (sewing machines, the locally made mills for grinding corn for tortillas, patent medicines) or for luxury items (felt hats, *charro* suits with silver embroidery, brass beds, and the like).

The material standard of living did not rise appreciably. Outside of town, people still lived in thatched huts; in the village and on the ranches men still wore huaraches, loose white cotton trousers, a red or blue sash, a shirt, and the palm-fiber sombrero with its extraordinarily high crown. It was known—although there were no eye-witnesses—that at the close of this era women were wearing under-clothes beneath their dresses. There do not seem to have been any innovations in diet, nor were any needed. The important fact was that the land was divided into privately owned parcels.

Modern Mexico's three great problems in connection with rural property (fixing of boundaries of unimproved land, breaking up and sale of property held in mortmain, and dealing with the institution of latifundia) did not exist in the San José area. For centuries, no land there had been known to exist without an owner. Neither the church nor the Indian communities had ever held any considerable amounts of property in the region. The large estate that had included San José and its *rancherías* had been broken up into 50 sections in 1851; because of legacies, each of these parcels had been divided and re-divided until, by 1910, there were 168 pieces belonging to an equal number of ranchers. This is not to say that along with the trend to-ward partition there had not appeared the contrary tendency toward the gathering of rural lands in the hands of a few owners. There were, also, absentee landlords, leaseholders, sharecroppers, and so on; but the fact remains that problems related to the ownership of land were nearly nonexistent here.

Labor continued to be the most problematical aspect of that life. Certainly, it was not held in high regard. Owners of small and medium-sized properties, merchants, and craftsmen usually carried on their occupations with their own hands, or, at most, with the help of their wives and children. Even so, the number of day laborers and share-croppers was growing. Wages were low—one and a half or two *reales* a day—but no one, unless he was a laborer on a hacienda, lived on that income alone. There existed no tradition of peonage or servitude. The common laborer and the sharecropper could make full use of their employer's land, unless that employer was the owner of El Sabino, the only surviving large estate.

Social life saw some upheavals, but many traditional elements per-sisted: the numerous "small family" groups, ruled by the husband; the "larger family," counseled by the patriarch; the strong family ties; the institution of *compadrazgo*, with its tightly knotted interfamilial relationships; the self-sacrifice and multiple, unceasing labor of women; the obstacles placed in the way of the daughter's marriage; the correct bringing up of one's children—by means of the whip, if necessary; and the search, never very far afield, for a wife. The innovations were the division of society into classes, the school, the church, the market, the growing ties with the city, the increasing use of firearms—completing the trinity of horse, dog, and rifle—and, above all, the rapid growth of the town of San José de Gracia and the rise of political passion.

In the years 1861–1910, traditional local rule was superseded, or nearly so. This did not prevent the husband from wielding the scepter in his own home, however, nor did it mean that the patriarch suffered any loss of respect within the larger family; but to these authorities were added others. These were not always strangers, but they were imposed from above by the *municipio*, state, federal, and episcopal governments. Civil government appointed and supported in the town and in each of the twelve *rancherías* a peace officer and a vigorous *juez de acordada*. It also compelled people to pay their taxes, and accommodated criminals with *jueces de letras* (justices of the peace who were also attorneys) and plenty of penitentiaries. But what most undermined the authority of the old men after 1888 was the power of the priest. It can be said, with some exaggeration, that the years from 1861 to 1910 saw the change from a patriarchal rule to a theocratic one.

Although it never compared with that of the priest, the influence of the schoolmasters was also growing. Their influence had begun at zero. Prior to 1861 there had never been even any elementary teachers. Four or five appeared in succession during the period that followed. It was the country people who hired them; they set up business in the largest *ranchería*, then, finally, in the village. With classes of no more than fifty children, they taught reading, writing, and keeping accounts. In 1900, by order of the bishop, the first proper school was established, with its own building, several teachers, more than a hundred pupils, and several primary grades. Education was mostly in the hands of the church.

In the fifty-year period from 1861 to 1910, there were some notable changes in religious life: a resident priest, the organization of devotional societies, daily attendance at Mass and Rosary, widespread religious education, vows to the saints, church festivals celebrating various occasions—especially March 19, the day of San José's patron saint—the bishop of Zamora's triennial visits to the village (along with retreats, and harangues by missionaries), penances during Lent (fasting, self-flagellation, public wailing), a deep awareness of sin, the sense of shame raised to its highest pitch, the nearly total suppression of extramarital sex, and long conversations between old ladies and the dead. In short, religious activities and their traveling companions came to occupy the greater part of the San Joséans' private and public life. The town of Mazamitla, their rival, gave them a richly deserved nickname: "the saints."

In spite of this new outbreak of religious thought and practice, many old ideas, attitudes, and beliefs persisted. Some of them were reaffirmed by the growing piety. This was the case with the ancient idea that the world is ruled by will, not by laws: first, by the will of God, second, by the will of the saints, and last, by the will of man— when God gives him permission. The ideal man still displayed the same characteristics: physical courage, cleverness, *machismo*, integrity, wealth in money and land and cattle, health, vigor, and, finally, "manliness." On the other hand, there began to appear the idea that wealth can be procured only at someone else's cost, as expressed by the saying that whatever one man seizes another man must let go—in other words, Foster's concept of the limited good.

It was after 1888 that many of the aspects of the fiestas still seen in the zone were introduced: that Moorish survival, the tower of fireworks;[39] the "little bull" with its rockets; the giant skyrockets; the crepe-paper decorations; and one or two other things. But the enthusiasm for fiestas fell off to a great extent when the priests came. They suppressed card games, general drunkenness, and dancing— including acrobatic performances. What had been a community of famous dancers was paralyzed. Many contests of skill survived: horse racing, and all the *charro* arts. San Joséans did not have many reasons to feel downhearted. "And they are never in a hurry / even on fiesta

[39] Arturo Warman Gryg, "La danza de moros y cristianos," pp. 41, 102, 157.

days. When there is wine, they drink wine; / when there is none, they
drink cold water. They are good people who live, / work, get through
life, and dream, / and one day, like so many others, / they go to take
their rest in the earth."

We can be sure that those who lived here before 1861 knew each
other very well but had hardly any knowledge of human beings or
events anywhere else. As time went on, they began to learn about other
people and places. Under the aegis of Porfirio's peace, there was a slow
increase in trade of all kinds. Little by little not only immigrants but
also other strangers began to appear. There were mule drivers, traveling salesmen, government and church officials, circus performers, and
gypsies. In 1906 came the mail service, and with it newspapers and
magazines. Local people started traveling, and not only to nearby
towns. More than a dozen went as far as Mexico City; at least one in
a hundred showed up in Guadalajara; and a small group of young
men went to study in Sahuayo and then in Zamora.

All these factors contributed to feelings of identity with a region
and with a large nation. On the eve of the revolution their lives were
beginning to be affected by nationalistic sentiments, an interest in politics, an awareness of the outside world, curiosity about new inventions,
and the desire to make money. Whether they liked it or not, the social
elite were coming to realize, to feel, and to welcome the fact that they
were inscribed in the diocese of Zamora, the district of Jiquilpan, the
state of Michoacán, and the Republic of Mexico. The better-informed
citizens knew who Porfirio Díaz, Aristeo Mercado, and the prefects
of Jiquilpan were; but the majority were unaware of the move toward
nationalism, or even toward regionalization.

Part Two

Thirty Years of Suffering

4. THE MEXICAN REVOLUTION (1910–1924)

The Madero Revolution

IN 1910 *El País* arrived filled with news. Since the president had announced that the populace was ready for democracy, political parties were forming to contend in the coming elections: the Democrats, the Antireelectionists, the Porfirists, the Science party, and the Reyists. Four of them agreed to support the reelection of General Díaz, while the most popular of all nominated Francisco Madero and his namesake, Francisco Vázquez Gómez, for president and vice-president, respectively. Madero set out on his campaign tour and was thrown in jail in Monterrey. There were elections that were not elections. Porfirio Díaz and Ramón Corral were declared reelected. Madero was taken to prison in San Luis Potosí, whence he escaped. A little earlier, the newspaper had described the splendid Centennial celebrations in the capital; now it began to carry stories exposing a series of plots, to tell of the Serdán brothers' heroic defense in Puebla, and to bring news of uprisings in the north.

Interesting news was also coming in from Zamora, San José's ecclesiastical capital. A new bishop had been appointed the year before. Señor Othón Núñez had arranged religious celebrations to commemorate the Centennial of the Independence. The civil authorities had organized bicycle races, student parades, recitations, speeches, banquets for poor children, allegorical floats, concerts, fireworks, and a "Mexican evening." "Three hundred horsemen, led by the prefect, raced through the streets; they carried pine torches, and acclaimed our heroes to the strains of the national anthem."[1]

Reports of Centennial celebrations came in from other places, too, and they were followed by more news of the revolution. All over the country, both the working people and the well-off were joining the Madero faction.

There were no Centennial fiestas in San José but three alarming events occurred in 1910. In May, Halley's comet appeared. The newspaper discussed the danger of its tail striking the earth. In the same year a frightening number of cattle died. It had been extremely dry the previous year, and there was even less rainfall in 1910. Much of the corn crop was lost. But even though people were preoccupied with the comet and the drought, they were swept up in the pro-Madero movement. Padre Juan encouraged this enthusiasm. Most people had no very clear idea of the merits of Madero's platform. Some thought that they would no longer have to pay taxes; others believed that he was an honest man; still others said that Don Porfirio was getting old and ought to step down in favor of a younger man. Don Aristeo Mercado, the governor of Michoacán who had been appointed by Don Porfirio, was held to be a good-for-nothing.

In 1911 the unrest began to spread; there were uprisings everywhere; Ciudad Juárez fell to Madero supporters; Salvador Escalante launched his pro-Madero proclamation in eastern Michoacán and was met with ovations everywhere; in Zamora, in the middle of a well-attended concert, Ireneo and Melesio Contreras let out the battle cry, "Long live Madero!" that was to be repeated in many other places. Don Ireneo wired his chief: "I am deeply honored to place Zamora and Jiquilpan, the principal towns of this district, together with their *municipios*, at your disposal. These places have been taken in the most orderly fashion, without bloodshed, and to the satisfaction of all their inhabitants."[2]

---

[1] Arturo Rodríguez Zetina, *Zamora: Ensayo histórico y repertorio documental*, p. 839.

[2] Ibid., pp. 841–845.

There was a rumor that the Madero forces would pass near San José and young people went out to cheer them; but they never came. When the young people returned to the village, they were overjoyed to hear Don Porfirio had been overthrown and that Madero had entered the capital. "The city was decked out as though for a great fiesta . . . The people were more enthusiastic than ever before within memory." And then came the electoral battle. There had never been an election in San José de Gracia until this one in 1911. Many people turned out to vote for Madero and Pino Suárez for president and vice-president, respectively. A vague feeling of nationalism came over the town.[3] Voting for these distant personages was a tacit acceptance of their authority. Until that time San José had been nearly independent; it had grown up without either help or hindrance from the outside. During the next three or four years—since it had begun having opinions about public affairs—it had set out on the road to becoming a politically minded town. In short, symptoms of a growing nationalism were appearing.

Padre Juan's *maderismo* spread in San José, but its champion returned to the seminary in Zamora, where he had been a professor. He was replaced by Padre Trinidad Barragán, son of a rich family from Sahuayo, who lasted two months—hardly long enough to tell a few of the jokes in his vast repertoire. Padre Marcos Vega, who was from right there in Los Corrales, took his place. Padre Vega got along with everybody. He arrived in March, 1910, giving off sparks. Without a moment's delay he organized a fiesta for San José's patron saint. Padre Vega will be remembered for the entertainments he devised, although he had his finger in more than parties. He was far from apolitical. He supported Madero, and ultimately he became a fervent *villista*. Like Padre Juan, he worked to get local landowners to take up residence in San José. He, too, believed that the rich were "useful to have around."

Local civil authorities maintained the best of relations with Padre Vega. The *jefe* and his *alcaldes de tenencia* had been appointed from among the town's most devout citizens: the *jefe* was Don Gregorio González, and his assistants were his son Luis, Matías Pulido, and

[3] As recalled by Luis González Cárdenas.

Juan Chávez.[4] In September of 1911 these were replaced by Don
Vicente Martínez and two other sons of Don Gregorio: Manuel and
Agapito. Under the *jefatura* of Manuel González Cárdenas, the dynamic businessman, a municipal project that aroused a great deal of
interest was undertaken: the improvement of the plaza. The sidewalk
around it was paved with cobblestones, new trees were planted, and it
was remodeled with an eye to its principal functions: the market and
the *serenata*. At that time, or very soon afterward, four gasoline lanterns were bought, one for each corner of the plaza. They took the
place, amid general admiration, of the red flames of pitch-pine torches.
The lanterns gave a light that was as bright as day, and they hissed
and blinded you, besides. Many were the Sunday evenings when
people regarded them and agreed that, aside from the fact that they
made everybody look dead, they gave the best light they had ever seen.
With the cobblestones, the benches, and the modern illumination, the
plaza was the equal of that in any important town.[5]

The plaza was ready for the many kinds of fiestas arranged by the
padre, and, in particular, for that of March 19, with its nine days of
deafening music, rockets, and fireworks (*toritos* and, especially, *castillos*). People still say, "We never had such great *castillos* as those
in the days of Padre Vega . . . What a lot of gunpowder we used to
use up!" In addition, the young priest encouraged *serenatas*; he urged
young people of both sexes to gather in the plaza at nightfall and
stroll around it, groups of boys going in one direction and groups of
girls in the other, complimenting each other as they passed with the
traditional gestures. Here they exchanged flowers, although in other
towns they threw *serpentinas* and handfuls of confetti.

Don Marcos Vega asked the nuns from Zamora, whom Padre
Castillo had not wanted, to come back to San José. Once again uni-
formed women taught kindergarten and primary grades. The sisters
organized the girls into a theatrical group for the presentation of
dramas, comedies, and sketches, as well as for school programs. All
the townspeople attended these shows given by "the Haven," as did

[4] ANJ, Correspondence.
[5] According to Luis González Cárdenas.

residents of the nearby *rancherías*, and even of other villages. This theater was doctrinal and of little artistic value, but it was of transcendental social importance; it was a kind of widely accepted catechesis for adults.[6] Padre Vega encouraged reading, too. He founded a library of three hundred volumes, which included both devotional and agronomic works.

In addition to all this, in Padre Vega's time there were cockfights, magnificent rodeos, and everything that was noisy and glittering. Young women began to wear colors again, although their dresses still reached the ankle. On the eve of the outbreak of war, everything was gay—just before the thunder of real gunfire drowned out the splendid fireworks. Since people knew that the revolution would reach San José sooner or later, many of them dedicated themselves more than ever to the noble tasks of having fun and reproducing— but with no great panic, without disrupting the usual peace and quiet of the village.

The population continued to grow at a great rate. According to the census of 1910, the increase was not spectacular; but the count was inaccurate. When that census was taken, war was in the air, and some people suspected that the information gathered would be turned to military use. Thus, not everyone showed up to be counted. In San José de Gracia, 980 people (454 men and 526 women) were recorded, and, in the surrounding *rancherías*, 1,419 men and 1,200 women.[7] The count for the whole *tenencia* was 3,599. There may have been no concealment among the country people, but we can assume that 250 San Joséans, nearly all men, hid from the census takers. Thus, we can say without fear of exaggeration that there were 3,850 inhabitants in the *tenencia*—450 more than in 1900. Thirty percent lived in the town itself—a greater proportion than at the beginning of the century. The population had grown at the rate of 2.8 percent a year. The density had risen from fifteen persons per square kilometer to seventeen. There were no notable changes in geographical distribu-

[6] According to Agustina González Cárdenas.

[7] Dirección General de Estadística, *División territorial de los EUM correspondientes al censo de 1910 (Michoacán)*, pp. 14–103.

tion, except for the disappearance of Auchen and La Arena and the
rapid occupation of Aguacaliente. The owner of Auchen and La Arena
did not like people living on his ranches, and it is said that when he
bought these properties he turned out the residents. In Aguacaliente
(which was part of the Sabino hacienda), on the other hand, workers
were attracted to the flour mill that operated there for several years.
Most of the country people still preferred to live along the border between the states of Michoacán and Jalisco. There were no apparent
changes in ethnic structure. The fact that the index of males had risen
gives the impression that this zone offered better working conditions
than did the surrounding areas. There can be no doubt that there was
an influx of outsiders—in addition to the wealthy people already
referred to—in the *tenencia* of Ornelas. Birth and death rates did not
change appreciably. There were still about four children born for each
hundred inhabitants, and of these one out of ten died within the first
year. There were fewer victims of smallpox, for vaccination had become widespread; but pneumonia and other endemic diseases still took
a heavy toll.[8]

Meanwhile, *El País* was still arriving, loaded with news; but, after
the first excitement, these reports had come to be regarded as something from another world, of no great importance. The town learned,
without much political fervor, that their candidate had attained the
presidency and that he was a spiritualist. They read of Zapata's cry of
rebellion from the summit of Las Tetillas, the capture of garrisons and
the sacking of towns by the *zapatistas*, the announcement of the Plan
of Ayala, the crimes of Juan Banderas, the return of Bernardo Reyes
and his trial for sedition, the insurrection by Pascual Orozco's followers in Ciudad Juárez, the advance of Orozco's forces to the south,
General González Salas's suicide upon his defeat by Orozco, Emiliano
Zapata's speech as he entered Jojutla ("All this belongs to you, boys,
and it must be given back to you"), the return of Francisco León de
la Barra, the overthrow of the *orozquistas*, the victories of General
Victoriano Huerta, the capture of Francisco "Pancho" Villa (the other
hero in the struggle against Orozco), the elections for deputies and

8 APSJ, Baptismal Records and Death Records.

senators, the battle of Bachimba, General Huerta's return to the capital, the *zapatista* attack on the reporter Ignacio Herrerías and the protests on the part of journalists and photographers, Félix Díaz's rebellion in the port of Veracruz, the fall of Veracruz into the hands of the federal troops—and many other events. In San José and its environs during this time nothing was happening—except for Elías Martínez's attempt to become a bird.

Elías had made himself a framework, with wings of grass matting; he strapped it on his back and climbed up into an ash tree. He called down to a friend standing below and asked him to frighten him out of the tree. His friend threw a rock at him, and Elías took wing. He was nearly killed, according to some because he forgot to make himself a tail and a beak; others said it was because his friend had not scared him enough.[9]

In those days Don Alberto González Cárdenas was the brawniest man in the neighborhood. His strength was prodigious. He could bend iron bars with his fingers. One day he overcame an armed enemy by giving him such a hug that his ribs rattled like bones in a sack. At that time there was no better horseman than a cousin of his, Don Francisco González Cárdenas.

Nineteen thirteen was another year when things happened as fast as they had in 1910. *El País* brought news of tremendous events throughout the nation: the imprisonment of Félix Díaz, the taking of the National Palace by the cadets, the liberation of Generals Félix Díaz and Bernardo Reyes and the death of the latter, the falling of the Ciudadela into the hands of the *felicistas*, the refusal of General Victoriano Huerta (appointed a few days before as military commander of the Mexico City garrison) to recognize the government, the seizing of the president and vice-president of the republic (who were obliged to resign), Pedro Lascuráin's fifty-five minute tenure as president, and Victoriano Huerta's self-appointment as president and his oath before Congress "unconditionally to respect and enforce the Constitution of the United States of Mexico, with its laws, legal additions, and amendments, and loyally and patriotically to discharge the

[9] As recollected by José Chávez Fonseca.

office of interim president of the Republic . . . always keeping in mind the good and prosperity of the Union."[10] At the conclusion of the ceremony, having promised to do everything he had no intention of doing, Victoriano Huerta went to the National Palace. From the coveted chair he appointed his first cabinet and ordered the murders of Don Francisco I. Madero and Don José María Pino Suárez.

Don Venustiano Carranza, the governor of Coahuila, refused to recognize Huerta; Don José María Maytorena, governor of Sonora, refused to recognize Huerta; in order to forestall further disaffection, Huerta removed and replaced governors, and he did not resist the temptation to murder Don Abraham González, the governor of Chihuahua. Pancho Villa rose again; several governors, well-known politicians, and prominent citizens were dragged off to jail in Mexico City; General Félix Díaz and Licenciado Francisco León de la Barra said "no" to their champions and supporters; Huerta, claiming that he was acting in the interests of peace, sent troops to put down the rebels; Emiliano Zapata rose again; the revolution spread, reaching as far as Michoacán; there Gertrudis Sánchez and Rentería Luviano fought the federal army; Zacatecas and Durango fell to the anti-Huerta forces; there were more murders and changes in the government; General Villa took Torreón; Senator Belisario Domínguez announced, "The present state of the Republic is infinitely worse than before"; Senator Belisario Domínguez was assassinated by Huerta's order; Congress was dissolved; the Catholic party backed Don Federico Gamboa for president; Pancho Villa marched into Ciudad Juárez, and Álvaro Obregón occupied Culiacán; the administration was faced with a new crisis, and the government made use of impressment to raise troops.

Local events began to be varied, abundant, and notable. The first occurrence worth recording was the eruption of the volcano of Colima. It was a little past noon. A heavy rain of ashes that blacked out the sky, a great noise, and flashes of fire on all sides did little to reassure the populace. In San José de Gracia, however, there was no great alarm. The better-educated citizens undertook to explain that it was a natural and transitory phenomenon. In the *rancherías*, though, people

10 Luis González, *Los presidentes de México ante la nación*, III, 51.

had made up their minds that the ashes and gloom and roaring and flashing lights that went on until ten at night were the prelude to the Last Judgment. The omens had begun in 1910 with Halley's comet and had continued with the revolution and confusion that had accompanied Madero's rise to power. Everything was beginning to fall apart. The revolution itself was turning into a bloody contest between political leaders.

The gritty ashes vomited by the Colima volcano very nearly brought catastrophe to the cattle ranches. The grass was covered with a crust several centimeters thick. The cattle would not graze even on the small trees and brush, for they refused to eat leaves covered with ashes. In the end, however, there was no catastrophe. There came a heavy rain, which washed the grass and brush clean; it was held to be a miracle. Life returned almost to normal: the dry season came, and a great many cattle died; the rainy season arrived, corn and beans were planted, and it was milking time again; then came autumn with its harvest. In winter and spring there was little to do, now that the beeswax refining industry had disappeared. This applied only to men, of course; women were still busy all year round, their toil only slightly relieved by the little mills for grinding corn and by the sewing machines. Merchants and artisans, like the women, worked on through the winter and spring. Life was ordered by the annual cycle of seasons—but not exclusively. After 1913 the disturbing developments within the nation and the modern world intruded into the life of San José and its environs more violently and more often.

Colima had erupted on February 6, when San José's better-informed citizens were still talking about what they had heard at the Great Assembly of the Confederation of Catholic Workers' Clubs that had been held in Zamora at the beginning of the year. Fifty groups, with 15,539 members, had taken part, not counting the archbishops and bishops.[11] Señor Núñez, of Zamora, had said in his welcoming speech that "he had at last seen his greatest desire satisfied—the organization of Mexican workers into confederations like those in Germany; naturally, these groups were only the first step toward syndicalism and

---

[11] Alicia Olivera Sedano, *Aspectos del conflicto religioso de 1926 a 1929*, p. 40.

collective action." The president of the confederation announced that
some groups had "already set up night schools" and savings banks.
The days that followed were filled with solemn masses, speeches that
were both bombastic and substantial, and resolutions: minimum wages,
regulation of female and child labor, family benefits, unemployment
insurance, mandatory arbitration, "provisions for sharing, as far as
possible, in the profits and even in the ownership of the company,"
and protection against money lenders. "As for the agrarian problem,
with due regard for the legitimate rights of landowners and proprietors," the members of the assembly promised "to assure, as far
as possible, the honest, hard-working rural worker of the possession
of, or the inalienable right to use, a portion of land large enough to
provide his family with a decent living." The hacienda owners had no
reason to be worried; three of them—the Garcías—gave a banquet on
one of their estates. The bishops gave the landowners their blessings;
and with that feast the Great Assembly of January 23, 1913, ended.[12]

Among those present at the Great Assembly was a young seminary
student who was to take orders that same year. November 21 is
memorable as the date of Padre Federico González Cárdenas's first
mass, especially since this priest, who to some degree incarnated the
spirit of the assembly, would be before long the outstanding personage
in the three phases of change and confusion that were to follow. It
would be his task to face and direct the growing modernization, po-
liticization, national awareness, and social unrest among the inhabitants of San José de Gracia. But he would be called upon first to
exercise his diplomacy on the military raiding parties that were beginning to appear in town.

Don Gregorio González Pulido had given up taking local products
to Mexico City, for bands of revolutionaries made the roads unsafe
for travel. The San José area began to return to the old practice of con-
suming its own products. Trade declined. Padre Juan's goal of increasing prosperity receded in the distance. From 1913 on, increased
poverty was the rule. Some people lost everything overnight, while
others watched their fortunes dwindle slowly as the storm of revolution gathered. The nascent nationalism had gone with the wind.

12 Rodríguez Zetina, Zamora, p. 415.

Everything in San José shifted into reverse. The revolution did no favors for the town or the surrounding *rancherías*.

Don Manuel González Cárdenas, Don Gregorio's son, went to Zamora to find some other way of making a living. He leased two vast haciendas there, and he lost all the money he had made earlier as a merchant when the rebels razed the property. Don Manuel then returned to San José, looking for peace and another opportunity. But there was no tranquillity in San José, for by that time the row had reached there, too. The church bells had added a new peal to their repertoire: the "curfew," ordering everyone indoors a little after nightfall.

The Agents of Revolution in San José

Parties of rebels often came to visit their friends in San José, either to rescue the girls from virginity, or to feast happily on the delicious local cheeses and meats, or to add the fine horses of the region to their own. At the head of the list of illustrious visitors were Don Antonio and Don Jesús Contreras from Jiquilpan, who rode under the flag of Madero. Madero's insurrection had not satisfied their hankering for revolution, however, for it was too brief. They and their men continued as belligerents, calling themselves followers either of Félix Díaz or of Venustiano Carranza. When they arrived in San José in June of 1913 they were, some say, *felicistas*; others think they were *carranclanes* at the time. They summoned all the rich residents and told them how much money in gold coin each was to contribute to the cause. In view of the rifles, no one protested. They were all very frightened as they handed over the money in canvas bags. Don José Dolores Pulido was not just depressed, like the other donors; he fell ill from grief and foresaw that he was going to die. He wrote in his will, "My illness dates from the day the rebels took the town." He added that, except for part of the Las Cuevas ranch, which he left to his nephew, his fortune was to be used for the support of San José's schools; this included some 250 hectares of pasture land, his house, and four thousand pesos in cash. This sum, together with the thousand pesos he had turned over to the rebels, represented his savings over half a century of toil and parsimony. Don José Dolores Pulido died about the same time as Don Antonio Contreras. The latter was killed October 25, when one of his men "crushed his head with a heavy stone when he was asleep."[13]

After this visit by the Contreras brothers, San José's enthusiasm for the revolution cooled, and with subsequent arrivals turned to disaffection. Several citizens agreed to organize a "home guard" to repel future invasions. The wealthy residents provided the weapons, and twelve young men volunteered as soldiers. Don Apolinar Partida was named captain; he was brave, clever, and decisive. Any stranger in town might be a spy. Therefore he would be led to the cemetery, the priest would hear his confession, the indispensable bullet would be meted out, and he would fall into the grave that had been dug beforehand. But very few strangers came to San José unaccompanied. The home guard's marksmanship and courage would not be exercised until some really dangerous situations came up.[14]

This local army could not prevent all the revolutionary and extrarevolutionary incursions. One day General Huerta's men came into town, allegedly to collect troops to drive invading gringos out of Veracruz. Nobody volunteered. The people of San José were disinclined neophytes in patriotism, and they had not yet come to identify with the state. Huerta's followers put an end to any incipient nationalism. They dragged men to the plaza, picked out fourteen or fifteen, tied them together in a line, and dragged them off to the dictator's barracks.[15] Not one was killed, or even fought. They all deserted at the first opportunity. Huerta was not popular; he was disliked as much as the *carrancistas* were.

Captain Villareal, a follower of Carranza, showed up with a handful of soldiers, looking for money and priests. Padre Vega had left in November of 1913, and he had been succeeded by two clerics from Sahuayo named Sánchez, who were against the revolution. A little earlier, General Eugenio Zúñiga had threatened to decapitate every priest in Sahuayo; they were saved by the community, who raised a

[13] ANJ, Judicial Records of Licenciado Zepeda, 1913. For the death of Contreras, see Esteban Chávez Cisneros, *Quitupan: Ensayo histórico y estadístico*, p. 45.

[14] My informant: Anatolio Partida Pulido, a member of the home guard and son of its leader.

[15] Data from Luis González Cárdenas.

large sum of money to buy their lives.[16] In San José, the Sánchezes did not reply to Captain Villareal's questions with the proper respect, and he carried them off. People were terrified. The *carrancistas* must be Masons, to be capable of such sacrilege. In the eyes of the San Joséans, they were representatives of the devil himself; and yet the region produced a small band of Carranza followers, headed by Salvador Magaña.

Although *El País* had suspended publication and people were getting no news, everyone knew that the antidote to Carranza was Villa. In June, 1914, General Villa broke off his friendship with Carranza. Then he dazzled the world with a series of lightning victories. At the time he was camped near Aguascalientes, where the Revolutionary Convention was being held, with eleven thousand men. On October 17 he made his entrance into the convention grounds amid roars of applause. As usual, Villa wept and blew his nose. The convention went on with its work, but Carranza refused to recognize it. Many declared in favor of the convention, and many more supported Villa. The *villista* uprisings increased; a large group of Sahuayans under Gálvez Toscano came out for the Centaur of the North. Enthusiasm for Villa overcame some San Joséans, mostly small landowners; but hardly anyone took up arms.

Parties of *villistas* came into town often. First it was the Sahuayans under Toscano; then it was the little band headed by Miguel Guízar Valencia, who bore the nickname of "Curlylocks" because of the long hair and beard he had vowed not to cut. After the leader from Cotija, came David Zapién, who "printed money sitting in his saddle."[17] Then part of General Fierro's army came to call.

People never liked the other revolutionary factions. The moment any group of armed men was rumored to be in the area, villagers hastened to hide their daughters, their horses, and anything else of value. Everyone knew that the invaders came with only two things in mind: looting and carrying off girls. Sometimes they left signed receipts for what they took, which (they said) would be redeemed when

---

[16] Francisco García Urbizu, *Páginas de Zamora y de Michoacán*, p. 86; and Chávez, *Quitupan*, p. 46.

[17] Chávez, *Quitupan*, p. 47.

the cause had triumphed. The anti-Villa faction under Ignacio, Vidal, and Mariano Cárdenas entered the village as plunderers; they demanded forced loans and took horses, weapons, and anything else they wanted. A little later Aceves and Don Luis Morales Ibarra swooped down. In 1915, at the end of June, Camilo López arrived with three hundred Yaquis; his party remained politely on the outskirts of town. People wondered whose side these sturdy Indians were fighting on. Don Camilo's answer was: "We are fighting the clergy, but we respect the 'Little Fathers.' "[18]

The one who was really anticlerical was Francisco Murguía. He came with an army of thousands, taking three days to pass through San José. On the first day, he began to plunder the church, and the priests, who fled in panic, were pursued with gunfire for many leagues. The intimidated populace provided food for Murguía's men and their horses. Aside from stuffing themselves and robbing the church, they committed no outrages. They were either on their way to or returning from a skirmish with Pancho Villa. The battle took place on a mountain slope near Sayula. A few days earlier, Villa had made a triumphal entry into Guadalajara. On February 13 he engaged and defeated Murguía at Sayula. After the battle, General Villa said, "Another victory like that, and the Northern Division is done for."[19] Two months later the Centaur of the North, who still believed in cavalry charges, lost several encounters on the plains of Celaya. Carranza's faction was finally victorious throughout most of the country. In 1916 Don Venustiano entered and occupied Mexico City. A Constitutional Congress was convoked. The Villa and Zapata forces did not surrender, and some of them turned to brigandage.

Bandits were not a local phenomenon. The revolution had been won by only one of the rebel factions: Carranza's elegant troops, who needed a victory less than anyone else. The poor people who had risen up to follow Villa and Zapata changed overnight into enemies of the revolution. It was the *carrancistas* who called them "bandits." There can be no doubt that they robbed, killed, and burned on a wholesale scale, just as they had done earlier when they were not called bandits

[18] According to Porfirio González Buenrostro, an eyewitness.
[19] Juan José Arreola, *La feria*, p. 22.

and had less enthusiasm. It is also true that many of them had not fought in the revolution. Many got into the fracas late, either because they had been unable to do so before, or because they were beginning to feel the rigors of hunger and injustice during 1915–1917, when the revolution was officially drawing to a close: times of terrible drought, shortage of food, and demoralization.

The war had three unhappy consequences: hunger, brigandage, and a slacking off of public morality. All three were felt in San José de Gracia. Young men who had not taken part in the civil struggle were beginning to display, by 1916, an exaggerated respect for physical strength, a contempt for law and order, and a passion for antisocial amusements. There were frequent feuds. Sometimes they were provoked by residents of the lowlands, and sometimes by San Joséans. These feuds usually ended in gunfire and a few deaths. In 1914, five men were shot to death; in 1915, three; in 1916 and 1917 no records were kept, but there were more.[20] One Sunday "La Custria" practiced his markmanship on the crowd of people standing around the greengrocers in the marketplace. One day a man stabbed another with a dagger. The victim's last words were: "Don't be so cruel; pull out the knife. Don't let me die with it in me!" The aggressor replied, "You keep it. You might need it in the next life."

Games of chance, so effectively opposed by Padre Othón, came back. Drunkenness, too, increased. Of course, it was not only the vicariate of San José that got out of hand. In every nearby village the priest was inveighing against killing and against indulging the appetites of the flesh. Don Mauro Calvario, the parish priest of Manzanilla, told his flock: "Learn from the people of San José. They do not kill, nor drink alcohol, nor are they filled with lust." While San José was celebrating its saint's day, the padre from Manzanilla took a number of his parishioners to the virtuous town so that it might serve as an example to them. The community so famous for its purity celebrated the day of Saint Joseph with four murders, a couple of rapes, and general drunkenness.[21]

While some were killing, others were fornicating. Year by year the

20 APSJ, Death Records, Book I.
21 As recalled by Sara Cárdenas.

number of illegitimate births increased. In 1918, 15 percent of the children baptized had been born out of wedlock. The town and its *rancherías* were filled with scandalous rumors and anonymous letters, not always unfounded. So-and-so had been seen climbing over the wall of such-and-such a woman's house; the Don Juan of the town often ended up in different bedrooms, having announced his arrival by tossing pebbles on the roof; several husbands had taken to wearing horns; so-and-so's spouse was astounded to find another man in his bed, and, instead of thrashing him, dove under the bed and remained there, trembling, until the combat was over. The gossips had many tales to tell, some of them funny, but most of them tragic.

The resentment toward Mazamitla increased, too, of course. Its citizens were accused of denouncing San Joséans to various revolutionary parties. The people of each town made up insulting verses about the other. There were rock fights between the boys. Juan Zavala, the wit of San José, had some funny things to say about the behavior of the Mazamitlans.

The Puntada Gang, José Inés Chávez García, and the Spanish Influenza

Those were years of depravity. The new priest, Don Silvestre Novoa, was unable to stem the tide of vice. Some people believed that schooling was the only salvation for boys faced with the temptations of fighting, lechery, gambling, and drunkenness.

Young males did not attend the school run by the nuns; there was room only for the smaller children and the girls. In 1915 the singer José María Ávalos opened a school for boys in the parish, but he was able to teach and thrash only a few of them. In 1916 Rafael Haro, an experienced teacher who had studied in Jiquilpan, came back to town. He took another group of young men under his wing. By dint of intelligence and tenacity he instilled reading and writing and good manners.[22] There were still many youngsters in the village and its *rancherías*, however, who had had no schooling.

Nineteen seventeen was known as the year of the famine. The least important of the shortages was that of small coins; these were eked

22 According to Bernardo González Cárdenas, aged 61.

out with scrip issued by the merchants in the larger towns (Sahuayo, Jiquilpan, and Cotija) and by the smaller villages themselves (Mazamitla, Tizapán, Quitupan, and San José). To the scarcity of money was added the loss of crops and cattle. A severe drought began in 1915 and lasted until 1917. For three years running the corn crop was lost.[23] The bones of cattle bleached in the fields. Those who had the money went to the Autlán area for corn; there they paid forty pesos a hectoliter (more than the price of a cow, and fifteen times what corn had cost in 1910).[24] Infant mortality rose to great heights. Some families left the village without a word. Others moved into San José from the surrounding *rancherías* for protection. Men who could not leave their crops unattended sent their wives and children into town. It was true that they could live better in the country, but they had to choose between danger and going hungry. The ranches had become fair game for bandits. Demoralization and hunger had led many men into lives of robbery and violence. There were several gangs of bandits.

The most famous of these were the crew from La Puntada. Its members were natives of Cojumatlán, Sahuayo, Jiquilpan, and the country around San José. Their lair was in Chicharra Canyon, twenty kilometers east of San José. Under the leadership of the *villista* Eliseo Zepeda, they made raids along the Tigre Range. Zepeda's rival was another famous *villista*: the doughty peasant Prudencio Mendoza. Around San José the Puntada gang took their orders from José Corona, a laborer on the Sabino hacienda. They made frequent sallies from their canyon. They once fell on San José, but they were able to rob and burn only a few houses before Apolinar Partida and his twelve stalwarts drove them off with a rain of bullets. The Puntada band numbered more than a hundred. They thought of themselves as revolutionaries and maintained that they could finance their rebellion only with money taken from the rich. When they found that they could not get it from the well-to-do citizens of San José, who were so well protected by Apolinar Partida, they began falling upon the wealthy ranchers in the *rancherías*. During one of these raids they

---

[23] Chávez, *Quitupan*, p. 152.
[24] My informant: Luis González Cárdenas.

killed Don Vicente Martínez. They also took to kidnapping moneyed
travelers and holding them for ransom.[25]

The Puntada band's principal bugaboo was the garrison from San
José. Apolinar Partida and his men often went to harass them in
their hideout, and they killed some of them. Another garrison that
distinguished itself was the one from El Valle, headed by Cenobio
Partida. Each one fought to defend its own area; occasionally they
fought each other. In San José, people said that some of Cenobio
Partida's followers were taking part in robberies and committing
outrages. It was proved that some were cattle thieves. Apolinar Partida's men once exchanged gunfire with Cenobio's group, who were
driving off a large herd of cattle from the Sabino hacienda. In any
case, these were not the worst of the local saviors. Don Jerónimo
Rubio surpassed them all, even the avowed bandits.

The terrible paladin Don Jerónimo Rubio, better known as "The
Black Hand," was not the best defender against brigandage, either.
His official residence was in Teocuitatlán, where he never let a week
go by without lynching someone. He was tall, blond, and a drunk,
and he never looked a man in the eye when speaking to him. He once
made a raid on Mazamitla "for no apparent reason except that he
thought the town was against him, and [he] ordered the arrest of
every man he met." The following day he chose "ten men in trousers
and another ten in *calzones*" from among the prisoners, and led them
to the gallows. "The macabre task was interrupted" when he had
hanged half of them.[26] Captain Rubio showed up in San José, vested
with military jurisdiction and in command of twenty-five soldiers.
When he heard that a certain Ambrosio Magaña, a solitary rebel said
to be a *villista*, was overrunning the *rancherías* in the northern part
of the *tenencia*, he rode out with his troops in pursuit. He found
him. Magaña was riding along singing to himself; Rubio's men
emptied their rifles into him and slung his body across his horse.
When they got to town they searched his pockets and found a letter.
The next morning three bodies were hanging from a tree in the plaza:
Ambrosio, and the men to whom the letter was addressed. From

[25] My informant: Anatolio Partida Pulido.
[26] Chávez, *Quitupan*, pp. 47–48.

then on, men hanging with their tongues lolling out were a familiar sight.[27]

It is said that the intrepid men of "The Black Hand" drove Inés Chávez García's hordes out of Quitupan.[28] They did not do as much in San José; they were the first to break and run when they heard the cry, "Here comes Chávez!" At a time when the president of the republic was Don Venustiano Carranza, the governor of Michoacán was Don Pascual Ortiz Rubio, the chief of the *tenencia* of Ornelas was Don Octaviano Plancarte, the military defender of San José de Gracia was "The Black Hand," and the captain of the civilian guard was Don Apolinar Partida, the country's most celebrated bandit, Chávez, made his entrance under Villa's flag. His tactics were "strike and run," and his triple purpose was to loot, to rape the girls, and to set fire to the ranches.

Inés Chávez García's antecedents were well known. He had been born in an Indian hut near Puruándiro. He never reached normal size—possibly because of malnutrition. He was short and ill-natured. In the war, he fought with General Pantoja, who was assassinated shortly thereafter. "Chávez García (a lad of twenty) took advantage of the indignation stirred up by the unjust murder of his leader to organize the first rebel party and made his forays under Villa's flag. His forces grew rapidly as he was joined by country people from small settlements [and] he was supported in his widespread raids by a vigorous body of followers . . . When the fighting was over they returned to their homes and once again assumed the aspect of peaceful farmers. If he needed a great many people for an attack, he could gather two or three thousand men. He was just beginning his incursions when he fell a victim to typhus. When he recovered from the disease, he was a changed man. Before, he would enter a town and ask for supplies without committing atrocities; afterward, his motto was 'blood and money.' "[29] Chávez García's men were experts in criminal behavior. In Tacámbaro, La Piedad, Pénjamo, Degollado,

[27] My informants: Luis González Cárdenas and Ángel Torres.

[28] Chávez, *Quitupan*, p. 52.

[29] Oviedo Mota, *Memorias*, II, 38, quoted in José Bravo Ugarte, *Historia sucinta de Michoacán*, III, 213–214.

and Cotija his men looted and killed, deflowered virgins, raped women in the presence of their husbands, and committed other excesses. The leader loved seeing his soldiers have a good time. Another of his pleasures was riding. He was an excellent horseman, although he was short and fat. He could boast many animal virtues and some human vices. The thousands of men the government sent to take him were powerless against this little commander who "slept on his horse and could endure hunger and thirst for days on end."[30]

In May, 1918, the word spread through Quitupan that Inés Chávez García "had just set fire to and taken Cotija, and had committed all kinds of outrages." The town "was terrified by the reports of atrocities, harassments, and high-handed acts."[31] His arrival in Quitupan seemed imminent; but it might be Jiquilpan or Sahuayo instead. It was, in fact, San José de Gracia that had been selected by Chávez García for his next visit. No one there had any idea he was coming until the laconic warning came from Quitupan: "Chávez is on his way."

Don Apolinar Partida stationed his men in the most strategic places in the village. Chávez García's pack came charging down Larios Mountain at noon, as local families took flight in terror. Everybody was running about, slamming doors, climbing on horses, and riding off without a backward glance. The garrison opened fire. Chávez's eight hundred men split to take up a pincers formation. Higinio Álvarez, one of the brave members of the garrison, fell dead. The attackers surrounded the town and started to set fire to the houses. The banging and crackling of gunfire went on until four in the afternoon, when the defending forces were nearly wiped out and Don Apolinar Partida had emerged from a burning house to be riddled with bullets in the middle of the street. The bandit chief was growing more and more furious. From his position in the open street he encouraged his men with a string of curses. While the contestants were locked in battle on the cobblestones of San José, and tall flames shot up from many of the houses, 90 percent of the

---

[30] Agustín V. Casasola, *Historia gráfica de la Revolución*, II, 1298.
[31] Chávez, *Quitupan*, p. 51.

populace was fleeing across country to neighboring villages. But those families, too, were in headlong flight. People everywhere were stampeding. No one had any confidence in the government platoons stationed in the villages. It was common knowledge that the twenty-five combat troops stationed in San José had been the first to break and run.[32]

Of Apolinar Partida's men, only one survived the Chávez attack; but before they died they killed from seventy to a hundred of the raiders. Chávez's gunmen collected their dead and threw them into the flames. The women who had not been able to get away in time were huddled together in Don Bernardo González Pulido's house. Some twenty men were taken to the plaza. They stood silently in a row, waiting to have their throats cut. For some time Chávez had been in the habit of executing prisoners to a musical accompaniment, and he carried with him an entire band he had captured during an attack on the train from Guadalajara. After the musicians had played a selection, the executioner, a man named Chencho, came up to the doomed men and announced: "General Chávez has granted each of you the privilege of listening to any piece of music you like while your throat is being cut." Then he rolled up his sleeves, grasped his knife, and asked, "Where do you want me to begin?" The shoemaker Don Juan González, who was at the head of the row, replied, "At the other end, Señor." Don Gumersindo Barrios, the last in line, called out, "Tell them to play 'Adelita' for me."

In all the confusion, it was Padre Federico who kept his head. He recognized two of Chávez's men, both of whom had influence with their leader. The young priest convinced them that they should take no further reprisal against the town. They in turn persuaded Chávez. The incredible happened: the lives of the prisoners were spared, and not another woman was raped. The next day Chávez rode off, leaving the village sacked and half burned. For days, weeks, and months afterward, families who had fled before the ferocious

[32] Informants: Anatolio Partida Pulido, surviving defender; Bernardo González Cárdenas, a child who remained in town; José Núñez, an eyewitness; and Josefina González Cárdenas, among those who fled.

marauder were still returning home. They arrived in time to be victims of another calamity: the Spanish influenza.[33]

The grippe was a grim welcome for the young people who came back home after Chávez's reign of terror. It was especially fond of children. "One awakened with a headache, then came fever and hemorrhages; the patient had to be nursed for about a week, for if he got up too soon he developed pneumonia—from which no one recovered." The flu carried off as many people as the *chavistas*: fourteen. In that year, 1918, forty died in San José (not counting Chávez's men), and forty-three in the outlying areas. In addition to Chávez and the grippe, there were epidemics of smallpox and whooping cough. There had never been a year as bad as this one. It not only took a heavy toll of lives, but it drove away some of the inhabitants. Of those who fled from Chávez, one out of eight never returned. That year the village lost twenty families—people who had no wish to come back to a pile of rubble.[34]

After Chávez and the Spanish flu, San José was left practically defenseless, with no garrison of its own. It was under the so-called protection of "The Black Hand" and fifteen troops of the line, ostensibly a respectable force. The only enemies in sight were the bandits of the Puntada gang, and there were not many of them since they had lost Eliseo Zepeda. One November day in 1918, about five in the morning, the twenty-nine survivors of the gang rode into San José. It could hardly be called a town any longer. Many of its houses had been burned to the ground; a large number of its inhabitants were gone or dead; and all the buried pots and sacks of gold had been dug up. There was a widespread feeling that the

[33] According to Porfirio González Buenrostro and Padre Federico González Cárdenas.

[34] APSJ, Death Records, Book I, and data from Luis González Cárdenas. According to Edwin Oakes Jordan's "Epidemic influenza," 21,642,283 people died throughout the world in the 1918 epidemic; 170,000 in Spain, 200,000 in England, 250,-000 in Japan, 350,000 in Italy, 450,000 in Russia, 500,000 in Mexico, 550,000 in the United States, 750,000 in the Dutch East Indies, and 8.5 million in India. It was called the Spanish flu because "some believed it came from Spain, where there had been a severe epidemic of influenza in the spring of that year" (*Selecciones del "Reader's Digest,"* February, 1952, pp. 51–54).

village would never recover from the blows it had suffered. When
"The Black Hand" saw the Puntada men in the streets, he fled, just
as he had when Chávez had arrived. Only one of his soldiers, who
was unable to run because of a hernia, held off the bandits until his
ammunition ran out. Then he tried to mount his horse; he was still
trying when they captured him. They led him to one of the trees
in the plaza, and at nightfall he was hauled up on a rope to swing
in the breeze.

The period between 1902 and 1919 must have been a disturbing
one, with the news in the papers, the camera, the excitement about
new inventions, the eagerness for wealth, the rich newcomers, the
promotion of San José to capital of the *tenencia*, political passions,
feelings of nationalism, Halley's comet, the drought of 1910, the rise
of Madero, the revolution, the fall of Don Porfirio, the *maderistas'*
contempt for San José, Padre Juan's achievements, Padre Vega's
fiestas, gasoline lanterns, the earthquake, Sunday *serenatas*, the introduction of aspirin, the murders of Madero and Pino Suárez, the volcanic eruption with its brimstone and ashes, the Assembly at Zamora,
the frequent visits by revolutionaries, the forced loans, General
Huerta's conscriptions, the attacks on the clergy, the looting of the
church, the looting of everything, cattle rustling, the abduction of
girls, the revolutionary songs and ballads, the passing of Francisco
Murguía's splendid army, Salvador Magaña's outrages, the people
from the lowlands, drunkenness, skirmishes at all hours of the night,
"La Custria's" exercise in target practice, the famine, the flight of the
villagers to the city, the flight of the ranchers to San José, the Puntada
gang, "The Black Hand," the hanged, the career of Inés Chávez García, the *chavista* raid on San José, the stampede, the slaughter of the
home guard, the burning houses, and the toll taken by the Spanish flu.

The inconveniences and worries of the time had different effects on
the various generations and social classes involved. Don Gregorio,
Don Andrés, Don Juan, Don Bernardo, and almost all those of the
older, founding generation, adopted an attitude of resignation. They
still could remember the banditry and unrest that had resulted from
the wars of the Reform and the Intervention. They also remembered
that after the storm had come a long and fruitful period of peace.

They were calmly confident that, when this new storm was over and the air had cleared, the good old days would come back again. They never believed that the calamities of the moment were the beginning of the end; besides, they were not inclined to forsake the land, even to avoid possible danger. The younger generation, on the other hand, saw their ambitions thwarted by war, pestilence, and brigandage, and they reacted with despair, disgust, and anger. Some had been killed; some, who had money, had moved away; the poor ones who were left could do nothing but complain. Of these young people, those born between 1878 and 1892 had grown up in adversity, and they were prepared to take their chances. More than a few took the path of delinquency and violence, and most of them, as we shall see, reacted in a fashion that was in no way meek. The members of this last generation can be perfectly described as "the volcanic generation"—and not only because they were on hand when Colima erupted. It was they who would stain the following chapter in San José's history with their blood.

Gathering Clouds

Newspapers began reaching San José again in 1920, although not regularly. Still, people managed to find out that Obregón had refused to recognize Carranza; that the generals had risen against the president; that he had been assassinated at Tlaxcalantongo on his way to Veracruz; and that Don Adolfo de la Huerta had been named provisional president. They learned that Obregón had assumed the presidency, had made peace with Villa, Murguía, Blanco, and other insurgent generals, and had gotten into difficulties with the United States and England. There were stories about the creation of a Secretariat of Education that, unlike that of the Díaz regime, was to disseminate culture elsewhere besides among the urban middle class. José Vasconcelos had the walls of public buildings covered with posters suggesting these new ideals; he built rural schools and founded libraries in the smallest and most remote villages. One of the libraries, of one hundred volumes, was opened in San José de Gracia. Obregón's watchword, "Literacy, Bread, and Soap," applied to other fields besides education. Although it was still not possible to increase production of food, it was beginning to be distributed in a better way under the agrarian reform. The inhabitants of the villages and ranches near San José that lay within the state of Jalisco were applying for their allotments of land. In eastern Michoacán there were no difficulties over land, but there was trouble of various kinds in the center of the state.

A former seminary student from Zamora, with friends in San José, became governor of Michoacán. General Francisco J. Mújica supported the socialists, who celebrated Labor Day with violent speeches against the clergy, the Catholics, and the rich, provoking a counterdemonstration that had to be broken up by police gunfire. The governor made himself unpopular with the president and was removed, but he assumed office again a year later. The legislature accused him of crimes against the constitution and of usurping authority; he was imprisoned December 1, 1923.[35]

In San José there was some alarm over Mújica's socialistic leanings and Obregón's violent attacks on the anticlericals; but that was all. There were still some robber bands in the neighborhood, but things were returning to normal in spite of them. People were able to travel the highways with greater safety than before. The economic, political, and social climates seemed to be improving.

Communications and transport were prospering. The Chapala Development Company put into service a railroad line between Chapala and Guadalajara and a fleet of steamships on the lake: the "Vickings" for passengers, and the "Tapatías" for freight. Both classes ran daily between the principal ports along the shore.[36] Both were patronized by the least ruined citizens of the vicariate of San José when they went to Guadalajara. They took the boat in Tizapán, crossed the lake to Chapala, and from there went by train to the capital of Jalisco. After 1920, shipments of cheese, too, were again put aboard in Tizapán, taken to Ocotlán, and there loaded on the train for Mexico City. People went to Jiquilpan as seldom as possible. Hardly anyone had business with the government or wanted any. Ties were very weak between the representatives of the *municipio*, the state, and the fed-

35 Bravo Ugarte, *Historia sucinta*, III, 215–218.
36 Antonio de Alba, *Chapala*, pp. 120–121.

eral government, who had offices in Jiquilpan, and the authorities of the *tenencia* of Ornelas and the citizens of San José.[37]

Only a few people crossed the boundaries of the *tenencia*: men in riding saddles or, sometimes, a woman perched on a pack saddle, with her right leg thrown over the horn and her left foot resting on the wooden cross brace. Most were on their way to some place nearby—from one *ranchería* on the mesa to another, or from some ranch to the village. Most village families spent the rainy season in the country, returning to San José in November. Many of the men stayed on the ranch during the dry months, leaving their wives and children in town. They were safer there. It was for this reason that the outlying settlements were gradually abandoned and San José's population increased—especially in women and children.

According to the national census of 1921, there were 3,258 inhabitants within the *tenencia* of Ornelas: 1,640 men and 1,618 women. Of these, 1,024 lived in San José de Gracia, while 2,234 were residents of the *rancherías* within its jurisdiction. This shows that there were 341 less than in 1910; but, as we estimate it, the loss amounted to only 314. This census, like the one in 1910, failed to account for all the inhabitants—and not through any fault of the census takers.[38] In any case, there were 8 percent fewer people because some had been killed during the uprisings, some had died in epidemics and endemics, and, above all, because some had moved away. Many of those who had fled from the bandits in 1916–1919 never returned. The loss was not compensated for by the new settlers who came in 1920: Timoteo Magaña and his family from Pueblo Nuevo, Padre Leopoldo Gálvez and his brothers from Jiquilpan, and several members of the Sánchez clan from Méguaro. Most of these immigrants came to San José in search of peace. There were still disturbances and bloodshed where they had been living. San José itself was not exceptionally peaceful, but in the country of the blind the one-eyed man is king. Three men were shot to death there in 1921,

---

[37] According to Luis González Cárdenas.

[38] Departamento de Estadística Nacional. *Censo general de habitantes, 30 de noviembre de 1921. Estado de Michoacán*, pp. 49–116 and 164–165.

four in 1922, and one in 1923—certainly not very many compared with the number of violent deaths in the surrounding *municipios*.[39]

Farming and the cattle business in San José and its jurisdiction recovered in 1921. After the winds of revolution had died down, the routine of seasonal planting was resumed, and dairy farming returned to normal. In addition, the practice of milking in the dry season as well as during the rains was beginning to spread. This was done out of necessity; but it was still not enough to bring farm production back to its prerevolutionary level. It was not easy to build up herds of cattle as large as those that had existed in 1910. Economic recovery was slow, in spite of the fact that the rainy seasons were better every year. Perhaps lack of enthusiasm on the part of the landowners had something to do with the slow pull up the slope of production. This gloominess had its origin in the recent calamities and in the news of agrarian reform. Stories about land redistribution were beginning to circulate. In Jalisco, agrarians were already demanding their employers' lands. Right here in Paso de Piedra, where there were 190 inhabitants over eighteen years old, people were applying for the property belonging to the Sabino hacienda.[40]

Ownership of land was changing in three ways: subdivision through inheritance, enlargement by means of purchase of neighboring properties, and redistribution under the agrarian reform. The number of individual parcels had increased since 1910, because the holdings of a couple of large landowners had been split up among a dozen descendants. This process of division was counteracted by purchase of contiguous sections; at least two ranchers were still buying land. Property here had been split up more than in nearby areas. The Sabino hacienda, owned by María Ramírez, the granddaughter of Manuel Arias, was still intact with its more than four thousand hectares. But aside from this estate, there were only three properties that measured between one and two thousand hectares; most ranches were of less than three hundred hectares, and many contained less than a hundred. Some two hundred families owned property; the rest—about four hundred—had no land at all, or even

---

[39] AJJ, Criminal Sentences, 1921–1923.
[40] ADAAC, file 1933.

any dependable way of making a living. The landowners had cornered commercial production. Some industries, like beeswax refining, had disappeared.

There had been no great changes in labor. The same techniques were still being used; but the falling-off of the cattle business had brought idleness and unemployment. Those who lived by their labor alone suffered because there was little work; they lived less comfortably and grew poorer. Most of these men saw that owning land was the only way out of their poverty, but the idea of a land reform had never occurred to them. Some of them knew that there were areas where it was apparently easy to make a living, but very few had the courage to go looking for them. Among the young men in San José there was talk of another attraction. They had heard of the postwar prosperity in the United States; they knew that thousands of Mexicans were leaving the turbulent areas of their own country to go north and earn good, solid dollars. Ten of them had the courage to take a chance: Apolinar Partida, Porfirio González, Ramiro and Socorro Chávez, Pascual Barajas, Benjamín Martínez, and four others went off to the United States in search of work and fortune. They got jobs as laborers at the Inland Foundry in Indiana. After two or three years, seven of them, disappointed, came back home with, perhaps, a phonograph, a couple of exotic shirts, a dozen English words, and very few dollars. They slipped back into the peaceful poverty of the village.[41]

For the rest, political and social life in San José and its *rancherías* slowly resumed its routine. The practically autonomous government of the *tenencia* was poorer than usual and almost unable to undertake any improvements. Gaudencio González Cárdenas, one of the *jefes de tenencia*, managed, with a great deal of difficulty, to have the garden paths in the town square paved with flagstones. Usually the authorities did little more than preserve peace and order, and their police activities were not always effective. Between 1920 and 1924 there were some remarkable ruckuses.[42]

Not everybody ate well, but it was a rare man who did not own a

---

[41] According to Porfirio González Buenrostro.
[42] AJTO.

pistol. It was not easy to wipe out overnight the attitudes and customs of *machismo* inherited from the past. The cult of violence, the habit of getting drunk, and the exaggerated sense of personal honor all persisted. Social distinctions were emphasized. The rich were not as rich as before, but the poor were poorer. The barrier of respect between the employer and his workers was crumbling faster every day. Still, the waters of social discord were far below flood level.

Schools and education in general reached a kind of apogee in the lustrum 1920–1925. Don Rafael Haro returned to teach the usual subjects to a class of small children and adolescents. In addition, he took up the reeducation of grown-ups by means of the theater. He wrote and presented one act farces in which he lampooned some new tendencies that were beginning to appear in town. In *El Alcalde de Panzacola* he made fun of braggarts; in *La Zahorina* he ridiculed the wave of irrationality and superstition that was leading the villagers to fall victims to quack doctors and gypsies.[43] Both of these plays—especially *El Alcalde*—were great successes.

The nuns from Zamora reopened their girls' school, which had been closed since 1918. The contract was signed January 9, 1922, by Don Luis González Cárdenas for the town and Lucía de Jesús for the school.[44] Padre Marcos Vega attracted two dozen young men to his preparatory school for the ecclesiastical seminary in Zamora. From 1920 to 1922 he taught Latin and Spanish grammar and some elementary arithmetic.[45] Not far away, in Cojumatlán, Padre Federico González Cárdenas had restored and begun directing another preparatory institution, where four youngsters from San José were enrolled. The two schools turned out some twenty aspiring priests, who went on to complete their studies in Zamora. By 1924 there were twenty-two young men from San José in the Zamora seminary, hard at work at Latin and scholastic philosophy. No other town in the diocese could boast as many seminary students as San José.[46] And yet, within the village and its *rancherías*, more than half of the children

---

43 As recalled by Rafael Haro.
44 From Luis González Cárdenas's private records.
45 According to Daniel González Cárdenas.
46 According to Honorato González Buenrostro.

of school age were either idle or working—not attending any school.
There was no teaching facility in any of the *rancherías*.

On the whole, everything was peaceful. Only Padre Emilio Ávalos
was worried about the dangerous innovations introduced by the
periodical press. He was upset with Rafael Haro because he subscribed to *Revista de Revistas* and, not content with poisoning his
own mind, was lending the publication to young people.

The circus came. It was a modest circus, typical of those that toured
the provinces: without wild animals—only some trained dogs; with
no great comedians—only a simple clown with his whitened face;
without famous trapeze artists—only a couple of apparently boneless
acrobats who were good at turning somersaults. It is reported that
the circus carried off Joselón (José Gómez), who was seven feet and
one inch tall.

The reception for the new bishop of Zamora was most spectacular.
Two hundred riders, with jangling spurs and stamping horses,
escorted him from above Cojumatlán to San José. He arrived in
the midst of a crowd, the air filled with the sounds of clanging church
bells and mariachi music.

In summation: the calm that came in the wake of the storm of
revolution had its pros and cons. The cycles of rain, dry seasons, and
frosts were on the whole favorable for the cattle raisers. An economic
step forward came with the practice of milking during the dry
season, and a step backward with the total disappearance of the
beeswax industry. The comforts enjoyed by the rich did not rise
again to the level of the first decade of the century; the misery of
the poor remained as it had been during the revolutionary decade.
There were few jobs, and salaries were low.

Prices rose steadily. Only 30 percent of the population owned
property. The landless aspired to ownership; but they did not dare
to apply to the government for land because of their respect for
private property, and because they did not believe that the government was really offering it to them. They were in the habit of
expecting only trouble from the authorities. Everybody agreed that
the government was bad—an opinion encouraged by their spiritual
advisers.

The clergy felt persecuted. No one bothered Padre Timoteo López, who had charge of the vicariate of San José in 1919–1920, nor his successor, Padre Emilio Ávalos. The anticlerical sniping on the part of Obregón and his governors was aimed at the rulers of the Mexican ecclesiastical structure, but it still disturbed the believing public— especially the citizens of San José, who identified so closely with their priests and seminary students. Huerta's rebellion was another cause for uneasiness. When the president insisted upon imposing General Plutarco Elías Calles as his successor, the army split into two equal factions, and war broke out again. The people of San José watched it approaching. There was a great battle, the like of which no one had ever seen, at Ocotlán, on the opposite shore of Lake Chapala. It was Obregón who carried the day.

The people of San José were like dry gunpowder, ready to burst into flame at the slightest spark. Clouds were slowly gathering on the horizon.

5. THE *CRISTERO* REVOLUTION (1925–1932)

A Few Months Before

GENERAL Plutarco Elías Calles became president of the republic on December 1, 1924, and lost no time in showing his hatred for priests. The bureaucracy echoed his sentiments. The anticlerical agitation fostered the creation of a "Mexican Apostolic Church," with a patriarch named Pérez, a cathedral called La Soledad, and hardly any customers. When the schism failed, Articles 3, 5, 24, 27, 32, and 130 of the republic's general constitution were rigorously applied. Article 130 called for the registration and reduction in number of priests. Shortly before the so-called Calles Law, speakers at the National Eucharistic Congress (the bishop of Huejutla, the historian Mariano Cuevas, the attorney Miguel Palomar, and others), held in Mexico City, October 4–12, spoke of "fighting for the Church and for the salvation of the country."[1] Two representatives from San José de Gracia were present at that congress. In a press conference, the old archbishop of Mexico expressed his dissatisfaction with several articles of the 1917 Constitution. General Calles's aptitude for polemics and his talent for leadership remained undiminished.[2] The

[1] Jorge Gram, *Héctor: Novela histórica cristera*, pp. 80–82.
[2] *El Universal*, January 27, February 4, and February 8, 1926.

regime advanced the tenet that the clergy were traitors to the fatherland.

General Calles is memorable not only for his disputes and battles
with General Serrano, the Yaqui Indians, the clergy, and the *cristeros*.
In addition to removing the obstacles to the enforcement of the 1917
Constitution, he laid the foundations for the subsequent development
of Mexico with agricultural and secondary schools, the Bank of
Mexico, the income tax, the Farmers' Credit Bank, and the Commissions of Irrigation and Highways.[3] All in all, Michoacán was
not aware of the constructive acts carried out by Don Plutarco. It
knew only of the many and varied destructive ones: the closing of
schools and convents; the prohibition of worship, "even when practiced by Catholics in the privacy of their own homes"; the confiscation of nuns' schools; and the closing of the educational institutions
for priests in Morelia, Zamora, and Tacámbaro.[4] On March 8, 1926,
the government closed the Consolidated Seminary in Zamora.[5] The
twenty-odd young men from San José who were studying there returned to their village to found the local group of the Catholic Youth
of Mexico and to begin a secret campaign of agitation. Printed antigovernment propaganda was pouring in, too. Speeches by Anacleto
González Flores and other Catholic leaders were read and circulated,
with striking effect. By far the most decisive event during those
heated times, however, was Padre Federico's return in 1924.

Padre Federico came back to raise the flag of the people, particularly those of the generation that had made itself felt at the time of the
eruption of Colima—those born between 1877 and 1890. The young
priest, who was sickly in appearance, had been born in 1889. His
personality had been shaped by three environmental forces: the
ranch, the family, and the seminary. During his childhood the em-
bryonic town of San José was merely a rural settlement in a region
dedicated to farming and cattle raising. His earliest occupations were

[3] Wigberto Jiménez Moreno and Alfonso García Ruiz, *Historia de México: Una síntesis*, p. 119.

[4] José Bravo Ugarte, *Historia sucinta de Michoacán*, III, 223.

[5] Arturo Rodríguez Zetina, *Zamora: Ensayo histórica y repertorio documental*, p. 576.

those of a life in the open air: playing marbles, riding horses, being punished for disobedience, roping calves, and doing occasional ranch chores—although this last was not really necessary, for he was the child of a rather well-to-do family, old settlers in the area. His father, Bernardo González Pulido, was peace officer in San José from 1891 to 1900; his mother, Herminia Cárdenas Barragán, who had been born on a ranch near La Manzanilla, was a passionate, emotional, active, and indomitable spirit. The boy inherited his mother's temperament and both parents' sense of honor and faith in the future. From his father, he took a strong religious bent, a love of horsemanship, and a feeling for leadership. At thirteen he entered the auxiliary seminary in Sahuayo, where he studied Latin, mathematics, and physics. In Zamora, where he took scholastic philosophy and theology, he acquired the duodenal ulcer that was to afflict him for the rest of his life, a dissatisfaction with the course of the Mexican revolution since the Reform, and a taste for reasoning. After taking orders in 1913, he went to Tingüindín as associate priest, worked with the Indians, and had dealings with the revolutionary guerrillas. He was in San José from 1916 to 1918, helping to defend the village against bandits. He was already regarded as a local hero when Chávez García came to call. He left his native village to go to Cojumatlán in the double role of priest and director of one of the seminary's auxiliary schools. In 1922 he appeared in Vistahermosa to straighten out a difficult matter and, in the following year, assumed the vice-rectorate of the Zamora seminary. When his ulcer began tormenting him again, toward the end of 1924, he returned to San José. Nervous, a light sleeper, active, always ready to expose himself to danger, intelligent, and strong-willed, he had every qualification for an excellent leader. He displayed these qualities when he involved his fellow townspeople in two delicate undertakings: the division of the Sabino hacienda, and the struggle against General Plutarco Elías Calles's anticlericalism.[6]

The Sabino hacienda came to be divided up because of its owner's dread of the agrarian reform. Several of her properties had been

---

[6] Information obtained from Padre Federico's family, and especially from Rosa and Josefina González Cárdenas.

threatened by those who were soliciting land under the laws of January 16, 1915, Article 27 of the Constitution, and the agrarian legislation of 1922. These agrarian winds were blowing out of Jalisco. We have seen that in 1921 the agrarian committee of Paso de Piedra applied for the Sabino land. The governor of Jalisco found the application to be in order and forwarded it to the local Agrarian Commission. This body proposed that the 190 residents of Paso de Piedra who were over eighteen be awarded 1,140 hectares: 826 hectares from Sabino, 99 from Ignacio Sánchez's Rancho Seco, and 117 from several smaller properties.[7] At that time there were still no eager proponents of land redistribution in the *tenencia* of San José. The villagers felt a certain shame at demanding other people's land. Padre Federico did not favor this method of creating landowners, either.

Padre Federico took advantage of Señorita María Ramírez Arias's terror—and that of her uncle and attorney, Don Mariano Ramírez—to persuade her to divide up the Sabino hacienda and sell parcels, on long-term contracts, to the landless citizens of San José. When she had agreed, a civil engineer was brought in to survey, make maps, and cut the vast latifundium into sections. After the first surveyor had been on the job for months, with no visible results, he was replaced by another. This was David Vázquez, who soon finished the task. Of the 4,232 hectares of Sabino, 1,872 were divided into 206 parcels measuring from 7 to 15 hectares each. The smaller pieces were to some extent suitable for rainy-season crops; the larger ones were almost exclusively pasture land. Of the remaining 2,350 hectares, 950 were made into twelve ranches of from 40 to 150 hectares each. The owner retained 1,400 hectares (which her relatives kept her from selling in parcels to the workers on her hacienda). In the same year— 1926—672 hectares of this land went to make up Paso de Piedra's *ejido*.[8] Both the small parcels and the ranches sold at reasonable prices; the average cost was fifty pesos a hectare, to be paid in ten years in annual amounts in cash or in kind. Thus, the number of landowners in the *tenencia* was doubled and every San Joséan's urge

---

[7] ADAAC, file 1933.
[8] Ibid., file 12558.

to own property was satisfied. Only two hundred families living out in the country still possessed no land.

Among these were forty on the Sabino property, who wrote a letter to Padre Federico González: "You have always taken such an interest in us poor people with no land of our own . . . who used to live on the hacienda only because they let us raise our animals and gave us a field to cultivate and who [now that those sections of the estate have been sold] find ourselves with no place to live or pasture our animals or grow crops . . . please help us by selling us parcels of the hacienda like those held by the people of San José, and at the same price."

The petition came too late. By July, 1926, all available land had been sold. Neither the padre, nor Don Guadalupe González, nor anyone else connected with its distribution could mend matters. The parcels had been apportioned by lottery. Two hundred eighteen heads of families from San José and Jarrero had already taken possession of their new ranches. The fact that everyone in town now had property of his own was celebrated with a delicious picnic lunch, as well as other manifestations of rejoicing and festivity.[9]

Another luminous event came about due to the initiative of Don David Sánchez, who installed a small electric generator, capable of lighting a few yellow bulbs in the church, the plaza, and two dozen houses. It also provided power for a mill to grind corn for tortillas— the second in town. A few years earlier, Don Juan Chávez's fondness for the ladies had led him to set up a corn mill. In 1926 the two mills woke the ladies before sunup with their harsh rasping; Don Juan's mill also boasted a roaring exhaust, which sounded like gunfire. The third happy occurrence of 1926 was the abundant rainy season; so much rain fell that the retaining dikes along the Swamp of Chapala were washed away.[10]

But it was not all good fortune. Several influential politicians in Sahuayo were not pleased by the subdivision of the Sabino hacienda.

[9] *Huanimba* no. 1 (1941); data from Porfirio González Buenrostro as well.

[10] Germán Behn, "El lago de Chapala y su cuenca," *Boletín de la Junta Auxiliar Jalisciense de la Sociedad Mexicana de Geografía y Estadística* 10, nos. 1–2 (September–October, 1956): 25.

Rafael Picazo declared that it was counterrevolutionary, and tried to have it declared invalid.[11] Others wanted the property split up into ranches and sold to the people of Sahuayo. Those who considered themselves heirs of the old-maid owner of the hacienda were not very happy about the sale, either. Many people, for one reason or another, declared war on the citizens of San José. The town had never been subjected to such abuse. San Joséans were denounced as *mochos*. People said that they were harboring a group of the Mexican Catholic Youth Movement. It was true that all the young unmarried men had been attending the MCYM meetings, just as in many other villages.[12] Like a great part of the country's population, the San Joséans had signed the memorandum to congress protesting the "Calles law." And they had not failed to obey the decree of the National League for the Defense of Religious Freedom: "Buy nothing, at least nothing that is not necessary; and when you have to buy, buy only from friends of the cause."[13] They also respected the episcopal order to suspend public religious ceremonies. They obeyed every order and recommendation issued by Catholic organizations, and they obeyed spontaneously and with enthusiasm.

The orders to suspend ceremonies in the church were carried out. The bells no longer rang; the town was silent. Padre Federico continued the daily saying of his office in private. People increased their religious activities: they went to Mass, confessed, and received Communion more often than ever. The village felt itself more and more identified with the church. It had been religious and proclerical from the beginning—which was not surprising. San Joséans had no reason to dislike priests. The clergy's paternalism and its role in temporal matters had been, on the whole, to San José's benefit. There were no complaints against priests; people had fond memories of the bishops of Zamora and of many of San José's pastors—especially Padres Othón, Vega, and Ávalos. Besides, at that time, they looked to a priest as leader. The officials of civil government had done nothing for anyone. The only case of San José's identification with the au-

11 According to Honorato González Buenrostro.
12 As recalled by Padre Federico González Cárdenas.
13 According to Josefina González Cárdenas.

thorities of the republic had been their sympathy with the *maderista* movement. For subsequent regimes, they had felt a marked dislike, which had turned to out-and-out hatred when Calles and his collaborators set to work persecuting priests and nuns and closing schools and churches.

The educated class of San José could not agree as to the attitude they should take toward the problem of religious persecution. Nearly all of them had studied at the seminary, although the teacher Rafael Haro was an exception. The majority maintained that it was their duty to take up arms against the government; they believed that the Calles regime was not only corrupt but also powerless, and that the two million Mexicans who had signed the petition to Congress demanding religious freedom were ready to go to war—especially since the Chamber of Deputies had answered them with double talk. The discussions were heated. Rafael Haro did not believe that Catholicism was as deep-seated in the rest of Mexico as it was in San José, and he doubted that the religious persecution had produced such a strong reaction elsewhere. Some felt that it was hopeless to go to war against the government, because it had the weapons and the army; the people had no means of defense. The advocates of violence met this objection with several arguments. They pointed out, among other things, that the *agraristas* of the neighboring towns in Jalisco would come with their rifles and fight beside them. They hoped, too, that the Catholics of the United States would help with money and military supplies. Some San Joséans were still skeptical—among them a man whose opinion carried a great deal of weight: Padre Juan González. After his death, the view of the educated elite and of Padre Federico prevailed.[14]

Eufemio, the "civil defense" commander in Sahuayo, had his reasons for resenting the powerful citizens of his town: he was a descendant of Indians who had been robbed of their land by the white colonists. But he took his revenge not only on the sons of the thieves; he often came to harass the people of San José. One day he arrived in the village with the intent of capturing Padre Federico and several of his friends. He was not able to find any of them, and, in

[14] As recalled by Rafael Haro.

order to get even, he looted several houses and stores. The inhabitants were furious, but not only with Eufemio, nicknamed "the Chiscuaza." They had reason to believe that the Federal District deputy, and, ultimately, the government itself, had a hand in these raids. These depredations on the part of the Sahuayan commander were the drop that overflowed the cup.[15]

The Uprising

Padre Federico chose the path of violence. But, although he was a man of quick decisions, in this case he hesitated. First, he sought the opinion of the bishops, some of whom were in favor of armed action. He had read books dealing with just wars of the past and concluded that in this case war was both just and necessary. He contacted the leaders of the Mexican Catholic Union. He surrounded himself with "a small group of men in whom he had complete confidence," and went to talk with parish priests and *presidentes* in neighboring towns. Eventually, he succeeded in winning over the municipal authorities in Cojumatlán, Valle de Juárez, Cotija, and other villages. Most people everywhere were ready for armed rebellion. Some of the other settlements had not suffered as much as San José, but they, too, were prepared to revolt. It was agreed that the insurrection would begin in San José on June 11, 1927, when men from half a dozen towns would meet to take up arms. Many other *cristero* bands were already fighting in various parts of the country.[16]

Luis Navarro Origel had attacked Pénjamo on October 29, 1926; when he was driven back, he withdrew into Michoacán.[17] Another outbreak had occurred at Chalchihuites, Zacatecas, on August 15. By August 22, the rebellion had spread, under the command of Pedro Quintanar and Aurelio Acevedo.[18] The National League for the Defense of Religious Freedom decided to encourage and coordinate

[15] As recalled by Honorato González Buenrostro.
[16] As recalled by Padre Federico González Cárdenas.
[17] Bravo Ugarte, *Historia sucinta*, III, 224.
[18] Jesús Degollado y Guízar, *Memorias de ...*, *último general en jefe del ejército cristero*, p. 26.

the armed movement. On January 2, 1927, Miguel Hernández took up arms in Los Altos de Jalisco, to be followed by "El Catorce," Valadez, Rocha, and the priests Vega and Pedroza.[19] At the same time several towns in the Bajío region of Guanajuato revolted.[20] In the Colima area the rebels were gathering forces at Coquimatlán, Villa de Álvarez, Pihuamo, and Zapotitlán.[21] Sparks were flying and setting fires in several places in Michoacán: in the mountain ranges to the southeast, and in Tajimaroa, Zamora, and Yurécuaro, not far from San José. There was also fighting in southern Coahuila, northern Zacatecas, San Luis Potosí, Tamaulipas, and in several towns near the capital.[22] It was reported that there were more than twenty thousand men under arms; that there was fighting in many different areas; that people were calling the *cristeros* "liberators"; and that the government was frightened. It was then that a piece of news arrived that led several men from San José to come to a decision: the extremely popular leader Anacleto González Flores was taken prisoner, tortured, and executed, in April, 1927. A little earlier, on March 3, the famous Don Prudencio Mendoza had raised his cry of rebellion a few leagues from San José, in El Calabozo and Cotija. "It was echoed by almost all the inhabitants of the mountain range."[23]

In San José there were about five hundred men of military age; but not all of them were eager to go to war, and there were not enough weapons available even for those who were. Of the forty who joined the ranks, only half were equipped with long-range firearms: .30/30's, .44's, and a few Mausers. León Sánchez was made a general, his brother David a colonel, and Anatolio Partida a major. Rafael Pulido, the *jefe de tenencia*, was given the rank of captain. The twelve members of the home guard joined the movement. Some of these men had come out of the Zamora seminary only the year

[19] Alicia Olivera Sedano, *Aspectos del conflicto religioso de 1926 a 1929: Sus antecedentes y consecuencias*, pp. 157–158.

[20] Ibid., pp. 160–162.

[21] Ibid., pp. 162–165.

[22] Ibid.; see also Antonio Rius Facius, *Méjico cristero*; and Aquiles P. Moctezuma, *El conflicto religioso de 1926*.

[23] Esteban Chávez Cisneros, *Quitupan: Ensayo histórico y estadístico*, p. 56.

before; some were small landowners and cattlemen (or their sons); and the rest were corn farmers or ordinary ranch hands. A third of them were married men with children. Their ages ranged from eighteen to forty; they knew something about firearms and horses, but they had no military training.

Not all the men in the San José contingent were simple idealists. Religious sentiments aside, many were motivated by a desire for vengeance against local petty politicians who had mistreated them in land dealings. Some were looking for fame, money, and power; some wanted excitement; and one or two were no more than ordinary criminals. Basically, however, they had been moved to action by an offense against their religious natures, by a feeling of humiliation, by a desire to avenge the injustices suffered by defenseless people at the hands of Calles's officials, and by the need to protect their small properties. The old hatred for the government had come to the surface again—a sense of hostility dating from time immemorial. The people of San José—and before them those of Llano de la Cruz—had long believed, as did the villagers of Luvina, in the Juan Rulfo tale of that name, that the government "only remembers them when one of their sons has done something wrong," or when it is time to collect the taxes the government called "contributions." The pacifists and, especially, the old people accepted this state of affairs as an irremediable evil; but the rising *cristero* army was confident that the man known as "the government" could easily be defeated.

As the rebellion moved ahead, groups from other towns joined the ranks. On July 8, 1927, the San Joséans learned that Cojumatlán was already mobilized and that its rebel forces were on their way to the village. On the following day San José's troop of forty rode out to meet their brothers. Together they made up an army of a hundred mounted men; they rode into San José at sunset, two abreast. In the plaza they raised their war cry, "Long live Christ the King!" Then they fired their first shots and received their first ovation. At eight that night, under cover of darkness, the Cojumatlán party under Lieutenant Colonel Enrique Rodríguez pulled out for Mazamitla. The San Joséans, under General León Sánchez, took the narrow road leading to Auchen.[24] For ten days they roamed about from one place to another, never far from home. Sometimes they hid out from the government troops in the Tigre Mountains; they gathered provisions, enlisted more men for "the cause," obtained more rifles, and consulted with Generals Jesús Degollado and Prudencio Mendoza at El Faisán, in the hills of the *municipio* of Quitupan. From there they rode forth, ready for battle; many were still without fear, with all the bravery of men with no military experience.[25]

They made their first strike on July 30, when they fell upon Cojumatlán at dawn. For four hours ninety-five *callistas* and thirty *cristeros* exchanged volleys. They were unable to hold the town, but they retreated with the satisfaction of having downed twenty-eight federal soldiers. They took the road leading west and cautiously, in a zigzag fashion, crossed the low hills and ravines of their plateau. At dawn on August 9 they descended upon the large town of Teocuitatlán. They routed the garrison; they rang the church bells; they snatched some matériel from the barracks; but they were forced to withdraw before noon. Bernardo González Cárdenas, from whose diary we have taken these facts, tells us that on the way back to San José they stopped at Pueblo Nuevo, in friendly territory, and at Toluquilla. They were, in fact, well received everywhere on the mesa, but nowhere were they greeted with as much enthusiasm as in San José.[26]

They came home with the news that the *agrarista* communities of Jalisco had taken the side of the government, but that the rest of the populace was sympathetic to their cause. With some confidence they rode out of San José again on August 15. They met four *agraristas* on the road to La Manzanilla and lynched them. Then they learned that a party of soldiers was on their trail. They made for the mountains[27] and rode into a vast zone ruled by Don Prudencio Men-

---

[24] Bernardo González Cárdenas, "Diario manuscrito, 1927–1929."

[25] Information supplied by Honorato González Buenrostro and Salvador Villanueva González.

[26] B. González Cárdenas, "Diario."

[27] Ibid.

doza, a lean, dark, just, and crafty man who was usually seen squatting on his heels and smoking. Old Mendoza's kingdom included parts of four *municipios*: Quitupan, Santa María del Oro, Tamazula, and Jilotlán. It was mostly mountainous and contained some fairly high peaks (Palo Verde, Cerro Blanco, La Cruz, El Cuascomate, El Faisán, El Montoso, and Chinito) and deep ravines (Agua Fría, Agujas, Burra, and Soledad). There were also large rivers: Las Huertas, Calóndrigo, Algodón, Santa María del Oro, and the broad Tepalcatepec. Mendoza's fief embraced tropics and cold country, a sparse population, and abundant vegetation and game. It was a rude paradise, where the *cristeros* were often to gather.[28]

On September 9 several parties joined forces and attacked Tecalitlán from three sides. The shooting went on without pause for seven hours. The town surrendered. The besiegers thronged in, with cries of triumph, and found seventy-four dead federal soldiers. They themselves had lost only six men. Shortly thereafter they were forced to retreat. They were always short of ammunition, hence could never hold a town they had taken for more than a few hours. This time they returned to the safety of Mendoza's country; they crossed the rising Santa María del Oro River and rode up into the mountains, where they celebrated the Sixteenth of September (Independence Day). There were speeches by the doctor, by Colonels Alberto Gutiérrez and David Sánchez, and by General Don Ignacio Sánchez Ramírez from Sahuayo. Shortly before this, Anatolio Partida and his men had left. Shortly after this, there was a visit from Luis Navarro Origel, alias Fermín Gutiérrez, who claimed to be the commander of the Michoacán *cristeros*. So did Jesús Degollado y Guízar.[29] Both had been appointed by the National League for the Defense of Religious Freedom, whose principal function was inventing and distributing military commissions. The most pious, silver-tongued, and blundering braggarts were made generals. City playboys arrived in the country expecting ranchers to obey them. Some of the local leaders humbled themselves, but the rest paid no attention to them

[28] Chávez Cisneros, *Quitupan*, pp. 56–69, 187–193.
[29] B. González Cárdenas, "Diario."

at all—especially Don Prudencio Mendoza. Before General Enrique Gorostieta the rebels had no military leadership at all. The league's leadership was invisible, impalpable, and ignored; local officers appointed by them turned out to be men who, not long before, had been lords of vast estates, engaged in writing their memoirs, for whom the publicity directors of the Acción Católica created ad hoc biographies, proving that they were men, saints, and martyrs. One of this number was Luis Navarro Origel, who came to strut like a peacock before the assembled *cristeros* and their real leaders in Mendoza's hideout.

On October 6 the insurgents from San José de Gracia came down from the mountains and headed for home. When they rode into the village the following morning, they received the greatest shock of their lives. San José had been "burned, destroyed, and abandoned." Like Martín Fierro, more than one of them felt "two huge tears running down his cheeks." It was a place of roofless walls, rubble, ashes, and charcoal, with green grass sprouting in the streets and on garden walls, and soot everywhere. The only sound was the howling of starving cats.

General Juan B. Izaguirre was responsible for the burning and devastation of San José. The federal government had sent him out at the head of a thousand well-armed men, thoroughly equipped and organized, to put down the rebels. He had moved into eastern Michoacán slowly and fearfully. Apparently he did not wipe out a single band of insurgents. At last he grew enraged at the pacific populace. He ordered the thousand inhabitants of San José, more than half of them women and children, to empty their village within twenty-four hours. They were forced to take refuge in other towns.

> He started up the mountain
> To wipe out the *cristeros*;
> But he didn't like the view,
> And came growling down again.
>
> He hardly gave us time
> To get our things and leave.

"Where can we go?" we said,
"Just look how hard it's raining!"[30]

Fifteen of the better-off families fled to Guadalajara; there they were able to get by—with difficulty, but without going hungry—by borrowing money on their ranches. About twenty-five of the poorer families set out for Mazamitla, where they were greeted by a sign that said, "No people from San José admitted here." However, Don Refugio Reyes ordered the notice painted out and gave shelter to some hundred refugees.[31] Other families found asylum in Jiquilpan, La Manzanilla, Sahuayo, and Tizapán. Everywhere they were avoided like the plague; even those who took pity on them were afraid to give them work, fearful of government reprisals.

It was Aguirre who gave the order
To set fire to the church,
And he and all his men
Will forever burn in hell.

In nineteen twenty-seven
The federal government
Sent soldiers from the city
To burn down San José.

General Izaguirre had brought in enough fuel to reduce the whole town to ashes. He burned houses wholesale. He piled up pieces of household furniture, drenched them with kerosene, and set fire to them; the flames rose above the rooftops. He also engaged in the sport of hanging *cristeros* from the trees. His soldiers and the poverty-stricken inhabitants of neighboring settlements had fun looting what was left of the town. To wind up the party, the generalissimo drove off thousands of cattle—where, no one knows.

After this kind of mistreatment the tide of rebellion rose. People who had not dared to revolt before did so now. In the *tenencia* of Ornelas the number of insurgents rose from forty to three hundred.

---

[30] This and the following selections from *corridos* composed at the time were supplied by Agustina and José González Martínez [my translations—J. U.].

[31] According to Margarita Orozco.

To the cry of "Down with the government, / And long live Colonel Partida! / Long live Christ the King!" the fighting spread.

After Tizapán

On October 8, rebels from San José and Cojumatlán, in greater numbers now, attacked Tizapán. Under heavy gunfire they bottled up the federal troops in the church towers. The fighting lasted all that day and into the next. The besieged forces were about to surrender when they were saved by the arrival of a sizable detachment of reinforcements. The *cristeros* pulled out hurriedly, leaving sixty-three enemy dead. They lost only six men.[32]

In the battle of Tizapán the division commander and chief of operations was General Luis Navarro Origel, alias Fermín Gutiérrez. In the name of the league he had tried to take command of the rebels from San José and Cojumatlán, but they refused to obey him. On October 11 he left for Tierra Caliente. The general was handy with both his tongue and his pen.

In several heated letters, he gave himself credit for a great number of victories. He blamed his defeats on the rural leaders ("El Guarachudo," "El Perro," and others), and on lack of support from the playboys in Mexico City who headed the *cristero* movement.[33]

The real leaders of the country people, held in such contempt by the Acción Católica officials in the capital, were given even less support than the splendid General Navarro. But they, at least, could count on the backing of their fellow country people, who supplied them with food and scouts. What equipment they had had been captured from the enemy. After Tizapán, they decided to try Jiquilpan.

The attack took place during the night of October 23. The *cristeros* took the town, but just before dawn they found themselves hemmed in by gunfire from all sides; they broke and fled about nine in the morning. Eleven were killed. Gaudencio González, Padre

---

[32] B. González Cárdenas, "Diario."
[33] See Martín Chowell [pseud.], *Luis Navarro Origel*.

Federico's brother, was taken prisoner. His captors knocked out his teeth with a rifle butt; they punctured his body with a stiletto; then they hanged him from a tree and finished him off by plunging a dagger into his breast. His comrades fled in total disorder, every man for himself. They were not to reunite until November 6, when they went to the aid of General Prudencio Mendoza, who was in difficulties.[34] It was the *cristeros* who burned the Jiquilpan town records.[35]

On November 9 and 10 there was fighting from Fresnal to La Cruz, for a day and a half without rest. If the *cristeros* had not run out of ammunition, perhaps they would not have been forced to retreat—some to Santa María del Oro, others to God knows where. Little groups began showing up at the pile of ruins that had been San José. They won a skirmish at Mazamitla. Padre Leopoldo Gálvez, the "Padre Chiquito," smashed the pots of the women selling tamales and *atole* when they refused him food and drink. He also tried to burn down the church.

The approach of General Juan Domínguez and a column of twelve hundred men changed the course of events. They rode up into the hills in Mendoza's territory. They found the area empty, the settlements abandoned. The general could hardly find a man to relay his offer of amnesty. Several *cristeros* were pardoned at that time, in particular those from El Montoso, under Don Prudencio Mendoza. When the general and the colonel of the San José party made their peace with the government, Anatolio Partida assumed leadership. From then on he was Colonel Partida.[36]

It was then that General Domínguez sent Doña Amalia Díaz, a woman widely know as "La Generala," to carry out negotiations for the pardon of the *cristeros* from San José and the surrounding ranches. She was from Concepción de Buenos Aires, now known as Pueblo Nuevo, and was related to the Sánchez family. She succeeded in getting her relatives to give in, but no one else.[37]

[34] B. González Cárdenas, "Diario."
[35] According to Don Jesús Mújica, of Jiquilpan.
[36] B. González Cárdenas, "Diario."
[37] According to Honorato González Buenrostro.

La Generala offered
(To avoid further trouble)
One of her many daughters
To every man who yielded.

"Even a mother cat,"
Answered my friend Othón,
"Wouldn't have enough daughters
For an entire battalion."

Honorato's answer was:
"What do I want with your hag?
There are plenty of flowers at home,
Just waiting to be picked."

Another incident came along to change the situation. When General Domínguez was passing through the devastated village of San José, he came across its only remaining inhabitant: Don Federico's aged mother, Doña Herminia. He seized her. Knowing of her son's intellectual leadership among the *cristeros* of western Michoacán, he hoped that this would bring about Padre Federico's capitulation. Although things did not turn out exactly as the general had expected, the priest did leave his followers and, with a brother, a cousin, and a couple of aides, came looking for his mother. Juan Domínguez's column rode down from the mountains on December 31; they passed through Santa María del Oro on their way to Tierra Caliente, which was by this time almost completely in the hands of the *cristeros*. There were encounters where neither side won. The federal army lost men, and the rebels lost ground. In the end, the weary Domínguez pulled his reduced and disheartened troops out of the zone and released Doña Herminia, three months after he had captured her.

During the first half of 1928, *cristeros* from San José, Sahuayo, Cotija, Tizapán, Pueblo Nuevo, Teocuitatlán, and other towns and hamlets were roaming from one place to another, in groups of ten, twenty, and thirty men. With no battle plan and no unified military leadership, short of food and even shorter of weapons, driven at times by fear and at times by sheer daring, they engaged in brief skirmishes, by turns with the federal troops, the *agraristas*, and the civilian defenders in the villages. There were good days and bad days, fun and misery—but hardly ever a major battle. Some of them operated in Don Prudencio Mendoza's mountains, some on the plateau, and others in the area near the volcano in the state of Colima.

According to the "Diary" kept by Bernardo González Cárdenas, who rode with Padre Federico, along with Porfirio González Buenrostro and others, there was not much happening on the mountain range or in Tierra Caliente. They spent the first ten days of 1928 at banquets and *serenatas* in Coalcomán, and the rest of the month traveling in the Jilotlán and Chinicuila area. They often hunted deer. At last they reached the sea. There were hardly any military encounters—merely the hardships proper to the tropics (ticks, vermin, malaria, and lethargy) and to the trackless and densely wooded mountains.[38]

Meanwhile, Major Honorato González Buenrostro left Santa María del Oro with eight men and orders to take charge of the operations on the mesa, where many *cristeros* from San José were moving about in a disorderly fashion. It was not easy. Among a thousand other incidents, they were ambushed by the men from El Montoso who had accepted the government's amnesty and were now anti-*cristero*. Most of the surprises, however, were pleasant ones. Insurrection among the people in the small settlements was at its height. Rafael Madrigal, from Ménguaro, commanded eighty men from the hills; Agustín Aguilar, from San Miguel, had no less than thirty followers. By this time Cojumatlán boasted four hundred rebels. "El Chaparro" led a good number of Sahuayans. In all, there were nearly a thousand insurgents roaming over the mesa, engaging in skirmishes from time to time with the *guaches* and the progovernment "home guards."

In February, 1928, Major Honorato González Buenrostro called a meeting of his officers in Cojumatlán. While they were discussing matters of strategy, they were set upon by three columns of well-trained troops and by the veteran soldiers led by the Indian, Eufemio,

---

[38] As recalled by Salvador Villanueva González.

"La Chiscuaza," who had been such a thorn in the side to the San Joséans. There was hand-to-hand fighting, in the midst of which "La Chiscuaza" fell. His soldiers gathered up the body of their illustrious leader and cleared out.

> "Ufemio, for you I say it:
> The cat was caught sleeping.
> It was a brave man who killed you
> In Cojumatlán."

The first half of 1928 was a time of heroic deeds and misfortunes for the *cristeros* of the mesa. In groups of from eight to thirty men, all skilled riders, they fought or ran away from, as the case turned out, the mounted troops under Generals Anacleto Guerrero and Anselmo Macías Valenzuela. On the average, there were four skirmishes and minor encounters a week. On two or three occasions formal battles took place, all of which turned out to be indecisive; the antirebel army suffered more casualties, although the *cristeros* had plenty of setbacks, too. More than forty *cristeros* were laid low in the engagement on the outskirts of Cojumatlán on Good Friday. The battle at La Sabinilla was not a bloodless one, either. But since this was guerrilla fighting, rather than a formal war, skirmishes were the rule: scuffles of little importance from the military point of view, offering more opportunities for minor leaders and individual soldiers to distinguish themselves than for generals. Here one could mention the heroic exploits of Ramiro, José, and Isidro Pulido; Adolfo and Antonio Ávila; Faustino and Salvador Villanueva; Luis, Manuel, and Honorato González; and Agustín Aguilar.[39]

Anatolio Partida's party, with 250 soldiers, was in the thickest of the fighting. Many of his men were from San José and the neighboring *rancherías*; others were residents of the western half of the mesa: La Manzanilla, Pueblo Nuevo, and nearby settlements. With these country people from many areas he undertook the major feat of taking Manzanillo. The plan for capturing the port was carefully laid by General Jesús Degollado y Guízar. Eight *cristero* leaders and nearly a thousand men joined forces to carry it out. On May 22 they

[39] Ibid.

assembled at Pueblo Nuevo; the following day they marched out in three columns (the left flank headed by Anatolio Partida). On the twenty-fourth they entered Manzanillo and attacked the customs house. A few minutes later a train filled with federal troops pulled into the port, and the *cristeros* beat a hasty retreat. It was a major and bloody military operation that cost hundreds of rebel lives.[40] In his recently published *Memoirs*, the general writes that during the fighting in Manzanillo "Majors Don Anatolio Partida and Don Rafael Covarrubias conducted themselves with great distinction."[41] In southern Jalisco and Colima there are still many old people who remember the *cristeros*—and not only those from San José—for the "loans" extracted from landowners and merchants, and for the way in which they made off with horses, weapons, and girls. It cannot be said that their wicked ways brought them the enmity of the rich, because they had never enjoyed their friendship; but they did incur the ill will of other sections of the populace.

At the beginning of the rainy season of 1928 there was a lull in the fighting. There were fewer federal incursions into *cristero* territory; and it did not occur to the rebel bands (there were more of them now, but they were smaller and more poorly equipped) to leave their "water holes." In Don Prudencio Mendoza's sector, from which Padre Federico was trying to coordinate the operations of the *cristeros* in northwestern Michoacán and adjoining parts of Jalisco, half a dozen skirmishes took place after the storm on May 22. The *callistas* set fire to *rancherías* in the mountains, two days later, on July 15, *cristeros* attacked the train from Los Reyes; there was action at Gallineros on July 18, at Lagunillas on August 12, and a battle at San Cristóbal on August 15. It was quiet enough for many of the hill people to return to tending their cornfields and milking their cows. Those who, like the San Joséans, were far from home spent their days and nights on horseback under the rain, receiving the encouraging news of the death of Obregón, taking part in religious services held by Padre Federico or some other *cristero* chaplain, writing letters to their fami-

---

[40] According to Anatolio Partida Pulido.
[41] Degollado y Guízar, *Memorias*, pp. 138–149.

lies and sweethearts, and celebrating at various times and in various places such events as the repopulation of San José.[42]

When the rains had come that year, San José was still a pitiful spectacle: empty, blackened houses with fallen roofs; tall weeds and thistles growing in the streets and among the ruins; no sound but the howling of coyotes and cats. But the rains had hardly begun when the civil and military authorities (perhaps because the "concentration" had not had the desired effect, perhaps out of pity for the refugees) allowed the town and its surrounding *rancherías* to be reoccupied. Almost the entire population, lean and ragged, returned to the village. The women and children set to work making the houses livable, while the old men went out to replant the cornfields and round up and milk the remaining cows. They also returned to the practice of serving as spies and providing supplies for the armed rebels. There was an attempt to move them out again, but it could not be done; they now knew how to defend themselves against the government, how to turn politics against the politicians, and how to practice the art of dissimulation. During June and July more than half of the villagers came back to their homes.[43]

Another piece of good news for those engaged in the revolution against Calles came when General Gorostieta was named supreme commander of the Liberation Movement on October 28, 1928. For some time people had been saying that he was an officer with excellent qualifications. He soon announced his manifesto, with its fifteen points, elucidating the goals of the *cristero* movement: all the guarantees of the Constitution of 1857 "without the Reform laws"; refusal to recognize the authorities; adoption of laws based on the people's wishes and on tradition; votes for women; syndicalism; agreements between holders of *ejido* lands and property owners for the payment of indemnities; distribution "of rural properties in a just and equitable way after indemnification"; plans to make land available to the greatest number; baptism of the *cristero* army as the "National Guard"; and adoption of the motto "God, Country, and

---

[42] B. González Cárdenas, "Diario"; and Federico González Cárdenas, "Diario, 1928–1929."

[43] Information obtained from several people who were present at the time.

Liberty." In line with these principles General Gorostieta would re-organize the *cristero* revolution; he would unify the Liberation Movement without "flinching under the obligation imposed upon him by the will of the nation."[44] Meanwhile, people were supporting José Vasconcelos in his campaign for the presidency of the republic, and the intellectual leaders of the *cristero* movement were lamenting the poverty, disorder, and irresponsible behavior of their forces.

As 1928 drew to a close, the rebels from San José de Gracia were still scattered. The largest group had been taken by Anatolio Partida to Los Altos de Jalisco, where they felt like dogs in a strange neighborhood. In any case, they took part in the battle near El Tarengo and in several minor encounters. They acquitted themselves well in the fighting, but not so well in the matter of other people's property and women.[45] A high-ranking officer drew Partida's attention to the amorous excesses committed by his soldiers. "I have men with me, not fairies," was Anatolio's reply. The many groups who remained on the mesa and in the hills spent October and November riding from one place to another, taking part in brief skirmishes, hunting deer, talking of more peaceful days, sleeping in one spot today and another tomorrow, and suffering the chills and fever of malaria. They had hardly any provisions, and their clothing was in rags; they had few chances for love and even fewer for drinking. They almost shot Porfirio González for having drunk a little of the alcohol kept for the wounded. They seldom had any news about the war, and it was always contradictory. On rare occasions they got hold of some ammunition. On November 12 each man received a change of clothing—which got rid of the lice for a while.[46]

The white lice were the worst; they produced an incessant itching, welts, and sores. They infested the *cordones de San Blas*, the scapulars, and the sacred relics—the very objects the defenders of Christ the King could not dispense with; they were a part of their religion, as precious as the masses celebrated by Padre Federico and the frequent

[44] Olivera Sedano, *Aspectos del conflicto religioso*, pp. 93–195, 203–205.
[45] As recalled by Anatolio Partida Pulido.
[46] B. González Cárdenas, "Diario."

confessions and communions. The religious zeal of San José's *cris-teros* was as complex and as aggressive as ever.

They were no longer so afraid. Now nobody, not even "La Monedita," vomited before a battle. They showed no signs of demoralization. During the fighting at the end of 1928 and the beginning of 1929, they showed considerable valor; this was as true at El Sauz as on the Cuesta de la Guerra.

On November 22 Padre Federico and General Sánchez Ramírez decided to consolidate the *cristero* forces on the mesa, in the mountains, and in the surrounding valleys, in preparation for an encounter with government troops that were approaching from every quarter. Since October rumors had been flying that they were on their way in enormous numbers. They were coming up from below, climbing, crawling, with a clatter of horseshoes and a flourish of bugles. The people of San José celebrated the fiesta of the Virgin of Guadalupe, with all its masses, confessions, sermons, communions, and its vigil of the Holy Sacrament, although everyone was aware that the enemy was not far away. On the night of the fifteenth the government forces reached El Sauz, "where there was a crowd of people," and set fire to the village. The battle began at dawn. About noon the soldiers ceased firing and had their noon meal, taking up their arms again at three. At dusk they retired to their base, from where they kept up a barrage all night. They were back the following day, but to no avail. They attacked both Aguacaliente and Agostero, but the defenders did not retreat. Since they were short of ammunition, the *cristeros* fired only when their targets were nearly upon them. The soldiers wore green uniforms, designed to be less visible against the trees; but the color only served to make them more conspicuous. When they were forced to fall back later that day (the sixteenth) they gave vent to their fury by slaughtering livestock and committing other acts of senseless destruction. But they did not withdraw to any great distance; they meant to return with greater determination and more effective weapons.[47]

Up until that time, the skies of San José and its vicinity had been strictly reserved for birds; but all that changed the day General

[47] Federico González Cárdenas, "Diario."

Bouquet (with more than five hundred troops) joined Honorato González and his men on the plain near Sabino. The roar of the planes was heard early in the morning, and soon the falling bombs were setting fires in the grass. That was enough for the *cristeros*; they turned and fled southward. They regrouped twenty kilometers away at El Zapatero, in a small meadow surrounded by high mountains and pine forests. About six in the morning, when the men were about to have breakfast, they suddenly realized that they were hemmed in by a circle of fire, behind which waited the federal forces. They succeeded in getting through both barriers, but with many casualties. For weeks afterward there lingered a penetrating stench of blood on what was from that day on to be known as La Cuesta de la Guerra.⁴⁸

The month of January, 1929, was one of uneasiness, sudden assaults, and skirmishes. Padre Federico wrote in his diary: "A year ago we were riding into Coalcomán with the hope that 1928 would see the end of it. Now it looks as if it may go on for another year." The news was all disheartening. The "government" was in Los Reyes; Santa Inés had been taken; a spokesman for the church tried to persuade Padre Federico to give up the cause, saying that "what the *cristeros* were doing was futile and prejudicial"; federal troops were stationed in Jiquilpan; the courageous *cristero* chief Ramón Aguilar was reported to have lost all his horses; there were rumors of a compromise; a newspaper carried the story that Archbishop de la Mora, addressing the diocese in a pastoral letter, had asked the rebels to lay down their arms. "We couldn't believe it," Padre Federico wrote. "We had chocolate and bread for breakfast . . . People said the government was going to fall upon us at any moment . . . We bought a pig for ten pesos . . . I had *chicharrones*, which I hadn't tasted for a year and a half. . . . We set out after breakfast . . . That night we had an unconfirmed report that Gorostieta had arrived . . . We went to see him in a driving rain."

Determined to reorganize his forces, General Gorostieta had come with an escort headed by Anatolio Partida to review the position of the Michoacán *cristeros*. "The task of organization was begun" on the

---

⁴⁸ As recalled by Honorato González Buenrostro.

twenty-ninth. On February 2 "the San José sector was established," under General Anatolio Partida. Some of the leaders wanted the San Joséans to take their orders from Sahuayo, and this made difficulties. Finally, the Sahuayans, with all their harangues, were put under General Sánchez Ramírez. Gorostieta inspired respect and affection, ratified and made changes in military ranks, discussed strategy, encouraged the men, and convinced everyone that victory was near. The new era began on February 5. The officers had a last drink together, and everyone went on his way. But the federal forces had got wind of the general's presence in the area; troops of the line and rural guards were activated. "It was before dawn [much before: it was about three in the morning] when we realized that we were surrounded. We tried to get away . . ." They had no ammunition.

At the beginning of March, Padre Federico returned to the town where he had been born. He talked with Anatolio Partida, Rubén Guízar, and the *cristero* leaders in Cojumatlán, and settled their disagreements. On the seventh, "after supper," he felt a very severe pain, and he spent the rest of the night in agony. On the ninth he was still "unable to walk"; but he recuperated on the twelfth, when Honorato González returned from Guadalajara with a good supply of ammunition. He had brought it across Lake Chapala in the still of the night in a fishing boat. The troops were mustered and prepared for action. Partida, now the brand-new general of the San José Division, took Pueblo Nuevo and captured more weapons. Delgadillo joined the movement, along with many others from Pueblo Nuevo. Major Honorato González occupied the sugar plantation at Contla. Gorostieta returned. The people of San José gathered to celebrate their patron saint's day. It was very gay, with phonograph music, liquor, banquets, and *serenatas* in the square. Gorostieta arrived on the twenty-first and made a most successful speech before the whole town. He urged them to carry on the struggle for freedom and religion. They were enjoying an interlude of peace while the government was busy putting down the Escobar rebellion.[49]

General José Gonzalo Escobar, impatient with Calles's political maneuvers, had, on March 9, instigated a series of uprisings in the

[49] F. González Cárdenas, "Diario."

outlying areas of the country, and had made a deal with the *cristeros*. The *escobarista* rebellion was particularly active in the north. General Calles appeared there, at the head of an army of loyal troops, and squelched the rebels almost overnight.[50] By May, Escobar's offensive had been totally destroyed, but the *cristeros* were arming again. Vasconcelos's campaign was crushed, too. But the *cristeros* in western Michoacán took part in two memorable encounters. A combined force of about nine hundred men, under several leaders, occupied Tepalcatepec on May 4, 1929, after shelling the walls.[51] It was not a lasting victory, but it was followed by other important battles, including one at Talayote, on the shore of Lake Chapala, and by several skirmishes in which the rebels were triumphant. But these were the last splendid moments of the struggle. Strange winds were beginning to blow; there were rumors that the bishops were coming to an agreement with the government; people were beginning to be afraid, and enthusiasm was waning.

San José de Gracia Lifts Its Head Again

On June 2, 1929, the newspapers carried the story of General Gorostieta's death in an ambush. Catholic leaders, who were at the moment negotiating a *modus vivendi* with the government, found this event to be providential.[52] On June 5, Don Emilio Portes Gil and two bishops—the papal delegate Ruiz y Flores, and Pascual Díaz, the archbishop of Mexico—had lengthy talks in Chapultepec Castle. Soon it was agreed that worship would be allowed to resume, that churches and other holdings would be returned to the church, and that amnesty would be granted to the armed rebels. The agreement was signed on June 21.[53] Church authorities urged the *cristeros* to lay down their arms, and the government called off its troops. "The churches of Mexico reopened on Sunday, June 30, 1929." San José's church did not open, however, nor did those of several other towns, for they had been burned. In San José, worship began again

[50] Olivera Sedano, *Aspectos del conflicto religioso*, pp. 224–227.
[51] According to Salvador Villanueva González.
[52] Olivera Sedano, *Aspectos del conflicto religioso*, p. 233.
[53] Ibid., pp. 235–237.

at the house of the *cristero* Juan Gudiño.[54] People celebrated religious services more fervently than ever; but very few celebrated the *modus vivendi*. A great many deplored it. Much against their will, the obedient *cristeros* accepted the amnesty that had been arranged by Archbishop Díaz.

It was agreed that San José's *cristeros* should lay down their arms in their own village. General Félix Ireta conducted the simple ceremony in the ruined portico on the north side of the town square, opposite the *churi* tree. One by one, the rebels surrendered their weapons—each man presenting the oldest and most worn-out gun he had, and keeping his best. "Don't think you're fooling us," said Rafael Picazo, who represented the civil authorities in the amnesty ceremony. "But since we want peace, we'll accept this heap of scrap iron instead of the guns you really fought with." The soldiers carried the junk away.[55] The townspeople lamented their dead: Agustín Aguilar, Demetrio Bautista, Salvador Buenrostro, Francisco and Román Cárdenas, José Gudiño, Manuel Chávez, Gaudencio and Jesús González, Luis Manjarrez, José Guadalupe Mancilla, Ramiro Pulido, Agustín Sánchez, and others. Almost all of them were to be privately enshrined, and many people would appeal to them as saints of the calendar: for favors, miracles, and all the things that are requested of the members of the celestial court. On the other hand, those who had not died in battle, or had not even taken part in the fighting, found themselves in the purgatory of poverty, injustice, and ill-will that their land had become.

Nineteen twenty-nine opened with severe frosts; the last of these, which did great damage to winter crops, struck on March 13 and 15. The years from 1930 to 1933 were cold and dry. For example, 1932 could not have been worse, with its niggardly summer rains followed by frequent bitter frosts. The corn withered in the hard earth and bent under the cold blasts of October. There was not enough of either corn or beans to satisfy local needs. Both had to be bought at terribly high prices: corn for 110 pesos a ton, and beans at 280 pesos.[56] And,

---

[54] As recalled by Juan Gudiño.
[55] According to Salvador Villanueva González.
[56] From the account book kept by Josefina González Cárdenas.

as if this was not enough, the cattle died in heaps during the frosts and drought that followed the meager harvest. The three or four thousand cattle that had survived the raids by federal troops and *cristeros* were reduced to half that number in the drought of 1932. There was want even in the homes of the middle class. The money-lender (San José had never been without one) sank his teeth in. People were saying that there was a "crisis"; there was not enough food or clothing; families were living in houses that had been only half rebuilt. Ruined cornfields, decimated dairy herds, unemployment—these marked a period of widespread misery.

The political climate was not encouraging, either. General Calles was still ruling Mexico from his position behind the presidents, the governors, and the local puppets. The armistice was not entirely respected in all branches of the governmental machinery. The president demanded the banishment of Archbishop Orozco y Jiménez. On July 27 he made a declaration that did not square with the agreement that had been reached with the prelates, and, ultimately, he refused to return many of the churches. Don Pascual Ortiz Rubio, the second puppet president, revived the policy of limiting the number of churches allowed to remain open and returned to the old Calles brand of anticlerical statements. Some state governors continued religious persecutions. General Lázaro Cárdenas, governor of Michoacán, tolerated the burning of holy images by groups of "defanaticizers," but the aims of his government were far higher than the excesses of the "Calles gang." The governor's tolerance toward San José was at first so broad that the former seminary student and declared pro-*cristero* Daniel González Cárdenas was appointed *jefe de tenencia*. Until 1930, local authorities had had complete control, but from that time on they were obliged to take orders from a military detachment under the command of Lieutenant "Ino," who owed his nickname to his inability to pronounce the word *himno* (hymn). Beyond making solemn public statements of all kinds, this man did no harm.[57]

San José's social atmosphere was something else again. When the

---

[57] According to Porfirio González Buenrostro.

cristero revolution ended, many soldiers in the army of Christ the King were no longer on friendly terms with their comrades, and some early sympathizers had turned against the *cristero* movement. There was less unanimity in San José than there had been in 1927. Quarrels arose, and some of the politicians who were interested in getting rid of the ex-*cristeros* fanned the flames. It is true that the San Joséans saw through these tricks, as the people of Cojumatlán did not, but that was not enough to restore harmony. In addition to personal quarrels, the town had to put up with exhibitions of barbaric behavior learned during the war: shooting off guns into the air, bullying, insults, gunfights, showing off, and drunken sprees. And then there was the robber band that seems to come along after every revolution. Manga Morada was their leader. One of his favorite amusements was sitting on the shoulders of his victims when they were being hanged. But personal quarrels, bad manners, and robbery were minor evils in comparison with certain emotional reactions to poverty and injustice.

Hatred was still the predominant emotion. On the eve of the revolution it had been the principal driving force behind the future rebels; throughout the struggle it had been responsible for the modest victories against the government. Before and during the war, anger played a role that was, if you wish, questionable; but it was not then useless or maleficent, as it turned out to be later. Targets of the postbellum wrath were—besides the machinery of government and the *agraristas*—the Mexican ecclesiastical hierarchy and anyone who had not supported the *cristero* movement or who had obstructed it. Among the factors of this hatred were impotence, the bitterness of having been unable even to attack the enemy, let alone crush it, the helpless desire for vengeance, and a relentless fury. This rage led many men into pure iniquity, into "evil-heartedness," so that they were ready to lash out blindly. Others became merely irritable. Around 1930 there were plenty of vicious and rancorous people in San José. In general, they were not the old people or the more mature adults, but those of other age groups. This hatred was reinforced, accompanied, stimulated, and nourished by other violent passions that circulated through the village.

Once again, as in the prewar years, this hatred was a result not only of misery and injustice, but also of humiliation. The ex-*cristeros* and their sympathizers felt doubly humiliated. They felt that the church authorities had laughed at them, and had not properly appreciated their sacrifice. Perhaps the behavior of Bishops Pascual Díaz and Ruiz y Flores, who had delivered them to their enemies tied hand and foot, had saddened and disappointed them most. The fiery *cristero* Don Leopoldo Gálvez, the "Padre Chiquito," composed his "Great Offertory of Opinions." He searched in vain for a Catholic association that would pay to have it published. But no one wanted to hear his grievances, expressed in such terms as "The Mexican people have now indeed been humiliated . . . I do not understand how the bishops had the heart to betray their children to their executioners without a second thought . . . Why was Catholic worship suspended three years ago . . . if it was to be resumed under the same unacceptable conditions? . . . Did the heroic efforts of thousands and thousands of humble Christians . . . with weapons in their hands, mean nothing? Or is it that the common people were not intended to have figs and apples—only prickly pears and magueys? . . . Since not everybody was man enough to take up arms in the name of God, . . . God has humiliated us by ordering us to bend our necks under the yoke."[58] Like the "Padre Chiquito," his neighbors and comrades in arms felt that they, too, had been humiliated—but they did not say so as openly.

Poverty, humiliation, and injustice produce fear and suspicion. The ex-*cristeros* felt persecuted. "Many men have lost their lives in a mysterious fashion since the amnesty." "In Cojumatlán there is not a single ex-*cristero* left alive." "They will get us all in the end." Each of the survivors saw danger on every street corner, a man lying in wait to murder him in cold blood. Overcome by fear, many broke and ran. They saw no way out but to flee from their persecutors, and they could find no better hiding place than the cities. From 1930 to 1932 they went to Mexico City to lose themselves in the crowd. There was danger there, too, of course; ex-*cristeros* were being

[58] Leopoldo Gálvez, *Grande ofertorio de opiniones y esperanzas para un sacrificio.*

slaughtered everywhere. The bad thing, the really bad thing was that this fear not only turned men into fugitives, but also turned the trusting village of San José into a nest of suspicion and a web of deceit.

Not only those who ran away, but also those who remained were suspicious. Needless to say, they had lost faith in the government long before, and after the *cristero* revolution they no longer trusted the bishops, who "came out *con una y un pedazo, con arreglos a medias*," as the "Padre Chiquito" said.[59] In fact, the mistrust had extended to include all one's neighbors. Everyone was afraid to trust anyone else. The sin of suspicion took up residence in the hearts of most San Joséans, perhaps in the corners once occupied by love, perhaps in the little gardens where truth once grew. People were still saying that it was good always to speak the truth; but now they said it to protect themselves from the deceit of others, or to deceive others by making them believe that they were telling the truth. It was a climate of deception, a vast network of lies, and, at best, a conspiracy of whispers. If anyone had asked them why they had this ridiculous persecution complex, they would have replied: "The children of darkness are wiser than the children of light."

We must not assume that Bishop Fulcheri y Pietrasanta was aware of this tangle of evil thoughts that was about to strangle the parishioners of San José de Gracia. Perhaps he considered that letting oneself be governed by hate, fear, and suspicion was only a trivial sin. Perhaps he did not classify as a sin of pride the belief, held by these former warriors of Christ, that they were, if not perfect, at least better than other people. They consoled themselves with the thought that they stood out above the multitude of cowards who had fled rather than take up arms against God's enemies. They allowed themselves the luxury of looking down upon those who had not fought or who had applied for amnesty before the end of the war. They had no doubt whatsoever that they were the elect, that the others were lost souls. They finally came to think of themselves as the creditors of God and man.

Padre Pablito had to contend with all this. Bishop Fulcheri de-

59 Ibid. [Phrases meaning to do things badly—J. U.]

cided to promote the vicariate of San José to a parish, and he appointed as its first parish priest Pablo González, a native of Cotija, who had taken orders on the eve of the *cristero* revolution and had taught for several months in the seminary. When the persecuted clergy were forced to flee from Zamora, the young priest had disguised himself as a laborer and had roved throughout the little city, "distributing the benefits of the sacraments in private homes."[60] Padre Pablito had come to San José in August, 1929, heavily laden with the virtues that were gradually disappearing within his new parish. The padre was charitable, gentle, honest, and peace loving, with a large dose of serenity, trust, and apostolic zeal. He was an antidote for San José's poisonous passions. After two years he had not succeeded in eradicating these passions, but he had kept them from destroying the village.

Padre Pablito encouraged Christian peace, piety, the monastic life, and culture. In his sermons he preached love, forgiveness, meekness, the virtuous life, and decorum. He summoned men, women, and girls to his religious retreats. Because of him, many of those who attended the Lenten ceremonies turned their hatred against themselves. The hundreds of people who took part in these retreats in 1930–1931— in the church with its new tile roof, its walls and floor still blackened with smoke, its altars still in ruins—listened in silence as the priest spoke of sin, death, the Last Judgment, hell, the prodigal son, and heavenly bliss. On two separate occasions, each lasting a week, they listened, meditated, scourged themselves, wept, and cried out, "Forgive us, O Lord! Forgive and be merciful!" They promised to forgive their enemies, to help one another, to be just and pure in heart; they promised more firmly than ever before, more convinced and confident than they had ever been. There had been retreats every year, but none as well conducted as Padre Pablito's.

In addition to retreats, there were many other opportunities for setting out on the road to piety and asceticism: confession, the daily Mass and Rosary, and meetings of religious associations. Besides the Daughters of Mary and the Perpetual Vigil, there were now other

[60] Rodríguez Zetina, *Zamora*, p. 365.

groups. Padre Pablito founded the San Luis Gonzaga Club for young men; as its name indicates, its purpose was to control eroticism and foster purity. For those young ladies who found the Daughters of Mary too austere, he organized a group known as the Daughters of Santa Teresita of the Child Jesus. Married men could belong to the UCM (the Mexican Catholic Union), and their wives to the UFCM (the Mexican Catholic Union for Women). Each of these clubs met at least once a week; they heard instruction for devotions from the governing committee in Zamora and readings from pious works, with comments by the priest; they recited short prayers and at least one set of five Pater Nosters and five Ave Marias, and they meditated.[61]

For the smaller children of both sexes, there was once again the school operated by the Sisters of the Poor and Madres of the Sacred Heart, better known as "the nuns' school" or "the Haven." It now occupied a private residence, since its own building had been burned and was in ruins. The government, too, decided to open a school in San José. It was staffed by the former seminary student and *cristero* Francisco Melgoza, by the fat, cheerful José González (also an ex-seminary student), and by the efficient and good-hearted teacher Josefina Barragán. About 1931 the authorities decided that the government school, with room for 150 children, was enough for a town with only 500 kids of school age, and they closed the nuns' establishment. This was done because it was the fashion to "de-fanaticize" the populace; and if the "defanaticizing" campaign brought no results in San José, it was for lack of "defanaticizers"; the three teachers who had taken the place of the nuns were "fanatics" who went to Mass every day.[62]

Padre Pablito forged ahead. It was one of his practices to scatter young San Joséans among the various religious orders. He sent a handful of young ladies into the order of the Sisters of the Poor (called "the nuns" for short) of Zamora; he enrolled several young men in the Brothers of the Christian Schools; and, finally, when he went to the capital to join the Jesuits in February, 1932, he took six

61 Private records kept by Josefina González Cárdenas.
62 As recalled by Josefina Barragán and Daniel González Cárdenas.

adolescents with him and entered them in the Santa Julia Academy, governed by the padres of San Juan Bosco. Nor did he forget his own seminary in Zamora, where he enrolled a trio of San Joséans. A total of fifteen young people set out on the road to holiness, and most of them ended up as businessmen.[63]

By then San José had inhabitants to spare—more than at any other time in its history. The destruction of the village had been like a good pruning. From zero (in 1927, when there had not been a single resident or an intact house) the town grew in a year and a half to 1,600 people (or 1,485, according to the national census of 1930), living in two hundred ruined dwellings in the process of reconstruction. After their exile and the *cristero* rebellion, the people who had lived on ranches tended to move into town. The rural population was only two-thirds of what it had been in 1921. The *tenencia* as a whole showed a considerable loss—490 inhabitants, according to the census, and a few more by other estimates. Many never returned after the revolution, and others lost their lives through war or disease. In short, the village residents increased by 55 percent, the rural settlements showed a population loss of 42 percent, and the area as a whole lost 15 percent of its inhabitants during the nine years between 1921 and 1930. The population of the *tenencia* was the same as it had been in 1890—numerically, if not structurally.[64]

In 1930, females accounted for 53 percent of the inhabitants within the entire *tenencia*, and for nearly 60 percent in San José itself. Half were under fifteen, and about 7 percent were over sixty. There was a shortage of adolescents and young men—a shortage that had little effect on farming activities, and none at all on sexual ones. The birth rate, still taken care of by Doña Trina Lara, reached forty-four per thousand. Married couples were furiously engaged in making up for the lives lost during the war years.[65] In addition to Don Juan Chávez, those dedicated to combating mortality now included Ana-

---

[63] According to José Castillo Mendoza.

[64] Dirección General de Estadística, *Quinto censo de la población, 15 de mayo de 1930. Estado de Michoacán*, pp. 67–68.

[65] APSJ, Baptismal Records, Book V.

tolio Partida (who had come back from his *cristero* career with the prestige of a surgeon who had specialized in extracting bullets and setting broken limbs) and Don David Sánchez (who had returned from the United States with a general practitioner's talents, without ever having studied medicine). These three cornered the patient market; very few people could afford the luxury of bringing Dr. Sahagún from Sahuayo, or Dr. Maciel from Jiquilpan. Many resigned themselves to home remedies or to the herbs prescribed by popular tradition.

6. THE AGRARIAN REVOLUTION (1933–1943)

*The Petitioners, the Petitioned,
and the Apportioners of Land*

Between 1918 and 1940 the revolutionary governments of Venustiano Carranza, Álvaro Obregón, Plutarco Elías Calles, Emilio Portes Gil, Pascual Ortiz Rubio, Abelardo Rodríguez, and Lázaro Cárdenas worked to remove the obstacles to the application of the innovational precepts of the 1917 Constitution and laid the foundations of national reconstruction. These foundations were reforms dealing with land, labor, politics, religion, education, art, and philosophy. General Obregón, through his minister José Vasconcelos, was the principal moving force behind the reforms in education, literature, the arts, and philosophy. General Calles chose to go down in history as the apostle of religious reform. Don Venustiano Carranza and, later, Licenciado Emilio Portes Gil are generally considered to have been the outstanding artificers of political renovation. In agrarian and labor reforms, there can be no doubt that the standard-bearer was General Cárdenas.

The intent of the agrarian and agricultural reform was to increase the number of landowners, encourage communal ownership of land, and improve and expand agricultural production by opening new areas to cultivation, making use of irrigation, exploiting tropical crops, improving farm implements, and extending credit to farmers. Labor reform called for protection of the worker through unions and federations, through such labor legislation as the federal work law passed in 1931, through campaigns for better health and living habits among the laboring class, and through government aid in improving housing, clothing, and diet. Agrarian and labor policies developed in different ways in different states.[1]

General Cárdenas, governor of the state of Michoacán from 1928 to 1932, made his attitudes toward agrarian reform and labor felt as soon as he took office. "Cárdenas's agrarian achievements consisted of dividing up and redistributing many large estates, and setting up four hundred *ejidos*, with an area of 408,807 hectares, for 24,000 *ejido* members." The general also saw to it that elected and appointed public officials—especially municipal officers, *jefes de tenencia*, and local peace officers—were people favorable to governmental reforms. Although Don Lázaro's successor, General Benigno Serrato, tried to hold back the avalanche of revolution, he could do very little; this was due partly to the fact that *cardenismo* became a national force when its leader became president of the republic.[2]

On November 30, 1934, Lázaro Cárdenas, a native of the *municipio* of Jiquilpan, was sworn in as president of the United States of Mexico. "His campaign promises led the workers to call a series of strikes that by June of 1935 numbered more than a thousand."[3] General Plutarco Elías Calles, who considered himself to be the Supreme Leader of the Revolution, made some public statements criticizing the prolabor policies of his friend Cárdenas. Shortly thereafter, General Calles left the country one night as an exile, escorted by an armed guard. From that moment on, General Cárdenas dedicated himself wholeheartedly to carrying out the agrarian and labor reforms; he also turned his attention to many other problems, foreign as well as domestic. It was the time of Franco's military revolt against the Spanish government, Mussolini's invasion of Ethiopia, Stalin's oc-

---

[1] Luis González, "México," in *Enciclopedia metódica Larousse.*

[2] José Bravo Ugarte, *Historia sucinta de Michoacán*, III, 219–220.

[3] José Emilio Pacheco, quoted, in Salvador Novo's *La vida en México en el período presidencial de Lázaro Cárdenas*, p. 11.

cupation of Finland, Hitler's advances, and, at home, the aftereffects of the religious conflict, political bossism, strikes, killings, the obstinacy of the oil companies, the innumerable aspirants to the presidential chair, and so on. General Cárdenas dealt with each of these situations to the best of his ability: he protested against European imperialism; he opened the doors of his country to the children and the intellectuals of the troubled Spanish republic; he called for the expropriation of the oil companies; he organized the Mexican Revolutionary party; and he put up Don Manuel Ávila Camacho as that party's presidential candidate.[4]

While General Cárdenas— in Mexico City or in his travels—was lending new stimulus to *agrarismo* and the labor movement, he was supported with singular enthusiasm in Michoacán by Colonel Gildardo Magaña, an ex-*zapatista* and former governor of Baja California. During his term as governor of Michoacán (1936–1939), Don Gildardo transformed the Michoacán Regional Federation of Labor into the Agrarian Communities League; he also handed over the University of San Nicolás to the students and the rectorate to Natalio Vázquez Pallares, a well-known socialist. In order to facilitate the revolutionary programs of the president and the governor, laws were passed and amended, and a bureaucracy and an ad hoc faculty were created.[5]

Among the laws favoring agrarianism, labor, and socialism, in general, were Article 3 of the constitution, as rehashed in 1934 ("Education imparted by the State shall be socialistic . . . and shall combat fanaticism"); the Agrarian Code of 1934, which had been preceded by the Land Allotment and Restitution law of 1929, by the Communal Lands Patrimony law of 1927 (repaired in 1932), and by the Ejido Members and Farmers Credit law of 1931, the precursor of Don Lázaro's legislation and his Ejido Bank. While governor of Michoacán, Cárdenas had been the author of the Idle Lands law, which called for confiscation of uncultivated properties.[6] In addition to laws, there was a flood of speeches, articles, and proclamations by

[4] González, "México."
[5] Bravo Ugarte, *Historia sucinta*, III, 228.
[6] Luis González et al., *Fuentes de la historia contemporánea de México*, II, 88–93.

professors, agronomists, and political leaders, so that the startling news of the Mexican revolution (agrarianism, unions, expropriations, schools) might be brought to everyone—even people in the farthest corners of the country and in the most reactionary communities, including those from whence the *cristeros* had sprung. Revolutionary ideology and practice had spread as never before in Michoacán, after Don Lázaro assumed the governorship, and even more after he had become president of the republic. This was especially true of the *municipio* of Jiquilpan, because Don Lázaro, like any good reformer, began with his own house, and because in his native town there were to be found such enthusiastic collaborators as Juventino Aguilar, the stocky *presidente* of Jiquilpan.

The vast reformative activity on the part of the legislators and executives of the republic, of the state of Michoacán, and of the *municipio* of Jiquilpan, together with the hard times and social unrest that had followed the *cristero* revolution, favored the division of San José de Gracia, its *rancherías*, and the *tenencia* of Ornelas into two parties: the agrarianists and the landowners. The civil government, as a rule, backed the agrarianists, while the church, with some exceptions, favored the landowners. The former promulgated agrarianism through the schools, and the latter proclaimed from the pulpit that "private property is a postulate of divine reason." Each party supported its thesis with a thousand rational considerations, while the people of San José merely organized, hurled insults at each other, went to court with their surveyors and shysters, and got into gunfights.

It was not easy to build an agrarian party in San José; there was a great deal of resistance to the idea. In the first place, many of the people were landowners; in the second, those who were not landowners had a concept of property that did not square with the principle of the *ejido*. They believed that there were only two honest and morally right ways to acquire property: by purchase or by inheritance. Obtaining land as a gift meant losing face; to be a landowner simply because the government had given you the land was not considered proper. Besides, for a man to feel secure in the possession of a piece of property, he had to own it outright—not merely have the right to use it, as promised by the Agrarian Reform government. In short, San Joséans believed that ownership of the earth should be not only absolute, but also individual; it should not be collective, as the *ejido* idea suggested. And, finally, potential agrarianists were depressed at the thought of taking anything from the government—an entity for which they felt little affection.

In any case, an Agrarian party was formed in San José; some of its members were local people, and some were agrarianist enthusiasts brought in from outside to propagate the new ideas. The depression that followed the *cristero* revolution led many people to take the agrarian path. The farmers of Sabino announced that if they were not allowed to buy land for crops and pasture, they would ask the government "to help them, not by means of *ejidos*, but by selling them parcels outright, with time payments." At that time they were still saying "we do not want to join the agrarian party . . . we are asking for a piece of the land we have tilled all our lives." And, since the government did not sell land, but only gave it away, and since their need for land was stronger than the shame of being supported, they fell into agrarianism. Honor was put aside by man's vigorous nature, by the age-old tradition of living out one's life on the spot where he was born, by the love for one's native heath and the desire to own it.

In the *tenencia* of Ornelas, the Agrarian party began gathering members in 1930. It grew up in the shadow of hunger. In 1934 it boasted about three hundred members, almost all of whom lived in the *rancherías*. Very few of them were inhabitants of the village itself. The reason was easy to see: most townspeople had been landowners since 1926. Those who lived outside were preponderantly share-croppers or simple laborers. The agrarianists tended to be of the younger generation, born between 1893 and 1905. Most of the older people did not dare to defy the landowners who employed them. Besides, the older generations still believed that it was dishonest to accept land without paying for it. The young members of the agrarian party recognized as their immediate leaders Camilo Chávez, from

Paso Real, and Don Antonio Ávila, of San José. Chávez had been
secretary of the *tenencia*, and Ávila was its *jefe* in 1934. In addition,
the residents of each *ranchería* produced their own leaders: Jesús
Contreras, Federico Cárdenas, and Juan Miranda in Sabino; the
Chávez brothers and Ramiro López in Paso Real; and José Contreras
in San Miguel. There were twelve of these leaders, and, like the
twelve apostles, they were old hands at fighting.

The landowners' party included all those with ranches of thirty
hectares or more. They were men of all ages. They were joined by
many landless businessmen, by some farmers with small parcels, and
by those who looked forward to inheriting property from their parents or relatives. A few of these landholders lived in Sahuayo,
Mazamitla, Tizapán, and Guadalajara, but most were residents of
San José. At that time they had no leader, nor had they organized
to defend their interests. Each man scratched his own back; with the
exception of Señorita María Ramírez Arias (who owned El Sabino
hacienda) and the smaller proprietors Arnulfo Novoa Sánchez, Abraham González Flores, the Sandovals, and the Arias family, none was
rich or powerful enough to defend himself alone. If Don Octaviano
Villanueva, the parish priest, sympathized with the antiagrarian faction, he did not show it; he fought with the leaders of the other party,
but over matters of education and not about agrarianism. Mazamitla's
priest took the side of the landless: those in Sahuayo aligned themselves with the property owners.

"The law-and-order party," as the landowners called themselves,
fell into Manichaeism. They came to believe that the world was divided into two groups: the good people who owned things, and the
wicked who did not. In wealth they saw a sign of divine predestina-
tion. They had not the slightest doubt that God had rewarded the
virtuous with material possessions and punished the wicked with
poverty. Virtue, in their minds, consisted of piety, good habits, hard
work, and thrift. They regarded these characteristics in a man as a
manifestation of the grace of God. While they did not absolutely deny
man's freedom to choose between the virtue of wealth and the sin
of poverty, they refused to concede that anyone without a large dose

of natural goodness or divine grace could aspire to belong to the chosen people—the pious, the moneyed, the lovers of law and order. They could not claim that they were virtuous because they had fought in the army of Christ the King—or that the agrarianists were evil because they had been anti-*cristeros*—because the largest landowners in the *tenencia* had been against the *cristero* movement, and several converts to agrarianism in 1929 had been among the "defenders." In any case, the landowners felt that they were the legitimate heirs of the people who had fought under the *cristero* flag.

The agrarianists' subversion was looked upon by the landowners as an aggression against the will of God. They sincerely believed that in demanding their land these people were committing a sin against nature. Thus, they called them heretics, blasphemers, hoodlums, or any of the synonyms: scoundrels, atheists, bad Christians, loafers, priest haters, libertines, drunkards, thieves, troublemakers, and desecraters. According to the landowners, agrarianists profaned the house of God whenever they went to Mass or the Rosary. If they received Communion, they were committing sacrilege, because they bore a multitude of sins—especially the sin of theft, which confession alone could not efface.

The Agrarian Reform was not only sinful, but also dangerous, the landowners declared. They considered themselves more intelligent, industrious, and cultured than their workers. Practically all of them could read and write, and many had studied in good schools or at the seminary. In addition, they were experienced and skillful cattle ranchers, and they had made their fortunes because they were smart and hard-working—or at least because their parents had been. Their employees, on the other hand, lacked these qualities. The owners were convinced that corn farmers and hired hands were incapable of handling any kind of business by themselves. To their minds, these people were idlers, spendthrifts, yokels, fools, and enemies of progress, devoid of learning or integrity. If they were given land, the region would deteriorate, fall into poverty, and eventually be completely ruined.

Most members of the Agrarian party did not agree with their

enemies' estimate of them. They knew that among them were many
who were both virtuous and poor. They believed in God, the saints,
heaven, purgatory, and the torments of hell. They were not possessed
of the devil. A few began to feel guilty, to believe that they were
bad; but this was not generally the case. Agrarianism had no quarrel
with God and his priests. Padre Pablito had never said that agrarianism was evil. In their own minds they were a little insolent, perhaps,
but not wicked.

About 1931 Francisco Melgoza, director of the government school,
made a speech during the Sixteenth of September celebration, in
which he stated that Jesus Christ was the first agrarianist. He also cited
several church fathers who supported this view. While a student at
the seminary he had read Saint Ambrose's words: "The earth was
made for all men, rich and poor, to hold in common." Members of
the property-owning group who had come to celebrate the national
holiday were terribly upset; some tried to shout down the orator,
while others improvised rebuttals. Many of them left in a fury. The
agrarianists, defended as they were by San José's teacher and
Mazamitla's priest, could not think of themselves as sinners. Even
those who admitted that the repartition of land implied robbery
pointed out that it was not the peasant who was the thief, but the
government. They themselves were not taking land away from anyone. Many of them had not even applied for it. One takes anything
people are willing to give him. What man complains when someone gives him bread?

Neither did they believe that they were "dumb," or lazy, or ig-
norant. Out in the country what counted was experience—not
whether or not you had gone to a good school. In fact, educated
people were inept when it came to raising crops and handling cattle.
They didn't know how to do anything. They couldn't drive a team
of oxen or do any of the other chores in the cornfield. They were not
usually much good at riding, or roping, or milking, or building and
mending fences, or any of the other jobs that have to be done on a
ranch. Physical toil was the province of field and ranch hands, and
none of their "bosses" could beat them at it; for them there was no

talent but manual dexterity, and no wisdom beyond their own empirical knowledge. Thus, they considered themselves more intelligent than their masters.

The arguments on both sides were highly charged with emotion. There were bad feelings—anger, especially—that Padre Pablito was not able to mitigate. Among the agrarianists, the old hatred for the government was now turned toward "rich people," and among the landowning class it was redirected toward anyone who aspired to join their ranks and toward the agronomists, the agrarian commissions, and the agrarian president. This hatred was expressed by insults, gestures, threats, and, on more than one occasion, by bullets. Landowners found some solace in reading *El Tornillo* or *El Hombre Libre* and the diatribes against the regime in the periodical press, in making up offensive jokes, and in hoping for a change in the situation. Nobody had the courage to revolt, although there were many who wanted to; but more than a few looked with sympathy upon the uprising led by Rubén Guízar, a former *cristero*; and more than one was accused of befriending the ringleaders, Jesús Hernández, Isidro Pulido, and José Cárdenas, who were marauding in the area. The agrarianists, with fewer opportunities for verbal relief, were occasionally driven to armed attacks against their masters.

But, in spite of the unhappiness, rage, and abuse that accompanied the agrarian struggle in San José, the quarrel never became as bloody as it did in Tizapán, Mazamitla, El Valle, or Quitupan. Perhaps this was because of the ties of kinship that existed between many of the property owners and petitioners, perhaps because many of them had only recently fought side by side against the government, or perhaps because neither faction produced any vigorous leaders. Another more obvious reason was (as we shall soon see) that the distribution of *ejido* land had already begun, to the detriment of a handful of landowners who, for the most part, did not live in San José and were not well-liked by the local small landholders. Thus the agrarian revolution never became terribly bloody or violent within the *tenencia* of Ornelas. This is not to say that it was entirely peaceful. The passions that had attended its birth did not fade away overnight. In addition, the underhanded machinations it gave rise to were bad for people's morale. There sprang up a new way of dealing with the authorities: the bribe.

The Origin of Nine Ejidos

In 1930 the communities of Paso de Piedra, La Breña, and Sabino applied for *ejido* land; the first two demanded the Auchen hacienda, and the last one asked for what was left of the Sabino hacienda. This last amounted to only 700 hectares; 2,000 had been broken up into parcels, 399 had been sold, and 672 had been given to Paso de Piedra.[7] In 1932 the petitions of La Rosa, San Miguel, and Ojo de Agua del Picacho were recorded. They involved properties belonging to J. Trinidad Montes, Ester Zepeda, Francisco Sandoval, José Luis Arregui, Amparo Arias, and Arnulfo Novoa—that is, the ranches known as La Raya, El Guayabo, and La Arena.[8] In 1933 about seventy citizens of San José de Gracia—one-seventh of the people who had just resettled there—applied for the lands surrounding the town, on the grounds that they were nonproductive.[9] In 1935 the residents of La Arena applied for the property owned by María Guadalupe Sánchez de Novoa and Jesús Barragán.[10] In 1936 the alleged inhabitants of Estancia del Monte and the genuine residents of Ojo de Rana declared that they wanted the lands surrounding them.[11]

The Consolidated Agrarian Commission which had been set up in Morelia published the applications in the *Periódico Oficial del Estado* (official state bulletin) and then ordered a census of the *rancherías* from which they had come. In La Breña, they found 84 qualified applicants; in Paso Real, 28; in Sabino, 85; in Auchen, 79; in La Rosa, 23; in San Miguel, 90; the same number in Ojo de Rana; 20 in Ojo de Agua del Picacho; 74 in San José de Gracia; 27 in La Arena; and none in Estancia del Monte.[12] In short, in the *tenencia* of Ornelas,

---

7 ADAAC, file 1933.
8 Ibid., files 10813, 12343, and 12863.
9 Ibid., file 11054.
10 Ibid., file 20010.
11 Ibid., file 21751.
12 Ibid., files 10813, 11054, 12863, and 20010.

with about 1,000 males of working age in 1934, they found 610 farmers who owned no workable land.

Each census was challenged by the owners of the lands in question. María Ramírez Arias's attorney forced twenty peasants from Sabino to appear before a notary and declare that the people who were demanding the property of the hacienda on which they lived were "from other places far away, and from villages in Jalisco"; as for themselves, they said, "they wanted to continue working as hired laborers."[13] Other landowners produced birth certificates and witnesses—not always truthful—to prove that the people counted by the census did not live in the *ranchería* mentioned, or that they already owned land, or that they were minors, or artisans, and not farmers, or that they were deceased, or imaginary, or even that they didn't want any land.[14] The agrarian leaders presented documents—not uniformly authentic—to show that the applicants were bona fide residents, adults, farmers, and still in the midst of life on earth.

Another cause for argument was the measurement and classification of land by the surveyors. Every day, men with theodolites and lines were to be seen checking boundaries, calculating areas, and making maps. Both landowners and agrarianists tried to bribe them with dinners, liquor, and money. One group wanted them to minimize their measurements, while the other asked them to exaggerate them. The surveyors usually accepted gifts from both sides. Armed with orders to apply the agrarian laws in a revolutionary spirit, and often merely hoping to extort money from the owners, these men would classify craggy terrain as pasture land, pasture as fields suitable for rainy-season crops, and the last as irrigable land. The terrified landowners gave what they could to the surveyors; the richer ones also resorted to shysters. Between the engineers and the lawyers they managed to have their holdings underestimated.

Then came the decisions by the Consolidated Agrarian Commission and the governor. About this time both the agrarianists and the landowners were wearing themselves out and going into debt running back and forth between San José and the capital. The governor an-

---

[13] ANJ, Records of Licenciado Miguel M. Mora (1930), fol. 57.
[14] ADAAC, file 13331.

nounced that such-and-such communities would be given such-and-such amounts of land. The engineers returned to arrange preliminary transfers. The agrarianists and the proprietors concerned entertained the engineers royally—the proprietors in the hopes that the surveyors might be befuddled enough to locate the appropriated parcels within their neighbors' ranches instead of theirs. Property was given and then taken away. On May 17, 1936, Antonio Ávila wrote to President Cárdenas: "We were given possession of the lands on May 4 . . . and on May 15 the order was countermanded."[15] The *ejidos* swelled and shrank; there were verbal battles, fights, and even some fatal shootings while the Federal Department of Agrarian Lands rectified or confirmed the decisions that had been made at the state level.

Months later the president's decision was published in the *Diario Oficial de la Federación* (the official federal bulletin). Paso de Piedra received 1,132 hectares (August 29, 1929); La Breña was given 102 hectares of land for seasonal crops and 96 hectares of pasture land (April 2, 1934); the 28 qualified residents of Paso Real were granted 222 hectares: 8 hectares for seasonal crops, 84 of pasture, and 130 of grazing land (April 2, 1934), all granted under collective title "in order to protect and safeguard the land for the community";[16] Sabino received 511 hectares: 157 of irrigable land, 65 for seasonal crops, 13 of swamp land, and 276 in the hills (September 10, 1934);[17] Ojo de Agua del Picacho, with its 32 applicants, was given 810 hectares, mostly pasture land, to be divided into 33 parcels, including one for the school (August 27, 1935).[18] No land was granted to San José de Gracia, because there were no affectible holdings within the legal radius (October 26, 1938.)[19] Ojo de Rana had the honor of educing two presidential decrees: that of March 3, 1938, granting 683 hectares, and another on June 28, 1939, which reduced the allotment to 372 hectares.[20]

15 Ibid., file 11054.
16 Ibid., file 13331.
17 Ibid., file 12558.
18 Ibid., file 10813.
19 Ibid., file 11054.
20 Ibid., file 19242.

The thirty-three applicants from La Rosa were favored with three of President Cárdenas's decrees. The first, dated March 2, 1938, awarded them 631 hectares—136 for seasonal planting and 266 of pasture land—most of which would be taken from El Guayabo, owned by Alfredo and Rosario Arias;[21] the second, on October 26, 1938, reduced this to 197 hectares, not, this time, to be taken from Don Alfredo, but from the helpless Don Trinidad Montes. On November 30 of the same year a third decree confirmed the second one; it gave the people of La Rosa "an area of 197.8 hectares, to be taken from La Raya hacienda: 113 in farming land and 84 in forest. This shall be divided into 14 parcels—13 for an equal number of qualified applicants and one for the school . . . This is without prejudice to the claims of the other twenty qualified applicants." And more: "Since it is for the public good that forests and groves be conserved and propagated . . . the community enjoying this grant must recognize its obligation to conserve, maintain, and propagate such forests and groves as lie within these lands . . . The community will be authorized to utilize these forests as soon as the Department of Agrarian Lands has incorporated them into the cooperative of *ejido* forest lands."[22]

In the same year, 1938, the president decided to grant 441 hectares—257 in forest and 178 in farming land—to some of the ninety country people in San Miguel; this property was expropriated from Emilio and Felipe Gutiérrez, owners of La Tinaja Seca.[23] The recipients expressed their gratitude with a letter written in pencil: "*Jefe*, please send us photographs of yourself and General Cárdenas so we can have an unforgettable reminder to hang up in our School Building so our children will know who to thank for the benefit and kindness we are enjoying."[24]

In March of that year—the same month when President Cárdenas ordered wholesale expropriations of, among other things, the oil company properties—the president decreed that 598 hectares were to

[21] Ibid., file 12343.
[22] DDF, May 16, 1945.
[23] ADAAC, file 12863.
[24] Ibid.

be handed over to residents of Auchen, Cerrito de la Leña, China, and Espino. These were taken from Abraham González (20 hectares in dry farm land and 115 in pasture), from Dionisio Arias (44 hectares of irrigable land), from Epifanio Arias (150 hectares of stony ground), and from Santos Barrios (265 of pasture and dry land). This decision stood for a year. On February 8, 1939, the president revised it, raising the figure to 621 hectares.[25]

The other two *ejidos* in the *tenencia* got their presidential decrees much later. The people of Izote, where the census showed sixty-six residents qualified to receive land, read the announcement in the *Diario Oficial* on August 3, 1942: "Of the 80 hectares granted, the usable farm land is only enough for three farmers at the rate of eight hectares each; the remaining 56 hectares are suitable for grazing cattle, and are to be used in common by the beneficiaries."[26] On July 19, 1950—fifteen years after they had submitted their application—the twenty-seven petitioners in the *ranchería* of La Arena received their land. The president gave them 298 hectares that had belonged to María Guadalupe Sánchez de Novoa.[27]

After the decrees came the process of taking possession—at first provisional, and then permanent. Almost all the *ejido* communities took formal possession of their land between 1935 and 1939; La Breña on March 30, 1936,[28] Paso Real on June 16, 1937,[29] Ojo de Agua del Picacho on October 21, 1935,[30] Auchen on April 14, 1939,[31] La Rosa [32] exactly one year before San Miguel.[33] On October 15, 1936, the people of Sabino were given partial possession, "in view of the overlapping that has occurred with the *ejido* lands of Paso de Piedra, which has had legitimate and unqualified possession

25 Ibid., file 14710.
26 DDF, August 3, 1942.
27 Ibid., November 25, 1950.
28 ADAAC, file 12054.
29 Ibid., file 13331.
30 Ibid., file 10813.
31 Ibid., file 14710.
32 Ibid., file 12343.
33 Ibid., file 12863.

since May 1, 1935."[34] On July 11, 1939, Ojo de Rana received 35 hectares less than the 358 it had been granted.[35]

The formal ceremonies that took place when the lands were handed over to the *ejido* members were lively occasions, with speeches, roast pig, mescal, conversation, and gifts in cash to the surveyors who had laid out the property. Sometimes the engineers advised the Agrarian Department by letter that they had been unable to carry out their orders because the amount of land available was too small. Often only partial possession was given. A great many extralegal and illegal things took place. The richer and better-educated landowners hired lawyers and fought tooth and nail.

The exchange of property was accompanied by dissension. Two or three of the landowners resorted to the device of offering the agrarianists other parcels in place of those that had been agreed upon—sometimes parcels not even belonging to them. Many of the peasants who stood to gain by the exchange accepted these offers; this in turn gave rise to new quarrels between the property owners, different *ejido* communities, and individual members of the communities. Perhaps the greatest source of discord was the distribution of parcels among the members of the communities. When this point was reached, the weapons (with which the *ejido* members had been provided to defend themselves against the rich) were turned on each other. Then the killings began. In Auchen and Paso Real rising tempers occasioned two series of incidents involving slaughter, Mexican style.[36]

To sum up, 4,284 hectares were redistributed within the *tenencia*—19 percent of its total area. A little more than half of the property handed over to the farmers consisted of grazing land and hilly terrain; a third of it was suitable for rainy-season crops, and 15 percent was irrigable. There were 300 beneficiaries: 178 were residents of the *tenencia* and the rest were inhabitants of Paso de Piedra and Ojo de Agua del Picacho, in the El Valle *municipio* of the state of Jalisco.

---

[34] Ibid., file 12558.
[35] Ibid., file 14242.
[36] Ibid., files 2941 and 20010. AJJ (see ANJ) correspondence.

Those outside the *tenencia* received 1,946 hectares, while those within got 569 hectares surrounding the village of San José. Individual parcels were not all the same size in different *ejidos*. They varied from 8 to 25 hectares. Of the 590 San Joséans over eighteen years old who had been landless, more than 200 were given land; according to the agrarian authorities, there was no land available for the remaining 66 percent—although, in actuality, there was, but it was in the hands of three or four influential people who had the money and the shysters to defend them.[37]

Within the *tenencia*, twelve large estates were affected. With the possible exception of two, they were all liable to expropriation according to the agrarian code. Almost every one was larger than it was claimed to be. María Ramírez Arias, who had owned the Sabino hacienda, was left with nothing; other estate owners still held more land than they had a legal right to, either because of the vastness of the property or because they owned other land outside San José's jurisdiction. When the tempest of reform had passed, naturally most of the properties that had escaped seizure became exempt—through sale to anyone who had the money to buy them, through transfer to legal heirs, or through having been declared inaffectible by the authorities.[38] Of the twelve landowners affected within the *tenencia* of San José, only five lived there. On the other hand, seven local residents who owned property elsewhere lost part of their holdings. In one way or another, during the 1930's, these rural lands were chopped up a great deal—in many cases more than they should have been, in a region largely devoted to cattle raising.[39]

During the years of the agrarian struggle, 1934–1937, San José benefited in various other ways. There was plenty of rain. Emigration fell off. There was a normal increase in population, which was helped along for a couple of years by Dr. Reynosa.[40] The cattle business recovered. In 1937 there were seven thousand head of cattle, eight hundred horses, an equal number of burros, three hundred mules, a

[37] See map of the *municipio* of Jiquilpan in ADAAC, file 12558.
[38] Ibid.
[39] In 1940 there were nearly 500 ranches and farms, not counting the *ejidos*.
[40] San José's first real doctor, there from 1933 to 1934.

thousand pigs, and a great many chickens. The yearly production of milk rose to 1.5 million liters, with a value of 250,000 pesos. The price of corn and beans remained low: between 4 and 6 pesos a hecto-liter. Daily wages rose from 70 centavos to a peso.[41] In 1935 the national telegraph system, which since 1930 had reached as far as Cotija, was extended to include Quitupan, Valle de Juárez, Mazamitla, San José de Gracia, and Pueblo Nuevo. A telephone was installed in each of these places. "Because of continual breakdowns in the equipment," customers practically had to scream to be heard.[42]

From 1932 to 1936 the *jefes de tenencia*, with one exception, were agrarianists: Pablo Ruiz, Juan Moreno, Antonio and Adolfo Ávila. The first of these, by dint of requisitioned labor and small contributions from the citizens, managed to get a narrow dirt road for automobiles built between Jiquilpan, San José, and Mazamitla. The job consisted mostly of widening and leveling the old path. Thus, during the dry season, one could travel the rather risky stretch by car. The road had been laid out and inaugurated by David Sánchez, whose automobile caused great astonishment among both children and adults. Many admirers ran after him as he drove through the streets of the town.

After Pablo Ruiz had frightened one of his neighbors to death, he was succeeded by Don Juan Moreno. During Don Juan's year in office, the bandstand was erected and the park put in order for the debut of the municipal band; Don Amadeo Padilla was hired as bandmaster and was soon to be directing his musicians in public concerts.[10] But the greatest thing that happened in 1933 was the movies. Don David Sánchez brought in silent films of the *Zorro* series, with a projector. He showed them in somebody's back yard for two or three weeks, and everybody came to see the "pictures." For several months they were the subject of conversation for all ages.

Of Antonio Ávila's many undertakings, the most remarkable were orders to plaster the red house fronts, to pave the dirt streets with cobblestones, to clear away the weeds, and—the most unheard-of—

---

41 Josefina González Cárdenas's account books, 1933–1940.
42 Esteban Chávez Cisneros, *Quitupan: Ensayo histórico y estadístico*, p. 237.
43 AJTO, Miscellaneous Papers.

an order forbidding men to wear the sarape, or *jorongo*. It fell to Don
Antonio Ávila to inaugurate the town band that had been organized
by Don Amadeo. On March 19, 1934, twenty-five musicians took
their places for the first time in the recently completed kiosk; thereafter, they gave a concert every Sunday. Their first director drilled
them well in marches; the second, Don José María, taught them to
play other, less noisy music;[44] and Alfredo Gutiérrez polished them
even more.

Antonio Ávila's secretary was Camilo Chávez, who used all his
oratorical resources and influence to have the priest's home turned
into a school building, but without success. It was decided that the
sparsely attended government school should continue to operate
in Fidel Fonseca's house. Even more rickety schools were built in
Sabino and La Breña. Many fathers, swayed by the priests, refused to
send their children to these institutions, which were said to be socialistic. The richer families resorted to various expedients to have
their children educated elsewhere. The government schoolmistress,
Señorita Josefina Barragán, was hired to give private lessons outside
her regular teaching hours. The ex-seminary students David González
Cárdenas and Daniel and José González Pulido ran a private school.
In 1936 Braulio Valdovinos, a native of the village, took charge of the
official school. At the time it contained thirty-seven desks, four black-
boards, and a writing table.[45]

Like his two predecessors (Pulido and Ruiz), Antonio Ávila was
ousted as *jefe de tenencia* because he had committed a crime. He was
replaced by Adolfo Ávila, an agrarianist and ex-*cristero*. During his
year of duty, fights among the agrarianists reached the critical point.
In 1935–1936 there were the greatest number of homicides ever recorded in San José: eight in a year. The great majority of the killers
and their victims were among those who wore the red *paliacate*
around their necks. When Camilo Chávez's group became annoyed
with Adolfo Ávila, a large-scale gunfight broke out right in the town
square one evening, just before the curfew bell.[46] Other less spectacu-

---

[44] According to Ingeniero Bernardo González Godínez.
[45] As recalled by Daniel González Cárdenas.
[46] AJJ, Correspondence.

lar fracases occurred in Paso Real, in Auchen, and in several *ejido* settlements.

Perhaps because of the belligerence of the agrarianists, which they were turning against each other, and the profound differences that had sprung up among the beneficiaries of the Reform, political power was taken away from them in 1936 and given to Rodolfo Sánchez of the landowners' party. Even so, the violence went on; nearly every month, as the villagers watched, the body of another victim was brought to the portico on the north side of the plaza. One of the victims was Antonio Ávila, the greatest champion of land repartition in the San José area.[47] Local people consoled themselves with the thought that there were even more fights and killings in neighboring *municipios*.

Padre Federico Returns and President Cárdenas Comes to Call

Every week a couple of copies of the magazine *Hoy* reached San José. The villagers read and discussed them. In September, 1937, the publication carried a story about the agrarianist president: "Cárdenas has frankly admitted that the air is filled with impatience and unrest, born of his unswerving agricultural program . . . The Department of Agrarian Lands has distributed 9,764,140 hectares, issuing 5,956 carefully considered decrees benefiting 565,216 rural inhabitants. To date a total of 17,914,982 hectares of land have gladdened the hearts of 1,324,759 farmers. The extraordinary powers granted to the chief executive in the field of agrarian legislation . . . have made it possible for him to issue land certificates and to expropriate property with no other consideration than the good of the farmers . . . By virtue of the same extraordinary powers the executive has enacted the Cattle Industry Development law, which confers a twenty-five–year exemption from seizure upon land devoted to cattle raising; for although there are at present twice as many cattle in the republic as there were in 1910, there are still not enough to meet the country's needs."[48]

[47] AJTO, Documents from the Jefaturas of Rodolfo Sánchez, Anastasio Partida, and Juan Moreno.
[48] *Hoy*, September 8, 1937.

In the Cattle Industry Development law the hundred cattle ranchers in the Ornelas *tenencia* saw their chance to save what property the land distributors had left them. They had a total of twenty thousand hectares, divided among more than four hundred individuals and eleven *ejidos*; they decided to set to work to have their property declared a cattle-raising zone—which in fact it was. Padre Federico González, who had just returned to the village, gathered them together with this purpose in mind; he persuaded them to forget the quarrels that had divided them for the past five years. No one had seen the padre since the *cristero* revolution, for he had been hiding in the cities. The police, on orders from the Supreme Leader, General Plutarco Elías Calles, had been combing the country for him. Once they had caught him and had taken him off to be shot; but he succeeded in persuading his captors to set him free. From 1930 to 1932 he had been a teacher at the Salesian school in Guadalajara; then he had hidden in Mexico City until 1935. Later he returned to Guadalajara, where he taught grammar and ethics with the Salesians until the school was closed and replaced by a "School for Soldiers' Children."

In 1937 the news spread through San José that Padre Federico was coming back. He arrived on horseback from Tizapán, and nearly the whole town went out to meet him, with the town band playing, the church bells ringing, and everyone cheering. The following day the padre reassumed leadership of the town and set eight projects in motion: the defense of private ownership of land; the celebration of San José's golden wedding—the fiftieth anniversary of its founding; a return to social solidarity; reconciliation with the politicians; the construction of the highway; the beautification of the village; the encouragement of cattle raising, orchard planting, handicrafts, and *charro* societies; and the improvement of children's education.

Padre Federico did not believe that the agrarianists were heretics, or blasphemers, or even wicked. He did not judge agrarianism from a religious point of view, but condemned it on economic and social grounds. Judging from the brief experience with *ejido* life in his village and in others nearby, and from the criticism of the Agrarian Reform carried in the periodical press, he did not believe that the *ejido* system would work. He considered it to be the cause of three great evils: decrease in production on small farms, misuse of the land by *ejido* members, and social dissension accompanying and following repartition. The drop in production to be seen among private land-owners he attributed to their fear of losing their property. He was convinced, too, that the *ejido* members—because of inexperience, or laziness, or poverty, or consciousness of not owning the land they worked—would never improve the area and would continue stripping the forests. But what worried him most was the deep social division and the bloody battles brought on by the agrarian revolution. Thus, he became the apostle of the small landowner. He gathered about him and organized four hundred ranchers, dedicated to arresting the agrarian movement in the San José area. His quarrel was with agrarianism, not with the agrarianists; he was in favor of the small property, but not the hacienda. If he lent his support to the owners of the larger holdings, it was because he knew that their children would be small landowners.

Padre Federico put as much enthusiasm into his defense of the small property owners as he did into the celebration of the fiftieth anniversary of the village. A man who was essentially active and emotional (passionate, in fact), he saw great significance in the so-called golden wedding. He set up collection boxes in all public places, where citizens could deposit money to defray the costs of the festivities. San José's colony in Mexico City, which consisted of some thirty families, was invited to cooperate and to take part in the celebration. *Charro* uniforms were bought for the town band, and restoration of the church was pushed forward. The remaining dirt streets were paved with cobblestones, weeds were cleared from the others, and the rest of the houses that had been destroyed during the *cristero* revolution were rebuilt.

The golden-wedding party consisted of two nine-day periods. The first of these, the religious preparation, was directed by two preachers, Padres Rentería and Ochoa. Six hundred people of all ages jammed into a church that could comfortably hold no more than three hundred, morning and evening, for nine days. They listened to thousands and thousands of words, delivered in declamatory tones, intended to prepare them spiritually for the commemoration of San José's fifty years of existence—this community that for twenty years had been mistreated, scattered, and filled with hostility and rage.

The second nine days was a time of *charro* exhibitions, pealing church bells, parades, bullfights, *serenatas*, banquets, and fireworks. The calendar was as follows. March 10: a sunrise concert with sky-rockets, a parade, and a free bullfight at eleven o'clock; then an after-noon bullfight with young bulls from Palo Dulce, Rosary, skyrockets, *serenatas*, and curfew. March 11: the same, except for a *charro* spectacle in place of the bullfight. March 12: about the same as on the tenth. March 13 (Sunday): the first *castillo*. March 17: day of the Partidas, with the best *castillo*, built by a fireworks maker in San Luis Soyatlán. The festivities were more exciting every day: a grow-ing throng of farmers in white *calzones* and fellow townsmen back from the capital in jackets and little city hats; parades, bullfights, kermises, *serenatas*, *toritos*, and *castillos*—each noisier and gayer than the last. A man called Palmito was outstanding in the bullfights, and he had many local imitators: Adrián Cárdenas, Porfirio González . . .

On March 19, before dawn, there was a deafening clamor of church bells, and the sun came up to the thunder of thousands of rockets. Then the bells rang for High Mass, and rivers of people flowed into the church. A thousand human beings crowded in to hear the sermon and to be inspired by the solemnity of the Mass, took Communion, and spilled out onto the plaza to wait for the parade. Under the ribbons of white and yellow crepe paper strung across the streets rode a throng of *charros* and *chinas*. The adults headed for the morning bullfight, and the youngsters scattered toward the merry-go-round and the games of chance.

There were many banquets that day. Pigs and steers had been slaughtered, and tubs filled with mescal. After the feasting, those who were still on their feet went reeling off to the bullring. Men in *charro* outfits and women dressed in bright colors climbed up onto the shaky framework of wooden planks that served as bleachers. The bulls were mere calves from a local ranch, and the bullfighters were only young boys. The spectators reacted by turns with gales of laughter, hailstorms of applause, and thunderbolts of insults. This uproar was succeeded by the concert in the town square, where, amid the boiling mass of humanity, the boys had a chance to mix with the village girls and even with some from other towns. Men and women wove in and out incessantly amid handfuls of confetti, *serpentinas* of every color; marches and romantic pieces were played by the San José band. The jubilee came to a close on March 20 with a fifth *castillo*—which, although not as impressive as the one on the seventeenth, showered everybody with sparks and set off Roman candles for more than an hour.[49]

The golden-wedding celebration helped reestablish the solidarity of the village. It brought the old and the younger generations together. Two old men were to be found at the center of the festivities: Don Gregorio González Pulido and his brother Don Andrés, members of the founding generation. The huge party reunited those who had abandoned the village in its time of trouble and those who had seen it through. But above all, men who had become enemies as a result of the agrarian struggle found themselves, amid the merrymaking and the drinks, falling into the embrace of reconciliation. This is not to say that San José's shattered social unity had been completely restored. Even with all the advantages of his position, Padre Federico had to work like a dog even partially to reestablish good feelings, to curb antisocial behavior, to drive away some of the ill will that was still fluttering its wings in village closets.

The other task that Padre Federico had set himself was to incorporate the town of San José into the Mexican nation by improving relations with influential people in politics. This was made easier by the fact that the Cárdenas brothers were from Jiquilpan, in the same *municipio* as San José. One was president of the republic, and the other was senator from Michoacán. Don Dámaso's friendly attitude toward San José, and Don Lázaro's personal visit to the village while he was still president both helped a great deal. Almost overnight the villagers turned progovernment—the poor because of the agrarian reform, and the rest because of the gestures of friendship on the part of these important figures.

---

[49] Luis González Cárdenas's private records.

As the magazine *Hoy* reported, "In the five-year period from December 1, 1934, to December 1, 1939 (1,825 days) President Cárdenas was absent from the capital for one year, four months, and four days—or 489 days and nights—while visiting a total of 1,028 towns in every state of the republic." One of the few villages that had not been so honored lay within his native *municipio*, a few kilometers from Jiquilpan; in San José there were even several citizens named Cárdenas, members of the same family. San Joséans attributed the rebuff to two things: the fact that they had been *cristeros*, and their lack of enthusiasm for agrarianism. Perhaps neither of these thoughts had even occurred to the general. Perhaps his decision to come had not been influenced, either, by their liking for General Manuel Ávila Camacho, as revealed by the voters of San José on Sunday, June 7, 1940. While only 20 had supported Juan Andreu Almazán, the opposition candidate, 373 had voted for Camacho, the man who had been picked by Cárdenas. This was the first time the citizenry of San José had shown any interest in a federal election since the time of Madero; perhaps this sudden electoral concern could have been explained by the gratitude they had felt toward Don Manuel ever since the time of the *cristero* revolution, when he had been a merciful and tolerant anti-*cristero*.[50]

The townspeople had only a few days' notice. They were all in a dither. Since 1938 they had gone through a cycle of lean years. Cows were giving little milk, and cornfields were producing very little corn; but, as people said, "After all, this is the first time a president of the republic has ever come to see us." It was imperative that he be given a royal reception. Padre Federico organized the villagers and the people from the *rancherías*. Agrarianists and landowners both gathered in San José and marched out of town along the road to Jiquilpan. It was an occasion for the embrace of reconciliation; General Cárdenas and Padre Federico gave each other the *abrazo* and entered the village arm in arm along the road lined with people, through cheering crowds and handfuls of confetti. The general was lodged in the padre's house, after having made a tour of the center

50 AJTO, Documents from the Jefatura of Juan Moreno.

of town, shaking hands with everyone while listening to their requests and complaints, and having embraced the widow and children of San José's agrarianist leader, Antonio Ávila. The general and the padre had a long talk in private. It was a splendid reception. Everyone in the town and its *rancherías* felt that Cárdenas was his friend. A few days later, on October 11, 1940, Padre Federico González received a letter from President Cárdenas, in which he said: "For your broad understanding of the nation's social problems, and for your dedication to the cause of improving the living conditions of your townspeople, I send you my warmest congratulations."

San José and its *tenencia*, which had been so unwilling to become a part of Mexico, so recalcitrant toward the national authorities, dropped a great deal of its traditional suspicion of the nation and its leaders after Don Lázaro Cárdenas's visit. In addition, the president's indiscriminate affability toward agrarianist and landowner alike helped to reconcile the two factions. At the same time, the villagers hoped that they would no longer be stigmatized as "pious reactionaries." The landowners were left with the impression that General Cárdenas was satisfied that the agrarian reform had been completed within the jurisdiction of San José. The four hundred who aspired to property were confident that the government would continue creating and extending *ejido* lands; and, soon after the presidential visit, there was a great increase in the number of these petitions.[51]

But it all had come at the wrong time. The land-distributing president was on his way out. The San José area remained almost totally divided. General Manuel Ávila Camacho, the man of compromise, had one foot in the presidential stirrups.

Incipit Vita Nova

The Agrarian Reform produced farmers. While the citizens of the town of San José de Gracia were engaged in cattle raising, cheese making, skilled labor, trade, and—on a smaller scale—tending their cornfields, members of the *ejido* communities spent summer and fall

---

[51] ADAAC, files 12343, 20275, 2491, 12054, 14760, and 12863.

preparing their *yunta* or half-*yunta* of ground for planting. According
to a report by the engineer Carlos Gómez del Campo, "As the terrain
is not level, for the most part . . . the hillsides that are planted produce very little . . . wheat does not do well." On one hectare a man
could plant, on the average, 15 kilos of corn and harvest 700; 10
kilos of beans would yield 200; 30 kilos of garbanzos produced 600;
69 kilos of barley would return 450; and 48 kilos of seed would yield
450 kilos of wheat. More corn was planted than anything else. The
ejido farmer could sell his corn and other crops for 550 pesos a year—
not even enough to cover household expenses for a country family of
six: three adults and three children. Their daily outgo was 42 centavos for corn, 11 centavos for beans, 10 for lard, 5 for chile, 5 for
onions and tomatoes, 12 for sugar, 20 for meat, 24 for milk, 15 for
rice, 5 for kerosene, 5 for soap, and 10 for cigarettes. This comes to
1 peso and 64 centavos a day: 598 pesos a year, without counting the
150 pesos spent for clothing.[52]

When the plowing season was over, some *ejido* farmers engaged in
other profitable activities to eke out their income. They worked as day
laborers for the landowners, sold the dry cornstalks and husks from
their fields for cattle feed, worked on the road being built between
Jiquilpan and San José, and cut firewood to sell in the market. There
was little work to be had during the dry season. The landowners who
hired laborers were usually hostile toward the agrarian reform and
preferred to deal out the little work they had to men who did not
belong to the *ejido*. In 1944 the highest daily wage was a peso and
a half. In short, the *ejido* members lived poverty-stricken lives, which
they hoped to improve by obtaining more land. Not one wanted to
return to his previous condition as laborer or sharecropper. They may
have been as poor as before, but they were freer and felt more human.

Every application for a new *ejido* or the expansion of an existing
one was answered: "Not granted, because there are no affectible
properties within a radius of seven kilometers." But these decisions
were without prejudice to the applicants. In 1942 the engineer Carlos
Hernández reported to the Department of Agrarian Lands that there

---

[52] Ibid., file 12558.

was no property legally accessible in the upper part of the *municipio* of Jiquilpan. He pointed out that portions of some of the largest ranches had already been seized (Auchen, Casa Blanca, Cerrito de la Leña, San Pedro, Estancia del Monte, Tinaja de los Ruiz, Divisadero, and Sabino). Others had been subdivided (Ojo de Rana among Doña Librada Sandoval's four children, El Guayabo among several members of the Zepeda family, Palo Dulce among the Arias family, and Sabino among all the purchasers mentioned above). There had been a rumor that the alleged subdivision of the Sabino hacienda had never actually taken place. An inspector from the Department of Agrarian Lands reported. "I made a personal inspection of the lands comprising the estate in question and found that the subdivision had been duly carried out and that the parcels are now being used by their new proprietors . . . Most of it is farming land, but so poor that it does not pay to work it every year; thus, much of it is used as grazing land. I learned that some of the proprietors have bought as many as three more parcels . . . and since it is very common for uneducated country people to buy and sell by means of private documents, very few of these transactions have been recorded in the Public Registry. But because everyone knows everyone else, they respect each other's boundaries . . . This subdivision was made in favor of working people who personally use their parcels."[53]

Thus, we can see that by 1942 the federal government considered the repartition of land in the San José jurisdiction to have been concluded. During the years that followed, only one favorable presidential decree was issued: that of July 19, 1950, which granted 298 hectares to the La Arena *ejido*.[54] All other determinations were negative.

There was undoubtedly less resentment between people in 1942 than there had been in 1936, but it was still far above the prerevolutionary level. There was a persistent undercurrent of ill will between the agrarianist and the landowning parties. The landowners continued fearing for their property and handing out a large part of their sav-

---

[53] Ibid.
[54] Ibid., file 20010.

ings to agronomists and shysters. The farmers who had no land lived in the hope that the repartition would go on and paid out the few pennies their poverty allowed to anyone who claimed to be able to do anything for them. As they wasted their money on futile litigation, both factions went on hating each other, exchanging calumnies and insults, trying to trip each other up. The landowners, so estranged at first, became more and more unified. On the other hand, dissension grew among the proletariat. *Ejido* members, and those who aspired to be, regarded each other with suspicion. There was no solidarity between the various communities, either; within the same *ejido*, hostile factions sprang up, occasionally reaching the point of bloodshed. From 1939 to 1945 thirteen *ejido* members died at the hands of other agrarianists.[55]

"There were many killings over land. One man, with an entire pistolload emptied into him, fell dead without shedding a single drop of blood. It must have been because he was so scared. If that was the case, there was another one who must have been very brave; they shot him only once, and the blood poured out. The people who had picked him up and were taking him to the doctor were covered with blood. He said to them, 'Come on, step on it, I'm dying!' But he was dead by the time they got him to Jiquilpan. I think it was over a piece of land. When a man's in his right mind he doesn't get into trouble, but once he gets drunk he starts arguing. Then off he goes to the other world. People were murdering each other. That's why there were so many widows in Auchen." This is what Doña Inés Betancourt has to say. She is one of the widows of Auchen, which came to be known as "The Widows' *Ejido*."

A third element in the discord was the Sinarquist party. In San José it had been organized by a native son, Gildardo González; he had joined the *sinarquistas* while studying chemical engineering in Guadalajara. Gildardo's charm, education, and youthful enthusiasm brought him many followers among his countrymen, and in 1945 he was chosen as party leader by thousands of *sinarquistas* throughout the nation. The San José group was organized about 1940 and had

[55] AJTO, Documents from the Jefaturas of Anastasio Partida, Juan Moreno, Salvador Chávez, David Sánchez, Adolfo Aguilar, and Salvador Villanueva.

reached its apogee by 1946. It was made up of about fifty land-owners who were disgruntled because of the agrarian reform, and some landless peasants. It published insults to the government and the opposing parties in two furious newspapers that expounded its doctrine: *El Sinarquista* and *Orden*. Padre Federico's hostility kept the group from making many converts or becoming a power in San José. When Gildardo González resigned as the national party leader, the small Sinarquist party in San José, under the command of Florentino Flores, collapsed like a punctured balloon.

Most inhabitants of San José had come to look to the village's military detachment for the maintenance of law and order. After having been antimilitarists, they had begun to like the soldiers. They felt that these men in green uniforms were the only ones who could keep peace between warring groups and individuals. Thus, there was considerable alarm when, in March of 1941, the detachment was withdrawn. The alarm turned to panic when Leobardo Pulido, the *jefe de tenencia*, was murdered. At that point, while the air still smelled of gunpowder, over a thousand of the citizens petitioned for the restoration of the military post. All they got for their pains was an order forbidding anyone in the village and its *rancherías* to carry a pistol. There was a storm of futile protests. Men considered carrying arms to be a sign of masculinity; they felt as though they had been castrated when their pistols were taken from them; they complained that they had been humiliated. But they soon found a way to rearm: Salvador Chávez, *jefe de tenencia* in 1942, appointed an extraordinary number of auxiliary police officers, and thus the men of San José were able to strap on their guns again.

However, the entire era of tribulation was entering its last quarter. It had been an epoch of the immoderate use of revolvers and Mausers, fighting over land, religious warfare, highway robbery, bloodshed, burning and destruction, mass banishments, hatred, and outrages. From 1941 on, one heard less and less the catchwords and boasting that characterized the destructive phase of the revolution: restitution of the rights of the proletariat, death to the scarecrow priests, sexual and socialistic education, "Consume what your own country produces," achievements of the Six-Year Plan, preparation of the working masses, feminism, necessity of transculturation, the class struggle, the Supreme Leader, the Political Institution of the Revolution, the Postulates of the Revolution, the rights of the laboring classes, the annihilation of those who are starving the people, the Message to the Nation, and all the other phrases employed by the revolutionary intellectuals who idolized laborers and peasants while sitting in their comfortable offices and conference rooms in Mexico City. Many of these expressions fell into desuetude and were replaced by others. The "constructive phase of the revolution" was at hand.

In San José the era of tribulation had begun with earthquakes and the eruption of the volcano of Colima, and it ended with more temblors and the birth of the volcano Paricutín, on February 25, 1943. Both sprinkled ashes on San José; their fire could be seen from the summit of Larios Mountain; they became the principal topic of conversation in the village; and there were many arguments about the hidden meaning in their message. Padre Federico organized a large expedition to San Juan Parangaricutiro to contemplate the explosions, the black clouds, the lightning bolts, the incessant discharge of red-hot rocks, the gusts of hot gases, and the rivers of lava that poured from Paricutín. Such a prodigious spectacle could not be without some meaning; it was an announcement of something, but it certainly could not be a warning that things were going to get any worse.

Thirty Years of Turmoil: Statistics and Concepts

It has been said of many places that "few towns suffered as much as this one during the revolution." That statement is certainly true of San José de Gracia. These three stages were a nightmare, but in the end fruitful. For thirty years people had lived with bullets whistling past their ears. First it was the Mexican revolution (1910–1922). The town was burned down twice. The most memorable event was the raid by Chávez and his horde. But the earth was never so defiled with the blood of crime and violence as during the period that followed. The most terrible time of all was the *cristero* revolution (1925–1932): uninterrupted fighting, total disorder, and the third destruction of San José. The Agrarian Reform brought notable changes in the system of landholding; it also sowed discord between brothers. But this does not mean that it was not beneficial.

During the revolution, San José's demographic history took new directions. There were times—1918 and 1927–1929—when the population was reduced to its minimum; there were sudden evacuations and rapid repopulations. On the whole, the population showed no increase during this period: it numbered 3,850 in 1910 and 3,859 in 1940. The birth rate remained high, as always. The death rate rose, particularly at the time of the *cristero* troubles. New settlers came, but the zone could not keep them. From that time on, there was a slow exodus.

Contrary to what one might have expected, the falloff in cattle production was not caused by technological stagnation. At the height of the revolution there were timid beginnings at new methods. New crops were introduced, such as the *urápeti* corn Padre Federico brought from Tingüindín. People began to milk during the dry season. In the midst of the agrarian revolution it became the custom to add concentrates to cattle feed. But still these were years of crisis, of poverty, of bony cattle.

Obviously, material and spiritual standards of living dropped during the revolutionary period. The introduction of electric lights (in 1926), of the mill for grinding corn for tortillas, of automobiles, and of the radio did not mean much in the face of the general impoverishment, the shortage of corn, and the fact that people had little to sell and very little money with much to buy. Many were up to their ears in debt. It was the era of usury; of the rapid enrichment of two or three men in the midst of widespread poverty; of sleeping on the ground again; of living on beans, chile, tortillas, and sometimes a little milk and meat; of being poorly dressed, of making sacrifices in order to rebuild the village and its shattered economy.

As these troubled times came to an end, the founding fathers were dying off, one by one. With them died the patriarchate. The large families were left headless. They survived as mere aggregates of small families, with some feeling of affiliation. More effective than the division by families was the division by class. The town was sharply divided into two social groups, who called themselves the rich and the poor. The Agrarian Reform had fostered class consciousness, hatred and contention between the classes, and social discord.

In no previous period had there been as many changes in land-ownership as there were from 1910 to 1942. The ranches that had appeared with the subdivision of the Cojumatlán hacienda were in turn subdivided by legacy. The Sabino hacienda was cut up into parcels and ranches. A new kind of private property was appearing: the small farm, the minifundium. The greatest innovation was the *ejido*, which corresponded to no local tradition and sprang from no spontaneous impulse on the part of the people. It was a form imposed by the government, from without.

The setting up of the *ejidos* did not mean the end of working for wages or sharecropping. There was not enough land for everybody. Labor structures suffered no change whatsoever. As the labor supply diminished, there could have come a real increase in wages; if there was none, it was because there was not enough work. The disturbances did not make all institutions obsolete—far from it.

In the years between 1910 and 1942 the rule of the patriarchs came to an end. There was a marked increase in the power of the priests, and a decrease in that of the *jefe de tenencia*, the tax collector, and the judge. The military authorities—the commander of the home guard, the leaders and officers of the *cristero* rebels and of the federal troops who fought them, and the army garrison stationed in San José in 1930—grew more powerful. San José lived under a rule that was at times theocratic, at times military. Both warriors and priests played very important roles during revolutionary times.

The upheavals of all kinds between 1910 and 1942 could not have failed to be an impediment to education. The influence of the home in child training was drastically weakened; there were more wayward children, and there was more delinquency. At the same time, the school widened its sphere of influence. In the first place, a new kind of institution appeared—the free secular school provided by the government; in the second place, more students went beyond the elementary grades to continue their studies in seminaries, secondary schools run by the church, preparatory academies, and real universities.

It may be important to mention that only one person—Camilo Chávez—suffered a loss of faith. People said it was because he had read certain books and magazines that questioned or denied the tenets of the church, the Immaculate Conception, and the like. But, on the whole, the level of religious fervor rose; there was even more faith, more intolerance, more self-denial; there were more vows, more retreats, and perhaps there was more virtue. In short, it was a time of inflexible dogma, resplendent and well-attended masses, and frequent backsliding and falling from grace.

Amusements went on as usual during the squabble. As for fiestas, some innovations were introduced between 1910 and 1942, such as the celebration of civil as well as religious holidays (the Sixteenth of September, the town's golden wedding, etc.). The golden-wedding jubilee in 1938 was an extraordinary festival, full of euphoria and general rejoicing. Games of skill were still popular; modern sports filtered in little by little; public spectacles began to appear. There was a greater consumption of alcohol. Card games came back, along with billiard tables.

Needless to say, one of the constants from 1910 to 1920 was the feeling that one's life was in danger—and with good reason. It was a time of strong emotions of all kinds, running the entire gamut. By virtue of this fury and violence the town became fused with the nation and gradually found itself less alone. Jean Meyer, one of San José's most illustrious visitors, was quite right: the war had wrenched the village out of its isolation and made it part of Mexico.

The triple revolution brought the end of isolation. Before 1910 people rarely ventured beyond their native heath. First, the Mexican revolution—and especially one of its by-products, bandits—drove people into nearby towns and distant cities. The *cristero* rebellion brought greater dispersion. Strangers appeared in the village; the radio came; newspapers became popular. The upheaval of this little world began. It became Mexicanized, with blood, fire, terror, bullets, thundering horses, anxiety, hatred, and newspapers. It took a step forward toward nationalization. But now it was no longer only the leaders of the community, but also the children of every citizen in it who came to know and feel that they were Mexicans. This does not mean full Mexicanization, however, nor did it mean identification with the government. They had hated every great figure of the revolution, with two exceptions: Francisco (Pancho) Villa and Lázaro Cárdenas, and these men became popular idols. They especially revered the agrarianist president, and not merely because he had handed out land. "He did not kill; he was merciful; he held back the religious persecution; he brought peace."

Part Three

Twenty-five Years of Change

7. WITHDRAWAL AND EXPANSION (1943–1956)

At the Mercy of the Outside World

GENERAL Manuel Ávila Camacho had to be a conciliatory president; his own good nature and public opinion demanded it. He put several catchwords of the time into practice. (1) "National Unity": Calles and Garrido were returned to the country; the uneasy *almazanistas* were admitted; it was declared that there had been neither victors nor defeated; the accusations following the election were forgotten. (2) "The Struggle for Production": protection was promised for the entrepreneur at home and a green light for those from abroad; the National Commission for Economic Planning was set up; trade agreements were made with foreign countries; the El Palmito dam was begun, as were the factories of Altos Hornos de México and Guanos y Fertilizantes. (3) "Machines and Schools": Torres Bodet set about the task of teaching the illiterate of Mexico to read and write—he built schools and created teacher-training centers. (4) "International Peace": there was condemnation of the Nazi-Fascist aggressions; an interview was arranged between Ávila Camacho and Roosevelt, and there was an agreement on indemnities for the oil companies; relations were renewed with Great Britain and the USSR; meetings were held, designed to bring an end to world strife, the last of which was held at Chapultepec. (5) "Government

for Everybody": Social Security was set up for the workers; conces-
sions were made to employers; farmers were given grants of land,
while other agricultural and cattle-raising properties were declared
inaffectible. In 1942 an agreement (without a catchword) was signed
placing Mexican rural workers at the disposal of growers in the
United States. Thus, Mexico contributed to the victory of the democ-
racies. By 1945 everyone knew that Licenciado Miguel Alemán, "the
cub of the revolution," would be the next president.

On December 1, 1946, "a generation of men uncontaminated by
the grudges of the revolution" took over the government of the
republic. "The ministers were university professors and specialists . . .
Everything was carefully planned: during his election campaign Miguel Alemán conducted round-table discussions of the great problems
of the nation . . . The United States granted us a loan of a hundred
million for the industrialization of the country . . . In spite of postwar difficulties—inflation, devaluation, loss of foreign markets—
there was an unflagging determination to lift the nation out of its
underdeveloped state; droughts were met by the construction of huge
dams; highways and new railroad lines were built . . . farming land
and cattle ranches were exempted from expropriation." The epidemic
of hoof-and-mouth disease was attacked with the sanitary rifle.[1] The
cattle business collapsed. In June, 1950, the United States sent its
men to war again—this time to Korea—and announced that it needed
"a large number of Mexican laborers . . . Mexico agreed to send
55,000 men . . . who would assemble at certain points to be trans-
ported across the border for distribution." The blond employers
would pay for the trip "from the border to their farms, and back to
the border." The United States government would provide funds and
police to "apprehend workers who had run away from their employers' ranches before the end of their contract." The Mexican government looked the other way; it accepted conditions that
turned its peasants into "exportable merchandise under the most favorable conditions possible for the importer."[2] The country people

---

[1] Salvador Novo, *La vida en México en el período presidencial de Miguel Alemán*,
pp. 11–17.
[2] Ibid., p. 152.

rubbed their hands in anticipation. They preferred the gringo's dollars, loud sports jackets, and radios to working on their *ejido* parcels.

Getting to California, where the pay was highest, was nearly impossible after 1948. From then on, the men ended up in Texas, New Mexico, or Arizona—but mostly in Texas, where they were treated badly and given dirty looks. Still, more and more workers wanted to go to the "Yunaites." Between 1943 and 1953 a million braceros made the trip with their papers in order, and perhaps an equal number illegally. In 1946 it was estimated that 130,000 slipped across the line under cover of darkness, in leaky little boats or simply by swimming, keeping an eye peeled for the Yankee police dogs. No power on earth could stop them. In 1944 an attempt was made to prevent men from Guanajuato, Jalisco, and Michoacán from going north as braceros, but without any noticeable results.

In 1941 Don Lázaro Cárdenas had returned to Michoacán; he worried, and he busied himself every day trying to pull the state out of its underdeveloped condition. The governors worked in harmony with the ex-president. General Félix Ireta, with his "conciliatory nature," like that of President Ávila Camacho, became governor in 1940 and was succeeded by José María Mendoza Pardo in 1944. In Morelia there were frequent disturbances among the university students, but in the rest of the state people were taking deep breaths of Ávila Camacho's atmosphere of machines, schools, solidarity, and government for everybody.[3] Three states led in the number of braceros shipped out: the Federal District, Michoacán, and Guanajuato. In 1942, 87 percent of all the men who were sent to the United States came from these three areas, and "81 percent in 1943 and 57 percent in 1944."[4] In addition, Michoacán was one of the regions where the most cattle were afflicted by hoof-and-mouth disease.

In 1950 a friend of San José de Gracia was elected governor of the state. Local people had not been in the habit of going to the polls, but a good number of San Joséans voted for General Don Dámaso Cárdenas. The new governor "promoted cattle production, the building of schools, hospitals, and highways, and public works

[3] José Bravo Ugarte, *Historia sucinta de Michoacán*, III, 228.
[4] Julio Durán Ochoa, *Estructura económica y social de México: Población*, p. 179.

throughout the entire state."[5] He was also known for his "peaceful nature." During this period Michoacán lost the championship for exporting the most braceros, but more and more of its people were moving to the capital.

The constructive aspects of the Mexican revolution began to be felt in San José. The townspeople opened their eyes wide when they heard that a highway was being built through their *tenencia*. The Cárdenas brothers had arranged it. At first, the engineers had specified that the Jiquilpan-Manzanillo highway should bypass the village; but Padre Federico had gone to his friend Don Lázaro, and the patriarch had had the plans altered.[6] It was decided that the road should run from Jiquilpan along the winding route that rose to the mesa, pass through the large Los Corrales *ranchería*, zigzag across the low hills of the Ornelas *tenencia*, pass through San José de Gracia, continue to Mazamitla, run through the pine forests of the sierra, drop to the cane fields of Tamazula, touch the towns of Tecalitlán and Pihuano, and go on to Colima, Cuyutlán, and Manzanillo. It would be a wide, paved, first-class federal highway, 317 kilometers long.

In a report dated September 1, 1942, President Ávila Camacho stated, ". . . among the national highways now being built, that between Jiquilpan and Colima should be mentioned for its exceptional military and economic importance."[7] Actual work on the road was begun in 1941. Hundreds of local men, with picks and shovels, dump trucks, and some light machinery, collaborated in the construction of Highway 110. There was a festive air about it. The San Joséans had work, good salaries, and high hopes for the highway. People laughed at Francisca Cárdenas when she dared to dissent from the general opinion. She said that the automobiles would run over the pigs and chickens that swarmed in the streets; they would make it impossible to milk one's cow at the front door, as had always been done; they would disturb people's sleep; and they would bring

[5] Bravo Ugarte, *Historia sucinta*, III, 229.

[6] As recalled by Federico González Cárdenas.

[7] Luis Gonzáles, ed., *Los presidentes de México ante la nación: Informes, manifiestos y documentos*, IV, 223.

in outsiders with evil ways who would rob the San Joséans of the little they had.

As work progressed on the highway, bars and prostitutes were installed. The workmen got drunk and fornicated. Automobiles and buses began coming and going. In 1941 and 1942 "a local car made the round trip between San José and Sahuayo every other day."[8] After 1943 its place was taken by the Flecha Roja buses running between Mexico City and Manzanillo. Transportation became swift and safe. The capital could be reached with ease in twelve hours; Guadalajara in three; Colima in five; and the beach resorts of Cuyutlán, Manzanillo, and Santiago in six or seven. One felt that he could be anywhere in the twinkling of an eye. Buses came by at all hours. The people of San José and its *rancherías* began traveling with a vengeance. With the highway under construction, local products— especially cheese—could be sent to Mexico City in large trucks.

World War II ended in 1945. The Jiquilpan-Manzanillo highway was no longer of military importance, and work on it was suspended. During the 1946 rainy season it became nearly impassable. Construction was begun again in 1949, to be completed four years later. In his 1951 report to Congress, President Miguel Alemán announced: "The road from Jiquilpan to Manzanillo is now completed except for the surfacing." In the last report of his administration he observed that "45 percent of the highway has been paved."[9] In 1950 many men went back to work on the road. Back came the road machinery and the high wages. The drought and the farm crisis, both dating from 1948, were hardly felt.

Another mode of communication had appeared in 1938, when Don David Sánchez bought a radio. Many people came to hear the music and the news. The music wasn't as clear as on phonograph records, but there was nothing like it for keeping up with national and world events. After 1939 there were always a dozen people clustered around the set, listening to the news of the World War. They were the town's leading citizens, of whom only two were rooting for the Allies. The rest, swayed by the traditional suspicion of

[8] AJTO, Documents from the Jefatura of Leobardo Pulido.
[9] González, *Los presidentes de México*, IV, 466 and 496.

their neighbors to the north and dazzled by the blitzkrieg tactics of the Germans, applauded Hitler's triumphs and told each other that Mexico's real independence would come when the Axis crushed the United States.[10]

In 1942 Don David's radio fell silent. The "light and power plant" which he operated had provided only enough electricity for the corn mill, for lights in a few houses, and for the village's only radio. A group of citizens who wanted more electric lights smashed Don David's generator, since its destruction was a prerequisite to being supplied with light and power from the hydroelectric plant just completed at Agua Fría, fifteen kilometers from San José. Don David left town in a rage. Months later the citizens greeted the new power lines with great jubilation. Although they received only a dribble of electricity, it was now possible to install more lights, about twenty radios, and two jukeboxes. News and music from the outside world reached more people and paved the way for the motion pictures.

Movies began to be shown, twice a week, in 1944. Leocadio Toscano built a primitive theater, with four hundred seats as hard as rocks. The priests forbade attendance on the grounds that the pictures were a school of immorality; but gradually their parishioners began to disobey. Leocadio had a full house whenever he showed films about singing *charros*, romantic ranchers, nightclub habitués, comedians in the style of Tin-Tan or Cantinflas, generous thieves, and saints. Then his audiences developed a taste for war movies and westerns in English. They liked the advertisements that preceded the features, too. They were beginning to live in an imaginary other world.

The leading citizens were still given to reading newspapers. After *El Universal* came *Excelsior*, *El Informador*, and *El Occidental*—the last two from Guadalajara. Only one magazine became popular with San José's elite: *Selecciones del "Reader's Digest."* It arrived first in 1948, and it soon had a dozen subscribers. Its pages were filled with stories about men who never gave up hope, reports of scientific

---

[10] I did not read or hear most of the information given in this and subsequent chapters, but took it from my own recollections and experiences.

miracles, descriptions of other countries, condensed novels, revelations of the benevolent and heroic side of capitalistic society and of the brutish aspects of the socialistic ones. It was, in short, a varied pabulum of fads, opinions, and tales of distant lands, indiscriminately passed around and swallowed by its small but influential group of readers. As for books, Martín Luis Guzmán's *The Eagle and the Serpent* was popular, as were other works dealing with the immediate past.

There was an enormous influx of outsiders: engineers and foremen working on the highway, tourists, traveling salesmen, and doctors come to fulfill their requirement for social service. Between 1944 and 1950 four of these young medical men appeared in succession: Jorge Solórzano, Rubén Gálvez Betancourt, Boris Rubio Lotvin, and Augusto del Ángel. Upon completion of their medical service in San José, each wrote a paper on the health, unsanitary conditions, and other aspects of the town. Some of the things they found had existed before the highway; others had appeared afterward.

In the reports by Jorge Solórzano and Rubén Gálvez we learn that the San José area was healthier than the great majority of the regions of Mexico. However, "the infant mortality rate is high." Two kinds of disease were continual threats to young children, and, to a lesser degree, to adults. The principal kind was "acute infections of the respiratory tract." The other consisted of "parasitic infections, from both tapeworms and hookworms." The reason was obvious. "It is common to find dung heaps in the houses." "Animals are butchered in the public thoroughfares." "Nothing is done without the least regard for cleanliness." It was conceded that the people were well nourished, however. "There is a very low incidence (one-half of one percent) of deficiency diseases." Nursing children were overfed. It was customary to give them the breast whenever they cried, and thus they suffered from diarrhea, the bowels being loosened often to the point of death. There was no venereal disease.[11]

Five years later we read, "In first place are the diseases of the

---

[11] Jorge Solórzano Márquez, *Informe general sobre la exploración sanitaria de San José de Gracia, Michoacán*, pp. 9, 17, and 19.

respiratory tract; the second is occupied by many forms of intestinal parasites; the third most common are venereal infections, particularly gonorrhea." These were followed by two other diseases brought in from outside: typhus and malaria.[12] Augusto del Ángel deplores the San Joséans' fondness for self-medication, the eight women who "assist in childbirth, and the woman who prescribes patent medicines," the fact that there is no pharmacy, and the lack of any prenuptial examination. He then discusses the three diseases that came in with the highway, with particular reference to the typhus brought by rats, riding "the trucks carrying cheese and eggs between the village and the Merced market" in Mexico City. First, the patient felt weak and had a slight temperature. "Then chills and fever; sometimes vomiting; invariably a loss of appetite, pain, and an eruption of pink and red blotches."[13] The highway brought all this, as well as chancres and gleet and malaria. "The source of infection was outside the village."

Besides doctors and salesmen, the highway brought some noted political leaders to San José. While General Lázaro Cárdenas was secretary of defense, he was a frequent visitor. Thanks to the new road, the governors of Michoacán fell into the habit of appearing in San José. The first to do so was General Félix Ireta. He and his successors usually came in the company of deputies and other important people in government. One of the most constant and rewarding callers was Don Enrique Bravo Valencia.

With the coming of the highway, episcopal visits became common; three bishops from Zamora, as well as José Garibi Rivera, the archbishop of Guadalajara, came to officiate at confirmations. The high point was in 1955, when Papal Delegate Guillermo Piani appeared. His reception was comparable only to that accorded five years earlier to the image of Our Lady of Fátima.[14]

[12] Boris Rubio Lotvin, *El ejercicio de la medicina en la población de San José de Gracia, Michoacán*, pp. 30–31.

[13] Augusto del Ángel Ochoa, *Informe general sobre las condiciones médico-sanitarias de San José de Gracia, Michoacán*, pp. 27–28.

[14] APSJ, Confirmation Records.

The highway brought other kinds of people, too; thieves of every stripe. There were political hangers-on who stole the spoons and liquor when they were invited to lunch; pickpockets who approached their victims as they emerged from church after mass; swindlers who went from house to house selling quack remedies, gadgets for locating buried treasure, and counterfeit lottery tickets; and, above all, cattle thieves. The last operated at night, driving the animals into huge trucks and speeding off, so that by dawn they were miles away. Rustlers would have wiped out the cattle industry in the area if the military authorities had not stepped in. The story got around that there was an executioner in Jiquilpan who would politely approach a captured cattle thief, hold a double-edged dagger to his heart, and gravely inquire: "Will you push, or shall I?"

In 1948 another beam of light from the city fell on the village: the telegraph. The telephone agency was transformed into a telegraph office. Advertising signs were appearing, recommending beers, Coca-Cola, liquors, clothing, gasoline, patent medicines, insecticides, cattle feed, and the hundreds of other products of an industrial society. Between 1943 and 1956 nine out of every ten San Joséans over fifteen years old visited Mexico City or Guadalajara, and they generally returned filled with wonder. The townspeople stopped resisting; they conceded that city life was, in some respects, superior to theirs.

Modern communications and transportation, and close daily contact with the outside world—especially with the city—gave rise to a consciousness of certain desiderata that were incommensurable, yet real and distinguishable: wealth, city life, new inventions, mobility, travel, and emigration. It was the younger men of the middle class who, in the forties, began to feel that they were living in a prison, that their village world was narrow, crude, and dull. They no longer enjoyed their lives. They wanted something more: to make money, to live more comfortably, to meet girls, to do anything they felt like doing, to escape to the "States" or even to Mexico City. An entire generation faced the alternatives of urbanizing San José or moving to the city. Acquisition of land was no longer the main subject of conversation. Instead of agrarianism and agrarianists, they discussed emigration and *émigrés* and talked of bringing home machines, comforts, and new ways of doing things.

The Symptoms of Transformation

Those born between 1905 and 1917 pioneered the acculturation. They were born and had grown up in a world of pistols and rifles, persecution, strife, poverty, injustice, hatred, fear, and suspicion. They had seen their village destroyed and rebuilt three times. Childhood, adolescence, and early manhood had been filled with calamities, and, upon reaching the age where they had a voice in the matter, they set out to obtain for themselves and their families the freedom and happiness heralded by the radio, the movies, and the magazines, which had been almost their only teachers. Feeling that their needs were greater than those of their fathers, they were determined to abandon many of the old patterns. Some had the enterprise to go to the city in search of a new life. Almost all those who stayed behind signed up as braceros, hoping to come back from the "States" with enough money to take up the bourgeois existence they aspired to. They were determined to wrest greater profit from the soil than their fathers had, to undertake new occupations, and, finally, to attain comfort, the apparatus of the good life, conveniences, and freedom to travel. Many of the more dynamic people left, feeling that it was either move to the city or transform the village. Those of this generation did not have as much love for the soil or the same community spirit their parents had. "My home is wherever I can make a good living," they said. They were fiercely individualistic, with no faith in anything or anybody. Only Padre Federico was able to make them part with some of their profits for the public good, occasionally convincing them that a man must contribute something of what he earns. On the other hand, some of these people had a strong sense of social unity and worked as hard for the community as for themselves.

Bernardo González Cárdenas is one of the best examples of the enterprising generation. He was born in 1907. He lived and suffered through the days of the bandit gangs. Although he was the son of a well-to-do man, the circumstances under which he grew up made any kind of comfort impossible. He took part in the *cristero* revolution, but his diary reveals how little enthusiasm he put into that struggle. Often he forgot to describe the battles, and, when he did, he never saw their heroic aspects. He loved to write about the good times. When the fighting was over, he came home, eager to go into business. First he set himself up as a manufacturer of candles, then he switched to making fireworks. When he inherited land and cattle from his father, he became a rancher unlike any other in the region. He bought magazines dealing with new, scientific farming methods. He never missed an agricultural fair. He visited other ranches that might serve as models. After collecting all the information on the subject, he launched into an entirely new enterprise: the *granja*. On a stony, dry hillside at the edge of town he sank a couple of wells, pumped the water with windmills, planted fruit trees, built chicken houses and pigpens, constructed stables and barns, dug a stock pond that held 25,000 cubic meters of water, and raised a compact, modern farmhouse, without patio or interior garden. The work was done gradually, whenever he had the money to spare. Everything was carefully calculated for maximal efficiency. He stocked the ranch with good milch cows, selected pigs, and the best laying hens. He fed his livestock with the choicest feed and grain, used both animal and chemical fertilizers on his crops, and brought in light farm machinery. He ran corn and beans (ears, pods, stalks, and all) through a chopper and stored the mixture in enormous silos to provide excellent cattle feed for the dry season. In fifteen years he created a model farm, with no equal for many kilometers around. In a short time, thanks to hard work, perseverance, and science, he became quite wealthy.

Today Don Bernardo follows a daily schedule that is without precedent in the area. He gets up later than his fellow ranchers—at seven or seven-thirty—dresses, and goes out to talk with his twenty-odd employees, assigning each one his job for the day. Here no one follows the principle of "Begin each day by doing the same thing you were doing the day before." After having looked over the entire farm (chicken houses, pigpens, stables, corrals, orchard, dairy, water tanks, barns, and workshops) and left instructions concerning feed, vaccines, horseshoeing, dehorning, milking, repairing machinery, castrating pigs, pruning trees, irrigation, and insecticides, he goes to the kitchen and has breakfast about ten o'clock. Then he may drive to Sahuayo or Zamora in his pickup to buy supplies and attend to various business matters. More often he goes upstairs to his office to look over and update his dossiers—the index cards on which he records the daily production of every chicken, cow, and pig; to take care of correspondence; and to read technical manuals, history, or fiction: *The Farm Repair Shop, The Eagle and the Serpent, The Lean Lands*. Often friends or customers come to call, and he receives them with his proverbial politeness; if a neighbor has a problem, he may pay a visit to his ranch and advise him. Other mornings he goes to inspect his alfalfa crop at Aguacaliente, the cornfield at El Zapatero, or the herd of yearlings at El Mandil. Don Bernardo has lunch at two, after which he naps for half an hour in his chair. Then he looks over the various operations on the farm again; he receives and weighs the feed that arrives in large trucks; he sells pigs, packs and ships eggs, and sets out beehives; and, some afternoons, he attends meetings to discuss community problems: water, schools, roads, and so on. He is usually a member of the committees that call on the governor or other officials to request some action for the common good. In the evening Don Bernardo recites the Rosary with the entire family, and then goes to the main house to visit with his brothers and relatives. After supper—if the little he eats at night can be called that—he goes to bed between nine and ten. In many of these daily chores he is assisted by his wife, Teresa. The daughter of a *cristero* general, she is invariably sarcastic but a hard worker. Don Bernardo's children attend the government school, and since an early age have helped their father on the farm, as well.

No other member of the enterprising generation followed Don Bernardo's example, but they all tried to modernize their farming and cattle-raising methods to some extent. Padre Federico urged the adoption of modern methods and the search for new markets. It became common practice to cross the old Andalusian cattle, with their yellowish hides, long horns, and scanty milk, with the Brown Swiss and Holstein breeds—both short horned and good milkers. Ranchers also began to provide feed for their cattle during the dry season, from November to June. In addition to cornstalks and straw, *tepame* pods, and *ojupos*, they gave them oil cake, bran, ground corn, and other foods to build endurance and increase milk production. The practice of dehorning became popular; thus, the animals were kept from harming each other in the corrals and out in the pasture. Stock was treated for ticks and given vaccines. A vigorous campaign against pests and diseases (mammitis, staggers, blackleg, etc.) was undertaken. One or two magazines began to circulate among the stockmen.

In 1941 a reporter for the magazine *Huanimba* calculated that about ten thousand head of cattle were owned by a hundred families in San José and its *tenencia* and estimated their annual production at half a million pesos. The journalist's figures appeared to be very nearly correct—but, of course, did not agree with the farm census. Beef prices were already on the upgrade in 1941, and from then on they rose rapidly. Fifteen years later there were about the same number of cattle, but milk production had doubled—in spite of the grave setback occasioned by hoof-and-mouth disease.

In 1947 all people talked about was the epidemic of hoof-and-mouth disease and the measures that were being taken against it. On October 28 a San José woman wrote to her son in Mexico City: "This terrible disease is doing great damage here, and the men who have come to wipe it out are doing even more. Their orders are to shoot the cattle. People are very angry, and the gringos in charge of the slaughter fear for their lives. They are afraid the ranchers will kill them, as they did up north."

The stockmen were drawn together by their fury. The towns on the mesa, in the mountains, and along the fertile crescent united to defend themselves from the prophylactic rifle. Don Salvador Romero, representing groups of ranchers in Jiquilpan, Sahuayo, San José, Cojumatlán, La Manzanilla, Mazamitla, El Valle, and so on, bombarded the president and the secretary of agriculture with six open letters. He wrote: "Hundreds of our people are engaged exclusively in raising cattle, and have done nothing else all their

lives . . . Not only is their business being wiped out, . . . but also
they are being condemned to idleness, for they know no other way
of making a living . . . The bullet that kills their cows also puts
an end to their ranches, which are exclusively grazing lands.[15] . . .
People are saying that the anti-*aftosa* campaign is being pushed by
powerful cattle ranchers in the northern part of the country . . . and
that it is in their interest to continue it, even if it means reducing
the center of the country to poverty.[16] . . . Imagine, Mr. President,
what a blow to the farmer's morale it must be to see these blond
foreigners come right into his own home, with the power to do as
they like with his property . . . The directors of the campaign like
to boast about how well equipped their teams are . . . but they have
forgotten one tiny detail: they haven't told us what they're offering us
in exchange."[17]

Like everyone else, the villagers and ranchers believed the rumor
that the gringos had spread the disease themselves, from airplanes,
because they wanted to get rid of their stocks of powdered milk left
over from the war. The Yankee-phobia spread, but it did not last
long. Only about two thousand animals had been killed when the
order came to put away the sanitary rifle. When the rifle left, so did
the hoof-and-mouth disease. Soon the epizootic and the gringo butchers were forgotten. The cattle business returned to normal. Now that
the big scare was over, the 176 stockmen in the *tenencia* went on
with their program of improving breeds, increasing milk production,
and converting the milk into easily marketable products.

Some of the milk was drunk with the morning and evening meals;
the rest was made into the traditional commodities—plus one new
one: cream. Centrifugal separators had been introduced at the end
of the thirties. But milk was still far from being fully utilized.
Bernardo González Godínez calculates that "50 percent of the milk
solids, with a considerable commercial value, is wasted when most
of the whey is thrown away"—a loss to the economy and a menace

[15] Salvador Romero Méndez, *Ensayos y discursos*, p. 97.
[16] Ibid., p. 104.
[17] Ibid., pp. 105–106.

to public health. The discarded whey "gives rise to malodorous and noxious putrefaction."[18]

There were nearly a hundred small cheese factories in the *tenencia.* While the great majority of the dairy farmers made their milk into cheese at home, a few sold their output to the two creameries in the village.

Now that the highway was in, people could send their cheese in large trucks to Mexico City. It was taken to the ancient Merced market and delivered to offices and warehouses of commission merchants from San José who had moved to the city five, ten, or fifteen years before. For a fee of 5 percent of the selling price, these agents would then distribute the merchandise to other markets, grocery stores, and restaurants in the capital. The cheese arrived somewhat shrunken. Some of this loss in bulk was normal and permissible, since the whey tended to ooze out during shipping; but the rest, attributable to the *mordida,* was unpredictable and costly. The truck drivers had to give "alms" to any highway police officer who might stop them on the way. The commission agents, too, had to pass out bribes to the various policemen and inspectors who infested the Merced market.

Two other industries that had been encouraged by Padre Federico never developed to the extent that the cattle business did. There was not enough electric power for mechanical arts, and not enough water for fruit trees. By 1941 the sarape makers, who washed, carded, and spun the wool, and then wove it on twenty ancient looms, were turning out 250 sarapes a month, with a value of 3,500 pesos. Their products were either black or gray, striped with blue, white, and mulberry. During the three years that followed, however, they were unable to exceed that figure. In 1946–1947 they began to reduce their output, defeated by the competition from bigger factories in the city and by the fact that the sarape was falling into disuse.[19]

Nor were the orchards as successful as Padre Federico had hoped.

[18] Bernardo González Godínez, "Industrialización de los subproductos lácteos regionales," pp. 7, 12, and 13.

[19] *Huanimba,* no. 1 (1941).

He had urged people to plant fruit trees—especially peach trees, which he imported and distributed. He succeeded in getting about twenty orchards started, setting an example by planting two of his own. But soon everyone was discouraged. Nineteen thirty-eight marked the beginning of a cycle of dry years, and there was a critical drought in 1940. People who had started orchards turned their cows into them.

One day a Spaniard in exile came to San José—a man with a greater gift for words than is usually found in his countrymen. Don Julián Enríquez assured everyone that the soil of San José was perfect for raising olives. The more affluent citizens were filled with enthusiasm and began planting the trees or grafting them to the wild olive. Many bought trees imported from Portugal; Manuel González Flores, the wealthiest Spaniard in San José, set out thousands of them. He nursed them tenderly for ten years or more; he went to Europe to learn more about the subject; he tried everything to make them bear, and, in the end, he admitted defeat.

The failure of the fruit-growing experiments created no crisis. Other elements in the economy were prospering. The cattlemen were making modest fortunes; merchants were pleased with the way business was picking up; the laboring class—the men working on the highway, on the dam at El Valle, and on gringo ranches as braceros—was happily spending with both hands. The great drought of 1948–1952, comparable only to the one thirty years earlier, produced no epidemics or shortages of food. People felt that they were gradually freeing themselves from the tyranny of the seasons and weather cycles.

The great drought, in fact, brought great expectations. The waters of Lake Chapala fell to an unprecedented level, exposing land that obviously belonged to the federal government; there were rumors that it would be made available to the people of neighboring villages for farming. Padre Federico went to work, and his efforts were rewarded with a telegram: "The Ingeniero Oribe Alva has authorized your townspeople to lease three hundred hectares of land in the Chapala basin." Those three hundred hectares were worth as much as the three thousand hectares of farming land in the entire *tenencia* of Ornelas. The San Joséans threw themselves upon the rich, fertile fields with joy in their hearts. For a whole year, and especially when they harvested their first crops, their faces glowed with pleasure. But there was no second harvest. The dike that had been promised to hold back the lake water was never built. With the return of the normal rains the lake rose again, and their hopes were dashed.

People began to multiply at top speed. General Cárdenas had fostered the institution of obligatory social service for graduating medical students, who were assigned to the various villages. Their influence was felt immediately. The death rate dropped with a thud. It had been fifteen per thousand; between 1949 and 1954 it fell to eight. The birth rate rose. San José's average had been thirty or forty per thousand; it moved to fifty-one in 1948, to sixty-two in 1949, to fifty-eight in 1950, to sixty in 1951, to fifty in 1952, where it stood until 1955.[20] This eagerness for children was equaled only by the new enthusiasm for health and cleanliness. People were beginning to be offended by the odor of armpits.

The desire for change could be seen everywhere, even in a wider use of soap and the eradication of lice by means of DDT. One no longer saw women and children sitting in doorways being deloused with brush and fingernails, or heard the snapping sound of lice being crushed between thumbnails. Short haircuts, shampoos, and DDT wiped out the ancient despots of the scalp.

Like soap, running water became a familiar commodity. Padre Federico's appeals to the authorities, with the help of Don Dámaso Cárdenas, at last bore fruit. In 1945 the water department of the Secretariat of Health and Welfare installed a small system. The water came from a spring (which in Mexican villages is known as *el ojo de agua*), from where it was carried downhill in an eight-inch asbestos-cement pipe to a reservoir 540 meters away. From this tank, consisting of two chambers holding forty cubic meters each, the water was distributed in galvanized-steel pipe, laid above ground, to fifteen

---

[20] Population figures are from the censuses of 1940 and 1950. Statistics for intervening years were estimated. Birth-rate figures are based on baptismal records in San José.

public faucets on street corners. One hundred and sixty citizens had it piped right into their houses.

But the dream was soon over. The system was inadequate. In the dry season only a trickle reached the village; during the rains the water, though plentiful, was contaminated.[21]

The postrevolutionary generation's eagerness for change showed in other aspects of its members' lives. First of all, they discarded the old costumes. Poor men no longer felt obliged to wear the traditional white shirt and *calzón*, and the rich abandoned the *charro* outfit. Men began wearing trousers, colored shirts, and modern jackets. Small hats or no hats at all became the fashion. People took to wearing shoes instead of huaraches. Young ladies' skirts went up and down with the fashions; their hair and make-up reflected the style of the city. The only thing they couldn't change was their mincing gait.

The second change had to do with the home. People began to spend all they could on modernization, starting with the interior. The wealthy added modern bathrooms (flush toilets, bathtubs, showers, and washbowls), equipped their kitchens with gas stoves and enamelware utensils, laid tile floors, and embellished porches, living rooms, dining rooms, and bedrooms with oil paint. New construction differed radically from traditional patterns. The typical older house had an interior garden open to the sky, an inner porch lined with potted plants, and rooms opening onto the patio. This was replaced in some cases by the compact city dwelling, with no sky, flowers, or birds inside. Thin brick walls were used instead of adobe, and the roof was supported by reinforced-concrete posts and beams. The old red-tile ridged roof gave way sometimes to a flat one of concrete. Four or five families made the unfortunate choice of building "cottages" with front yards. The poorer people who could not afford modern houses continued to erect traditional ones, but they substituted brick for adobe.

The third innovation was beautifying the town. Padre Federico distributed some three thousand ornamental trees (casuarinas and *truenos*) among the citizens of San José, to be planted along the streets. He saw to it that ash, eucalyptus, and cedars were set out along

21 Ángel Ochoa, *Informe general*, pp. 33–34.

the highway, on the road leading to the cemetery, and within the cemetery walls. He concluded his efforts at forestry by dotting the slopes of Larios Mountain with young pines. He directed the re-paving of the village streets, with two lateral gutters replacing the single central one. Padre Federico also succeeded in getting everyone to pitch in for a new façade and bell towers for the church. The design was his, and the work was done by the engineer Morfín. The construction was finished in time for the celebration on March 19, 1943.[22] The broad steps leading up to the entrance of the church and the new front door were used for the first time on that date. A little later, when Salvador Villanueva was *jefe de tenencia*, the road to the cemetery was paved.

The fourth improvement consisted in leading the populace out of barbarism by, first, suppressing the dangerous sport of celebrating high spirits or drunkenness by firing pistols and, second, trying to put an end to the custom of killing a man for an offense to one's honor. The *jefes de tenencia* during those fifteen years (Adolfo Aguilar, Salvador Villanueva, Delfino Gálvez, Luis Humberto González, Isaac Ávila, Napoleón Godínez, Gildardo González, and Antonio Villanueva) worked assiduously to reduce the number of gunfights and killings. They were assisted in this task by Don Alberto Cárdenas, commandant of the Zamora military zone, and by the garrison of soldiers who returned to the village in 1945 at the request of Salvador Villanueva and the majority of the citizens. In San José homicides dropped to one per year, but in the *rancherías*—Auchen in particular—people were still killing each other over *ejido* parcels. Between 1943 and 1955, twenty-eight farmers were shot to death, at the rate of two per year and one for every thousand inhabitants. There were three times as many killings in the outlying areas as in town.[23] "Since everybody went around wearing a pistol, people were killing each other. Many times the shooting was over nothing at all—just because they were drunk and had guns. They fought over girls, too. Three men were killed because of Carmen, whose parents wouldn't

22 According to Guillermina Sánchez.
23 AJTO, Documents from the Jefaturas of Salvador Villanueva, Delfino Gálvez, Luis Humberto González, Isaac Ávila, Gildardo González, and others.

let her get married. In Paso Real there were a lot of killings over women. Gabina was murdered out of jealousy. Jerónimo came home with two friends. When she went to get the basket of tortillas for their supper, Jerónimo pulled out his gun and said, with a laugh, 'This is the way to use a pistol.' And he killed her then and there. And just because his mother had put the idea in his head that he ought to be jealous of El Cantero, who she said had been calling on his wife. There wasn't a word of truth in it. Anyway, Jerónimo killed El Cantero one Palm Sunday. He came riding along, all unawares, and Jerónimo and some friends of his, waiting behind the stone fence on each side of the road, put a bullet in him. First they shot his horse; he was trying to get away on foot when they dropped him." San José was suffering more and more from the barbarism of the automobile. Drivers on their way to the coast were in the habit of shooting through the village streets like meteorites, scattering children and old people right and left. This savagery was a daily occurrence that the local authorities could not control.

Public education flowed in three streams: parochial, private, and governmental. Catechism was taught by the church school, which was headed by Padre Federico from 1940 to 1944, by Padre Rafael Ramírez from 1945 to 1948, and from then on by Don Pascual Villanueva. Every child in town came to learn by heart Cardinal Gasparri's catechism, which had replaced Padre Ripalda's in 1937. In 1941 Padre Federico sent for the "madres" from Zamora, who had left the village in 1933, and rebuilt and reopened "the Haven." It was operated by four nuns who taught kindergarten for children of both sexes and the first six primary grades for most of the young girls. Private elementary schooling for boys was irregular, informal, and not gratis. Enrique Villanueva, a former teacher and capitular of the Christian Brothers, taught rudiments of grammar and arithmetic to fifty boys for two or three years. Héctor Ortiz, ex-student from the Colegio de México, settled in San José at the end of 1946 and gave elementary English lessons in stores and bars to aspiring braceros. In 1948 he had about two dozen students. Meanwhile, now that the townspeople no longer felt hostile toward it, the government school was making progress. In 1938 it received a grant of five thousand pesos for a new building. It was still classified as a rural school. Señorita Josefina Barragán was a member of the faculty. A shortage of teachers and furniture made it impossible for more than two hundred children to be instructed in primary subjects. It was coeducational, but, in 1940, Leobardo Pulido, the *jefe de tenencia*, ordered "the boys and girls to be taught in separate classrooms . . . since [according to him] coeducation is bad for children."[24] It may be pointed out that the number of girls attending the government school was insignificant. It should also be mentioned that there were official schools in six of the neighboring *rancherías*, each with one teacher and a maximum of fifty students. Finally, Padre Federico made the wealthier parents send their sons away to school. Some attended the Institute of Sciences in Guadalajara, while others went to the Consolidated Seminary in Zamora; a good many entered the order of San Juan Bautista de la Salle. At least four were to go on to complete their university work years later.

Perhaps even greater than the desire for an education for oneself and one's children was the thirst for entertainment. There were more family parties, and they were more elaborate. "Modern dances, such as the waltz," which Padre Octaviano Villanueva had prohibited, became more popular than ever. The "fandangos" at the Lupe Sánchez home attracted the most distinguished lads and lassies of the region. They drank whiskey and cognac, which had recently been imported into the villages; they tried out the latest dance steps; they told jokes they had heard on the radio, at the movies, or from the out-of-town visitors who were always on hand for these soirées.[25]

Public amusements multiplied. Power provided by the hydroelectric plant at Agua Fría, although inadequate, made it possible to operate

[24] According to Daniel González Cárdenas, and AJTO, Documents from the Jefatura of Leobardo Pulido.

[25] Ingeniero Bernardo González Godínez tells me that the parish priest Rafael Ramírez reaffirmed the ruling against dancing "when the first queen was chosen for the national holiday celebration, and a dance was planned in her honor, after the coronation. Don Andrés Z. González was in charge of the festivities. In his attack on the projected ball, Padre Ramírez made some reference to the struggle between God and the Devil (*Satanás*). That was how Don Andrés came to be nicknamed 'Don Sata.' "

jukeboxes and radios. Three stores bought deafening "dime-in-the-slot" phonographs in order to delight their customers with selections by Lucha Reyes, Jorge Negrete, Tito Guízar, Emilio Tuero, and other singers of romantic songs and *rancheras*. There were plenty of movies and movie fans, too.

Padre Federico tried to maintain the traditional amusements at all costs. He devoted himself to reviving the sport of *charrería*. He organized the young men; he promoted rodeos; he petted the horses; he was pleased to see the enthusiasm with which some of the men relearned the *charro* skills of riding, roping, throwing the lasso, and fighting bulls on horseback; and he succeeded in making the *charro* exhibitions the highlight of the March fiestas.[26] Beginning in 1944, the San José rodeos drew people from miles around; this was partly because from that year on they were augmented by some distinguished members of the Mexico City Charro Association.

In crowds and excitement, the fiesta of the town's patron saint surpassed all the others. But second in popularity (and this is highly significant) was the national holiday, the Sixteenth of September. Prior to 1930 this fiesta had been unpopular and a little forced; but almost overnight it came to be greeted with jubilation. Apolinar Partida was usually in charge of the events, which included the election of a queen, a children's parade, and speeches by the director of the government school and by Ramiro Chávez, the town's greatest orator.

And yet life was not all that it might have been. In the fourteen years from 1943 to 1956 San Joséans had outdone themselves in producing children, had spent more money on their homes, and had been led into buying things they would not have thought of buying before—either because they had been unwilling to spend the money

26 In 1944 a local *charro* association was formed. According to Salvador Villanueva González, the founding members were Jesús and Juan Chávez; Guadalupe, Honorato, and Jesús González Buenrostro; Bernardo and Federico González Cárdenas; Abraham González Flores; Gregorio González Haro; Everardo González Sánchez (treasurer); Rogelio González Zepeda (secretary); Arnulfo Novoa; Anatolio and Apolinar Partida; Miguel Reyes; León and Rodolfo Sánchez; Antonio and Salvador Villanueva (president). Later there was a schism in the group, but the Michoacán Charro Association was not dissolved. It still exists. It was responsible for the construction of the bullring and the *lienzo charro*, and has usually been in charge of the secular festivities during the celebration of the town's patron saint's day.

or because they had not known these things existed. Now they took "tours" and went in for expensive entertainment. They were no longer satisfied to own very little, or to live simply, or to put up with hardships, privation, and the uncertainties of crops and markets. They felt the attractions of the city, and they did their best to urbanize their community by beautifying and modernizing it; but it was not enough. Many people felt that the town could never be as attractive as the city and the outside world. Money, comfort, and exotic pleasures were now within the reach of everyone. As a result, people moved away; for many of them it was like being set free.

After 1943 San José and its district progressed internally, but not at the rate demanded by the explosions of population, necessities, and spending. Only a small number of its inhabitants stuck to their guns; very few believed that they could attain their new goals without outside help. Many people left for a time, "to see what they could bring back from out there." Many more went away forever.

Seasonal Migration to the United States

Prior to the end of the Second World War, very few people from San José went to the United States as braceros; but, after 1945, when they were no longer worried about being "hooked" by the army, there was an increase in short-term emigration. In the five years between 1946 and 1950 no less than sixty workers went north every year. After 1951 the figure tripled and remained high until 1956. Some years more than two hundred men obtained contracts—20 percent of all males of working age. After the highway was completed, many had found themselves unemployed and accustomed to higher salaries than those they could earn at home.

We can describe the migrants as follows. The great majority were under forty when they signed up for the first time. At the beginning most of them were from the village; later it was the men from the rancherías who predominated. In the early years, the larger part were young men of the middle and upper classes; but, as time went on, most of them were poorer people. Needless to say, the migrants' cultural level was low. They knew no English, of course, in spite of having attended Héctor Ortiz's classes just before they left. It is interesting to note that many of the men who did not have the rough, scaly hands of laborers put them in lye or abused them in some way in order to give that appearance. A large percentage of them were unemployed, although some left full-time jobs to embark upon the great adventure.

Many who left the *tenencia* of San José to go to the United States as braceros did so, by their own testimony, because they hoped to bring home enough money to start them on the road to riches. Some were tired of begging for work from door to door, in vain; some were no longer willing to put up with want and miserable wages; some, who had been working their small plots of land, wanted to be able to stop worrying about bad weather and puny crops; a large group, among them sons of the well-to-do families, were eager to have adventures, to see new lands, to measure themselves against the gringos, to have a pleasure trip, and, in passing, to free themselves from their parents' tutelage. They were able to behave like prodigal sons without risking disaster.

The chief worry of the poor men was raising the money for the trip and, above all, for the services of the "coyote" (the labor contractor). Hardly a man among them had enough money saved to pay his way to the contracting centers—the capital or Empalme—much less to pay the labor contractors a thousand or fifteen hundred pesos in bribes to get a job. Some sold their animals or their land. Most got the money from loan sharks. There were two or three of those in San José, and usually the sum had to be repaid to them twofold at the end of six months. The migrants, confident that the high wages in the "Yunaites" would take care of everything, went into debt in this way with no fear or trembling—or, at most, they trembled with gratitude. All they wanted was to get away; they had no particular desire to "work for the victory of democracy," as people were saying in high political circles.[27]

Men were signed up without their families, and not always exactly

---

[27] In addition to what I have seen myself, I have heard accounts of their experiences from braceros. Other data are from the files in the *jefatura de tenencia* of Ornelas. There, for example, can be found lists of the migrant workers who went north each year.

according to the terms of the 1942 agreement: "Mexican workers shall be paid the same wages" as the Americans. "All costs of transportation, food, lodging, etc. . . . during the round trip will be paid by the employers. As for occupational illnesses, accidents while working, medical attention, and health services, they shall enjoy the same rights accorded the American workers under the laws of that country. They shall be assured employment for at least 75 percent of the period stipulated in their contracts, and shall not be victims of any discrimination."[28] These provisions were only partially complied with, but always to a greater degree than were most provisions of labor legislation in Mexico. Thus, the migrants, instead of feeling cheated by the derelict gringos, thought they were being treated like kings.

Their destinations were not the most attractive in the country; they were usually in the south instead of in the north, in the country instead of in the city, and in areas where wages were low and the climate was severe. They were the sites of ancient slavery and lawlessness. The braceros liked it except in the winter; when December approached they returned in droves to San José and the *rancherías*. After all, they were not used to freezing temperatures. Besides, they had not been eating enough; trying to keep their expenses down, they had spent no more than a dollar for their three daily meals. They had been cooking for themselves—badly and too little. Besides, they had been living in areas where there was not much to choose from in the way of food, and—in short—where they found few of the comforts of home. Until the cold months came, they had been able to sleep fairly comfortably in the huge sheds set aside for dormitories.

Perhaps it was because they demanded little in the way of comfort; perhaps it was because of the amendments of 1943, 1948, 1949, 1951, and 1956 to the 1942 agreement; perhaps it was because the governments of Mexico and the United States showed a growing interest in enforcing the terms of the agreement; perhaps it was because of the attraction of suddenly earning ten times as much as they could at home. In any case, the braceros from San José rarely felt that they were badly fed or housed. Very few of them thought the work was too hard; and later some would recall with pleasure

[28] Durán Ochoa, *Estructura económica y social*, pp. 176–177.

the good times they had in the recreation halls, on the playing fields, and in the bars and whorehouses. The inconvenience of not being able to communicate with their employers and the hazardous nature of some of the jobs were balanced by the fact that they enjoyed some guarantees they had never known—such as accident, health, and life insurance.

The braceros worked principally at picking cotton, tomatoes, lemons, apples, olives, and other farm products in California, Texas, Arkansas, and in most of the states in the west and the south. Very few got a chance to work on dairy farms or cattle ranches, much less in industry. Generally, the man who succeeded in avoiding field work had made an illegal contract. They labored like ants on the vast Yankee farms, engaged in purely physical toil, not seeing or knowing anything of the overall picture. They were like mere harvesting machines. Nearly all of them sent home goodly sums of money— either to be saved, or for the support of their families.[29]

The economic results of this venture were varied. Local farm production did not suffer from the loss of the braceros. Those who stayed behind every year were more than were needed to tend the corn- fields and the livestock. The emigrants earned good hard dollars; and if a few left every penny in bars, stores, and whorehouses, the vast majority brought their money home to their village or farm. Up north the average bracero was able to live on one dollar and save nine. During his first three-month period he was able to save a considerable sum, to be used at home for buying cows or pigs, making a down pay- ment on a piece of land, buying a house, contracting to buy a car or pickup on time, moving his family out of San José, drinking with his friends, going on binges, opening a shop of some kind or a little store or a barber shop, gambling, playing the tourist, or supporting himself until he could go north again, with enough money left for the trip and the bribes he would have to pay.

There were other evidences besides the economic ones. Many men showed that they had been braceros by their loud shirts and jackets,

[29] It can be roughly estimated that between 1948 and 1960 each bracero was able to save from eight to ten thousand pesos for every year he spent in the United States.

their cowboy boots, their gringo swearwords, their rolled hat brims, their radios, their repertoire of stories brought back from the north, their admiration for the way people spent money up there, and their pretentiousness. Almost all of them came back unwilling to work for the traditional wages paid in San José, and many proved it by starting independent businesses, or becoming vagrants, or going back to live permanently in the United States, or moving to Mexico City. They did not come back *pochos*; hardly any of the culture or customs of their American cousins stuck to them—neither language, nor habits of sanitation, nor gestures, nor attitudes. Nor did they bring back any new ideas that might have been useful to them at home. They returned with their souls untouched—or nearly so.

When everything is added up, it turns out that the bracero program took more than it gave. Many San Joséans never came home again; and some are sorely missed. One of these is Ramiro Chávez, who had always been the secretary of the *jefatura de tenencia*. He was the son of the artisan Narciso Chávez, a man of many talents. Ramiro and Apolinar Partida introduced the Sixteenth of September celebration, and other patriotic events. Ramiro spoke English, as did Apolinar; he directed and acted in plays, did wonderful and artistic wood carving, was an amateur archaeologist, collected birds and butterflies, took an interest in statistics and history and, in general, every sort of activity, art, and science. He was a unique member of the uprooted generation, those born on the eve of the revolution. In 1956 or 1957 Ramiro Chávez crossed the border, and he never returned.

Some of those who had traveled—temporary emigrants, tourists, or braceros (but mostly braceros)—came back determined to leave their native heath for good. A few wanted to return to the United States, but most felt the pull of Mexico's capital. "La Borrachita" came back into style, along with "Canción Mixteca." Leaving the land where one was born produced a flood of tears, reproaches, and some envy, and there was a permanent popular argument over the relative advantages of staying home and of moving to Mexico City. The polemic began about 1940 and is still going on. On one side are the men who are old or comfortably fixed; on the other side the women and the younger men.

The Permanent Move to Mexico City

In their sermons against moving to Mexico City, the old people and the well-to-do advance many arguments:

Better a known evil than an unknown good.

In the city everybody's in a hurry, and they live on top of each other.

Children and women fall into evil ways.

You can't get anything good to eat. They put water and tallow in the milk and inject things into the eggs.

Men live like slaves in the city.

All you get from the pleasures of the capital are diseases like syphilis.

With all that smoke from the factories, you can't even breathe.

People die suddenly, without a chance to confess.

All the enemies of the body and soul are gathered in the city.

You spend it as fast as you make it.

Some people are happy, but others are so miserable they commit suicide.

Why go to all that trouble? Where can you go to escape death?

Young people, eager to leave, support their view with just as many arguments:

People don't have to work so hard—especially women.

You can't have any fun here.

It's easier to make money in Mexico City.

Almost everybody who's gone to the city has done well.

If a man lives carefully, he can make a fortune.

Living in the country is no life at all.

There's a man here I've got to kill; if I leave I won't have to do it.

I had a run-in with so-and-so. I'd rather have people say, "He ran away," than "They buried him here."

I'm tired of putting up with bad weather that comes along and ruins the crops.

I can't stand it here any longer; I'm getting out.

I want my children to have a good education, and Mexico City has the best schools.

The plaza of San José de García, with the village offices at the right (photo by John Upton)

Don Gregorio González Pulido, another of the village founders

Don Andrés González Pulido, a leader in the founding of San José in 1888

A group of *cristeros* with their spiritual leader, Padre Federico González Cárdenas (*middle row, third from left*)

Don Juan Gudiño, *cristero*

Don Guadalupe González Buenrostro, businessman and rancher

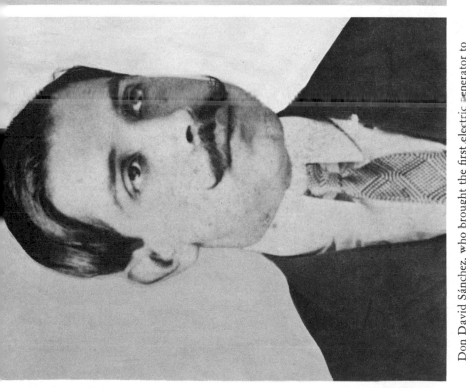

Don David Sánchez, who brought the first electric generator to San José

Don José Martínez, a wealthy landowner, and his wife

Don Honorato González Buenrostro in his *charro* costume

The kitchen of Doña Inés Betancourt

Traditional house with interior garden

Modern house of a businessman, with a large exterior garden

Farmers at the entrance to the village offices

The parish church of San José de Gracia, facing the plaza

Doña Rosa González Cárdenas, an active force in village improvements

General Lázaro Cárdenas, president of the republic, during a visit to San José

Partial view of the José María Morelos primary school

Padre Federico González Cárdenas

Don Agustín Arriaga Rivera, governor of Michoacán,
during a visit to San José

Street scene in the village

When almost everybody in our family is in Mexico City, why should we stay here?

Nobody likes me here. I'm leaving.

Between 1941 and 1960 there were 614 permanent emigrants from the *tenencia* of Ornelas; since 1961 at least 300 more have left. Before the middle of the century the great majority of them were from the village itself, but during the next seventeen years it was the farms that spewed out the most people. Some of the farmers got only as far as the village, but many moved on to the capital or toward the United States. The largest *rancherías* lost population most rapidly: San Pedro, San Miguel, Sabino, La Rosa, Paso Real, Ojo de Rana, Breña, and Auchen. Except for San Pedro, they all had *ejidos*; but the *ejidos* were in a state of hopeless stagnation.

Not every *ejido* community had the same experience, but the small differences between them do not invalidate the following conclusions. Most able-bodied men in an *ejido* community had no land of their own. Men who did own land either planted it, leased it for pasture, or sold it to some local political boss. Some *ejidos* were left in the hands of only two or three individuals—who surely could not complain about their lot. *Ejido* members who worked no other land than their assigned parcels could by great effort make a living in good, wet years—which were not common. Their parcels could not produce enough to provide the most basic necessities, much less provide them with the capital for increasing production. If they remained within the *ejido* they had no chance to get ahead; they were doomed to remain poor, and they were convinced that wealth was not something that grew, but something that had to be snatched from someone else. Many men could not even remain in the community. Some had quarreled with their associates; some were not suited to communal projects; some boasted that "nobody was going to order them around," and when anyone tried to do so he ended by being shot to death, or badly wounded, or, at best, he had to listen to some remarks concerning his mother.

There were, of course, many factors in the emigration picture: problems brought about by population pressure upon available resources, the influence of those who had already moved to the city, the universal urge to improve one's social position. Every man's mind is a world apart; some left for one reason, some for another. But nearly everyone was ready to make the move.

Those with the shallowest roots—the young, the landless, the people with no fixed occupation—were most eager to leave. There were many young men from fifteen to twenty-five, most of them unmarried, unskilled, and unemployed; they were in their most productive years, but there was no one to hire them. Some were boys filled with ambition, and some were merely looking for fun. Only a very few had had any experience—as blacksmiths or carpenters, for example—or had gone through elementary school. Most had no trade and were illiterate, ready to work at anything, anywhere, and, for the moment at any rate, for any wages people cared to pay them. Once they "got to Mexico City," they would try to improve their working conditions: do less or earn more.

Also among the emigrants were small landowners and *ejido* members, with from six to twenty-five hectares of land for their own use, a cornfield, a team of oxen, and from two to a dozen milch cows. Some sold their cattle and land before they left, and often even their houses. They would use the money to set themselves up in some small enterprise in the capital, as the merchants had who left the village when business had fallen off. Most of the exiles aspired to go into trade, although there were some who went away to become entertainers. "La Rosa Michoacana," "Los Oros," and the "Mariachi México" made a go of it.

From 1941 on, an average of thirty people left San José and its environs every year; men, women, and entire families went to the big cities to live better, or worse, or at any rate in a different way. Usually it was the man who went first, with the hope that he would soon be able to send for his wife and "the brood." While some were leaving, others were getting ready to leave. Almost all of them had relatives in the city, or someone who would help them get started: Renato Roura, Amelia Aguilar's husband, was the head of La Ciudad Deportiva; Gildardo and Honorato González could get people jobs in the Rastro or Merced markets; others who could help were José Castillo,

Ezequiel González Pulido and his sons, Jesús Valdovinos, Don Francisco and Don Jesús Partida (the first arrivals), and many more.

Three-quarters of those who have left during the past twenty-five years now live in Mexico City; one out of every ten lives in the United States, usually in Los Angeles; some are distributed among the border towns of Matamoros, Mexicali, and Tijuana; the rest are in Acapulco or scattered among neighboring cities in Michoacán and Jalisco: Zamora, Uruapan, Apatzingán, Tangancícuaro, San Pedro Caro, Tizapán, Chapala, and, above all, Guadalajara. Naturally, most of those in Mexico City and Los Angeles live in the suburbs. The former are residents of Nueva Atzacualco or some other quarter where the streets are either muddy or dusty, or they live in rundown, dirty buildings near the Merced market, or they have modest houses in Colonia Balbuena. There are some, of course, who are lucky enough to live in more pretentious areas: San Rafael, Viaducto-Piedad, Villa de Cortés, Marte, Navarte, Ciudad Jardín, Lindavista, Tacuba, and Atzcapotzalco. And two or three are to be found in Lomas de Chapultepec, among the upper crust.

Those who went to Mexico City got jobs in the Merced market area, working for the Federal District. Many went to work in stores in different parts of the city; others became manual laborers. The La Azteca chocolate factory hired many women from San José who preferred not to work as servants. Few women went to work as domestics, and when they did they usually worked only in the houses of people from San José. Only a very small number of young men went to the city to study; after becoming lawyers, engineers, or teachers, they usually forgot their native village, although they might visit it occasionally. A large group of exiles was made up of members of the religious teaching orders employed in various private schools. Thus, the emigrants went into all kinds of work. No less than twenty heads of families have made fortunes, and half of these have cooperated in the improvement of their native village by investing money there and making donations for public works.

The authentic "emigrants"—those who went to live in the United States—have reached a total of about eighty during the past few years. In Chicago there are two or three descendants of the original emigrants of 1923, and they all have huge families. The most numerous are those who went north after 1950. Of these, the most important group is the one in Los Angeles, whose members are killing themselves working in a dog-food factory. They live in the poorest wooden houses. They can barely get by, if they have their families with them, on the twenty or thirty dollars a day they earn. If they live alone they can save something, support their families in San José, and make preparations for going home. Only a tiny fraction of those who are now in the United States intend to spend the rest of their lives there; most hope to save a little money and go into some good business back in their home town. There are others, working on cattle ranches, who are accumulating not only dollars but also knowledge they will use later to improve production in their native area. Nearly all of them return to the village for two or three weeks every year, and nearly all swear that they are coming home for good the following year. Although they make good money up north, and there are many things to buy and a lot of things to see, they say they are not happy; the gringos don't like Mexicans, they insult them and treat them as inferiors.

Some of those who went north to live or to spend some time returned against their will. They had crossed the river illegally under cover of darkness; they were "wetbacks," who had been picked up by the *chota*. Others who sneaked across expect to be deported at any time. Most of the exiles look forward to coming home, willingly or unwillingly. Here I do not refer only to those in the "Yunaites." There are many Mexicans scattered about their own country who are dying to get back to their native villages.

Not all of them remained in the cities. Many people did not like living in the capital. They came back convinced that the fields of home were the best and the most livable in the world. One man changed his mind because he loved to hunt; in the city it was impossible—unless you counted hunting pedestrians with an automobile. Another returned because the food in Mexico City was nothing but "slop"; another because he was old and sick, and, "If you want to die in peace, the best place is where you were born."

8. FROM YESTERDAY TO TODAY (1957–1967)

Priority of the Economic Factor

Don Adolfo Ruiz Cortines assumed the presidency when he was in his sixties, with the kind of background that would not allow him to let himself or the country run wild. In his youth, as accountant, paymaster, and public official, he had learned to be careful with money. He built huge dams and many kilometers of highways, but these were not the most characteristic acts of his regime. People said that it was because he was born in a port town that he devoted so much energy to his maritime development program. He concerned himself principally with modest and immediate needs. He was the president of the family and of the *municipio*. Municipal projects were his specialty: slum clearance, water supply, Mexico City's flood control, paving streets, and building markets and hospitals. He was concerned with the home: he fought high prices; he worked for better schools, for emancipation and the vote for women, for more and better consumer goods; and he introduced the Christmas bonus for employees. He was the president of López Velarde's beloved fatherland, the advocate of village aviculture; the promoter of moral, civic, and material improvement in towns and on farms; the tutor and patriarch of braceros. Like General Cárdenas, he was the president of the underdog, but without oratory or loudspeakers. Think of Cárdenas without Luis I. Rodríguez and all the brave splendor of that regime. Don Adolfo (or whoever it was) decided that his successor should be a man of the opposite type: a college professor, public speaker, alpinist, a man accustomed to the contemplation of broad horizons, whose *zócalo* was the mountain, and, ultimately, the nation. Ruiz Cortines handed over the sash and the rest of the presidential apparatus on December 1, 1958.

Professor Don Adolfo López Mateos resumed the blaring marches. He created a multiparty congress. He called in seven ex-presidents to work with him. In his messages to Congress he gave his views on self-determination and nonintervention in the life of the villages, on peace, democracy, the meaning of the Mexican revolution, total agrarian reform, "stability and progress," and "liberty and justice." He tried to set the world straight. He preached peace in the United States, South America, Europe, and Asia, and he was host to some twenty heads of state. He issued "joint declarations." He did everything in a big way. He built double-width highways; to the roll of drums he announced the nationalization of the electric-power industry, and he ordered the construction of great hydroelectric plants. He inaugurated dazzling art and history museums. The diffusion of a national, nationalistic, and technical culture was spurred by an eleven-year plan to wipe out illiteracy, by a commission to distribute free textbooks with a liberal hand, by work-training centers, and by public celebrations of sesquicentennial, centennial, and semicentennial anniversaries of the great moments in Mexico's history. The INPI (Instituto Nacional de Protección a la Infancia) distributed medicines and millions of breakfasts; the National Housing Institute and other agencies built sumptuous and comfortable cities within cities. It was forgotten that we are poor; the people who were living without material comforts were forgotten. No one noticed that the bracero situation was deteriorating. The revolution got down from its horse; it got into the automobile and raced away, leaving the slow-moving country people behind. Tough luck, peasants. The institutions set up by Ruiz Cortines for aid to small communities languished.

Michoacán lived through two state governments. The administration of David Franco Rodríguez (1956–1962) continued in the direction pointed out by General Dámaso Cárdenas; it undertook public works and built roads and schools. It was remarkable for the financial aid it lent to the University of Michoacán. It promoted programs for moral and material betterment. It made the most of the state's meager budget. It was a constructive regime.[1] Agustín Arriaga Rivera's government (1962–1968) aspired to reach everybody. Of its educational efforts, only the difficulties with the university in Morelia were heard about—and not the hundred thousand farm children it brought into the school system, or the doubling of the number of teachers, or the 600 percent increase in secondary technical schools. His administration disseminated information on new methods of farming and cattle raising; it built dams and planted trees. Communications leaped ahead, with telephones and good roads to facilitate commerce and encourage tourism. Electric power was brought to 250,000 people in small towns in Michoacán. Many municipal governments and minor officials— such as *jefes de tenencias*—were caught up in this dynamic program.

In the Ornelas *tenencia* the *jefes* were Bernardo González Cárdenas (1956–1958 and 1963–1965), Jorge Sánchez (1960), Rigoberto Novoa (1961), Bernardo González Godínez (1962), and Elías Elizondo (after 1966). The first of these *jefes* served the town with the same energy he had put into building his own dairy farm. By means of special taxes, public entertainments, and fines he collected enough money to provide San José with an attractive building for the *jefatura de tenencia* and other governmental offices, a cemetery surrounded by a stone wall, and an all-year drinking water system. He extended the sewer lines, built barracks for the military post, ordered citizens to sweep the street in front of their houses once a day, and encouraged people to keep their homes in good condition—especially those that faced the town square.[2] San José had never had such an active administrator. Don Bernardo was extraordinarily hard-working and exacting; in the latter, however, he was surpassed by his nephew.

Ingeniero Bernardo González Godínez was determined to keep the village immaculate, to suppress drunkenness, to enforce rigorously

1 José Bravo Ugarte, *Historia sucinta de Michoacán*, III, 229.

2 AJTO, Documents from the Administrations of Bernardo González Cárdenas, Jorge Sánchez González, and Bernardo González Godínez.

the basic municipal code laid down by Franco Rodríguez, and, in short, to make San José de Gracia a community with all the conveniences and none of the defects of a city. He closed twenty-seven bars; he forced businessmen to pay municipal taxes; he succeeded in having the *juzgado menor* reopened; and he refused to argue with merchants and saloonkeepers. He was able to stand the job for only six months. He left ten thousand pesos in the treasury. Like his uncle, he didn't mind when people called him "Uruchurtu."[3]

Elías Elizondo has tried not to gain the reputation of a tyrant, although he did not raise the money to build the school simply by being easygoing. All three *jefes* have been severely criticized by the townspeople, although each one has merely tried to achieve what everyone wants: the urbanization of the village. In any case, this attitude on the part of the villagers reveals an uncommonly ferocious individualism, along with some other characteristics of the new trend among human beings.

The generation born between 1920 and 1934 seems to be quite different from all the previous ones. It has less power, because most of its members have moved away. In 1960 its members made up only a fifth of the population. They are equal numerically to the generation they are trying to displace, but they are not as well-off. They are weak and ambitious. They want to move too fast. They show little respect for tradition. They want to be famous, and they are slaves to a mania for mechanical devices and money. There seems to be no limit to their individualism. They have seen more of the world than their elders. They recognize no authority—neither patriarchal, nor civil, nor that of Padre Federico. They are rebels in attitude, but not in deed. Older people say they are "nothing but talk," quick to criticize things but incapable of doing anything about them. And yet some of them have achieved a great deal—although principally for themselves and only secondarily for others. There are a couple of highly competent professional men among them; some are dynamic businessmen and enthusiastic political leaders. Among the last are one or two women.

---

[3] Ingeniero Bernardo González Godínez said, "I quit because it was the kind of job I didn't like; besides, I had done the essential things."

Not all the changes that have taken place in the area since 1957 can be credited to the faultfinding generation. They have not yet had a chance to do much. Padre Federico, now in his seventies, is still the principal agent of progress in the community. After him comes Don Bernardo González Cárdenas. In third place are the young men of the unruly generation, who bring in good ideas on economic development and household comforts. All of them together, with some outside help, are bringing about the transformation of their native village—although less radically than in the previous fifteen-year period and more in the direction of economic greed and personal profit.

The local census of 1957 recorded 11,950 head of cattle; of these, 3,615 were dairy animals, producing a daily average of 10,232 liters of milk, or more than 3 million liters a year. At least 50 percent of this was made into cheese, with smaller amounts of cream, butter, and ricotta, and taken to market in Mexico City—less and less profitably. During the fifties cattle raising and the local milk industry faced several problems: the drought of 1949–1953, a drop in productivity, and competition from city factories, "some of which manufacture the so-called filled cheeses from powdered skim milk, vegetable butter, and potato starch, while others make use of reclaimed decomposed products."[4] And, as if the makers of this bad cheese needed further protection, the Secretariat of Public Health on several occasions prohibited the sale of good cheeses, on the grounds that they were not made from pasteurized milk. The dairy industry had never experienced such a crisis; nor had there ever been proposed more and better measures to assure its survival and expansion.

In his thesis on rural industrialization of milk by-products, Bernardo González Godínez suggested as a general solution "the total utilization" of dairy products, "the formation of an association to solve . . . the problems," and, more concretely, the construction of a couple of factories. One would be for making "one or several types of cheese and butter," and the other would extract the residual lactic acid from the whey; since there was a good demand for this product, it

[4] Bernardo González Godínez, "Industrialización de los subproductos lácteos regionales," p. 14.

"should be very profitable." He presented a detailed plan for this second plant. He also asserted that once it was in operation "it would be a simple matter to extract other products . . . by merely adding other small pieces of equipment to modify the process." Finally, he showed how easy it would be to put this plan into effect by setting up a cooperative.[5]

The Secretariat of Public Health and UNICEF had other suggestions. The former recommended installing a pasteurizing plant. The latter had a much more attractive idea: build a factory for making powdered skim milk. In addition, UNICEF offered to furnish all the machinery, which would cost half a million dollars. It would top off its gift by sending a pair of experts to instruct the farmers in modern methods of increasing milk production and improving cattle feed. The Mexican government promised to cooperate with UNICEF's technical-assistance program. The authorities agreed to set the pasteurization process in motion. After some discussion, it was decided that the best location would be Jiquilpan.

Of the three proposals, the dairymen favored the solution offered by UNICEF and the Mexican government. A ranchers' association was formed; the factory was built; the machinery promised by the organization to aid undernourished children arrived; and a couple of advisers appeared. They made a careful study of the region's potentialities and explained what could be done to increase milk production within a short time. Two local chemical engineers were put in charge of the machinery. The Secretariat of Public Health sent a manager—and that was when the trouble began. The enterprise died a few months after it was born. But, even so, the dairy farmers of San José got some good out of the brave experiment. They learned the lessons the experts had taught them; they put some of them into practice, and milk production rose.

Since 1956 modernization on the dairy farms has consisted mostly of improving the breed, butchering the yearling calves, milking twice a day, building silos, using green corn for silage, increasing the feed during the long dry season, using more vaccines and medication, and

5 Ibid., pp. 15–16 and 181.

other such refinements. In spite of the fact that scientific procedures were adopted slowly and erratically, milk production doubled within a decade. Although the price of milk did not rise as fast as that of feed and consumer goods, the dairy business enjoyed a modest prosperity. The beginning of this period coincided with the increase in poultry raising. The years 1957 and 1958 brought good times to some two hundred families engaged in dairying and farming.

Ruiz Cortines's campaign to build the poultry industry had its effects in San José. The young parish priest Pascual Villanueva was the pioneer; he built the first chicken house in 1956, and many citizens followed his example—particularly younger people. The egg market was good at the time, and suppliers of baby chicks and feed were ready to help the chicken farmers get started. No less than fifty of them set to work erecting chicken houses with good light and ventilation, tile roofs, cement floors, chicken wire on the windows, and whitewashed walls of adobe or brick. They built long sheds equipped with drinking fountains, feeders, laying platforms (or sometimes cages), and they filled them with selected chicks. The pullets and hens were inoculated and fed in accordance with scientific principles.

By 1958 there were seventy-five such chicken houses and more than 200,000 laying hens. Every week their owners sent off 3,500 or 4,000 cases of eggs to Mexico City. Poultry production that year amounted to 27 million pesos, with a profit of nearly nine million directly benefiting a hundred families.[6] There was great jubilation in the town and the surrounding hamlets. Many people were in the process of building chicken houses of their own when the blow fell. The price of eggs dropped. Most of the poultry farmers, who were loaded with debts, suddenly found themselves wiped out; they lost their homes, their equipment, and their chickens. The rumor was that Doña Eva, President López Mateos's wife, was to blame for the disaster, because she had imported enormous quantities of eggs from the United States for the schoolchildren's breakfasts that were to make her famous. Everyone furiously denounced the First Lady for engaging in

---

[6] I have Pascual Villanueva to thank for these figures.

"smuggling." Poultrymen went to the capital to ask the government for protection, but it was all in vain. Nobody was going to let mere farmers interfere with the exalted matters of politics. The San Joséans could not comprehend why their country had to feed children eggs from the United States, nor did they understand that in those days it was more important to restore harmony between the two nations than to worry about the price of eggs. The chicken farmers were told to "go bother somebody else."

San Joséans were hounded by bad luck during the six years between 1958 and 1964. We have seen what happened to the poultry raisers. On three occasions the cheese manufacturers were accused of poisoning the city, and they were hard put to prove that the poisoners were actually in Mexico City. Those who hoped to become braceros saw the institution dying out. Recent contracts with the gringo growers had been so unfavorable that workers could not earn enough even to pay their transportation. Those who aspired to a parcel of *ejido* land spent the little they had earned running back and forth from one government office to another. The officials wouldn't say no, but they wouldn't say yes, either. "They gave us the run-around." "Things began to get better with President Díaz Ordaz and Governor Arriaga Rivera," according to people with money. For people without money, nothing changed very much—except that "they didn't lie to us as much."

Health, Water, Electricity, Education,
Telephones, and Television

The introduction of new practices in personal hygiene, preventive medicine, and modern therapeutics began thirty years ago, but these have been accelerated in the past decade. There has been a resident doctor since 1953. Daniel Ruiz, who was born in Chicago and had studied at the University of Michoacán, served his social service in San José in 1961; upon receiving his license he returned to the village to live. In a short time he had wiped out the quacks, discouraged belief in miraculous cures, and brought in modern medical apparatus. In 1965 he opened a small, well-equipped hospital, with its own laboratory and pharmacy.

People began to discard the old, traditional remedies: the *cordón de San Blas* for throat trouble, the *bálsamo de Fierabante*, the *bálsamo magistral* for rheumatism and skin diseases, poultices, plasters, foul-smelling ointments, palm branches that had been blessed, chicken fat, infusions made from a thousand different herbs, lime, lye, and salt for stomach disorders, the prayers to St. George, the belief that "the bark protects the tree." Privies were built for many houses that had never had them. The well-to-do installed "English toilets" and shower baths. Gas stoves appeared in the kitchens. Stone or tile floors were installed in many houses. People began taking the precaution of boiling doubtful drinking water.

Sanitation started in the house and overflowed into the street. A sewer system had been put in when Luis Humberto González was *jefe de tenencia*. Cleaning up the village became everybody's principal concern. Water, which had always been plentiful, began to be in short supply, because almost overnight many people began taking baths regularly. The water shortage became critical during the dry months. Padre Federico used all his influence to get the government to help, and all the authorities, from the secretary of water resources down, promised to solve the problem as soon as possible. Once they sent a crew with a huge well-drilling machine. It stood there for several months, but the operators did little or nothing with it. In his report, the governor referred to the project of supplying San José with water as though it had been completed.

At last Don Alfredo del Mazo, the secretary of water resources appointed by López Mateos, disillusioned the petitioning committee. "Stop fooling yourselves," he said. "The government can't help you." Then the two men named Bernardo González—uncle and nephew— came to the village council with a simple solution: "Let everybody who wants water contribute three hundred pesos, and we'll drill our own well." Don Bernardo González Cárdenas took upon his shoulders the task of raising the money, with the blessings of most of the wealthy citizens and against the will of a grumbling minority. A deep well was sunk, and on March 19, 1965, water was brought up at the rate of twenty-four liters a second. The dry-season water shortage was no longer a problem. It was not possible to put in new water mains or bring running water to every house, but the principal goal had been attained.[7]

In 1951 the town found itself without electricity, although not without radios. The Agua Fría hydroelectric plant had been selling power right and left, until there came a time when the lights were more like glowing embers than incandescent bulbs. It finally got so bad that people had to burn candles to reinforce the electric lamps. As the illumination dwindled, public indignation rose. The owners of the power plant did not wait to be lynched; they took down their wires and fled. People went back to using paraffin candles, oil lamps, and gasoline lanterns. Padre Federico set to work to get electricity for San José. Don Dámaso Cárdenas, the governor, sent the town a large, expensive power generator that had been lying unused in some city in Michoacán. An engineer was sent to operate it, but he was unable to make it work.

As the generator rusted, Padre Federico continued his efforts to get electric power. At last, after a fifteen-year struggle, he succeeded. The authorities asked for financial assistance from the village. Don Federico established quotas for the wealthiest families; between the residents and the native sons who lived out of town, he was able to collect the necessary 150,000 pesos. The villagers were astonished to see the government keep its word. Poles were erected and wires strung. Seventy percent of the citizens signed up for service. On March 18, 1965, the governor arrived to inaugurate the new system. People flocked in from the ranches and hamlets, and the plaza was filled to overflowing for the ceremony. At eight o'clock that evening Licenciado Arriaga pushed the switch, and strings of light bulbs blazed amid applause and *dianas* from the band. No previous March 19 fiesta—in celebration of San José's founding—had ever been as grand as the one that took place the following evening.

The governor saw that there was another serious deficiency in the area: not enough teachers, and an inadequate school building. The

---

[7] When Don Alfredo del Mazo learned of the villagers' plans for supplying themselves with drinking water, he had the Secretariat of Water Resources send technical advisers to assist in the project.

government school had been dragging itself feebly along for some time. There had never been very many students, and in 1956 attendance had fallen to a new low—perhaps because the parish priest took a notion to disparage the school. In one of his Sunday sermons he said: "Parents who send their children to the government school have a heavy load on their consciences. Take them out, before it's too late. It's better for them to learn nothing at all than to be corrupted by the government." In 1960 he had to drop his unfriendly attitude, for Daniel González Cárdenas—a local boy whom no one could suspect of heresy—was named director of the school. Attendance increased; in 1961 there were 394 pupils enrolled—one-third of all children of school age. Now there were not enough classrooms, and there was an excessive teaching load for the four teachers. Besides being too small, the schoolhouse had no doors, no drinking water, and insufficient furniture. Its playground was "a yard that was mud during the rains and dust in the dry season."[8]

The state authorities asked the town's cooperation in providing a new school building. The federal government and the state would each put up a third of the cost, and San José would supply the rest. The citizens handed over their share—although not with the same enthusiasm as in the case of the electric lights—and construction began, on a 10,000-square-meter lot. The inauguration was set for March 19, 1968. Its twelve classrooms would accommodate half of San José's children of primary school age. The other half would not be deprived of education; there were the nuns, who had been teaching for twenty-five years, and there was the "Libertad" school, which Padre Federico had started at the beginning of 1966. Both were private and semigratuitous. In 1967 a fourth was added: a secondary school headed by Miguel Homero Rodríguez, who was also to be principal of the government primary school. Education has received an unprecedented impulse in the past few years; but, as we shall see, it is still not adequate.

The people of San José often remark that "the town has never gone through so many changes and been given so many advantages as it has in the past few years." That is true. Another unexpected boon,

[8] This information from Daniel González Cárdenas, the school's director.

the telephone, appeared in 1966. The jubilant populace gathered en masse for the formal inauguration of the telephone line. Once more, schoolchildren waved their little flags and adults applauded—this time for the instrument that would enable the villagers to contact their relatives in the city. For parents, neither letters nor telegrams were adequate as a means of sharing in the lives of their children in Mexico City, Guadalajara, or Los Angeles. "If you're in any kind of trouble, there's nothing like the telephone." "All you have to do is talk, and you're there." "Let me talk to so-and-so." "How's everybody? You hardly ever write these days. Be sure to come for the fiesta, and bring the kids. As you can see, we're getting very modern here; we have lights now, and telephones, and lots of television sets."

As soon as the power lines were up, the merchants from Sahuayo and Zamora came to sell television sets on time. Aside from a few old people who were "not interested in such things," and many poor families (who couldn't see "any way to get hold of one of the gadgets," and for the time being had to get along with the radio somebody or other had brought back from the United States), everybody bought one. Since then, even the devout have stopped going to Rosary; it is as though they can't hear the church bells.

Padre Esquivel, convinced that soon people would no longer pay any attention to the bells, bought a public address system to announce church services. Then the *tenencia* office bought one, and so did the movie theater. At all hours of the day and evening all three tried to make themselves heard above the noise of the automobiles, the radios, the televisions, and the sound trucks with loudspeakers mounted on top advertising miraculous medicines, artifacts for the home, and clothing. Since 1965 all the racket of modern mechanism has reached San José. There is even a plane going over twice a day. "They say it's the jet from Guadalajara to Acapulco." Some people, however, think it's the Mexico City–Puerto Vallarta flight.

Many San Joséans thought that there would be less traffic on the Jiquilpan-Manzanillo highway as soon as the new one built by Governor Agustín Yáñez across the Sayula and Zapotlán valleys was opened. The stream of tourists on their way from Guadalajara to the coast dwindled, but more trucks, loaded with bananas from Colima and paper from Atenquique, roared through town. The bus service did not change. Two "Tres Estrellas de Oro" buses still come by every day, heading south in the morning and east toward Mexico City in the evening. At all hours, no less than twenty buses belonging to other companies still pass through San José, where few outsiders ever get off.

San José does not have enough accommodations for tourists. The old inns fell into decay when the mule trains disappeared. The last to close was the one operated by Isabel Reyes. There has been nothing to replace them except a small hotel with a dozen rooms. People say it was a first-class establishment, with private baths and hot water, in the days when it enjoyed the personal attention of its owners, Salomón Mercado and his wife, Rosa González Flores. Construction was begun on another hotel, but all that ever went into operation was the gasoline pump next door.

Two Hundred Words More about Change

Other changes within the past decade, aside from the advent of inadequate technology, inadequate affluence, inadequate urbanization, and inadequate education, have been most numerous and varied—as the following lists of words in alphabetical disorder suggest.

Since 1957 we find more actuality, adaptability, alcoholism, anxiety, authority, bicycle riding, bribery, bureaucracy, cancer, capital, class consciousness, class struggle, comfort, competition, concourses, consumer credit, contracts of sale, coquetry, cosmetics, cowardice, cupidity, dancing, discrimination, dispersion of possessions, division of labor, enmity, envy, eroticism, ethical dualism, exhibitionism, exogamy, feminism, freedom of assembly, free love, free speech, fruit, gas, gossip, help wanted, hyperdulia, imitation, impatience, inequality, insolence, insults, isolation, kissing, leisure, lodging, maladjustment, mendacity, mendicancy, middle class, nationalism, necessity, opposition, ornaments, pastimes, pauperization, peonage, permanent emigration, pessimism, photography, politics, population pressure, pressure, propaganda, publicity, public opinion, robbery, satire, secularization, selfishness, sewing, short skirts, simulation, slenderness, smuggling, social capillarity, social parasitism, social rivalry, spectacles, sport, taxes, tenderness, tourism, transportation, unemployment, utensils, vaccination, vagrancy, vehicles, and vices.

Since 1957 there has been less altruism, appealing to a higher court, asceticism, astonishment, autarchy, barter, bastardy, births per thousand, boredom, braggadocio, caste, cavalry, church attendance, cohesion, collective conscience, community of interests, compassion, concubinage, confidence, confluence, conformity, congruence, conservatism, cooperation, corporal punishment, courtesy, crime, criticism, diarrhea, disease, donkeys, ethnocentrism, etiquette, fasting, fatalism, fear of ghosts, forests, gerontocracy, happiness, homicides, horseback riding, horses, hunting, ignorance, immigration, inertia, invitations, justice, latifundianism, mercy, modesty, mortality (especially infant), mourning, multi-individual conduct, mustaches, mutual aid, necrodulia, oaks, oxen, personal leadership, possession of firearms, professional mobility, puritanism, quackery, rape, rational conduct, regional costumes, resignation, ritualism, rural population, sanctimony, saving money, seasonal migration, self-discipline, shame, social coaction, succor, superstition, taboos, thaumaturgy, virtue, and work.

Among the innovations during the past twenty years are antibiotics, Coca-Cola, contraception, DDT, drug stores, plastics, transistor radios, silos, polio shots, vitamins, television, automobiles, and refrigerators. Nevertheless, San Joséans are still living beyond the frontier of industry, cybernetics, abstract art, existentialism, Marxism, psychoanalysis, neuroses, psychedelics, racism, yoga, the philosophy of Teilhard de Chardin, Mexican mural painting, tests, nuclear energy, surrealism, concrete music, rebels without a cause, relativity, and other contemporary forms of humanism.

The casualty list includes mule driving, the *Alabado*, the arroba and other ancient units of measurement, esparto baskets, the prognostic value of the *cabañuelas*, the dog days and their retinue of illnesses, the mariachi, the Judas burned in effigy on Holy Saturday, the owl and his evil omens, and other equally concrete things—none of them really nuclear.

Since 1957 some old sayings have disappeared. "A good marriage, like the hour of death, is decided in heaven." "The devil's so wise because he's so old." "The words of old people are tiny Bibles." "May God make you lucky, and never mind about being wise." "Man's place is in the field, and woman's is in the kitchen." "Between the saintly woman and the saintly man, keep a wall of stone." Other proverbs have come to the fore: "First earn your living, then be a Christian." "If you have the price, you can buy anything—even the cathedral." "Once you've used a china cup, you can't drink from clay." "Don't pray to the saint—tempt him." "There are more devils than holy water." "Only what a man has eaten and enjoyed does him any good." "Dead men do not walk again."

Ten years ago one would not have believed that the people of San Jose could change in so many ways. A lot of notions have been driven out of their heads, and many more new ones have taken their place. Yet they have kept more than they have thrown overboard. The geographical surroundings are not much different from what they were. The changes in props have not yet had any effect on the stage itself. So far, structural alterations have been minor ones. Basic attitudes have suffered hardly any modifications, and the repertoire of beliefs is still much more typical of Mexican villagers than of contemporary man in the large cities. In statistical terms, San José ceased to be a village in 1950, when its population rose above 2,500. From then on it could have been called a city; but nobody has dared to tell it so, for it is still just as much a village as on the day it was founded. Although it is pursuing urbanization, at the present time the distance between it and the urban centers is a vast one.

It has not been a unanimous pursuit. Not all San Joséans aspire to urbanization, and efforts in that direction on the part of various social groups have differed widely. Among those who do not want to move completely into the new world are the old people. They are satisfied merely to have some of the advantages of modern life: medicine, communications, convenient transportation, and electric lights. Among those who have been unable to acquire even these conveniences are the poorer villagers and the people who live in the *rancherías*. The youngsters in the vanguard are leading a column that is very long and very broad; in spite of the fact that they are young they are not precisely revolutionaries. They are not in pursuit of a different world, they merely want to develop the one they have. It is not a question of a new way of life, but of rising out of material underdevelopment. There is no awareness of any spiritual underdevelopment.

In the pages to follow, my ambitious aim will be to show where—in the first days of 1968, four hundred years after the first settling of the region, eighty years after the founding of the town, and twenty-five years after the beginning of the race toward modernization—the runners who are still living on their native heath find themselves. Those who have leaped over the fence—the San Joséans who now live elsewhere—will be the subject of another volume.

New Aspects of the Landscape and the Town

The terrain granted to Francisco Saavedra, Pedro Larios, and Alonso de Ávalos four hundred years ago is different today. The fifteen thousand men who have lived on it, and particularly the most recent of their offspring, have left their mark by cutting down trees, hunting, laying out farms and orchards, running cattle, building towns and hamlets, stringing electric lines, and stretching ribbons of asphalt across it. They may not have altered it beyond recognition, but it is quite different from what it was in pre-Hispanic times, or even thirty years ago, in all four elements: earth, air, fire, and water.

The damage that has been done to the crust of the earth, that thin layer of vegetable and animal life, has been done by the ax, the rifle, insecticides, fungicides, and many other tools of destruction. Woodcutters who pay a small bribe to the forestry agents chop fallen trees (and standing ones, too) into firewood; they fell oaks that it will take centuries to replace; they strip hillsides and mountains; they take the logs by burro to the highway and load them on trucks so that city people can have charcoal-broiled steaks and decorate their houses. The tourists have free rein to hunt deer and rabbits, and they have just about finished them off. Local hunters have stripped the land almost bare of destructive animals (opossums, coyotes, squirrels, rats, hawks, and snakes) and edible ones (armadillos and doves). On the other hand, insecticides and poisons, which are more widely used every day, are far from effective in eradicating flies, mosquitoes, fleas, ants, caterpillars, and worms. Each season arrives with its own pests and takes them with it when it leaves.

The ravagers have not finished the job by half, and they do not expect to see it completed. The present generation will probably see Larios Mountain and the rolling mesa stripped of trees and bushes. The pasture grass and brush will probably continue to be brownish during the seven months of the dry season, sprinkled with flowers in October, and green from July to September. Probably the local economy will not suffer from the total absence of oaks, live oaks, madroñas, thornbushes, and clumps of cactus. Padre Federico thinks, however, that the loss of the trees will bring catastrophe. "It will stop raining; the lowlands will be covered with stony patches, and the fields and hillsides will be nothing but rocks." He is fighting deforestation; he has asked people to scatter pine cones, and he has asked the Subsecretariat of Forestry for help. It has all been in vain. The pines refuse to grow, and the forestry inspectors go right on taking their *mordidas* and allowing the trees to be cut.

Most people don't worry about the loss of the trees. They don't believe that it will cause droughts; they are not saddened by the thought of a bald-headed Larios Mountain; they don't expect to see any increase in the whitish stony patches, or any desert of rocks. *Ejido* members, and some who aren't even that, know that they can make enough cutting firewood to cover household expenses. If they strip someone else's property, they have the satisfaction of knowing that some "rich guy" is gnashing his teeth; if they cut on their own land, there is more room for corn. On the *ejidos*, cleared areas become cornfields—less and less productive and more and more extensive. Erosion advances slowly, in no hurry. The mere loss of trees is less detrimental than their replacement by corn, beans, and garbanzos.

Every year more land is planted to corn; there are now more than two thousand hectares, and probably three. The *milpas* begin to show signs of life in June, in the ravines and on some of the hillsides. Patches of green here and there, clearly visible from the top of Larios Mountain—spots that appear, disappear, and change color with the seasons. But these days there are also some green patches that do not fade away: orchards, like moles on the skin of the earth, growing near the warts of the village and its *rancherías*. Manuel González has thirty hectares of fruit trees; there are more than a dozen other orchards of a hectare or less. Peaches predominate. Olive trees, relieved of the responsibility of fruiting, have been retained for their decorative value. The natural flora is giving way to the domestic.

Animals foreign to the region have multiplied tremendously in number, if not in variety, in recent years. As the bovines increase, there are fewer horses, mules, and burros. Sheep have disappeared, but there are many more pigs and chickens. Dogs probably outnumber cats. A new development that everyone deplores is the arrival of the European sparrow. The ranchers call these birds "agrarianists," because they take over and destroy other nests and are always squawking and quarreling. They have undoubtedly done more than the hunters to crowd out other birds and thus have contributed to the general trend toward reduction in varieties of animal life. There is another tendency: domestic animals are living more sedentary and cloistered lives. The practice of driving cattle to different grazing grounds is dying out, as they are kept more and more in corrals and stables. Almost all chickens are now kept in runs, and many live in cages. There are more doghouses and pigpens every day.

Unproductive uses of the earth are responsible for the remaining disfigurements of the original landscape. In first place are the means of communication and transportation. A federal highway of gray asphalt crosses the *tenencia*, fed by the paved road from El Valle, the dirt track from Ojo de Rana, the cobblestone lanes from San Miguel and Sabino, and the rutted trails connecting San José, Aguacaliente, Auchen, Paso Real, and Espino and Ojo de Rana, La Rosa, Cerrito de Enmedio, and La Española. In all, twenty-six kilometers of all-weather roads and about forty kilometers of dirt roads (passable during the dry season). The mule trails are still there, more rocky and slippery every day, less and less trod by mules and burros. Along the main highway three rows of poles stand guard, carrying telegraph, telephone, and power lines.

There is still a lot of sky. On the whole mesa there is not a single factory, and the smoke from cooking fires and automobiles is not enough to discolor it. The windstorms that come up in February raise momentary clouds of dust. On winter days the sky sometimes turns gray. During the wet season it is filled with towering clouds, rain, thunder, and lightning. After seven at night only San José shows a yellow glitter of lights; none of the surrounding hamlets has electricity. The reddish glow of pitch-pine torches has disappeared; the *rancherías* are lighted by candles, oil lamps, the moon, and the stars. It is the same transparent air that Pedro Larios knew—with a little more illumination and fewer birds.

There is more water: the same rivers and creeks found and named by the Spaniards, and, in addition, twenty liquid mirrors. When Fray Alonso Ponce (sometime around 1585) saw the only small natural lake in the area, it was teeming with geese. Toward the end of the colonial period three man-made bodies of water appeared, and, in Don Porfirio's time, five more. They were called ponds, or watering holes. Lately, about fifteen ranchers have decided to construct *bordos*, as they now call these small reservoirs; almost all are for watering cattle. People have started pumping water from the earth, too; there are now three deep wells, and some of the more dynamic farmers are hoping to be able to drill others. There is a rumor that a large dam will soon be built on the Pasión River. Getting more water is the principal concern of every inhabitant.

The rivers, ponds, and watering holes cover a little more than one-half of 1 percent of the terrain; the remaining forests account for 4 percent, 12 percent is planted with corn, beans, barley, and other crops; the scars made by highways, lanes, and trails cover 1 percent; 70 percent of the area is grazing land; 11 percent is escarpments. Less than one-half of 1 percent is taken up by human habitations and supplementary structures, distributed among several *rancherías* and a town on its way to becoming a city. On all sides are to be seen the results of labor and ingenuity: plowed fields, roads, wires, stock ponds, domesticated animals, rows of trees, shocks of corn, stone walls, irrigation ditches, machinery, motor vehicles, antennas, and, above all, shelters for men and livestock. The last are centered in small, scattered groups that make up the *rancherías* and in a larger network, a kind of lattice, that is San José de Gracia.

There are twenty *rancherías*. Some consist of nearly a hundred houses, while others have five or less. The largest are Ojo de Rana, Sabino, and San Miguel. Some sit in the gully of the Pasión River or along the creek beds; others perch on the hummocks and hillsides. They all look alike: a single, rocky street, stone walls, pigpens, houses scattered about—one here, another a hundred or two hundred meters away—as though thrown down at random. Each house has its guardian tree standing inside the patio fence near the porch, in the midst of the chickens, where the horse is tied. The porch leads to two rooms and, at one side, to the kitchen. The walls are of adobe, except in the case of a few new houses which are of brick. Sloping tile roofs. Walls whitewashed or the earth color of adobe. Dirt floors. A few pieces of furniture: a table, chairs, a radio, beds—no one sleeps on grass mats these days—a small leather trunk, farming tools, sometimes a kerosene or even gas stove, a gasoline lantern, a *metate*, or small corn mill, and a number of pots and utensils. As always, pictures of saints; in recent years, photographs of family members; even more recently, calendars and chromos of such heroes as Cuauhtémoc, Hidalgo, and Morelos. The houses are small, poor, and very clean. Usually there is no toilet. On the back of the doors, blessed palm branches to protect the house, and outside the door, the dog. A rifle in one corner, and a machete hanging on the same wall with the saints, the heroes, and the relatives. In the three largest *rancherías* the church is the tallest building; it is a miniature one, but it has its bell tower and steps in front. Sometimes one sees a little two-room schoolhouse, too. In most of the *rancherías* the original old mansion of the hacienda has disappeared, or at most it is represented by a few ruined walls melted by the rain, or merely by the foundations. In some places its courtyard still serves as a plaza.

The village of San José now covers all of the low hill that meets the western slope of Larios Mountain. It measures forty hectares. It is an oval, with its long axis lying north and south: an oval marked off in squares by thirteen streets running east and west and eight at right angles. There are now ninety-one blocks. The highway street is paved; the rest are cobblestone, except for a few on the outskirts. As the streets run downhill, the rain does not stand in puddles, but the

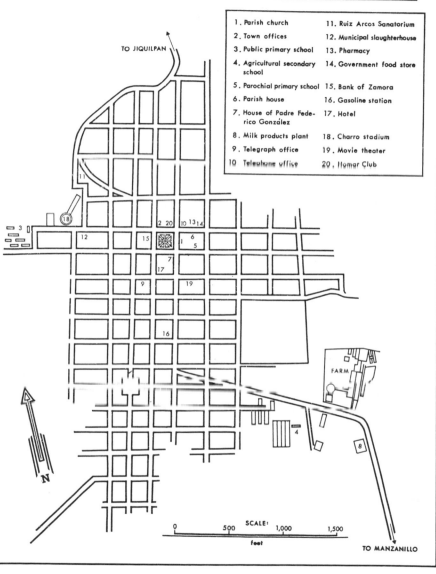

Plan of San José' de Gracia

TO JIQUILPAN

1. Parish church
2. Town offices
3. Public primary school
4. Agricultural secondary school
5. Parochial primary school
6. Parish house
7. House of Padre Federico González
8. Milk products plant
9. Telegraph office
10. Telephone office

11. Ruiz Arcos Sanatorium
12. Municipal slaughterhouse
13. Pharmacy
14. Government food store
15. Bank of Zamora
16. Gasoline station
17. Hotel
18. Charro stadium
19. Movie theater
20. Homar Club

FARM

N

SCALE:

0   500   1,000   1,500

feet

TO MANZANILLO

streets become roaring rivers during the rainstorms, from June to October. As in other Mexican villages, the streets are officially named Hidalgo, Morelos, Juárez, Quiroga, and so on; but the inhabitants continue to use the traditional names: the King's Street, the Ditch, the Highway, the Road to the Cemetery . . . The streets are monotonous because they are so straight, and because of the reddish color of most of the houses and their roofs. San José is still a sea of tile roofs, out of which rise the church towers and the tops of the trees that grow along the sidewalks and in the patios. The great majority of the houses, and all those built before 1950, have retained the traditional elements: the interior patio, its surrounding porch, and the rooms opening onto them. The patio brings in light, fresh air, and space, for the doors and windows on the street side are generally kept closed. The porches are furnished with potted plants, chairs, calendars on the wall, and cages housing canaries, *clarines*, mockingbirds, and linnets. Three-quarters of the larger houses have kitchens with gas stoves.

In 1963 there were 849 buildings in San José de Gracia: 766 homes, 29 chicken houses, 22 stores, 8 warehouses, and 17 structures devoted to other uses. A small number measure from one to two thousand square meters, while the majority occupy from three hundred to five hundred square meters of land.[9] The houses are comfortably large; the five or six people who occupy each one do not all crowd into one room to sleep—with the exception of a few extremely poor and prolific families. Only eight of these dwellings have more than one story; half of them have dirt floors. There is electricity in 70 percent of the homes, and running water in 48 percent.

The plaza is the geographical and cultural center of the town. There, right in the middle, is the bandstand; it is surrounded by a garden that Nacho Gálvez keeps filled with flowers and shaded by healthy green trees. The garden is encircled by a promenade furnished with handsome cast-iron benches; a prominent element in the design of the backrests is a Phrygian cap. The church rises on the east side; the office of the *jefe de tenencia*, together with a few stores, stands on the north; there are more stores on the west; and the south side is occupied by an arcade of pink stone, in which are the entrances of

---

9 AJTO, Documents from the Jefatura of Bernardo González Cárdenas.

Padre Federico's house, of María's restaurant, and of Luis Manuel's store. The plaza is still the place where government, church, and commerce meet, although it is no longer the center of all entertainment, or the principal gathering place for prominent citizens. The district near the cemetery has a corner on sports (the bullring, the *lienzo charro*, and the soccer field), and it contains the largest school. In the Ojo de Agua section there are two villas and several structures for raising chickens; the lower part of La Huerta *barrio* boasts four of the noisiest bars and, in the upper part, Dr. Ruiz's hospital and half a dozen houses in the modern style. Other aspects of village life can be seen in the old La Morada section and in the newer areas called El Durazno and Baja California, where there are, among little rickety shops, cantinas, and unpretentious dwellings, one or two rather expensive homes. Large houses and small ones, traditional and modern, are to be found side by side in every *barrio*.

In spite of emigration, the population of San José and its hamlets grows larger every day. The most recent census, that of October, 1967, recorded 8,360 inhabitants—4,553 in the town and the balance in the *rancherías*. We must not take too literally the assertion that people from the *rancherías* move into the village, and from there to the capital, or to the United States. Neither is it entirely correct to say that the villagers wait only until they are fifteen years old to leave. In 1967, of the 42 per thousand who were born, 9 died and 8 moved from the village. The net gain was 2.5 percent. Fifty-four percent of the population were women; 47 percent were under fifteen; 10 per cent were between fifteen and twenty-four years of age; 15 percent were between twenty-five and thirty-nine, 4 percent between forty and fifty-nine, 4 percent from sixty to seventy-nine, and 2 percent were over eighty. The population density was 36 per square kilometer. The average family had a little over 6 members.

There were more than 1,300 small families, or households. In the village alone there were 760. All of them acknowledged membership in some larger family, identified by one surname or another.

The 4,500 citizens of San José de Gracia shared 114 surnames, denoting larger family groups. Half of them were distributed among eight families, representing only 7 percent of the total number of family trees. The González and Chávez families each had between 300 and 400 members. The Martínez, Pulido, and Cárdenas groups accounted for from 200 to 300; the Sánchezes, Torreses, and Partidas numbered between 100 to 200. Another 25 percent of the population belonged to 16 other major families. These were Haro, Valdovinos, Moreno, Villanueva, Gómez, Bautista, Zepeda, Silva, Aguilar, Ávila, Castillo, Betancourt, Rodríguez, García, Cisneros, and Toscano.

The social frontiers were not nearly as imprecise and much more economically oriented than they had been. There was an important elite, or landowning, class, consisting of 3 percent of the total. According to the poor people, everyone in this class was rich. Their annual per capita income was over five thousand pesos, and, on the average, about ten thousand. If they had lived in Mexico City, they would have been members of the lower middle class. San José's middle class, which was 18 percent of the population, had a yearly per capita income of about three thousand pesos. The poor, who were 79 percent of the total, earned, on the average, twelve hundred pesos per person per year. To sum up: a rich family's income was five thousand pesos a month; a middle-class family earned fifteen hundred; and a poor one took in about five hundred—or the equivalent in goods.

9. THE UPPER CRUST

The Rich and the Middle-Income Group

ALL BUT three of the forty "rich" families own ranches of from 30 to 500 hectares. Eight of the families own more than 300 hectares, twenty-two own between 100 and 299, and six own between 30 and 99 hectares. At one time there was an exact correspondence between wealth and owning large sections of land. This no longer holds. Of the eight families with the largest incomes, at least half are not large landowners; one of them owns no rural property at all. Nor do the old families any longer have a monopoly on wealth. Of the forty, fourteen are *nouveaux riches*. Ninety percent of them live most of the time in the village of San José. Some of the larger *rancherías* (Ojo de Rana, San Miguel, and Paso Real) have from one to three wealthy families. Almost all are of *ejido* origin. The heads of these families are or were *ejido* leaders.

These "rich" people are one or two of three things: owners of land and cattle, merchants, or professional men. The vast majority fall within the first group; those in the last category can be counted on the fingers of one hand; and the fingers of both hands will suffice for the second. Many of the property owners and merchants are partially engaged in industry. It is the primary processing of the goods they produce or supply that brings the greatest profit, and they know it.

They are aware, too, that wealth and the professions go hand in hand today. "Any professional man, no matter how unsuccessful he is, makes as much money as a small farmer, and has less to worry about. Knowing is better than owning, in a one-horse town like this. Just look at the doctor."

The principal occupation of the rich and the middle-income classes today is cattle raising. Seventy percent of the land is devoted to pasture. About fifteen thousand cattle are grazing throughout all or part of the year within the *tenencia*: about seventy animals per square kilometer. Discounting land that is used for other purposes, we can see that there is only a hectare for each head of cattle, instead of the three hectares needed because of the quality of the grass. The mortality rate among the herds is probably now about 8 percent a year, whereas in the past it has reached 25 percent. Twenty thousand liters of milk are produced daily during both the dry and rainy seasons. All this is because the natural pasture is supplemented today by ten thousand tons of feed each year, of which half is imported and half is supplied by twenty-nine silos; veterinarians, vaccines, and medicines are in demand; breeding bulls of good stock have been brought in; the cows are milked twice a day; the male calves are butchered; and ranchers are beginning to make use of stabling and artificial insemination. Dairy men complain that prices of milk and milk products rise slowly in comparison with the rapidly increasing costs of feed and consumer products; but they realize that, even so, they are making more money than they used to, although it is still not enough to permit them to live well and to increase their operations. Their purchasing power is becoming greater, but it does so slowly.

Some San Joséans are fascinated by machines, speed, chemical science, markets, transportation facilities, and increased production. There is no resistance to technical advances or industry. What they lack is capital and the solidarity to build a large factory. Some, like Luis and Rafael Valdovinos and José Partida, have started small plants where they turn some seven thousand liters of milk a day into process cheese. The cream is removed, and vegetable butter is added to give the appearance of whole cheese. Here and there in the various *rancherías* some twenty-five centrifugal cream separators are in use;

the butterfat is made into a cheese that must be eaten fairly soon, before it turns to stone.[1]

The domestic cheese industry is on the decline. Most of the dairy farmers prefer to sell their milk to industrial firms: The Nestlé Company in Ocotlán, which powders it; Lacto Products of Jiquilpan, which pasteurizes it; the *chongo* makers in Zamora; the three native San Joséans in Mexico City who manufacture cheese on a large scale—odorless, adulterated, and cheap, the way city people like it; and twenty-odd processing plants. In this way, the dairymen avoid difficulties with the Secretariat of Public Health and the merchants in the capital. They make more money with less trouble. Even so, some of them have maintained the tradition of making good cheese. Don Luis González Cárdenas, who is eighty-seven, turns out the best *panelas* in the area. The cottage cheeses produced by Agapito, Antonio, Bernardo, Everardo, and Luis Humberto González, Elena Villanueva, and some others are justly famous. But one sees cheese ripening on the rack in very few houses these days.

As for commerce, all is not well. About a hundred individuals are engaged in buying and selling—seven at the wholesale level. Some, like Eliseo Toscano and Federico Castillo, take local products to the city markets, particularly in the capital; others, like Antonio Villanueva, deal in feed for farm animals. Food not produced locally is bought from shopkeepers in Sahuayo, to a lesser degree in Guadalajara, Zamora, Jiquilpan, and Mexico City, and least of all in the many little grocery stores in San José and the *rancherías*, and at the Sunday market that is set up on the west side of the town square.

There are thirty-nine stores in the village, and there are nearly as many in the rural settlements. Their proprietors—with the exception of Abraham Partida and David Cárdenas, who do a considerable business and have the best stock—are happy if they take in a hundred pesos a day. Their tiny shops are really operated merely for amusement. They have little to sell, and their prices are high—even for

---

[1] "The worst are the butter and cream that come out of the process cheese factories. The butter is mostly colored vegetable fat, and the cream consists of a very small amount of natural cream, a somewhat larger quantity of vegetable oil, and the rest corn-flour."

alcoholic drinks, which account for most of their business. Their minute establishments look like cantinas filled with drunks if they sell liquor, or like empty houses if they do not, or if the proprietor is grouchy. They give their owners something to do. In addition to the grocery stores, there is a pharmacy, a shoe store, a hat shop, Braulio Valdovinos's funeral parlor, three little restaurants, and a gas station. The druggist's customers are mostly poor people who cannot afford a visit to the doctor; he prescribes the medicine and then sells it to them. Ambrosio's clientele comprises the indigent and the auto-therapists. The bakeries, of course, do more business than the drug store, but not as much as the shops that sell tortillas. The busiest are the merchants who deal in cattle and chicken feed.

Many of the middle class make their living driving taxis (Alfredo Barrios, Manuel Córdoba, Rafael Miranda, Manuel Vargas, Fernando Vega, José Chávez del Paso, Don Timoteo Magaña's son, and Don Joaquín's boy). Every morning and evening they make the run between San José and Sahuayo with their *colectivos* crammed with passengers. They charge each person ten centavos per kilometer— that is, four pesos to Jiquilpan, a peso more to Sahuayo, and one peso to Mazamitla. They use roads still under construction and cut across country on others that are mere parallel ruts. They pass through all the *rancherías* and neighboring villages.

Others butcher and sell meat (David, Jesús, Juan, and Rafael Chávez, Juan López Haro, José Núñez, Anatolio Partida, Rafael Sánchez, and Eliseo Valdovinos). Some, like Elías Elizondo and Napoleón Valdovinos, are tailors.

The new trades, too, are the province of the middle class. Ignacio Vega is an automobile mechanic, but he also repairs radios, televisions, clocks, and any other kind of appliance. Others who enjoy working at several different occupations are the Martínez brothers, Francisco Partida Chávez, Florentino Torres, and his sons. Jesús Torres Santos has already become "rich."

Barbers and bakers may not earn much money, but they are respected. Salvador Pulido cuts hair and in addition is a political leader and acts as an attorney for poor people. Manuel Álvarez is the oldest barber. Alberto and José Martínez are among the younger ones. Some of the bakers are Ignacio Ochoa and Pachita Moreno, Adolfo Pulido, and Roberto Toscano.

Some of the neighboring towns have fallen into the temptation of trying to attract tourists. In San José the temptation has never been more than sporadic, perhaps because the community is one of those "societies with an almost neurotic urge to conceal itself from the eyes of outsiders." The people of San José "have a fear of opening their windows and letting others look in at them." No entrepreneur has taken the simple step of building a hotel or motel for tourists. People talk about how easy it would be to make Aguacaliente into a spa as famous as San José Purúa. They say that such a tourist center would bring many badly needed pesos to the *tenencia*. But it never gets past the talking stage. There is no real desire to see foreigners there. They treat strangers courteously, even at times with too much kindness; but it is always with the precaution that "nobody sees them doing it."

This privacy complex, while present in all San Joséans, is particularly noticeable among those of the middle class. They are mostly shy and modest people: 250 families who work small farms, or keep tiny shops, or make their living as teachers, clerks, or government employees. Eight out of every ten middle-class men own property. Most have farms that measure from twenty to a hundred hectares. Some own three or more parcels of land in different areas. Almost all of them use their land for pasture and for planting two or three hectoliters of corn. They are principally dairy farmers. Almost without exception, they own from ten to a hundred head of cattle. The middle class are the owners of half the cattle in the area, and half the land.

The land is fairly evenly divided among 422 private owners and about 300 *ejido* members. Including absentee landholders, there are more than 700 proprietors. Eleven have tracts of over 300 hectares, accounting for 29 percent of the *tenencia*; 22 own farms of between 100 and 299 hectares, constituting 18 percent of the rural area; 35 have from 30 to 99 hectares, representing 10 percent of the total land. The small holdings, of less than 30 hectares but almost invariably more than 5, are distributed among more than 650 farmers, called parcelholders or *ejido* members. Half of the latter group are not residents of the *tenencia*.[2]

The middle-class farmer, scourged by unpredictable weather and limited to only a small operation, worries about ending up as in The Magnificat—"sent empty away." He lives in fear that his property will be expropriated and handed over to the agrarianists. The newspapers, radio, and television bring reports that the president is distributing land in all parts of the country; it seems obvious to the farmer that these properties will not be taken from the large landowners, who have the money to defend themselves, but from small ones like himself. He hears rumors about so-and-so, who had only twenty hectares and was left with nothing. These rumors are always somewhat hazy, and they are probably spread by the shysters; but they are enough to discourage the small farmer from making any effort to improve his property. He prefers to hand over the little money he might be able to invest in his farm to the "coyotes" who promise to protect him from the specter of agrarianism.

One makes money by perseverance or self-denial, not from business profits. The middle class has a very small capacity for self-financing and investment. Nor is it possible to get sizable long-term loans from the banks. The Alliance for Progress has lent some money, through various banks, to four individuals for improving their land and livestock; it is to be repaid within ten years. In short, there is no local capital or outside help available to lift the San José area out of its underdevelopment.

The middle class are given to theorizing about their situation. They know very well how difficult it is to attain a better life on their native heath, and they do little to dissuade their children from leaving. Sometimes they even encourage it. "It's easy to see that there's nothing for a man to do here. It would be better for them to go somewhere else, where they can make something of themselves, than to hang around their home town like bums." "Idleness is the mother of all vices." Besides, "here you're scared to death all the time." "In the capital nobody takes anything away from you, except for taxes."

2 Information from the files of the local tax collector's office in San José de Gracia, obtained through the kindness of Guillermo Barrios.

"When you live in the country you're never sure of having work, and your property isn't safe." "City rich people are very intelligent and very sympathetic; there's no doubt about that. They keep saying that the poor people must be helped—but with somebody else's money, with the little we manage to earn here." "They all get together [the government, the rich, the communistic professors, and the loafers] just so they can cheat people."

The hatred felt by those who own small and medium-sized farms is directed mainly at the agrarianists and the central government. Their hostility toward those who are demanding land has sprung up again during the past decade. They no longer condemn the agrarian movement as immoral and sinful, as they once did; now their arguments are based on economic and social considerations. They repeat, in everyday language loaded with hatred, Padre Federico's antiagrarianist sentiments. The landowners claim that "these people who are demanding land are not real farmers; they know nothing about living in the country; they are cunning, irresponsible, without dignity, troublemakers; they don't want to work the land; they want to do the same as a lot of *ejido* members: sell the pasture rights. Giving land to people who expect to get it without paying for it is bad business. They're too shiftless and unreliable to get any good out of it themselves, and they won't let anybody else do it. And not only that; once they take over, these agrarianists start killing each other."

They not only hate the government; they fear it, they respect it, they try to appease it. Sometimes they are grateful to it for some small service; but they nearly always blame it for the evils that befall the area. They have progressed from expecting everything from it to expecting nothing. Nobody believes that it represents the people. Few dare to show their antipathy in the elections, or choose to express their fear by voting for it. The majority stay away from the polls; they prefer to keep their feelings to themselves. Those who own something hate and fear it because it distributes land and collects taxes; those who have nothing feel the same way because it imposes penalties, makes promises, and does not fulfill them. The upper crust and the underdogs are united by their dislike for the government.

This repudiation of government and law may be due to some extent to the individualism that blocks the progress of any farmers' organization. This individualism finds expression in a thousand ways: disparagement of one's neighbors by means of gossip and jokes; extreme sensitivity to insults and public opinion; an excessive introversion; emphasis on the proverb "Take care of your own house, and never mind your neighbor's"; refusal to work for wages; determination to be in business for oneself; "Don't interfere in my affairs"; "Nobody orders me around"; "Let every man scratch his own back"; thinking of oneself as very *macho*, and regarding all other men as competitors; and reluctance to keep appointments.

Important factors in their antigovernment attitude are the new national feeling and a vigorous provincialism. Even though national awareness, sentiments, and loyalty are growing, marked patriotism is evident only during the national holidays and the fiesta of Our Lady of Guadalupe. There remains a fear of the outside world, and of other people in the region. Consciousness of being part of a national whole, while marked, is still insufficient. In spite of the factors that have tended to dissolve it, individualism is still a potent force. All San Joséans—even those who have emigrated—believe their community to be morally superior to any other; they are proud of their miniature nation. They can hear Mexico insulted, but they will not stand for jokes about the area where they were born. They can make fun of it themselves, but outsiders must not.

Ideologies play no part in their rejection of the government, although they did at one time. "If that is the case, then why do you hate the government authorities?" The usual answer is: "Because they're a bunch of bandits." "What makes you think they're thieves?" "Why, just look at them: they're all rich."

Politics from the Top Down, and Vice Versa

If we take a cross section of life in San José and its *tenencia*, we see that politics hardly figures at all. The activities of federal and state governments go almost unnoticed. Political ideas and actions among the citizens are nearly nonexistent. Relations between the town and governmental agencies are tending to improve, but slowly, with no enthusiasm, and without much sincerity. The high purposes of the state, on the one hand, and the farmers' hostility toward the authorities, on the other, might explain why these relations are so fragile, cold, and hypocritical.

San José and its *tenencia* are so insignificant, in fact and in economic possibilities, and so far removed from the center of power, that governmental justice and aid seldom reach them. They are still orphans. In 1967 only three federal agencies were functioning in San José: the tax collector, the post office, and the telegraph. Indifference on the part of the government was most pronounced that year. There was merely a decree published in the *Diario Oficial* informing 178 applicants from San José (who had already been told the same thing in 1938) that there was no affectible land within the legal radius of the *tenencia*. Oh, yes! It also intervened by sending a few soldiers to prevent some *ejido* members from taking over several pieces of property at the suggestion of the Independent Farmers' League. And there was something else: the Secretariat of Water Resources sent a plane to fly over the Pasión River to find a site for the dam the people of Tizapán had been asking for.

The Michoacán state government, which had begun to make itself felt in San José in the thirties and became more active under the governorship of General Dámaso Cárdenas, has not been so indifferent. In the opinion of the people of San José de Gracia, Agustín Arriaga is a good governor, and he has kept some of his campaign promises. They say he promised lights, telephones, and schools; the lights arrived in 1965, and the telephone in 1967. Now he is waiting for the San Joséans to do their share toward the construction of the schoolhouse before he comes for the inauguration, bringing a teacher for each of its twelve classrooms. Local committees often call upon the governor to ask his help in some project. Don Agustín is young, conscientious, and accessible; sometimes he grants their requests, and at other times he raises a thousand objections—as he did in the matter of the *municipio*.

There has been a movement to promote the *tenencia* of Ornelas to a higher category; San José, they say, is now large enough to be the head of a *municipio*. In addition, there are great natural, economic, and ethnic differences between Ornelas and the rest of the *municipio* of Jiquilpan; and, it is claimed, the Jiquilpan municipal government ignores the Ornelas people as though they were invisible. Of the three levels of government, that in Jiquilpan is the most meaningless for the eight thousand inhabitants of Ornelas's 230 square kilometers. And, when Jiquilpan does take a friendly interest in the western third of the *municipio*, as it has under the leadership of Jorge Romero, it has been unable to translate that friendship into works; the little money it has at its disposal must be spent on Jiquilpan.[3]

San Joséans worry more about money, religion, education, and amusements than about politics. Nobody loses any sleep over world affairs, and not more than twenty people ever discuss them; national politics has some slight interest for the middle and upper classes; state matters concern these same groups a little more; but it is only local politics that arouses some real enthusiasm, even among the poor. Of those who do pay attention to politics, the elderly show the least interest, the young, the most. The most politically minded is undoubtedly the generation born between 1920 and 1934. Another thing that seems certain is that women—aside from the few young ladies who were fascinated by sinarquism in the forties—have concerned themselves only with local politics. Rural people are less politically conscious than those in town, and in the *rancherías* the small property owners pay less attention to such matters than do *ejido* members. Of course, there is not much interest in politics anywhere in Mexico these days.

Political ideas are extremely vague and imprecise. Everybody, more or less, still believes that being in politics is an inferior and immoral occupation, fit only for scoundrels. The great majority of the population obviously has no political ideology at all. There are perhaps no more than a dozen people who have signed up voluntarily with one of the political parties. A few bureaucrats and *ejido* farmers may appear on the official rolls as members of the PRI, but they ignore it.

---

[3] In 1968 the state legislature promoted the *tenencia* to a *municipio*. See the epilogue and postscript, in chap. 13 below.

Five percent of the citizens voted in the 1964 national elections. In 1967 the propaganda put out by the parties and by the priests to persuade more people to vote brought 22 percent of the voters to the polls. PRI beat PAN by two votes, and the PPS got eleven.[4] Votes for PAN, in general, indicate two things: repudiation of the government, and the widely held belief, especially among women, that a vote for PAN is a vote for the church.

The restrained enthusiasm provoked by local politics can be seen in a recent event. Jorge Romero, *presidente* of the *municipio* of Jiquilpan, renounced his right to appoint a *jefe de tenencia* in San José for the two-year period 1966–1967 and called an election instead. Three groups formed: the dissidents of various leanings (PANistas, Sinarquists, landless agrarianists) gathered round a former estate owner and ex-leader of the local Sinarquists, Rafael Anaya; *ejido* members followed Juan Gudiño, a small landowner; and those in favor of the status quo recognized the leadership of the tailor Elías Elizondo. The last two factions had no quarrel between themselves, and they were ready to join forces if necessary. Anaya's party, however, unleashed a kind of propaganda unheard-of in San José and showed an unprecedented virulence.

The election was held on the first Sunday of 1966, with the voters of each party assembling with their respective group. The results were 312 votes for Elías Elizondo, 310 for Rafael Anaya, and 274 for Gudiño. These figures represent the local citizens' maximum participation in politics and show their lack of any real interest in formal democracy.[5] That Sunday in 1966 there were at least 3,000 citizens within the *tenencia* of Ornelas, and only 898 voted—30 percent. It seems clear that most people could not care less who is or is not the *jefe de tenencia*; it is obvious that the majority prefer to see the continuation of the system of personal bossism—either because they hold the man himself in high regard, or because of sheer political indifference. It seems equally certain that the survival of the town assembly detracts in some small ways from the influence of the other

---

[4] AJTO, Documents from the Jefaturas of Bernardo González Cárdenas and Elías Elizondo.
[5] Ibid.

powers—the legal one of the *jefatura*, and the extralegal one of the local patriarch.

Although the *jefe de tenencia*'s powers are limited by the organic municipal law, they are still numerous. He appoints the fourteen peace officers stationed in the *rancherías*, as well as his immediate assistants: a secretary, a couple of typists, and two policemen. The *jefe* also chooses the public project to be completed during his term of office. Elías Elizondo has elected to finish the schoolhouse and has dedicated a large part of his time to the undertaking. He has the responsibility of preventing quarrels, gunfights, and other kinds of disturbance. He walks into bars and disarms drunks. He tries to keep the streets clean by fining housewives who do not sweep the cobblestones in front of their houses. He often serves as a judge, or as an official of the Department of Public Records, and he does anything else not forbidden him—by the municipal authorities in Jiquilpan, on the one hand, and by the other elements of local government, on the other: the patriarch, the church, the Committee for Civic Improvement, and the town assembly.

Patriarchal rule and the intervention of the church authorities within the sphere of government are two institutions that are not as vigorous as they used to be. Since 1962 the *jefes* have been acting without consulting Padre Federico, and at times, against his express point of view; this does not prevent the old priest, in his position outside the bureaucracy, from making decisions on various matters of general interest, or from having those decisions respected. Neither does it imply any open hostility between him and the *jefe de tenencia*.

Padre Federico was at one time the village's undisputed ruler, but no longer. Today there is argument about it. Among those who attack him, not all live in the village. Most of them are young. Some people think that these criticisms are no more than a manifestation of the unspoken rivalry that exists between the large families, the silent struggle between those with the surname González and several others. But it is more than that. Some people have been annoyed by Padre Federico's way of taking matters into his own hands. Their struggle is against the patriarchal system. Others say that the patriarch is not impartial, that he favors some citizens above others.

In any case, the vast majority of the villagers love and respect him. His terse oratory and his sermons delivered in a conversational tone, without gestures or quotations from verse and chapter, have earned him many friends. Others admire him for his wise counsel. He holds a public audience every day at dusk on the porch in front of his house, hearing petitions, solving problems, and dealing with arguments, uncertainties, and matters of conscience. In addition, it is rumored that he gives people money from time to time. Certainly his dynamism and shrewdness are the principal reasons for his fascination. Most people have great faith in the padre's intelligence, wisdom, and actions. Any reforms he suggests are certain of public support. "We all owe him a lot," says a taxi driver. "Anybody can tear things down; but for building up, there are very few men like the padre," a storekeeper observes. The farmers say: "He's the only one who has tried to improve the town." "He may be skinny and dressed in a cassock, but he's a very brave man." "Old, but tough." "Let's hope we have him around for a long time."

The truth is that the patriarch, bowed down under his eighty years and the afflictions of old age, is not as strong as he once was, although he is just as eager to be of service. But the people who live in San José today are not the same, either. They do not believe in patriarchy, or in government by priests. Not only Padre Federico, but the parish priest, also, has less power and importance than he did. Even the bishop's pastoral visits are no longer remarkable events. The parish priest, for his part, interferes less and less in the affairs of the patriarch and of the *jefe de tenencia*. His relations with the agencies of local government and even with the peace officers in the *rancherías* and the *ejido* leaders are excellent, but on a basis of mutual respect. Even so, the priest could veto any decision by the governing bodies, and his objection would most likely be respected.

Another political institution that Padre Federico is determined to keep alive is the town assembly.[6] All adults are called together— these days with a public-address system—whenever any important

[6] The town assembly is a recent institution. It was inaugurated in 1962, during the term of office of the *jefe de tenencia* Bernardo González Godínez.

issue is to be decided. These meetings are not on any calendar, nor do they take place in any special location. They are usually called on Sunday, in the movie house or in one of the schoolyards. Normally it is the *jefe*'s secretary who makes the announcement, but it may be the *jefe* himself or some other prominent person. Attendance is unpredictable; it is assumed that those who stay away are willing to accept the decision of the rest. In 1967 there were three assemblies. The first was called to consider a proposal by the Secretariat of Water Resources, which had offered to install the plumbing for a water system if San José could raise 700,000 pesos. The majority voted to postpone the final decision until the next meeting. At the following assembly the project was voted down, after heated debate. The third meeting that year was called to discuss taking up a collection to build a secondary school; after some argument, the project was approved, and a committee was appointed to carry it out. A fourth assembly had been planned to decide whether they should petition the governor and the Michoacán legislature to raise the *tenencia* of Ornelas to the category of a *municipio*; but the promoters of the plan went ahead and presented the petition without consulting the town. This raised a furor, even though everyone knew that the proposal would have been unanimously approved.

None of the local leaders have much power, because they have no money. In 1966 the *jefatura de tenencia* took in a little over 60,000 pesos, or 5,000 pesos a month. It went for miserable salaries and inadequate street lighting. The patriarch spends his small income on formal applications to the authorities and gifts to individuals who can be helpful to the town. The assembly imposes taxes for special purposes every year. Local authorities do not have the resources to provide for such essential services as sewer systems, roads, drinking water, elementary and technical schools, recreation centers, free medicine, markets, electric lights for the entire *tenencia*, and accident, health, and old-age insurance . . .

Only the state and federal agencies have the funds to provide these services at an adequate level. The outlying settlements and half the town are without potable water, and the ranches are in darkness;

many of the roads are impassable during the rains; sports fans have no playing fields; half of the hamlets have no schools, and the other half do not have enough teachers. People say, and with good reason, that if San José had some local people in politics it would be a different story. It already has the church in its pocket, because the area has turned out so many priests. But the entire zone has not produced a single *presidente municipal*; the only politician of any importance from San José rose to be a leader, but of the opposition party.

Religion and Some of Its Environs

In San José it is easier to see the influence of the church than that of the state. The bishop of Zamora comes to call more often than the governor of Michoacán. There are fewer church representatives than civil ones, but they do more. Three or four priests and five or six members of monastic orders are usually on hand. In addition to the parish priest, there is a vicar, a resident priest, and generally some visiting padre. Aside from the four nuns who teach in "the Haven," there are nearly always one or two other nuns in the village. And within the past two years two or three seminary students have joined the ecclesiastical team. There is no precentor, but there is a sacristan.

The parish priest, Don Carlos Moreno, keeps the parochial records of baptisms and marriages, administers the sacraments, says two Masses and a Rosary every weekday and three Masses with their respective sermons every Sunday, visits the larger rural settlements with some regularity, gives advice to troubled parishioners, and runs a vocational academy for girls from poor families. Don José Luis Garibay, the vicar, supplements his priestly duties by directing a school for more than two hundred children, with the assistance of two seminary students. The nuns preside over a girls' school and an academy for young ladies who can afford the tuition. Many times during the day one hears the sound of church bells, and, in addition, the voice of the parish priest, from a loudspeaker, calling people to services, making announcements, or giving some suggestion or other. He, like the vicar, belongs to the new school of churchmen. Instead of preaching the joys of poverty, they suggest and put into practice schemes to remedy it; instead of saying, "You must attend Mass, Rosary, and church meetings," they urge the practice of Christian virtues, work, and progress.

Religious beliefs, ritual, and commandments still play important roles in San Joséans' private and public lives. With the exception of an occasional elementary-school teacher, they all profess Catholicism. Not one questions the National Catechism, or those of Padre Ripalda and Cardinal Gasparri. In their everyday conversations they often make reference to the Creation, Redemption, the Last Judgment, and the four realms of the next life: limbo, purgatory, hell, and heaven. Today there is less intolerance of other creeds. Superstitious beliefs have lost ground. One can see at a glance that very few people wear amulets around their necks these days.

The people of San José want not only conveniences and freedom in this life, but also salvation in the next. The way of the sacraments is well traveled. No infant goes unbaptized; no child reaches the age of ten without confirmation. Everyone over eight goes to confession and takes Communion at least once a year; 50 percent or more do so every month. Very few people are allowed to die without extreme unction. Marriages, without exception, are performed by the priest in the approved way after the civil ceremony. Although everyone feels that a church wedding is the only real one, the priest himself insists on the civil one as well.

Monday through Saturday there are three or four Masses every day, and from six to eight on Sundays. The daily attendance at week-day Masses is about five hundred; no one, unless he is sick in bed or out of town, is absent on Sunday. Many people come in from the *ranchos* then, too. Needless to say, many men take advantage of Mass to look at the girls, and the girls, in turn, make the most of the chance to wear their gaudiest and most revealing dresses.

Observance of the Ten Commandments, the five mandates of ecclesiastical law, and the seven virtues is not as vigorous as it was twenty years ago. Most people try to comply with the precepts learned as children at home and in the church; even so, there are frequent and widespread infractions, periodically pardoned by the priests after proper confession. Among the sins, drunkenness and lust are said to be much more common now, although restricted, as always, to the masculine circle and the rare professional among the women. Miniskirts and greater social contact with men have not diminished feminine modesty and rigidity. Women have great respect for the Decalogue, of which they violate only the second, fifth, and eighth commandments. They still take the name of the Lord in vain in order to convince people they are telling the truth, and they kill by means of words; they leave the physical act to their men.

At one time the peasants were obliged to give a tenth of their gross income to the diocese. They are now expected to contribute much less, and often give nothing at all. They are no longer willing to pay tithes.[7] However, people are not stingy in other church matters. The alms given at Masses and Rosaries, the coins dropped in the plate passed by the sacristan or one of the padres, and the parish priest's honorariums come to almost as much as what is collected by the local government, legally and under threat of punishment. Everyone voluntarily hands over whatever is needed to support the church and its ministers, participates in raffles and kermises to raise money for parochial projects, and contributes small extra amounts for diocesan and worldwide activities. People are more than willing to give for missions to propagate the faith and for the training of priests.

Both religious faith and social pressure assure observance of other church disciplines: fasting and abstinence on Ash Wednesday, Good Friday, December 7 and 23, and the surviving abstinence on Fridays during Lent; the yearly retreats; the repeated breast-pounding, kneeling, and crossing oneself; attendance at weddings and wakes; visits to His Holiness; the fulfillment of vows; the ceremony of atonement; the *Via Crucis*; the Rogations and the greater and lesser litanies; the *gracias* following Communion; the short prayers; the novenas, the three Sundays of San José, and the three Tuesdays of San Antonio; the Act of Contrition; Hail Marys, Pater Nosters, *Salves Reginas*, and

---

[7] In recent years tithes have brought in between eighteen thousand and twenty thousand pesos a year; this amounts to .10 percent of the total production within the parish.

Credos; and the Rosary service, which is losing its customers to television these days.

The influence of religion is falling off in other spheres. At one time all children were named after some saint (usually the one on whose day they were born, one who happened to be in fashion at the time, or the town's patron), or the Virgin Mary, or, as a last resort, they were adorned with the name of their father, a grandfather, or some other relative. Today no name in the hagiology, with the exception of San Martín de Porres, plays a very important part in the baptismal ceremony. In many cases names are borrowed from public figures, or from stars in the world of movies, radio, television, and nightclubs: Yolanda, Georgina, Patricia, Sandra, Lilia, Nidia, Eréndira, Noelia, Laila, Moraima, Fabiola, and so on. Some everyday expressions taken from the vocabulary of religion are disappearing. When someone sneezes, people now say "Salud!" instead of "Jesus bless you!" The phrases "God willing," "With God's help," "May God reward you," and many others are used less and less. The devil continues to suffer devaluation, and his machinations are mentioned only in jest. Another forgotten figure is the Guardian Angel.

There are about ninety religious holidays during the year: fifty-two Sundays with High Mass, when no one works (although it is not forbidden); the Circumcision of Our Lord Jesus Christ, on January 1, when everyone makes his predictions for the coming year; the Epiphany, on January 6, when children leave their shoes outside their doors; Ash Wednesday, when no one fails to observe the ceremony of the ashes; the festival of the village's patron saint, on March 19; the eight days of Holy Week, with the blessing of the palms on Palm Sunday, the Stations of the Cross, the general seclusion, the sermon of the Last Supper and the washing of the feet, the sermon of the Seven Last Words, and what little else has remained since the recent liturgical reforms. What people miss most of the former splendor is Holy Saturday and the burning of Judas. Holy Week has been torn to bits.

May, the month dedicated to the Virgin, when children bring offerings of flowers and skyrockets are set off at the hour of the Rosary, has lost its special holidays; the Day of the Finding of the Holy Cross now comes and goes with no particular festivity. On Saint Isidore's Day, May 15, more than a thousand people hear Mass in the soccer field. In other villages,

> Three Thursdays in the year
> Are more splendid than the sun:
> Holy Thursday, Corpus Christi,
> And the Day of the Ascension.

But in San José none of these differs from an ordinary Sunday. Even Saint John's Birthday (June 24), the Assumption (August 15), All Saints' Day, and All Souls' Day are now rather seedy. On the other hand, December 12 and Christmas Day have become important holidays. On the feast day of the Virgin of Guadalupe (December 12) there are Masses and Solemn Rosary, and a procession along the street leading to the highway. The nine days of *posadas* and Christmas Eve, neither of which has a long tradition in San José, are observed today with crèches and Christmas trees, piñata parties, noisy pageants in "the Haven," and Midnight Masses. People still play tricks on each other on Innocents' Day (December 28), and give thanks on the last day of the year.

Pilgrimages have never been especially popular with San Joséans. Two annual peregrinations have been introduced recently: the former *cristeros* make a journey to Cubilete one Sunday in October, and a few members of the Zamora diocese go to Tepeyac one day in February. Unorganized groups attend the Santiago fiesta in Sahuayo and that of San Cristóbal in Mazamitla. Trips are still made—but fewer every year—to Totolán, Talpa, and San Juan de los Lagos in payment of vows. Padre Luis Méndez raised an enormous concrete cross on the mountain peak that watches over San José, in the hope that it would become an object of pilgrimages; but, aside from the one that took place at the dedication in 1964, it has never attracted many people.

Nor have religious associations been able to keep their heads above water in recent years. Very few citizens show up at the meetings of the various Catholic Action groups (UCM, UFCM, AJCM, JCFM) and even less attention is being paid to the directives issued by the AC.[8] The Daughters of Mary are not even a shadow of what they once were; instead of young girls, the society now attracts little old maids. Today's Daughters must be dynamic, rather than devout, and the San José membership is no longer young enough to do much. One traditional society that is holding its own is that of the Perpetual Vigil. On the other hand, the Family Christian Movement, which was fashionable in 1963–1964, has been reduced to a mere letterhead.

The parish of San José is still a heavy contributor to the religious vocation. It is the birthplace of seven living priests, and an equal number are completing their studies. Eight San Joséans are in the Order of Brothers of the Christian Schools; the Sisters of the Poor and the Madres of the Sacred Heart have twenty-three members from the village. Many more girls have taken refuge in other religious orders. There are about thirty-four nuns. Not counting acolytes, sacristans, and dropouts, sixty local people are now in the religious profession.

In addition to the professionals, San José has a number of thorough-going Christians. They have a profound knowledge of the basic principles of Christian doctrine. They regard themselves as creatures of the Lord, redeemed by Jesus Christ, and participants in his church. In everything they do they are mindful of the presence of death, and they rarely fall into sin. Their virtues shed their light everywhere, at all hours, quietly. They receive the sacraments, and attend Mass and Rosary daily. They treat the clergy with great respect. They would avoid heretics, if there were any. They carry out as many charitable works as they can. They pray often, but it is not mere lip service, cant, or sanctimony. They are not "sacristy rats"—although San José has those, too. They are just and devout, and number less than a dozen. The villagers say they will go to heaven, shoes and all.

The demon of pleasure comes knocking at their doors just as he does anywhere else, and they let him in.

---

[8] The most popular of these is the UFCM (Mexican Women's Catholic Union). It has about ninety members.

Pleasurable Occasions and a
Digression concerning Happiness

Perhaps the citizens of San José are not having any more fun than they used to, although there are more kinds of entertainment and they have the time and inclination. All they lack is the money. In the opinion of some local moralists, if they had the means they would be just as licentious as the people who live along the prodigal Marsh of Chapala. They feel the call of sybaritism, but are restrained by poverty. There is less enthusiasm than before for games of chance, *charrería*, reading, and conversation. Today San Joséans enjoy modern sports, tourism, and spectacles. A large percentage of the population spends a good part of the day glued to the radio or television.

Pleasures of the table have survived unharmed. Most people still enjoy admirable digestions; the rich and moderately well-to-do prefer food that tastes good, without worrying about whether it is nutritious, fattening, or harmful. Housewives and restaurateurs realize that food must, above all, be delicious. Among the dishes that meet this condition are *minguiche*, cheesecake, tamales, Lenten *capirotada*, *corundas*, corn soup, fritters, *ates*, refried beans, *chiles rellenos*, and everything that is greasy, highly spiced, or sweet. Everyone drinks *atole*, *pajaretes* (milk laced with alcohol), *aguamiel*, milk, Nescafé, hot chocolate, beer, rum-and-Coke, mescal, and soft drinks. They chew vigorously on peaches, fried meat, jerky, barbecued goat, sugar cane, *quiote*, and *chicharrones*. Easier to chew but noisier are the *tostadas* sold by Chole Partida and María Valdovinos in their restaurants, the *buñuelos*, the golden-yellow *chongos*, the tacos browned in pork fat, and other snacks. All of which shows that the people of San José love to eat.

Sleeping has lost ground in the past few years, because of speed, noise, and electric lights. Before, you could doze off in the saddle, or catch forty winks whenever you felt like it while you were working, and at night you slept soundly from nine until dawn. "Now it's impossible," some say. This is obviously an exaggeration, because automobiles do not race their engines or blow their horns very often, because the jukeboxes, radios, and televisions all together do not make a thousandth of the racket one hears in the city, and because San José is not really a metropolis glittering with lights. Things usually move slowly, work schedules (when they exist) are very flexible, and very few people's nerves are on edge. The great majority of the population enjoy a full and well-earned night's sleep.

Sports are popular with younger people, adolescents, and children. *Charrería* is not; its three champions (Rodolfo Sánchez, Miguel Reyes, and Ignacio García) are in their seventies, and its promoter, Padre Federico, will soon be eighty. When the young men don *charro* outfits, all they prove is that clothes do not make the man, and that sometimes they unmake him—as is happening in the case of Chema García and his brother, "El Piporro." The *charro* parade has ceased to be the main attraction of every fiesta; it now draws no more attention than the crepe-paper streamers strung across the streets. As for hunting, only Alberto Partida Chávez takes it seriously. These days, most children and adults are soccer and volleyball fans. There are four adult soccer teams in San José, and one in each of the larger *rancherías*. The village soccer field is in frequent use. Local players compete with teams from other towns and have matches with Padre Cuéllar's boys from Guadalajara, who come to spend their vacations in San José. Winning seems to be more important than playing. In any case, interest in sports is growing.

The Sunday evening *serenata*—when the girls and boys stroll round and round the village square for the romantic purpose of seeing and being seen—is dying out. Now, lovers prefer to sit on the benches in the plaza or around the tables in María Valdovinos's café, or to walk along the streets—and not only on Sundays. Sweethearts meet any time, anywhere; they paw each other in the darkness of the movie theater while their elders pretend not to notice. Premarital contact is no longer as shocking as it once was. In this, as in other things, the tinge of puritanism is disappearing—slowly, but with no particular fuss. Young people of both sexes can now go swimming together, attired in the customary bathing suits. With no shyness at all they plunge into the ocean or into Lake Chapala or into the region's only swimming pool: the natural one at Aguacaliente. And all without the dreaded downfall from the Christian life.

Cards and other games of chance have many mature devotees—and an occasional young one. These amusements, like *charrería*, are going downhill not for lack of enthusiasm but because they do not interest young people. Several of the card players would be living in Mexico City with their families if it were not for the long and serious card parties organized by Alejandro Salcedo and Leocadio Toscano in their respective homes. Two dozen or more gamesters spend most of the day there, exchanging their meager funds. They could not be quieter or more absorbed if they were attending Mass. There are others who play only the lottery. Since no one sells tickets in the village, they go to Jiquilpan or Sahuayo to buy them; they are delighted whenever they get their money back, and jump for joy if they win a prize—which is never "the big one."

People read very little; instead, they talk, listen, and watch. Not many are expert conversationalists. They do not work any more than they used to, but they talk less—especially the younger people. The new means of communication tend to make them uncommunicative. Even so, at any hour of the day one finds groups of people talking in the plaza, on street corners, in stores, and in bars; these are mostly older citizens, or ones who have just returned from Mexico City or the "Yunaites." They have many things to tell about the city; they exaggerate their adventures, offer highly colored narratives, and sprinkle their accounts with all kinds of lies—not to impress anyone, but to amuse their listeners. "These days, nobody believes anything you say, anyway."

Old people talk about the perennial subjects: the weather, crimes, everyday affairs, horses, and cattle. They also reminisce. They tell and retell the history of the village, from the time of Martín Toscano to the present, and recount the events of the *cristero* rebellion. They concern themselves, too, with the future—their own, their family's, and that of their native region. They make hardly any reference to what may be happening in the world or in the Mexican republic. Their view of the future is very narrow and, in general, optimistic. They do not discard the possibility that the village may become stagnant, or even that it may be abandoned; but that is not the usual view. It is more common to speak of it as an area that will one day take advantage of all the advances of science, to assert that, when the sleeper awakes, San José will be heard from.

The youngsters talk a great deal less—and about other things. They discuss fabulous business deals, women, and politics—and little else. They prefer billiards and sports to any kind of spectacle. They do not enjoy plays. There is a local theater, as there is in every town in the country; it is in the school run by the nuns. Every year there are one or two performances. The actors are primary-school girls, and the audiences consist of children from the other schools and an occasional old man or old woman. The plays and the acting are usually ingenuous.

No house in the village or the *rancherías* is without a radio, which is turned on for many hours every day. Old songs are the most popular, although the youngsters like the new rhythms. They also enjoy the broadcasts of the big football games. The radio has had something to do with the falling-off of movie audiences. Leocadio's noisy loudspeaker brings very few people to see the films, and the average weekly attendance is not more than three hundred. The causes of this withdrawal seem to be the radio, the fleas, the uncomfortable seats, and television.

San José's first television set was installed in 1965. At the end of 1967 there were 114—one for every forty inhabitants, or one for every five houses. They bring in three channels: 2, 4, and 6. In their own houses or their neighbors', people watch the movies that hardly anyone goes to the movie theater to see. Adults enjoy the episodes of *Bird without a Nest*, *The Right to Be Born*, and *The Storm*; not many watch the bullfights or the news programs. Those who learn English from watching television can be counted on the fingers of one hand. Most of the younger adults and teen-agers see the football games.

In their grandparents' time everyone was eager to see a bishop; now it is the idols of movies and television who fascinate people. Since these personages do not deign to visit San José, some villagers make trips to the city to see them in person. Many more are content with their imitators. Three or four times a year caravans of entertainers come to the village: a second Cantinflas, another Javier Solís, a resuscitated Jorge Negrete, and other pseudo bishops of song, come-dy, dance, and related arts. They draw crowds of at least a thousand, who perch on the bleachers of the *lienzo charro* to listen, watch, and applaud. In the matter of spectacles, people are easy to please.

These caravans of pseudo stars, starlets, and asteroids are more popular than the one formal bullfight, the one *charreada* with *charros* from Mexico City, the sporadic puppet and marionette shows, the annual nine days of cockfights, or any other live presentation in San José during the year. The circus no longer comes; nobody thinks of reviving the greased-pole contest; in March there are always fire-works, but they don't create much of a stir. Kermises are held to raise money for this or that, but they bring in very little.

There remain weddings with music and dancing, family or group picnics, midnight serenades, tourism, photography, a little reading (the *Guide, Selecciones del "Reader's Digest," Life, Siempre, Super-man*, the dailies from Guadalajara and Mexico City, and some light fiction). There are few readers, even among those who have finished school. Family gatherings are probably less popular than they were. We know very little about the pleasures of the night. A great deal could be said about innocent nonsense and jokes.

The large fiestas have grown more splendid, but they have di-minished in intensity. The one on September 15–16 includes speeches by the school teachers, and by the *jefe de tenencia*'s secretary. There is a reading of the Declaration of Independence that was proclaimed in Chilpancingo. Small boys stand on the stage and recite poems about the priest from Dolores, and Morelos, and other heroes of the time. School children and mounted *charros* parade through the streets. The flag is raised and unfurled; at that moment, hundreds of men wearing pistols (there are still a great many who do) have the fun of firing into the air. In fact, this is a common amusement: drunks do it every night. Of all the fiestas, only San José's most important one—that commemorating its founding—has been depistolized.

There are three days of the year when San José undergoes a tre-mendous expansion: March 17, 18, and 19. Many emigrants return to visit their relatives and friends, and men come up from the *rancherías*. The bars, especially the large one set up for the occasion in the arcade, fill up with drunks. The elderly men never miss the cockfights and the betting; the youngsters enjoy the *serenata*; the ranchers gather to watch the *charros*. Many outsiders come to see the formal bullfight. Children stay up past their bedtime to watch the fireworks; during the day they wander from the parade to the eleven o'clock bullfight, and from there to the merry-go-round, the shooting gallery, the gimcrack stalls, and the tents housing monsters and other fascinating things. Side by side with the profane merrymaking, there is a religious celebration.

And, as if all these amusements were not enough, it must be pointed out that San Joséans even enjoy working. To put it another way, their day of routine occupations is usually a mixture of work and relaxation. The separation between the two is not as sharp as it is in the city. Shopkeepers play solitaire between customers, and when one comes in, they have a good chat. Is this working? Women knit and sew as they cut their neighbors down to size, thus killing two birds with one stone. It is hard to say where work begins and amusement leaves off in many farming activities: looking for a stray animal, taking a walk around the pasture to mend fences, getting up very early in the morning to do something or other, bringing in the harvest and joining in the cornhusking, going out to pick cactus leaves, mushrooms, prickly pears, purslane, and the like, and hunting doves.

To sum up: life in San José is less comfortable and offers perhaps fewer opportunities for prefabricated pleasure than that in such places as Mexico City; but the joy of existence, or earthly happiness, seems to be present in larger amounts. Either people here are never as unhappy as they are in the cities, or they are better able to cope with it. In any case, there are no suicides and few signs of neuroses in San José de Gracia and its environs. Life is not idyllic, certainly; but neither is it sad or monotonous. It is more reminiscent of the poetry of Ramón López Velarde than of the prose of Juan Rulfo.

The desire for a better life does not contradict any of the foregoing; it indicates merely that San Joséans—or most of the young people, at any rate—are not satisfied with their world. Even so, there are a good many houses with happy men in them. Miguel Reyes, Rodolfo Sánchez, Juan Gudiño, Juan Chávez, Porfirio González, and many more find no fault with their native village and would not exchange their life for any other—not even for that in heaven. If they were not a minority, these men would set the tone for the community. Today that tone is set by those who are ambitious for comfort, wealth, and progress—or, more accurately, by those who are only a little ambitious: the really ambitious ones move away as soon as they can. The people who remain do not aspire to many of the pleasures of modern city life, or they do not believe that fabulous wealth, easy living, and a great variety of amusements bring happiness.

Happiness and opportunities for pleasure are not uniformly distributed. It cannot be said that members of the village "upper crust" have everything they need, because they want more. The poor, certainly, are seldom happy. They have less fun. Many of them admit that they are fed up with sucking on cigarettes rolled in cornhusks, gagging down cheap liquor, and gabbing about the same old things with the same old friends. Now, especially since braceros are no longer in demand, they are short of money for amusements and for alleviating the misfortunes that cash can remedy. Women of all classes seem not to have found happiness, either. In short, all the underdogs (the poor, the women, the children, and the zeroes) go around most of the time in a state of sadness—a meek kind of sadness, with frequent lightning flashes of hatred.

10. THE UNDERDOGS

*Small Landowners and Men
Who Work for Other Men*

THE THOUSAND poor families are divided into landowners and day laborers. One-third of them have parcels of land, either as *ejido* members or by private title. Their holdings are, on the average, about twelve hectares, which is usually enough to plant a *yunta* of corn and keep four or five head of cattle. From a functional point of view, they are small farmers who have no way of lifting themselves out of poverty. Their "scrap of land" produces hardly enough for them to eat, to dress miserably, and to have a little fun once in a while. Theoretically, they are free to rise to the wealthy or middle class; but they have no backing or funds to increase the productivity of their farms or to buy more land. They are at a standstill, without capital, without education, without machinery, without influence. Some cling to their patch of earth, while others are on the point of getting out and abandoning the whole thing.

The landless poor are in the majority. Except for the young men who are expecting to be called to Mexico City or to get a visa for the "Yunaites," poor people who do not yet have one foot in the grave and want to continue living in the traditional way in their native region have concentrated on a single goal: getting hold of a piece of land that they can work as an independent entity. They will not in this way raise their standard of living, any more than *ejido* members have raised theirs in the course of three decades, but they will have the satisfaction of knowing that nobody can order them around. Some, like Zenaido Martínez, the father of twelve children, are able to save enough out of their modest wages to buy a parcel. Others prefer the way of the agrarianists; they spend their lives sending in applications for land and making references to the rich people's mothers. The DAAC's answer is always the same: "No land is being granted because there are no affectible properties." The landless poor, like the landed poor, go on, as always, tending their cornfields.

Farm production is as low as ever. People continue planting the same crops. They are working more land, but they are not doing it any better. They are still employing the ancient systems of clearing and planting—using a plot of ground only on alternate years. Traditional methods of crop rotation are still employed. Mules have replaced oxen for plowing. Hoe agriculture, which is known locally as "making an *ecuaro*," is becoming little more than a hobby. There has been a notable improvement in farm tools. Tractors are not used as yet, because (they say) of the rocky terrain, and perhaps also because the farms are too small to justify individual ownership of such machines. The use of fertilizers is still beyond the reach of most small private owners and *ejido* farmers. Cereal crops are not yet grown regularly or in any quantity. A man thinks he is lucky if he can get a ton of corn from a hectare of land.

In addition to planting corn, which barely feeds them at a subsistence level, many poor people have marginal incomes as woodcutters, day laborers, or distillers. A woodcutter can bring home two burro loads a day, which he can sell for twenty pesos; if he makes the wood into charcoal, he can get a little more. Charcoal is still used for baking bread, and for cooking in kitchens that have not been modernized. Setting up a still and selling one or two barrels of mescal is sometimes a way of earning extra money. It is said that some farmers have found a good source of income in raising marijuana. The rumor is that the drug is sent to the United States and brings a high price.

Several crafts have disappeared. There are no longer any shoemakers. In 1960 Francisco Chávez, Isaac Pulido, Antonio and Raúl Orozco, and Dolores Vargas were still listed in the census as harness makers, but the fact is that their products (leather covers and cases, saddles, stirrup straps, whips, halters, riding crops, and saddlebags) are falling into desuetude.

There are no more blacksmiths, although José Chávez Fonseca and Rubén Vergara still claim to be of that profession. José is over eighty and now merely goes from house to house with a stock of tools he buys in Sahuayo. More tools are in use these days, but they are imported. The same thing has happened to sarapes. The only people who weave them today in San José are Isidro Ávila, and Ramón and Moisés Ceja. Carpenters are not flourishing, either. In San José they are José Pulido Cárdenas, Luis Partida, Adelaido Rodríguez, José Valdovinos, and some others. In short, imported, mass-produced products, cheaply made, are about to wipe out local craftsmen.

It is only the building trades that are still going strong. The following are employed as masons: Filemón Becerra, Isidro Martínez, Ignacio Partida, Daniel Pulido Córdova (the well-known, stocky individual who has built a large percentage of the poorer people's houses), Gonzalo and Manuel Villalobos, Guadalupe Vergara, and several others. Today the principal occupation of many poor families is molding and baking bricks and roof tiles. During the dry season more than a hundred people are engaged in this work. In one season a man can turn out thousands of bricks. In 1968 these were selling for 350 pesos a thousand.

The raw material is dug from muddy areas near a river or a spring. The men perform a frenzied dance in the mud, mixing it into a smooth mass. This is packed into wooden forms that give it the shape of bricks or tiles. When they have dried in the sun, the bricks are loosely stacked in towers, leaving a hollow space beneath, where the wood fire is built. When the baking is completed, and the bricks have turned red, the oven is carefully taken apart. The bricks and tiles are then loaded on the backs of burros or mules, or into trucks driven in by the buyers. These brick factories are usually family enterprises; only rarely do the operators hire paid helpers, as does Gabriel Torres.

A little later, I shall discuss the feminine occupations: candymaking, sewing, and embroidery.

There is little to be said yet about the spinning and weaving shop next door to the government primary school. It has just been opened, thanks to the energy of the school's principal, Miguel Homero Rodríguez. It is already turning out tablecloths with Oaxaca designs. These are made by the children, and they are selling like hotcakes. More looms are needed.

Very few of the local poor people bring commodities to sell at the Sunday village market, which is set up in the western arcade of the plaza. The vendors, who are usually outsiders, arrive Saturday evening to unpack their merchandise. Selling begins at seven Sunday morning and closes at five in the afternoon. The market supplies whatever is not produced locally: vegetables, crockery, fish, notions, dry goods, *rebozos*, spoons, plastic toys, sandals, and shoes. There are also local vendors on duty every day, selling things to eat; in addition to fresh beef, they offer tripe in tomato sauce, roast goat, hot corn on the cob, *atole*, tamales, fritters, hotcakes, roasted yams, *chayotes*, heart of maguey, sugar cane, and so on. Customers always haggle and examine the merchandise. They rap the crockery to see if it is cracked; they squeeze the fruit and demand pieces to taste. The cloth is checked over thread by thread. Most of these buyers are women.

Another source of income for the proletariat is wages—an insignificant one, since there is little work to be had and the average pay is fifteen pesos a day. There cannot be more than seventy cattle ranchers who need the services of milkers or cowhands. Fewer than a hundred people are working as employees on dairy farms. The cheese industry probably provides jobs for two dozen men, trade and transportation employ about sixty, and public and domestic service account for twice that number. There are not five hundred salaried workers with permanent jobs. There is even less seasonal work: the corn harvest in December, mending fences and preparing silage in October. Since there is little work and wages are low, the wife usually supplements the family income by doing embroidery and sewing, and gathering food (wild fruit, mushrooms, cactus leaves, purslane, and wild yams), while the husband goes hunting for armadillos, doves, and so forth.

Poor men must be healthy, if they are to survive. They live by their hands and by their physical strength; thus, their fear of falling ill is sometimes greater than their fear of death. They also worry a great deal about the waning of their physical and sexual powers. Keeping themselves strong, virile, and healthy is their greatest concern. This accounts for their determination to have three meals a day—one with milk and another with meat, in addition to the usual beans, tortillas, and chile. It also accounts for their panic when they are sick; they go into debt to pay the doctor and buy medicine; they swallow and grease themselves with everything prescribed by the doctor, the local quack, and their neighbors; and they pray to the greatest possible number of saints, all so they can recover their health and go back to work—if there is any.

The number of able-bodied men who are totally unemployed is very small; but 60 percent are engaged in low-paying occupations or in part-time work. At any time during the year—but particularly in the dry months—unemployed men can be seen at all hours in the plaza, in the village streets, and in front of the houses in the *rancherías*. They are willing to work, but incapable of begging or even asking someone for a loan—especially if they are young. The wealthy people claim that there are not as many unemployed here as in other towns in the area, and that no one is ever allowed to starve to death—which is true. No one is totally indifferent to their plight, but they live in the midst of insecurity.

There are no labor organizations. Each worker looks out for his own interests and defends himself as best he can. If he gets a steady job, he does everything in his power to keep it. When he has seasonal work, he tries to get into his employer's good graces in order to be put on the permanent payroll. There are, of course, some men who are unwilling to take steady work, and others who are just plain bums—but they are a tiny minority, and held in contempt.

The peasant cannot save money. Whatever he can make as a small farmer, sharecropper, woodcutter, or day laborer is hardly enough to provide the barest necessities for himself and his family: food and a few "rags" to wear. It is fortunate that he has no rent or utilities to pay. He owns the house he lives in, and only rarely does he have electric lights or running water. He cannot save anything, and his purchasing power diminishes every day. His position is considerably worse since the contracts for braceros were discontinued in 1964. Now only a miracle can lift him out of his misery. Today, however, there is a new attitude in evidence everywhere: the poor man is not as patient or as courteous as he used to be. "Times have changed."

People have become rather ungracious, and many social amenities are disappearing. Some of the youngsters have dropped the old custom of greeting everyone they meet on the street or along the road. There is less politeness in daily intercourse. Formerly, it was only the people of Sahuayo who gave their neighbors unkind nicknames, but now the habit has spread to San José. Voices are still soft, and gestures are restrained; but San Joséans no longer think that anyone who speaks loudly or behaves in a theatrical way is crazy. Loud colors are beginning to appear in women's dresses and men's shirts. It is no longer unusual to hear people speaking of intimate matters. The poor of San José are politer and more reticent than their counterparts in any city; but they seem rude when compared with their fathers and grandfathers.

When they see that their income from farming, sharecropping, and wages provides only the bare necessities, while others, with no more effort, live in ease and comfort, take a trip once in a while, eat whatever they want to, wear good jackets and shoes, build big houses, have electric lights, running water, and television, and sometimes even a pickup truck, go in anywhere without being asked, "What was it you wanted, Mister?" get drunk without being called a sot, break the law without going to jail, send for the doctor when they are sick, and sometimes even have something left over to expand their operations; when they see other people with all this, and feel that they themselves are just as deserving of the good life—then the old rancor rises. The small landowner, the day laborer, and the unemployed feel that they are being kept down by those whom they regard as rich; they cast hostile and envious glances at the employer class, and even at the middle class; they begin to hate them, and they are usually repaid in the same coin. The climate of hostility broadens and deepens, because of envy, because of "hating to see other people get ahead," because of the conviction that, if others have gotten rich, it has been at their expense, or through sheer luck.

Many of the older people still speak well of their employer; they feel satisfaction in being of service to him; they are grateful for a kind smile, a gift, any mark of regard. They take pride in the fact that their wives or daughters are asked to help their employer's wife in emergencies—when she has company, or is ill, or is called away, or has arranged a picnic, or is in mourning. Of course, any manifestations of affection are most discreet; San Joséans are not demonstrative.

But most young people and some of the adults are not like their fathers. They have no inclination toward loyalty, gratitude, or affection. Gifts and tokens of esteem and confidence from their employer leave them unimpressed. They may not say anything against their boss, since they are not so foolish as to bite the hand that feeds them; but they speak of the employer class with rancor. According to the employers, the young workers are money-hungry; they are interested in nothing but high wages; while they were in the United States they got into the bad habit of making a lot of money, which they will never be able to do in the village, where business is so poor. The employers wish they would go somewhere else, and there are many who do them that favor. Others, however, are unwilling to leave their native heath. They prefer to live badly but in familiar surroundings, or they are too lazy, or they lack the courage. So they remain where they are, grumbling, cursing the rich, and listening to rebellious proposals by radical groups.

To sum up, then, there are many factors that have contributed to the present state of discord, the contention between the young proletarians and the property owners: the still-smoldering embers of the hatred that accompanied the agrarian reform of the thirties; the suspension of the bracero program, which had acted as a safety valve; the low productivity of the area; the unequal distribution of wealth; the dissolution of ancient bonds of friendship (the godparent-parent-child relationship, the unity of the family, and so on); *machismo*; individualism (the feeling that one is "just as good as anybody else"—that one is a "man's man"; the doctrine that "everybody should solve his own problems"—insisting that "I can take care of myself"; the suspicion, and extreme sensitivity); the obsession expressed by "I wonder what those rich sons of bitches are plotting now"; social unrest; envy; "hating to see other people get ahead"; the unshakable belief that wealth can be obtained only at someone else's expense; the certainty that some men are rich only because other men are fools; the idea that the rich live off the poor; the notion that wealth is not to be obtained through labor ("and if that's wrong, just tell me, and I'll kill myself working"); and the conviction that "people get rich because they know how to steal."

The man who accepts the sordid aspects of life as something natural and inevitable is a rarity these days, and so is the man who does not malign somebody. The destitute country people are continually hurling insults at those who own three-quarters of the land. Although violence is less common than it used to be, the poor are threatening to make use of it. "Don't try to weasel out of it, you rich bastards. We'll see who gets the short end of the stick this time. You have your lawyers, and we have ours." They all chip in to hire attorneys; only to this point are they capable of cooperation. The menacing poor man, like the apprehensive rich man, is radically and fundamentally an individualist. Because he does not want to have to depend upon a boss, he aspires to own a piece of land of his own. But it is that same strong sense of individualism that keeps him from working with others in order to obtain it.

The Woman Produces Children, Meals, and Art

Unlike some other places, San José has not yet become a village of women and children, although these are, of course, in the majority. Forty-seven percent of the population consists of little people under fifteen. According to the census of 1967, there were 2,476 women over fifteen: 30 percent of the total. It can be seen that families tend to be smaller these days—the average number is six. Nevertheless, the ideal family is still a large one, especially among the poorer people. Nearly all unions have been sanctioned by the church and the state, and they are so stable that legal divorce is unheard-of and separation is very rare.

Women have risen to a higher position. The father is still the head of the family, but today he wields less authority over his wife and children. In many cases the wife seems to share the authority with her husband. Only rarely is she completely dominated by her spouse, allowing herself to be beaten or otherwise mistreated. This is not to say, however, that they have fallen into the practice of showing their fondness for each other. The man expresses his love for his family in actions, not in kind words; he provides the basic necessities for the home and does not concern himself with expressions or gestures of affection. Kissing is just now beginning to appear among the younger people. There is little intimate contact in the home, and even less in public. Although the wife receives no more caresses than she used to, she has more freedom every day, thanks to the revolution against male authority and the advent of some modern conveniences. Public mills for grinding corn, together with the tortilla factory, have liberated her from three to five hours a day of slaving over a *metate*. Sewing machines, gas stoves, and running water have lightened the load of a third of the female population.

With the exception of about fifty who work in shops and offices, a dozen schoolteachers, and an equal number of gossipmongers, women still conform to the tradition of spending most of their time at home. In the *rancherías* it is not unusual for a woman to help her husband in the field and in caring for the animals; but generally she leaves the house only to go to the river to wash clothes. Those in the village may attend church services, take a walk, or go shopping. Most feminine occupations and amusements take place indoors. Today's woman is free and active, but within her own home. This varies according to her status as a mother, an old maid, or a girl of marriageable age: each group has its own rules. In general, women's activities are more flexible and indeterminate than men's.

Although many mothers have been liberated from the toil of grinding corn and making tortillas, they are still the ones who have to face the hardest jobs in the home. They bear, on the average, one child every two years for two decades. Thirty percent give birth with the help of a doctor, and the rest depend upon a midwife. They follow the traditional diet prescribed for a good supply of mother's milk, and they nurse their children. They have the exclusive care of them—

for the first seven years, in the case of boys, and until they leave home, if they are girls. Except for a few who have maids, they are "roasted alive" during their many hours in the kitchen, cooking meals for the family. They wash dishes, sew, mend, sweep, dust, and beat. If they have daughters to help them, they have time to gossip, to listen to the soap opera on the radio, and to watch television. Scolding their husbands, putting up with them, and keeping them in line are other very important tasks they perform with resignation and little fuss. They often add to the family income by doing various kinds of work. The phenomena of the unfaithful wife and the licentious single woman do not appear—at least not noticeably. The sex life of these women is the most highly controlled thing in the world.

If one of the unmarried girls gets pregnant, it is the greatest tragedy imaginable. The unwed mother goes through hell. She is disgraced for the rest of her life. In fact, however, this seldom happens. Only 2 percent of all children born these days are illegitimate.

The few girls who have been carried off by lovers who refuse to marry them, or who have had premarital relations, are held in very low regard. Sexual liberation for women is not even in sight yet.

In cases where the young couple must force the girl's father to give his consent to the marriage, she is sometimes carried off to spend the night with the young man; this practice is tolerated, but not looked upon with favor. Girls who "run off" under any other circumstances almost always end up unmarried, for a man's honor demands that his wife be a virgin. In fact, a woman's good name is like a piece of glass· it can be shattered or smudged very easily. Even when she is no longer a virgin, she must think like one. A girl who has lost her virginity may find that her life is in danger; her parents or brothers may give her a terrible beating. The worst happens when the men of the family feel obliged to wash out the insult with blood. "A woman's dishonor does not affect her alone. Her humiliation is contagious; it besmears her parents and her brothers and sisters. That is, if she's unmarried. If she's a widow, a wife, or living with some man, then naturally it isn't so serious. As the old saying goes, 'Between a saint and an angel, put up a stone wall.' You have to be on your guard; otherwise, there's trouble. Girls have to leave town, people talk about them, and more than one ends up living as a loose woman, loses all her shame, and gives herself to anybody."

Old maids "hardly ever leave their corner, their hidden lookout, and yet they know everything that's going on." "They end up by learning more about human nature than someone who walks about in the open air, whipped by the winds of fortune." Like the mothers, they are seen most often in church, where they are indispensable for draping and undraping the statues of the saints, tending to the parish's charitable activities, and watching over public morals. At home the old maid is the babysitter and the prototype of the industrious housekeeper. Old maids have turned the village into an enormous factory for needlework and embroidery; they have to some extent made up for the missing dollars with the pesos they earn with their tablecloths, bedspreads, and, in particular, their Spanish shawls. In the past seven years they have become the greatest competitors of the shawl makers of Granada, and many other local women have followed their example. Today two hundred needleworkers turn out an equal number of Spanish shawls every month; but they sell for very low prices, and the annual production does not exceed 900,000 pesos.

Sewing and embroidery are the favorite occupations of young single girls, too. After the trauma of their first menstrual periods, special care is taken to make them into "proper young ladies"—which is to say good seamstresses, cooks, ironers, housekeepers, and guardian angels for their younger brothers and sisters. They must also be devout, clean, sweet, and home-loving. When they reach puberty they lose many childhood liberties. They are forbidden to loiter in the street, play with boys, or give their opinions about anything. Their reading and entertainments are supervised, and they are impressed with the importance of several virtues: chastity, obedience, self-denial, resignation, and thrift. Their education follows the same pattern as their mothers' and grandmothers'; but they are allowed to use makeup and dress according to the fashion.

The current vogue for short hair is observed, along with other abbreviations demanded by the worship of the body. The girls of San José, always a little behind the young ladies of the city, are raising their hemlines higher every day, showing more leg than has ever been seen before. They worry about their hips and suppress their curves by means of dieting and wearing certain articles of clothing. San José girls use cosmetics and perfume, of course; but their make-up makes them look less artificial and mechanical than most city women. They keep their distance from fashions in the capital; they are even giving up the local habit of smoking, just to be different from the snooty city girls. Once out of school, they give up sports completely; they say they get all the exercise they need doing housework.

Much more could be said about the women of marriageable age. It is their attitude toward marriage that is most surprising. Although they worry less than their mothers did about finding a husband, they find one more easily. In the past, girls hardly ever considered marrying outsiders; today they prefer them. (And the predilection is mutual, because San José girls are chock-full of virtues, and good-looking, besides.) "They adore birds and flowers, children and old women." Today things are a little different; now they adore, above all, boys from Guadalajara and Mexico City, because they are eager to leave the village and live in the city.

In the slow abandonment of San José and its *rancherías*, women are playing a very important role. They soften up fathers who are unwilling to let their children leave their native soil. Young wives try to persuade their husbands that the family's future lies in the city. At family gatherings it is they who remind everyone how well some of their former neighbors are doing in Mexico City. They argue with those who worry about the moral degeneration that takes place in the city. They insist that the only people who go astray are those who are naturally wicked; they point out that youngsters are in greater danger if they remain in the village, where so many fall into vice because there is no work for them.

Women have taken the lead in making another important decision (here we are speaking of mothers of about thirty-five, not of old women, and certainly not of the ones who have been "passed by"). Mothers with four children or more have taken to using birth-control pills, with or without the approval of their husbands. It is said that this group includes only a few of the poorer women; they are mostly of the middle class, although it was the women of the "upper" class who introduced the practice. The most modest among them get their pills and instructions from the druggists in Sahuayo. Others go to local doctors. Birth control is still such a new idea that women have not yet formulated any precise justifications for making use of it; they know only that they do not want more children. About seventy—a tenth of the potential mothers—take the pills faithfully.

Women are the champions of the little art that is produced in the community of San José. If we leave out Enrique González, the painter, and Ramiro Chávez, a writer, sculptor, and actor who has left town, we find only women in the field. They decorate the church for fiestas and weddings; they turn out beautifully woven and embroidered bedspreads, Spanish shawls, and tablecloths; they plant patio gardens; they do dressmaking, make floral arrangements, and create a thousand kinds of exquisite decorations from crepe paper; and they raise flowers. In spite of the fact that the modern woman does not neglect her looks or her attire, the art that is practiced least by the girls of San José is that of keeping themselves beautiful. After they marry they become careless of their appearance—especially if they live out in the country. They either grow fat or become dried-up and wrinkled, and they make no effort to be attractive.

It is in the art of cooking, of course, that they show their greatest talent. If women are so insistent that their men eat well, it is because they know they are champions in the kitchen. Among the famous dishes are Olivia Cárdenas's tamales, Sara Martínez's *buñuelos*, and the desserts made by Elena Alcázar, Toña Martínez, and Lola Pulido. Josefina González Cárdenas's *chongos* and cheesecake are without parallel. They all make excellent corn soup, *corundas*, and *toqueras*. Some of the all-around culinary artists are the Villanueva sisters (Elena, Eduwigis, Pepa, and Rita), Elpidia González, Chela and Mariquita Sánchez, Esther Godínez (a dressmaker as well), Amelia Sánchez, Lola Magaña, María Álvarez, María Pulido González, Librada Chávez, Rita Anaya, Leonor Arias, Soledad González, Antonia González and her two daughters (Carmelita and Pina), Consuelo Pulido, Emilia Novoa, and Herminia Sánchez.

Finally, it is the women who are most concerned with their children's education. There are, of course, more women teachers than men; but it is not there that one sees the greatest interest. It is the mothers, more than anyone, who insist that their children go to school and who concern themselves with the progress of education. The director of the government school calls a meeting of parents every two months. He insists that it is more important that the fathers come than that the mothers do; yet there are usually about 150 women present and never more than 40 men, and it is the women who take part in the discussions.

Today Many Youngsters Go to School

Children are half the population of San José and its greatest sta-bilizer. There are 3,947 under fifteen. About half of them are girls. Little men are treated with more respect than little women. The birth of a son is a happy occasion; more will be expected of him than of a daughter, and he will be brought up more carefully. Each stage in the life of a child calls for special handling and for supervision by different people. Infants up to seven are cared for by their mothers and their elder sisters; this is a centuries-old tradition which is now disappearing.

The aim of early training is to emphasize the difference between boys and girls, to teach them the correct hand to offer when greeting someone, and other social niceties, and to endow them at an early age with a few accomplishments. A week after birth, the infant is taken in his swaddling clothes, with his godparents, to be baptized and recorded in the Registry. After this first excursion into the world, he is taught to tell somebody when he wants to make *pipí* and *popó*, to cross himself, to say *papá* and *mamá*, and to show where God is.

In early infancy, children depend almost exclusively upon their mothers. Some fathers, in spite of other men's ridicule, are brave enough to help their wives care for the younger ones. There is a growing practice of buying toys, brightly-colored clothing, and shoes for babies. Their mothers do their best to keep them clean. In the past, children under seven were never punished to any extent, and today, even less. Physical punishment is resorted to only rarely, and it is never severe; the mother who spanks her little ones is looked upon with disapproval. Children are punished less; they are allowed to play more; and now it is acceptable to show signs of affection, to kiss and pet them. People still hold the view that a child should not be spoiled, that too much indulgence makes him insolent and unruly, and that obedience should be the first virtue. The other virtues, in order, should be piety, industry, and learning to read and write.

Blind obedience is demanded of children. Boys are taught to be courageous and daring so that they may be able to take care of themselves. Both boys and girls must be able to stand pain, to suffer without whimpering, from an early age. They must not be allowed to criticize others, or they will grow up to be faultfinders, like everybody else. They should not be buttinskies, or go around showing off. When adults get together, children are not allowed to hang around. There are certain things they are not allowed to hear. When they are present, sex is not mentioned and no one criticizes his neighbor.

As soon as they are seven or eight, almost all children help their parents in different ways: the girls lend a hand with household chores, and the boys assist their fathers in the fields, the workshop, or wherever they can. At the same time they are beginning to work, they learn to pray. They are given instruction at home and are enrolled in catechism classes held in the church. Today's children devote less time than their parents did to becoming good workers and Christians, and more to playing and studying. These days most youngsters from seven to fourteen spend more than half their time at school and doing homework.

On Saturdays and Sundays a swarm of small fry offer their services as shoeshine boys. Sometimes there are just enough customers to go around; at other times a boy may get only one shoe to shine, or even none at all. It isn't a big job, and the boys are very fast. A San José boy needs no more than five minutes to transform a pair of shoes that are gray with a week's dust into two dark, glistening objects. During the week one never sees a bootblack. Some are in school, and the rest are helping their fathers. The latter are the boys who have left school. Some of them have completed their six years of primary education; but the majority have been taken out after two or three years, hardly able to read and write any better than their parents.

If we are to believe the census figures, 72 percent of all San Joséans over seven can read and write; but a great number of these "literate" citizens read with difficulty, syllable by syllable, and their writing is a scrawl. It is only since 1967 that nearly everyone has had access to the primary grades. There are three institutions offering the first six years of education: the government school, the church school, and "the Haven." The first of these has had the worst building, but soon it will have the best (a new plant with twelve large, well-separated, comfortable classrooms). In the *rancherías* there are seven schools, where the rudiments of reading, writing, and arithmetic are taught by nonprofessionals who are often absent and by rural teachers who are not distinguished for their punctuality, either. Still, they are considerably better than they were. The education provided offers hardly anything useful for those who live in the community; but, even though it conflicts to some extent with home training, parents are not unwilling to enroll their children in school.

Resistance on the part of some farmers toward the schools is disappearing. Interest in education falls off as one moves farther away from San José and the highway; but fathers who live outside the town will allow their children to be enrolled in school, and sometimes they even ask for it. In the village itself the middle and upper classes take an interest in the education of their offspring; they make sure they go to school, and many mothers supervise their homework from day to day. Most of them want their sons to be people of some education, instead of laborers; there are men, and especially women, who worship learning to the point of believing that it is more important to build schools than churches. In Sabino, the largest *ranchería* in the *tenencia*, two hundred children were without instruction for six years, and you should have seen the mob of women making pilgrimages to Jiquilpan to confront the inspector of education and demand a teacher.

In the entire *tenencia* there are two thousand children from seven to sixteen; only a little more than half of them were in school during the year that began in November, 1967. Thirty-three percent were in the first grade, 23 percent in the second, 12 percent in the third, 8 percent in the fourth, 5 percent in the fifth, and only 4 percent in the sixth. The remaining 15 percent included 9 percent in kindergarten,

4 percent in the young ladies' cooking and sewing academy, and 2 percent in the new secondary school.

The three schools with the most pupils, and the only ones offering all six years of primary instruction, are in the village of San José de Gracia. Four hundred and eighty girls and boys attend the government plant, "José María Morelos"; "the Haven," or nuns' school, or "Colegio Guadalupe," has 325, including those of kindergarten age (after the first year of primary school it accepts only girls); Padre José Luis Garibay's "Colegio Libertad" has an enrollment of 236, all boys. The three schools are in constant competition; there is a running argument about which has the best scholars, the best orators, and the best soccer players. Each one tries to teach more and with better methods. The competition is a healthy one. There are other aspects of the educational picture, however, that leave something to be desired: a shortage of teachers, overcrowding, student absenteeism, and withdrawals.

The fact that more than half of the children leave school after one or two years is not the only problem. A large percentage are often absent, especially in the *rancherías*. The highest absence rate is found at planting time, during the harvest, and while fiestas are going on. The teachers say that parents give higher priority to farm work than to education. They think, too, that this is why some youngsters are taken out of school as soon as they are barely able to read and write; but in this case there is another reason. The *ranchería* schools offer only the first and second years; after that, the farmers are unable to send their children elsewhere to continue their studies. Teachers do not complain of discipline problems, or of low achievement levels. Those who have served in other towns say that in San José the pupils are superior: they are less unruly, more attentive, more studious, and they do not display the mental laziness to be found among people with faulty nutrition. Students seem to present the greatest problems during their first and fourth years.

Although the content of education has not been adjusted completely to the needs of the community, the school has considerable influence. In addition to teaching youngsters to read and write, it accustoms them to cleanliness and hygiene, it instills the concept of and love for their country, and it helps to moderate their extreme individualism. It encourages better understanding between the sexes, makes children feel less oppressed by their elders, intensifies their competitive spirit, and gives them a liking for sports: soccer, volleyball, swimming, basketball, and the rest.

The taste for these physical exercises has brought a falling-off of interest in the traditional sports and in some ancient forms of amusement: steer roping, horseback riding, practicing the *charro* arts, hiking, flying kites, playing marbles, making *runfadores*, spinning tops, and so on. Sports of Anglo-Saxon origin are encouraged because they are credited with thousands of effects leading to the development of the mass-produced personality. It is claimed that they teach cooperation and competition simultaneously; that they curb eccentricity; that they have the virtue of turning wolves into sheep and of producing an excellent flock. The youngsters of San José are undoubtedly going full speed ahead toward the modern passion for sports, and these small competitors will probably grow up to be healthy men, with little or no individuality—happy, robust, and submissive to the umpires and rules of the social game.

On festive occasions, both civil and religious, the small fry have more fun than the adults. A hundred or so gather at the door of the church on Sunday mornings. Baptisms take place from eleven to one, and anywhere from three to six new godparents will come out and throw coins into the throng of children. Anyone who fails to do so runs the risk of being insulted, or even attacked. Godparents must also give their godchildren their "allowance" once a week and provide a special present on Twelfth Night. The little ones leave their shoes or huaraches at their godparents' house and, early in the morning on January 6, pick them up with a gift inside. After they pass the age of ten, youngsters begin to take an interest in the pool hall and in sports—the road to ruin and the road to virtue.

When they are fifteen or sixteen, young men must decide whether they will remain in San José or go to seek their fortunes in the city; until this decision has been made, they are a headache to their parents, for after they reach thirteen there is no longer any school they can attend, and they have nothing to keep them occupied. They begin to smoke, drink, have love affairs, stay out all night, swagger around, masturbate, fight, and engage in sports. They become good-for-nothings, hell-raisers, and ruffians. They play pool or wander aimlessly about. The young men of today are smarter than their predecessors, yet their bad habits can turn them into a swarm of insects, a wasp's nest of vicious human beings.

Human Pests and Other Sources of Annoyance

In spite of today's higher tolerance in such matters, many villagers believe that there is more abnormality in San José than there used to be. A study made by experts might come up with some serious conclusions concerning the local pathology and its possible causes. Here we can only list some of the types of behavior that the inhabitants find annoying: either rebellion or absolute conformity, idiocy, insanity, chronic alcoholism, pugnacity, unsociability, vagrancy, prostitution, and disease.

Thirty years ago the most troublesome personages in the *tenencia* of Ornelas were the "ghosts," which now have just about disappeared. In first place were the souls in purgatory, like those of Martín Toscano and Doña Pomposa. They were formless spirits, made of smoke, who begged one to return some money they had borrowed from so-and-so, or asked to have some buried money dug up, or wanted some religious matter taken care of. Then there were the flaming souls of the damned, who came back from hell to inform the living of their eternal torment and the reasons for their presence in the army of the condemned. In third place came the demons who specialized in breaking plates and cups; the devils seen by those who were gravely ill— red all over, with horns and tails; those who dragged chains at all hours of the night; the ones who appeared in the shape of black dogs or howling cats; and those who took the form of a rich dandy from the capital. These ghostly figures are no longer encountered in San José, where few people still believe in them; even out in the *rancherías* they are becoming rarer. Ghosts and comets keep no one awake these days. Atomic bombs and flying saucers have not yet become things to be afraid of. Bad storms do not frighten people as they used to. Every day there are fewer reasons for terror. Even villains are going out of business.

The living devils, the crafty desperadoes, the evil-hearted men, capable of sinking a knife into anybody, at any time, or of putting a bullet into someone just because they felt like it, of committing any crime for a price—if there are still any of these people around, they are keeping their inhuman natures very well hidden. Today there are no professional criminals in the *tenencia*. Those who were left over from the era of violence have put aside their evil ways, or have gone away to join some famous police organization, or (and this is the most common) they have been killed by their victims' relatives. Crimes against persons still occur, but they are fewer every day. Every year someone is shot to death, and a couple of people are wounded. There is more aggression, but it is taken out in words or gestures, or suppressed; it seldom draws blood. Although there is less solidarity, people are not as tolerant of homicide as they once were. Bravado is no longer admired; it is looked down upon and ridiculed, especially in the village itself.

Professional thieves are not found in San José and its outlying settlements. Highwaymen have been wiped out. The few robberies that occur are not the work of local people. One hears employers saying that hired hands are not as respectful of other people's property as they used to be. It seems that some of the milkers and field hands do a little business of their own behind their employer's back—with commodities they have no right to; they cheat in small ways and betray their boss's trust; they eke out their miserable wages with petty thefts. Thus, they make their lives a little easier, or find the money to meet some extra expense: illness or death in the family, a wedding, or a baptism. Many men, however, do not dare to commit even these tiny crimes. In case of an emergency they ask for a loan, which they never repay.

Pests that are on the increase these days are alcoholics, reckless drivers, idiots, and beggars. San José has its own, and, in addition, it has taken on its shoulders some from neighboring communities, particularly Mazamitla. There are a dozen full-time drunks in the village, and twice as many in the *rancherías*. These have increased since men started going north as braceros. Half of today's chronic alcoholics took up the habit with money earned in the United States. They began by celebrating their happy homecoming and ended up by becoming professional drunkards. The rest did not carry things quite that far, but they are not as abstemious as they were. Drunkenness began to be more common in the forties, and it is still on the rise. While it has ruined many poor devils, it has been the making of some fifty dealers in alcohol and firewater.

No priest has succeeded in wiping out backbiting, the habit of constantly criticizing one's neighbors. People say this man is a jackass, and that one is swell-headed. "So-and-so doesn't bother to ask you for something; he would just like you to put it where he can reach it." "That old woman's a busybody." "They're all a bunch of good-for-nothings." "He's talking just because he's got a big mouth." And so on.

The mentally ill have always been a small percentage of the populace. Today there are no more than two harmless madmen and half a dozen retarded individuals. No drug addicts or sexual deviates are to be found. There are few prostitutes, but quite a few oligophrenics. Márgaro spends his days singing the same song, accompanying himself on the guitar, and hurling insults at anyone who tells him to shut up. There are some other less spectacular half-wits and there is more than one complete idiot. A psychiatrist could find some paranoiacs, manic-depressives, and people crazed by old age or alcohol, but perhaps not in such a high proportion as in the cities. There are undoubtedly a few neurotics, especially among the women. Everyone, except the doctors, attributes such disorders to organic disease or to "weakness."

Although San José has twenty or thirty beggars, the problem does not seem serious when compared to the situation in Sahuayo or Cotija. Those who go around with their hands out represent only a small number of the destitute. The others rarely ask for alms; generally they begin by making a request for a loan. First they ask how the family is, talk about how hard the times are, say something nice about their intended victim, explain about the pig they are going to sell as soon as it is fat enough, and how that will put them back on their feet again, tell about their illness, and then ask for a few cents. With very few exceptions, they are extremely courteous.

San José differs from modern, more highly developed communities in that old people are not thought of as pests, or treated as though they were of no importance. They are respected, esteemed, and pampered. For their part, they try to continue being self-sufficient. They do not stop working until the day they fall into bed paralyzed or on the point of death. In the *tenencia* of Ornelas there are about two hundred people over seventy-five, with wrinkled faces and vacant eyes, trembling in hand and limb. Most are women. They are loved and respected, whether they work or not.

San Joséans do not respect idle people. Anyone who works less than he should to support himself is looked upon with disfavor, and so is anyone who works harder than he has to. Thus, there is some tolerance for laziness, and a certain contempt for excessive ambition. Hard work is not a highly regarded virtue; this is because, among other things, people do not look upon it as an inexhaustible source of good, or even as a source of wealth. They are fond of saying that idleness is the mother of all vices; but an idle man annoys them only if he has some vice: playing pool, or drinking too much. They do not welcome such vagabonds from outside as the Gypsies, or "Hungarians," who tell fortunes, mend pots, and steal.

The zoology of the imagination was meager in the past, and now there is none at all. Not even the bogyman has survived. As has been said, the fauna—especially destructive animals—are in full flight. It must be a hundred years since there were any wolves or mountain lions. The coyote, the fox, the opossum, and other enemies of small domestic animals have just about disappeared. Rattlesnakes, hognoses, coral snakes, and all venomous serpents are dying out. There are fewer scorpions, wasps, fleas, lice, and ticks. St. George, who killed the dragon, and who is our protector against poisonous creatures, has no devotees in San José; and neither has St. Anthony.

The inanimate world, too, has become less terrifying, as can be seen from the falling-off of prayers to St. Barbara, St. Isidore, St. Christopher, and St. Serafín del Monte Granero. There are just as many thunderstorms, but fewer people are killed by lightning. This is partly because of the introduction of lightning rods. Every river that rises during the rainy season carries off one or two men each year, and a larger number of domestic animals. Earthquakes in these parts do little more than scare people, and less every day. Comets no longer frighten even children. Diseases, however, are another matter.

Among the ailments there are both ancient and modern names. The ones mentioned most often are diarrhea, catarrh, grippe, cancer, rheumatism, the itch, worms, tapeworms, amoebic dysentery, chills and fever, typhoid, measles, cough, melancholy, pinkeye (they call it conjunctivitis today), *aires y punzadas*, bronchitis, pneumonia, colic, whooping cough, diabetes, asthma, appendicitis, varicose veins, onchocerciasis, toothache, heart trouble, high blood pressure, *mala cama*, pimples, sprains, hernia, stitch in the side, prostate trouble, palpitations, tumors, gangrene, hepatitis, constipation, hot flashes, fever, sweats, stomachache from eating hot food (or cold food, as the case may be), pains brought on by sudden changes of temperature or by fright, children's convulsions that turn their faces black and their fingernails purple, the falling-in of the "soft spot" on an infant's head, indigestion from eating unpeeled peaches, and, above all, the "bile," which, if you are lucky, merely makes you lose weight and, if you are not, turns you yellow, feverish, and hollow-eyed, makes you vomit a bitter, green fluid, loosens your bowels, and produces "weakness"—which, as everybody knows, brings on a multitude of other diseases, of which some go away by themselves, some can be cured by the doctor or by ancient remedies, and some kill you.

To observe that fewer people die these days is no more than a manner of speaking. Fewer children die, probably, and more individuals may reach old age; but who knows? No one escapes death. Old Nick carries off everybody sooner or later; nobody recovers from the last illness. Thoughts of the tomb drive us all mad. We can still accept the idea of heaven, but what about death and hell? The Reaper squeezes through every crack; he comes unseen and may fall upon his victim suddenly or make him suffer for a while. The Bony One, Old

Bare Bones, is the greatest cause for worry among the peaceful inhabitants of San José.

Everyone talks about death. Priests love to dwell on the subject. In daily conversation, people often refer to the end of this life, to passing on, making the last journey, cashing in one's chips, giving up the ghost, turning stiff, going to God, being eaten by the worms, giving an accounting to St. Peter, appearing before the Judgment Bench, turning in one's huaraches, folding one's tent, and taking the road to the cemetery.

The traditional concept of death has survived intact: it is an end, and it is a passing over. If there is less respect for life here than in more civilized areas, it is because of the ever-present thought of death. Life has little value, because of death. One fears dying because one loves living, and at the same time death is desirable because one yearns for paradise. But not all deaths are the same.

It is not good to die unbaptized. The souls of children who do so are destined for limbo, where they are denied the sight of God and yet do not suffer. They exist there without either sorrow or glory. The best death is that of the *angelito*, the child who has been baptized and departs before reaching the age of reason. There can be no doubt that he will play the harp with the heavenly choir. There is little mourning when such children die. The grief of losing them is balanced by the certainty that they have passed to a better life and that they will be able to intercede for their parents and their brothers and sisters. At their death there is both sorrow and rejoicing.

The demise of young people, adults, and oldsters is much more complicated. It includes a will, confession, anointing with oil, assistance in dying properly, candles, prayers, the death knell, the *media hora*, sobbing, words of praise for the dying, having the coffin made or buying it from Braulio Valdovinos, weeping and wailing on the part of the women, the Rosaries, the wake, the Requiem Mass, the procession to the cemetery, the responsory, the burial, the novena of Rosaries, the Masses for the dead, the mourning, and the gradual fading from memory.

The will is usually dictated in the presence of a group of friends and a priest, and rarely before a notary. Property is generally left to the widow, or, if there is none, to the children. Land and savings are distributed equally among the children. This practice would have led to the most economically disadvantageous kind of small holdings, had it not been for the tremendous demand for land. Many heirs sell their portions. The house usually passes to the unmarried daughters or to the youngest member of the family. There is no shortage of difficulties brought about by the distribution of legacies, especially if the deceased has no children. Some legators avoid complications by turning over their property within their lifetime by means of a contract of sale. They give title to the property, but retain the use of it as long as they live. People often die intestate.

Dying without a will is not nearly as serious a matter as dying without receiving the last rites of the church. Confession is essential. There may be no doctor present, but there is always a priest to hear one's confession, offer comfort, provide the sacred viaticum, hold the crucifix, and pray for mercy on one's soul. Meanwhile, the Perpetual Vigil society orders the tolling of the death knell (twenty-four strokes for a man, eighteen for a woman) and the half-hour prayer in the parish church, where many mourners have gathered.

When someone dies, the women in the family wail; the men feel a lump in their throats; in the more prominent families, the mourners put on dark glasses, as is the custom in the city. It is the women who prepare the body for the wake and the funeral: they clothe it, cross the arms over the chest, close the eyes, lay it in the coffin, and place wax candles at the four corners. Mourners file by, one Rosary after another is said, and the women serve food. The wake goes on all night. Between Rosaries, those present speak of the deceased's many virtues, and repeat the time-honored observations: "It comes to all of us"; "Death is something none of us can escape"; "May God not take us before we have confessed"; "God took him from us"; "He'll go to heaven, shoes and all"; "He was so good"; "We're the ones we should feel sorry for—we're such terrible sinners"; "He looks as if he were asleep." "Who made his coffin?" "They bought it from Braulio." "At least they had enough for a casket; so many poor people still go to their graves wrapped in a *petate*." "Do you remember so-and-so? When he was dying after his last drunk, his wife gave him the crucifix to kiss, and he said, 'Take the cork out for me.' He died thinking they were offering him a bottle of tequila.''

On the following day the deceased, if he was an important citizen, lies in state in the church. After the Mass, he is taken to the cemetery at the head of a long procession. There are four pallbearers, or more, if he is very heavy. The cortège is made up of a few women and many men, all bareheaded. At the cemetery the burial ceremony is held, the grave is filled, and everyone removes his mask of solemnity. People put their hats back on and talk about the weather, their cattle, the crops, and the harvest.

The remaining ceremonies—the nine days of Rosaries, the assumption of mourning attire by the deceased's widow, children, and brothers and sisters, the celebration of Masses for the eternal rest of the dead—are not as solemn or as rigorous as in the past. The ritual of death has tended to become simpler. Widows no longer remain in mourning for the rest of their lives, or even for three years; there are not as many prayers for the dead, and they do not go on for such a long time. Perhaps this is because no one really believes that his loved one is waiting in purgatory. Nobody can imagine heaven without his relatives and friends.

Three Conclusions

Timeless Things

The great periods in San José's history do not coincide exactly with those in the career of the Mexican nation. There was no pre-Hispanic culture to merge with that of the New World; the Spanish explorers found no indigenous people or society here. The area was thinly populated in the sixteenth century and abandoned in the early 1600's. Its truly formative period, corresponding to the colonial era in the country as a whole, began at the end of the eighteenth century and lasted until fifty years after the War for Independence. The second stage (1861–1912) coincides in time, if not in spirit, with Mexico's liberal era. The third period (1913–1942) belongs to the destructive stage of the Mexican revolution, while the fourth (from 1943 to the present) falls within the constructive years of that revolution. Each of these four periods shows us a community with a different aspect, but they are not four different communities. There is a continuity of environment and population, a series of unchanging elements.

By the end of the eighteenth century, when human beings became an important part of the landscape, the inhabitants of the rolling plateau of the Cojumatlán hacienda had been set apart as *alteños*, highlanders; occupying a mesa surrounded by lowlands, they were given to a peculiar way of living, unlike that of those about them.

They were more isolated from the outside world, more turned in upon themselves. They lived in a scattered fashion, not jammed together in cities and towns. Their land was not the level plain with its rich, arable soil, but rolling hillocks covered with brush, suitable for grazing animals. They were driven to a cattle-raising economy, less profitable than that of growing cereal crops. Lacking the qualities of serfdom, their natural inclination was to rule themselves, to command instead of obey, to attack instead of defend. They were destined to find their friends among supernatural beings, rather than among the ants who lived on the plain below.

Being an *alteño* also means being a horseman and a cattle owner. Not even modern means of communication and transportation have been able to diminish the San Joséans' love of horses and of skillful riding. It may be that the *charro* tradition is about to disappear from the world; but from the beginning of San José's history until the present time its men have distinguished themselves in the art. Cattle raising, too, is probably on its way out, to be replaced by other ways of making a living; but so far most of these people have been professional cowboys, milkers, or cheese makers. Not that they have not engaged in other occupations, but none has been held in such high esteem. Today they are beginning to see that there are quicker ways of getting rich with the same amount of effort, and yet . . .

Another constant in the life of San José has been poverty. No one ever made a fortune raising stock on a small scale. Many men on the mesa have been called rich, but only to distinguish them from others who were poorer. No San Joséan, no matter how well-off, has ever had an income to compare with that of a landowner on the plain below, a ranking politician, a *rentier* in the city, or any of the thousands of businessmen and industrialists in Guadalajara and the capital. All the land, cattle, and houses within the jurisdiction of San José are worth less than a single skyscraper in Mexico City. If one man owned all of San José and its environs, he would still fail to qualify as a member of the Mexican aristocracy. Only in other high regions in the country has wealth been distributed among so many. It is a community where everyone is more or less poor; but no one is miserably so. People have never been destitute here, as they have in so many areas of Mexico. Rarely has anyone lacked food, clothing, or shelter. Most of them have even had enough money left over to provide some small luxuries and to save something.

Constant poverty goes hand in hand with lagging technology. Not even the advances of the past twenty-five years have brought San José into the ranks of modern communities. Its inhabitants are still living under the hegemony of the hoe and plow, the tortilla griddle and the *metate*, natural pasturage, range cattle, the lariat and the machete, and the cattle-raising practices introduced by the Spaniards in the sixteenth century and modified by the environment and indigenous cultures. The lack of progress in methods of production becomes obvious the moment one compares San José with other cattle regions in Mexico; the state of the industry is revealed in all its backwardness when placed beside that in the United States. Technological advances may never have been rejected, but they have not always been understood and put into practice by local people. It may be that outsiders, prominent capitalists from the city, will mechanize the area and destroy another of San José's traditional ways of life: private ownership of land and livestock, and with it individual enterprise, the unwillingness to depend upon anyone else economically, and the reluctance to take orders in other areas of activity. For centuries they have been declaring, "Nobody tells *me* what to do." They have tried to maintain this attitude at all costs—although not in absolute terms, as witness their respect for the aged, their willingness to obey the priest, and their grudging recognition of the civil authorities, not to mention their dependence upon an outside market and familial solidarity at home. They have never meekly put up with domineering people; but they have avoided falling into anarchy, disorder, and social discord, in accordance with an immemorial table of commandments.

San Joséans have always been bound by a code of honor. It derives largely from the precepts of Christian morality, but there are elements from other sources, as well. Among the qualities and modes of behavior they have traditionally admired are physical agility, having money and a woman of one's own, contempt for death, saving money, hard work, keeping one's word, industry, female chastity, generosity, telling the truth, and puritanism tinged with a certain Don Juanism.

They have always tried to avoid those things that bring dishonor: cowardice, physical weakness, having illegitimate children, theft, cheating, begging, sodomy, usury, pandering, sexual relations in unmarried women, female adultery, treachery, mocking other people, bragging, and even pulling another man's beard. Following these precepts has made the man of San José a punctilious human being, curt and serious in his relations with other people, introverted, and at times homicidal. The need to maintain his honor, avert disgrace, and keep his dignity has robbed him of spontaneity, the joy of living, and a sense of humor; on the other hand, it has lent him the air of an old Castilian, such as one finds in *Fuenteovejuna*, the drama from Spain's Golden Age.

The people of San José have often been called religious reactionaries, sanctimonious prudes, pharisees, and "Peter the Hermit Catholics." This has come about because of their never-failing submission to the divine will; faith in God's mercy and justice; belief in the intercession of the saints; credence given to miracles; fear of ghosts and the devil; prayers addressed to God, the Virgin, and St. Joseph; recitation of the Rosary; attendance at Mass; respect for the sacraments; desire for early baptism; elaborately celebrated confirmations; frequent confession and Communion; lavish weddings; insistence upon extreme unction; love of sermons; reading of devotional works and lives of the saints; familiarity with the catechism; clericalism; submission to papal and episcopal decrees; love of priests; intolerance of other religions; violent opposition to secularism; hostility toward the enemies of the church and toward unbelievers; readiness to take part in any crusade or holy war; moral code more or less based on the Decalogue and the commandments of the church; familial puritanism; approval of good deeds and public charity; fear of sin; belief in hell, purgatory, and limbo; hope of paradise; willingness to contribute money for the support of the church, its priests, and propagation of the faith; and massive participation in religious celebrations.

It has been at all times a community characterized by religious fervor and political tepidity. The new feeling of patriotism and the diminishing piety of recent years do not invalidate that statement. There never have existed a clear-cut national consciousness, a strong love of country, a true veneration of the flag or the national anthem, or a reverence for Mexico's heroes. Some of the ever-present manifestations of San José's deficient civic spirit are: hostility (sometimes violent) toward the federal government; unwillingness to pay taxes; a tendency to stay away from the polls except under pressure; the absence of any political ideology at all in the mass of the population; and jokes about politicians and their infamous profession. In short, an indifference toward the progress of the nation and, to a slighter degree, toward the development of their own region is contrasted with a rather strong attachment to their native heath and an enduring provincialism.

San Joséans have shown their love for their community in many ways. Sometimes it appears in an excessive praise of the climate, the drinking water, the cooking, the intelligence and industry of its inhabitants, the customs, or its patron saint. It has also been revealed in endogamy, in their marked suspicion of strangers, and in their contemptuous attitude toward people who live elsewhere. There has always been plenty of local pride: a belief that theirs is the best of all possible worlds, a narcissism combined with a certain false modesty. Their way of making outsiders share their self-esteem is to belittle themselves in their presence. This self-disparagement takes many different forms.

The people of San José have used language more to conceal thought than to reveal it; they have good reason to be aware that actions speak louder than words, and that what a man says does not tell us what is in his heart. Many of their expressions cannot help disclosing their way of thinking, however.

An extensive anthology of these expressions could be assembled; the following collection, while far from exhaustive, is very nearly representative.

Sayings of Yesterday and Today

We've had no rain here. This year has been the worst yet, with the rains coming late like this. The cattle are dying, and we keep getting further in debt. Nobody can give me even a little milk for the children. I put on the kettle and make them some tea with orange leaves, or whatever I happen to have, and give it to them with a tortilla or two, and when they've finished I thank God I had something to kill their hunger. This heat is terrible. Here it is June, and not a drop of rain. Francisco spends all day shooing away flies, but he isn't selling a thing. I'm really worried, because I haven't got any feed for the cows. This wind will bring rain, I'm sure. It's raining now, thank God. All the animals have diarrhea; it must be on account of the new grass. The fields are beginning to turn green. Your father's out planting. He goes out every morning and doesn't come back until evening. I send him his lunch. I planted three hundred peach pits. There was a storm yesterday, a real cloudburst. For the first time this year the Pasión River came up, and it carried off eight of your father's calves. Three of them got ashore, half-drowned. Polino Partida left very early in the morning, to milk his cows. It was still dark, and he hit a dead animal lying on the highway. He went over the cliff and landed on some rocks and was killed. Agapito's cows are giving a lot of milk. I follow the milkers from one place to the next. We went to El Mandil to drink milk fresh from the cow. If you have a headache, or feel weak, there's nothing like some warm milk squirted into half a cup of chocolate with some alcohol. That's how my *compadre*'s children got started drinking. These are the winds that blow away the rain. Just look how many flowers there are in the fields! Some people say the world will end in fire, some say in ice. I think it's going to stay cold. We've had the first frost. I didn't even make expenses on my corn and beans. Don Bernardo used all his corn for silage. If I just had something to feed my cows, they wouldn't go dry. A lot of people get just as much milk in the dry season as they do during the rains. This cold is going to be the death of us. Honorato sent some blankets to the poor people. January and February are the months that carry off the old folks.

Every year people die, but even more are born. My mother was left a widow at thirty-eight, with ten children. Who knows how many more she might have thrown if my father hadn't died. The other day the priest told us to keep track of our cycle, and he said nothing can happen for twelve days in the middle of the month. I didn't understand it very well, but I'm expecting, anyway. But you're not; go talk to the priest and write down everything he tells you. But what man is going to be patient that long? They say that's the only way that isn't a sin. Well, no rhythm system is going to work in my house. There's no holding off the men in my family, even when they come home dead tired. Rich people are the smartest—they have three children, and that's it. They use all kinds of tricks to keep from getting pregnant. And you can't blame them, when you think of all the misery we go through: miscarriages, varicose veins, and things like that. It would be nice if husbands and wives took turns having the children. The trouble is, children are brought up just any old way. You can't hope to feed them the way you should, or even give them proper schooling. Look at them: running around like monkeys, dirty, with runny noses. My sixth is on the way, and my man shows no signs of stopping yet. They say it's a sin to refuse your husband. And when they come home drunk and insist, what can you do? They say the town already has nearly five thousand people, and the tree is still bearing. A lot of men are leaving, too. Jesús wasn't able to go north this year. Why don't you get them to give my boy a visa for the United States? For a long time now he's been trying to get back with the boss he worked for during the bracero days. Here he does nothing but wander around town like an engineer: measuring the streets. I tell my children to go away and make a life for themselves, to try and see if they can't find something to do somewhere else. Every month whole families move to the capital. If only there was work to be had in San José! No. The more people go away, the more there's left for us.

Mr. Governor: Unlike the rest of the *municipio* of Jiquilpan, the *tenencia* of Ornelas is principally a cattle-raising area; its people make their living by milk and cheese, not crops. There is hardly any money to be made by planting corn, garbanzos, beans, or wheat. Chickens and pigs were profitable about 1957, but there is no money in them today. Many women embroider mantillas; they ruin their eyes and their backs to make a few centavos. Some 150 poorer people manufacture bricks in the dry season. Business is in the hands of a hundred or more storekeepers, who sell very little, and at high prices. A dozen men who own trucks haul cheese and eggs to sell elsewhere, and bring back cattle feed. Taxes go up steadily.

No matter how hard we try, we can't find any way to get ahead. We're in a bad way, and the government won't help us. We need machinery. Why don't we form a cooperative? If we could set up a plant to homogenize and pasteurize milk, there'd be no stopping us. We ought to have a factory for making cheese. Dairy farms and orchards are the coming things. I've never tasted peaches as good as the ones we grow here. Yes, everything does grow beautifully, but we've got to do something about it. Nobody's in any hurry. People here work like dogs. I like to see that our people are so hard-working; they *want* to work. Your father's managed to keep busy. He comes home exhausted every night. My husband can't find anything to do. We ought to demand a minimum salary. The *presidente municipal* of Jiquilpan says he'll stand behind us if we do. What I'd like is a business of my own, where nobody can order me around. Rafael Degollado says what we need is a union. That's what he said when he was a deputy. When a man's stomach is full, he forgets that other people are hungry. All I want is a job. Yes, what's what you say, but when the time comes, you don't show up. They want a man to work himself to death for nothing. They pay starvation wages. When I was in the United States . . . When I was in Mexico City . . . Why don't you go back, then? The best thing we can do is stick with agrarianism. They're really going to give us land this time.

Mr. Director of the Department of Agrarian Affairs: In the jurisdiction of San José de Gracia 75 percent of the heads of families own rural property. The principal cattlemen, 130 individuals with more than ten head apiece, have ranches whose average size is eighty hectares. About 500 have parcels of between five and fifteen hectares. There are 300 *ejido* members. Like the ranches, the smaller parcels and the *ejido* sections are, with very few exceptions, devoted exclusively to cattle raising. The land has been divided among too many people.

Mr. Director of the Department of Agrarian Affairs: We are applying for an *ejido*. We have never been given any land. The engineer who was here the other day said there was land available.

What we need is another Cárdenas regime. We want land and work. The man who works has money, and the one who doesn't watches him make it. If you have chocolate you beat it, and if you don't you watch somebody else beat it. The only way to get what you want is to work for it. This agrarian business doesn't interest me. My father could never support us with the parcel they gave him. I'll trade any piece of land they want to give me for a job in Mexico City. I wonder why God wants us to always be poor. The poor man's lot is to spend his life in toil. God gave you what you have, and the rich people took what they have. That guy has money because he never spends any. If you'd inherited as much as he did, you'd have to be a complete idiot to be broke. A lot of people had money at one time and lost it, because they were lazy, or drunks, or fools. If you have any clothes you don't need, let me give them to some people who are poorer than we are. If only we could remember that we're all brothers! If only we all had the fear of God! All of us, poor and rich, are members of the same family. But not even all the fingers of a man's hands are alike. Nobody is going to make fun of me, or look down his nose at me. Everybody has somebody who doesn't like him. We just heard that they shot José Martínez in the head, and he may not live. We were very upset about Rubén Zepeda's death. The day before yesterday he was on the way to his ranch when they emptied a pistol into him. The man who shot him was the one who killed his own mother-in-law. He shot him in the back, and the bullet went right through him. They say he had a fight with Rubén over nothing. They took José Cárdenas to jail in Jiquilpan after he killed somebody. Death has been very busy around here lately. There's been a run of sickness. Adolfo Pulido was killed because of jealousy. He was beginning to sell more bread than Ignacio Ochoa, the baker who shot him. I'd rather they killed me than say bad things about me. A good name is worth more than a life. If there were fewer talebearers, there'd be fewer fights and murders. Those old ladies who are always making trouble ought to be shot. If we punished criminals properly, more people would be afraid to commit murder. When are we going to have a decent government? Don't tell *me* there's any such thing as an honest politician! Politics and corruption always go together.

They make promises, but they never keep their word. They talk just because they have mouths, and embrace you only because they have arms. Nothing but promises. They're used to living on other people. They get rich at the expense of fools. People say somebody has to give orders. Some of us make the laws, and the rest of us obey them, as little Alberto used to say. He would have liked to be a politician. So would Luis Manuel. That's not saying anything against them. Besides, we don't have to dislike *all* the authorities. You have to be sensible, boys, because they can do us a lot of harm. If we're patient, we can accomplish something. We've already made some progress. Well, I'll tell you. The man who's running for deputy sent word that when he arrives he wants to be met by the prettiest girls in San José, with plenty of confetti, *serpentinas*, and flowers. He thinks two hundred pesos worth of confetti should be enough. Yes, sir. You're probably right, but we don't bow down quite that far. When I bend over, it hurts, and it's hard to straighten up again. We have a powerful friend right here in the village: our patron, St. Joseph. No saint in the heavenly court, not even St. Martín de Porres, can work miracles like the carpenter. I have more faith in St. Isidore. When I need help, I go to Father Pablito. Whenever you leave the house put on your hat and commend yourself to the Virgin of Guadalupe and St. Joseph. Go to confession and receive Communion in the proper way, for the good of your own town. Good Lord, how many people I have to pray for at Mass and during Communion! Prayer is the only comfort we old folks have. We should pray for the youngsters, who only go to church when they have to. It's always been that way: when a person is young he never thinks about death. Boys are thinking about girls, or what they want to be when they grow up, or making money. A man's main concern is the salvation of his soul. If you know how, you can fit everything into a little pitcher. Put your oxen to the plow and pray to God. I remember Don Agapito: he spent all his life praying and was always poor. Where do you learn such things, my boy? I wish you'd be more reverent. The priest says he'd rather see fewer churchgoers and more virtue. According to one of the *testamentos de Judas*, the village girls

Are hoping for a chance
To run off with their lovers;
But the poor things never see
How they're sullying their good name.

At the prayer meeting it was decided that we should try to persuade people living in sin to change their ways. I'd be glad to contribute, but I just gave something for the school. Every time you turn around, somebody asks you for money. I really feel like giving, though, when I see how smart the youngsters are, how they remember everything they're taught. When I realized that my children wanted to go to school, I began begging for money to send them to the seminary, or anywhere where the tuition was free. I was ashamed, but how else could I see that they got an education? Who could I ask but the rich people? With a little here, a little there, I don't really know how, I was able to send them. My children are all grown up, thank God. I have a priest, a nun, and two Christian Brothers. Only one got married. A lot of parents don't use their heads. It's a shame to see so many children doing nothing, like bums. Today anybody who wants to can learn to read and write. If he can't get to school, he can always find somebody to teach him. The government acts as if we didn't exist. I see that in Jalisco they have schools even in the poorest *rancherías*. Well, we can't complain about Governor Arriaga, or about Padre Federico, either. María González Zepeda gave a lot of money to the padre's school. What we need here is a secondary school. Even without schooling, the boys learn, these days. But the things they pick up from the movies and television! They'd be better off learning nothing at all. No, anything is worth knowing, *comadre*. Telling your troubles makes you forget them. What everybody likes is a little fun. Last night a lot of people were having a good time. All the yelling and gunfire kept me awake. Salvador Villanueva wants to celebrate the national holidays. He's chosen three candidates for the queen: Estela Toscano, Esther Reyes, and Consuelo Pulido. They're all so pretty, it's hard to choose between them. They're not going to have the Sixteenth of September fiesta this year. Last year it lasted three days. The town was bursting with people. Every house was full. The church was all decorated, the streets cleaned up; there was a good band, a marvelous preacher, and a fine chorus. We had all kinds of fireworks every day. Lupita came from Mexico City, as she does every year, to make dresses for the rich girls to wear at the fiesta. A lot of girls found boys. That's what the *serenata* is for. María has a Three-S boy friend: strong, serious, and ugly as sin. My father wouldn't mind having him for a son-in-law. Yes, if they get married: all girls want to do these days is run around with boys. No, it's the boys who back away from marriage. There aren't any men any more. Or women, either. Don't kid yourself: life is full of suffering. Anyway, let's go to the wedding. There were some outsiders there, and some politicians. They went for a stroll around El Zapatero and then had beer and mescal at the priest's house. My Aunt Sara made dinner for them: young, tender squash with *minguiche*, chicken in *mole*, and beans. Some people got drunk and didn't eat. I was left with almost all the food. Rain! The rains began yesterday, and I was certainly glad. This is where God put me, this is where I've spent my life, and whether a lot of people like it or not, this is where I'll die.

A Small Epilogue and Postscript

The belief that small towns will disappear in the more or less near future is entertained, if ruefully, by many people of importance. Some villages will be left with nothing but empty houses. Some will be engulfed by large cities and transformed into residential areas for the rich or slums for the poor. Others will grow and become cities themselves. San José, so far removed from the megalopolis, runs no risk of being swallowed up by any city. It will not die like Tonalá, Zapopan, and San Pedro—the towns absorbed by Guadalajara. It may be extinguished with the emigration of its citizens; it may soon become a village of women and old men, and then, a little later, an uninhabited corpse, and finally, a pile of ruins and sorrowing ghosts. At the moment it is a community hanging in the air; its position is insecure, unstable, fragile, precarious, touch-and-go; it is held together with pins, teetering, built on sand, with no foundation.

San José is on a mesa, two thousand meters above sea level. The mesa is poor in agricultural resources, and, outside of its pasture lands, which are meager, it is not productive country in any way. It is a lean land, and natural erosion and deforestation at the hands of human beings have joined forces to make it leaner. It could ultimately become a wind-swept plain, with stony outcroppings here and there, without grass, or brush, or flora, or fauna. Today it is an unprofitable region; but just as it could become totally worthless, it could also do the opposite. Up until now no one has investigated its hidden resources, and it could easily have some. But even though San José has no solid geographical foundation, it possesses a vigorous demographic potential. It is possible to live without one's feet on the ground: suspended, but not necessarily insecure.

The events of the past quarter of a century indicate that San José de Gracia and its satellite hamlets are still growing—stumbling, tottering uphill, without much help from the outside world—and that they will continue to do so, in spite of the great number of deserters. Since 1943 the area has had a population explosion, a modest economic miracle, a higher standard of living, an ever-increasing and fruitful intervention in its affairs by the government, dissension in some ranks, more interest in education, more patriotism, and some idiosyncrasy that is not incompatible with modern times. Today, neither the local inhabitants (with a few exceptions) nor the government of the state of Michoacán foresee any imminent collapse in the community; they predict, rather, a prosperous future. Thus, Governor Arriaga Rivera was gratified toward the end of 1967 to receive an application from the local citizens asking that the *tenencia* of Ornelas be made an autonomous *municipio*, independent of that of Jiquilpan.

For half a century San José and its environs have been suffering from hemorrhages of some magnitude, although not fatal ones. Many people have left, but many more have been born; and there have even been some immigrants. The birth rate has dropped recently, thanks to birth-control pills; but from 1940 to 1966 it reached incredible heights, in some years as many as sixty births per thousand. On the other hand, with improved medical services, the death rate has fallen to a nearly ideal minimum. Permanent and seasonal emigrants have been nearly all over eighteen years of age, since 1946, at least; but there has been no seasonal migration since 1965, and the other has not increased much. In other words, even with emigration the population of San José and its *rancherías* has doubled, and the village alone has three times as many citizens as it had in 1940. There you have the population explosion. The economic miracle is not so striking.

The leap forward has been marked by an increase in cattle production, some use of new agricultural methods, more nonfarming activities, and a greater desire to make money. In San José the classic thesis that "all wealth is based on cattle" persists. The volume of cattle production—but not the income from it—is four times what it was twenty-five years ago. Poultry raising had its apogee, but it has fallen into a decline in the past ten years. Fruit growing has never been profitable. More land has been planted to corn and other crops, without any visible benefit. Whatever slight improvements there have been in farm production are attributable to the increasing application of scientific methods. Although the land is capable of producing even more, the younger generation prefers other types of work that are more profitable and less laborious.

Half of the economically active population no longer lives by farming and cattle raising. Most of the inhabitants of San José, and an appreciable minority of country people, are engaged in manufacturing bricks, embroidering shawls, adulterating cheese, buying and selling, driving taxis and trucks, working as barbers, carpenters, masons, public officials, and teachers. There is still no important industry, although many young men in their twenties are looking in that direction. There is not enough money. Parsimony is on the decline, and most people still cannot save much. The days of burying money are over. Those who have any profits today put them in the bank. The Bank of Zamora is about to open a branch in San José.

The desire for money has grown of late and so have earnings; but neither has increased as much as the love of comfort. If people save very little, it is because they spend a considerable amount on things that make their lives pleasant. Like any village, San José has a central square with its garden, bandstand, shade trees, benches for sitting and a promenade for strolling, cobblestone streets laid out in straight lines, one-story houses with red tile roofs, and quiet, unassuming inhabitants. But, unlike other villages, it has a paved highway, a steady

flow of automobiles, buses, and trucks, a dozen taxis, a taste for traveling, electric lights, drinkable running water in its houses, the telegraph, the telephone, a roomy cemetery, a hospital, and many homes
where the *metate*, the *molcajete*, and the rest of the equipment of
the ancient wood-burning kitchen have been relegated to the back
yard to make room for sewing machines, radios, television sets, gas
stoves, clocks, electric irons, pressure cookers, articles of glass and
plastic, refrigerators, and other fashionable possessions. The people of
San José are poor. The average annual income is about 2,500 pesos
per person, yet there are not many signs of poverty. There are plenty
of fat people—mostly among the men, for the women are more determined every day to get rid of their curves. Like the vast majority
of Mexican villagers, San Joséans eat corn, chili, and beans; but they
also stuff themselves with meat, milk, and wheat bread. Although
dressing well is not one of their dominant preoccupations, one sees
few men without modern trousers, shoes, and jacket. They gave up
living in huts years ago; most people live in houses with adobe walls
and tile roofs, although more dwellings are being built of concrete
every day. They aspire to live in the same way as the better people
elsewhere.

There is not as much inequality as one finds in the cities; the gulf
between rich and poor is not as wide, partly because of the more or
less equal distribution of the means of production. It is an economy
of small producers. Big business is conspicuous by its absence. This
does not mean there are no classes, or that there is no struggle between them. Those who own no land are fighting constantly with the
seven hundred who do; small wage earners malign those who make
more money. It is not that there are any more people without land, a
trade, or steady employment than there were twenty-five years ago;
there is just a stronger urge toward a better and more secure way of
life.

When the first steps were being taken to make the *tenencia* of
Ornelas into a *municipio*, some of the better-off citizens were against
it. They said: "The *municipio* will create more division among us";
"The people from the *rancherías* will try to get more power than
those in the town"; "If we have elections, people will get killed";

"Here nobody can agree with anybody else about anything"; "It is our very nature to be at odds with each other"; "The power will no longer be in the hands of those who believe in law and order."

There is disagreement. Rich and poor watch each other out of the corner of an eye; so do the young and the old, the ranchers and the villagers, this family and that family, the newcomers and the old settlers, those of one trade and those of another. Still, those in the social struggle in San José are far from coming to blows, and rivalry is not nearly as serious as it is in other rural areas of Mexico.

It was people from the wealthy class who initiated the project of making San José the seat of a *municipio*. "Then the government will pay more attention to us," they said. In the past, any intervention on the part of the higher authorities was looked upon as something to be avoided; but within the past twenty-five years, since the government has assumed the role of the great builder and has set in motion a vast program of public works (dams, highways, schools, manufacturing centers), everyone is ready with a warm welcome. Where once people spoke of the government only as an agent of retribution and spoliation, now they also mention the services it can provide. They are coming to realize that in order to reap its benefits they must make themselves visible, instead of trying to hide, as they have done in the past.

Padre Federico came out in favor of the *municipio* movement. Don Bernardo González Cárdenas and Dr. Daniel Ruiz Arcos made many trips to Morelia to enlist the support of the governor, the legislature, and Carmelita Herrera, the deputy from the district of Jiquilpan.

A state inspector arrived one day in San José, sent by the legislature to determine whether the *tenencia* of Ornelas was ready to assume the status of a *municipio*. Don Bernardo showed him around the town, and the inspector returned to Morelia filled with optimism. He had found the village to be even more advanced than its citizens had claimed, and he was convinced that it was ready for self-government. He exploded the legend that the Mexican revolution had not reached San José; in some respects, he said, it had made itself felt there earlier than it had in some other places. In San José he had found none of the alarming exploitation of man by man; people worked in earnest and with enthusiasm; some of the better social institutions, such as the family, had survived intact. The tremendous changes brought by the past quarter of a century had not caused any great weakening of the bonds of loyalty between husbands and wives—mutual dependence, the rule of the husband, and the tacit acceptance on the part of the woman of her man's missteps.

In the country of the blind, San José could be king. For several years it has been more up-to-date and in closer contact with the world than many other villages. No less than two hundred of its inhabitants leave by bus and car every day to see what is going on elsewhere. In addition, the great majority go to the movies, listen to the radio, and watch television, and more than a few read newspapers and magazines. The number who can read and write is above the national average. They take a lively interest in their children's education; besides the two primary schools, the villagers support a secondary school also. It is a remarkably well-informed community. It is a rare citizen who does not know—accurately or otherwise—what is taking place and being said in Washington, Moscow, Rome, and, of course, Mexico City.

Being informed does not mean identifying. The village mentality persists in many respects. The temptations of wealth, power, and fame are felt, but not as strongly as in the cities. The notion that when some become richer others must necessarily grow poorer is still widely accepted. To own land is still the greatest ambition of adults; the youngsters dream only of getting away from their home town. Boys are not as afraid of making love to girls as they used to be. The desire for freedom is still strong. Individualism is more pronounced than ever. More and more one hears that "you can't trust anybody." Introversion subsists and finds expression in the statement, "We don't like to show our feelings." Criticizing one's neighbors, envy, and gossip are nothing new, either. The feeling of attachment for one's native village does not rule out a growing nationalism; the latter, in turn, does not exclude the possibility of hating the government. Their suspicion of the authorities does not keep San Joséans from hoping that the government will do more for the area. Only the state can lift them out of their underdevelopment.

After the tour of inspection and a census carefully taken by Jorge
Partida and Alfonso González Partida, there could remain no doubt
that the *tenencia* of Ornelas was fit to become an autonomous *municipio*. On June 4, 1968, Governor Agustín Arriaga announced a
bill that had been passed by the Michoacán legislature providing that
"the *tenencia* of Ornelas, which is at present a dependency of the
municipio of Jiquilpan, and which shall be known in this and further
documents as the *municipio* of Marcos Castellanos, in memory of that
illustrious insurgent, is hereby declared a *municipio*." The seat of
the 112th *municipio* "shall be Ornelas (formerly San José de
Gracia)." The name "Marcos Castellanos" had been requested in the
petition to the legislature; but the legislators decided to change the
name of the town to "Ornelas." This made the people of San José
very unhappy. There were several reasons for their reaction; their
love for the name that had been chosen by the founding fathers, the
offense to their religious sense, and the unpleasant stories people told
about General Ornelas.

Although the traditional dogma, moral code, and liturgy have suffered some wear and tear during the past twenty-five years, the
people of San José are congenitally Catholic. Their faith is a stubborn
and potent one. Their devotion to the major saints, and particularly to
their patron, is abounding. Changing "San José" to "Ornelas" strikes
most of them as heresy. ("As if General Ornelas were somebody. . . . How can you have any respect for a man who let an army
of four thousand be cut to pieces by four hundred? . . . If we had any
pride, we wouldn't want to remember that disaster, much less the
man who was responsible for it . . . But then, who ever said he was
being honored because he was a hero? It's probably because he was
a martyr, just as people worship San Lorenzo because he was roasted
over a slow fire, and San Sebastián because they shot so many arrows
into him he looked like a colander.") It is well to remind our readers
that General Leonardo Ornelas died with a French bullet in his neck.

One also hears: "After all, what does it matter what name the government gives our village? We'll go right on calling it San José de
Gracia." However, what concerns us here is its promotion to the
seat of a *municipio*.

On August 9, the day appointed for the installation of the first
municipio government, the town square was as jammed as if it had
been the day of a major fiesta. Two thousand people were there,
showing their delight in a thousand different ways. They applauded
the speeches by the governor's secretary and by the principal of the
government school. There were fireworks, sporting matches, and
other demonstrations of joy. The mariachi played all afternoon and a
good part of the night. The only person from Jiquilpan who showed
up was the deputy from the district.

(Local politicians, too, were notable for their absence. The fact is,
there aren't any, and from now on they are going to be needed. Perhaps the return of Padre Rogelio Sánchez's brothers—Gildardo, Isidro, and José—will be the best match to light the lamp of politics. The
inhabitants of the new *municipio* must provide themselves with politicians, and the Sánchez brothers would be good men for the job. It
is better to have politicians picked out by the residents of the political
community than to bring in incompetents from outside.)

"On August 9, 1968, at 19 hours" [according to the minutes],
"there gathered in the council hall . . . the members of the first council, appointed by Citizen Licenciado Agustín Arriaga Rivera . . . by
virtue of the powers granted him in the second provisional article of
Decree no. 157 [the same one providing that the *tenencia* of Ornelas
be raised to the category of a *municipio*, Municipio 112 of the state
of Michoacán]." Then, in the presence of the governor's secretary,
the deputy María del Carmen Herrera, and the judicial delegate, Salvador Villanueva took oath as first president of the *municipio* of Marcos Castellanos. "Then, Citizens Elpidia González Sánchez, Bernardo
González González, Rafael Valdovinos González, and Rigoberto
Novoa Blancarte, the regular council members, and Arcelia Sánchez
González, Francisco González Flores, Ramiro López Arias, and Juan
López Haro, alternate council members, took oath before the *presidente* of the *municipio*, according to the terms of Article 18 of the
Constitutional Municipal Law. . . . Then the council secretary was
appointed: Señorita Rosa María Partida Cárdenas. Then Señor Jorge
Partida Cárdenas was named treasurer." Finally, Salvador Villanueva
"took the chair" and adjourned "the solemn and public meeting."

The first council "will hold office until December, since the first constitutional council will be elected . . . in November of the current year."

The new council was chosen in December. Several factions had sprung up in San José; one favored Abraham Partida for *presidente*, a second supported Guillermo Barrios, and a third Juan López. The state government, however, wanted no dissension and ordered the various parties to reach an agreement. They decided upon Juan López Haro, a successful butcher and a capable man. He assumed office as president of the first constitutional council on January 1, 1969.

The beginning of the new regime in San José coincided with the loss of the town's leader, Padre Federico. His health had been failing for several months, and about the first of February he was confined to his bed. He must have suffered a great deal, but he was never known to complain. His labored breathing could be heard for a month and a half. On March 11 every door in town was hung with a black bow. No fewer than three thousand people, both villagers and visitors, accompanied him to the cemetery.

Padre Agustín Magaña wrote in his obituary: "Padre Federico lived eighty years . . . He was tall and slender, with a noble and dignified bearing . . . He was a man of outstanding practical talents, wise, courteous, always ready with advice for anyone who asked for it . . . Under a different electoral system he would have been a bishop, and a good one . . . His sympathy with certain anti-Catholic elements could only have earned him criticism, and it did . . . Some regarded him with suspicion and disapproval, but he never ceased dealing out his good deeds to anyone who would accept them . . . The mass of the people were behind him."

Now that Padre Federico is dead, many of his burdens have been assumed by his brother, Don Bernardo. Antonio Villanueva is another notable leader who has emerged recently. And lastly, Dr. Daniel Ruiz Arcos is proving to be an extraordinarily dynamic agent of progress since his assumption of the post of *presidente municipal* on January 1, 1972. Don Bernardo González Cárdenas has succeeded in his efforts to provide San José with a new secondary technical school of agronomics and animal husbandry. He is also the director of a newly

formed association of cheese manufacturers, whose plant for the production of dairy products will be erected and put into service in 1972.
Antonio Villanueva has done his part in keeping Padre Federico's
memory alive with a recently unveiled statue, and he has been very
active in the various groups dedicated to developing local industry.
The doctor has set up a plan for bringing electric power to the *rancherías* within the *municipio*, and he is working to improve the
drainage system and the urbanization of San José. The three men
work without getting in each other's way, with the multiple support
of the residents and the state and federal governments. Don José
Servando Chávez, the governor, is doing everything possible to erase
the San Joséans' conviction that "all the government does is make
promises, and then when the time comes, nothing happens." Ingeniero Garza Caballero and Licenciado Abelardo Treviño, executive
officers of the Secretariat of Public Education, are keeping an af-
fectionate eye on the nascent secondary school.

These are encouraging signs. San José is on the verge of ceasing
to be a village in transition.

GLOSSARY

abrazo: an effusive embrace.

aftosa: hoof-and-mouth disease.

aguamiel: a white liquid extracted from the heart of the maguey plant. It is fermented to make *pulque* (q.v.).

aguardiente: "burning water." The cheapest and most inferior of distilled liquors, sometimes made from the juice of the maguey plant.

aires: maladies thought to be caused by sitting in a draft.

Alabado: a hymn formerly sung by Mexican peasants in the fields at dawn and sunset, at the beginning and end of each working day.

alcalde: the executive officer in town or district government, sometimes with judicial powers.

alcalde de tenencia: a police judge, something like a justice of the peace.

alcalde mayor: the governor of the political subdivision known in colonial times as an *alcaldía mayor*.

alicante: a small, harmless serpent.

alzador: a worker in the cornfield whose principal task is to uncover the young plants that have been buried during the plowing.

arroba: a unit of weight, equal to about twenty-five pounds.

ate: a sweet paste made of guava, quince, mango, or papaya.

atole: a sweet gruellike corn drink, served hot.

audiencia: a governing tribunal.

Bajío, the: a table land of Central Mexico, mainly in the state of Guanajuato.

barrio: any one of the quarters of a town or city.

belén: star-of-Bethlehem, a common garden flower.

birria: roasted sheep or goat.

buñuelos: deep-fried, sugarcoated pastries.

caballería: a unit of land measurement equal to about a hundred acres.

cabañuelas: a very complex system of predicting the weather for each month during the coming year by observing that of each day in January.

cacique: originally, a chief or leader among the Mexican Indian tribes. It now means a local political boss.

calzón: the white, pajamalike cotton trousers formerly worn in the fields by Mexican farmers.

capirotada: bread cubes dipped in batter and deep-fried, served with a sweet cinnamon sauce and pine nuts.

carnitas: tender pieces of fried pork, used as a filling for tacos.

carrancistas, or *carranclanes*: followers of Venustiano Carranza, political leader and president of Mexico (1914, 1915–1920).

castillo: a towerlike framework of bamboo, on which an elaborate fireworks display is mounted.

charreada: a *charro* exhibition.

charrería: the practice and display of *charro* skills.

charro: the traditional, richly costumed Mexican horseman.

chayote: a small, apple-green squash.

chicharrones: cracklings; crisp bits of pork remaining after the lard is rendered.

china: girl attired in the traditional *china poblana* costume.

chirimía: a high-pitched Indian flute.

chocho: a kind of beetle.

chongo: a lump of sweet, cheeselike pudding, served with syrup and cinnamon.

chota: a slang word for police, or border guards, "the fuzz."

churi: a luxuriant shade tree.

clarín: a slate-colored solitaire thrush.

colectivo: a taxi that takes as many passengers as possible, each paying separately.

comadre, compadre: mode of address used between people sharing the parent-godparent relationship. It can also mean a close friend.

compadrazgo: the bonds uniting parents and godparents.

conceptismo: a movement in seventeeth-century Spanish literature, characterized by subtle and ingenious concepts, double meanings, and plays on words. Its prophet was the Peninsular poet Francisco de Quevedo y Villegas.

cordón de San Blas: a strip of flannel worn around the neck to ward off diseases of the respiratory tract.

corregimiento: a political division ruled by a magistrate-governor, who was called a *corregidor*.

corrido: a traditional and typically Mexican type of narrative popular song.

corundas: small tamales made of corn meal, with no filling, wrapped in cornhusks (a Tarascan word).

criollo: a person of Spanish blood born in the New World.

cristero: a member of the "Army of Christ," which rose in rebellion against the anticlerical legislation in the 1920's.

cuicacoche: a yellow-and-black songbird of the thrush family.

diana: a short musical phrase played over and over to signify "Bravo!" It is used by town bands everywhere in Mexico during fireworks displays and other public events.

ecuaro: a Tarascan word meaning a plot of ground cleared for planting. It also refers to the ancient system of clearing and planting, as opposed to preparation of a field by plowing. It is the equivalent of the Náhuatl *coamil*.

ejido: land handed over to farmers when the large estates were broken up at the time of the Agrarian Reform. It is held in common by an *ejido* community, which has the right to use it but not to sell it.

encomendero: the holder of an encomienda.

encomienda: a territory, together with the income from it, granted to an individual by the Spanish crown. Its encomendero was, in essence, a feudal lord.

esposa: a bishop's ring. The word also means "wife."

fanega: a unit of dry measure equal to about two and a half bushels.

gachupín: a Spanish-born resident of Mexico. The etymology is uncertain; some authorities believe the word derives from the Náhuatl *catzopini*, "man with spurs."

gongorismo: the literary school headed by the Spanish poet Luis de Góngora y Argote in the seventeeth century. It created a private, hermetic poetic language by coining new words from Latin roots, reworking Spanish syntax, and employing the rhetorical devices of the classical tongues.

granada de china: Chinese pomegranate; a climbing plant.

granja: a dairy farm, often devoted to pigs and chickens as well.

guache: a soldier; a contemptuous term.

guamúchil: the tamarind, a large tree with an edible pod (from the Náhuatl *cuauh-mochitl*).

güero: a person with light skin and fair hair.

guitarrón: a six-string bass guitar.

huaraches: leather sandals.

ingeniero: an engineer. It is often used (cap.) as a title by men with a degree in science or mechanics.

intendencia: a political subdivision in New Spain, ruled by an *intendente*.

jarabe: a brisk, intricate dance performed by a couple.

jefatura: the position and term of office of a *jefe*; also, his headquarters.

jefe de acordada: a police court judge.

jefe de tenencia: the executive officer of a *tenencia*.

jocoque: the curd of raw milk.

juez de acordada: the same as a *jefe de acordada*.

justicia mayor: a magistrate.

juzgado menor: a local police court.

licenciado: the holder of a university degree between the bachelor's and the doctorate. The word can also mean an attorney, and is often used as a title (cap.).

lienzo charro: a kind of bullring for *charro* spectacles.

machismo: the obsessive concern with being "all man."

macho: male, aggressively manly.

mala cama: a miscarriage.

mariachi: a peculiarly Mexican type of strolling musical group, including guitars, violins, trumpets, and singers.

media hora: a half hour of prayers for the dying, offered by the townspeople gathered in the church.

metate: a rectangular mortar of pitted stone for grinding corn for tortillas.

milpa: a cornfield.

minguiche: curds or sour cream mixed with cheese and chilies.

mocho: a contemptuous term applied to supporters of the church during the *cristero* troubles, meaning religious zealot, hypocrite, and reactionary.

molcajete: a round, three-legged mortar.

mole: a thick sauce for meat or poultry, made with chili, spices, and sometimes unsweetened chocolate.

mordida: a bribe exacted by public officials.

municipio: a political subdivision of a state, something like a county.

nopal: the prickly pear cactus. "El Nopal," nickname for Francisco Gutiérrez.

ojo de agua: "eye of water"; a spring.

ojupos: undersized or imperfect ears of corn.

paisano: the Italian *paesáno*, Yiddish *landsman*; a person from the same town or district as oneself.

panela: a soft white cheese, made in small discs.

paliacate: a bandanna.

papaqui: a mock battle with confetti-filled eggshells, accompanied by games and dancing.

Pésame, El: The Condolences.

petate: a large straw mat.

piñata: an earthenware jar concealed within a fanciful figure made of colored paper. It is filled with candy and favors, hung from a roof beam. and broken with a club by blindfolded contestants at children's parties.

pizcador: a pointed tool made of bone, used to tear open the corn husks at harvest time.

pocho: a Mexican who has adopted the speech and way of life of the United States.

posadas: the traditional Christmas reenactment of the Holy Family's search for lodging, often performed by children.

pozole: a spicy soup of pork and hominy.

presidencia: the *presidente*'s office and the building housing it.

presidente municipal: the chief official of a *municipio*.

pulque: a kind of beer made from the fluid secreted in the heart of the maguey plant.

punzada: sharp pain.

quiote: the flowering stalk of the maguey; it is eaten boiled and roasted.

ranchera: a kind of lively "country" music, usually performed by singers accompanied by a mariachi band.

ranchería: a cluster of houses in the country.

rancho: rural property of more than 10 and less than 1,000 hectares.

real: an old coin worth 12.5 centavos.

rebozo: the traditional Mexican shawl.

requesón: a kind of cottage cheese.

runfador: the humming toy made from a tin-can lid with two holes in it and a twisted loop of string running through the holes.

Señor Mío Jesucristo: a Catholic prayer used in the Mass.

serenata: the traditional Sunday-evening band concert, with groups of young people strolling around the plaza.

sitio: approximately 4,340 acres; 1,755 hectares.

sopes: snacks made of tiny tortillas topped with refried beans, shredded cheese, and sliced radishes.

tacha: a cooking pot.

tapanco: an attic, used for storing grain and fodder.

tenencia: an administrative subdivision of the *municipio.*

tepame: an acacia with an edible pod.

Tierra Caliente: "the hot country." In Mexico this usually means the coastal regions.

Todo Fiel: a prayer.

toqueras: small tortillas covered with crumbled sausage and cheese.

torito: a figure of wood and paper in the shape of a bull, strung with small rockets. A man puts it over his head and shoulders and charges through the crowd, spouting fire and scattering spectators.

torreznos: bits of crisp bacon.

tostadas: crisp-fried tortillas topped with refried beans, shredded cheese, ground meat, lettuce, sliced onions, chiles, and nearly anything else.

trueno: a large, handsome tree, widely used in Mexican parks and promenades.

valonas: popular songs or compositions made up of recitatives accompanied by three simple musical chords.

Yo, Pecador: a response—part of the Mass.

yunta: a land measure; it is the area that can be tilled by a team of oxen in one day.

zapote: the sweet, fleshy fruit of the trees of the sapodilla family, of which there are about a dozen varieties in Mexico (from the Náhuatl *tzapotl*).

zócalo: the main plaza (in Mexico City, and in some other cities and towns as well).

WORKS CITED

Aguirre Beltrán, Gonzalo. *Problemas de la población indígena de la cuenca del Tepalcatepec*. Memorias del Instituto Nacional Indigenista, vol. 3. Mexico City: Instituto Nacional Indigenista, 1952.

Alba, Antonio de. *Chapala*. Guadalajara: Publicaciones del Banco Industrial de Jalisco, 1954.

Amaya, Jesús. *Ameca, protofundación mexicana. Historia de la propiedad del valle de Ameca, Jalisco y circunvecindad*. Mexico City: Lumen, 1952.

———. *Los conquistadores Fernández de Híjar y Bracamonte*. Guadalajara: Edición del Gobierno del Estado, 1952.

Ángel Ochoa, Augusto del. *Informe general sobre las condiciones médico-sanitarias de San José de Gracia, Michoacán*. Mexico City: Instituto Politécnico Nacional, Escuela Superior de Medicina Rural, 1949.

Arregui, Domingo Lázaro de. *Descripción de la Nueva Galicia*. Estudio por François Chevalier. Seville: Imp. de Hijos de A. Padura, 1946.

Arreola, Juan José. *La feria*. Mexico City: Joaquín Mortiz, 1963.

Basalenque, Diego de. *Historia de la provincia de San Nicolás de Tolentino de Michoacán del orden de N.P.S. Agustín*. Mexico City: Editorial Jus, 1963.

Beaumont, Pablo de la Purísima Concepción. *Crónica de la provincia de los santos apóstoles de S. Pedro y S. Pablo de Michoacán de la Regular observancia de N.P. San Francisco*. 5 vols. Mexico City: Biblioteca Histórica Iberia, 1873–1874.

Behn, Germán. "El lago de Chapala y su cuenca." *Boletín de la Junta Auxiliar Jalisciense de la Sociedad Mexicana de Geografía y Estadística* 10, nos. 1–2 (September–October, 1956): 23–39.

Bora, Woodrow, and Sherburne F. Cook. *The Original Population of Central Mexico on the Eve of the Spanish Conquest*. Ibero-Americana, 45. Berkeley and Los Angeles: University of California Press, 1963.

Bravo Ugarte, José. *Diócesis y obispos de la Iglesia Mexicana (1519–1965)*. Mexico City: Editorial Jus, 1965.

————. *Historia sucinta de Michoacán*. 3 vols. Mexico City: Editorial Jus, 1962–1964.

Cambre, Manuel. *La guerra de tres años en el estado de Jalisco. Apuntes para la historia de la Reforma*. Guadalajara: Biblioteca de Autores Jaliscienses, 1949.

Casasola, Agustín Víctor. *Historia gráfica de la Revolución*. 4 vols. Mexico City: Archivo Casasola, n.d.

Cavo, Andrés, *Historia de México*. Mexico City: Editorial Patria, 1949.

Censo de la Población de los Estados Unidos Mexicanos, verificado el 27 de octubre de 1910. 2 vols. Mexico City: Oficina Impresora de la Secretaría de Hacienda, Departamento de Fomento, 1918.

Censo y división territorial de la República Mexicana, verificado en 1900. 12 vols. Mexico City: Tipografía de la Secretaría de Fomento, 1904.

Chávez Cisneros, Esteban. *Quitupan: Ensayo histórico y estadístico*. Morelia, Mich.: Fimex Publicistas, 1954.

Chávez Orozco, Luis. *Breve historia agrícola de México en la época colonial*. Mexico City: Banco Nacional de Crédito Agrícola, 1958.

Chevalier, François. "La formación de los grandes latifundios en México." In *Problemas agrícolas e industriales de México*. Mexico City, 1956.

Chowell, Martín [pseud.]. *Luis Navarro Origel: El primer cristero*. Mexico City: Editorial Jus, 1959.

Constitución Política del Estado libre y soberano de Michoacán de Ocampo. Morelia, Mich.: Poder Ejecutivo, 1960.

Cosío Villegas, Daniel, ed. *Historia moderna de México*. 8 vols. publ. Mexico City: Hermes, 1955–1965.

————. "El Porfiriato: Era de consolidación." *Historia Mexicana* 13, no. 1 (July–September, 1963): 76–87.

Degollado y Guízar, Jesús. *Memorias de . . . , último general en jefe del ejército cristero*. Mexico City: Editorial Jus, 1957.

Departamento de Estadística Nacional. *Censo general de habitantes, 30 de noviembre de 1921. Estado de Michoacán*. Mexico City: Talleres Gráficos de la Nación, 1925.

Díaz, Severo. "La desecación del lago de Chapala." *Boletín de la Junta Auxiliar Jalisciense de la Sociedad Mexicana de Geografía y Estadística* (Guadalajara) 10, nos. 1–2 (September–October, 1956): 5–22.

Díaz Navarro, José C. *Ameca, Jal. y sus costumbres en 1910: Agricultura, ganadería, industria, comercio y minería. Diario Oficial del Gobierno.* Mexico City, 1964.

Dirección General de Estadística. *División territorial de los Estados Unidos Mexicanos correspondientes al censo de 1910. Estado de Michoacán.* Mexico City: Departamento de Talleres Gráficos de la Secretaría de Fomento, Colonización e Industria, 1917.

————. *Octavo censo general de población, 8 de junio de 1960. Estado de Michoacán.* Mexico City: Talleres Gráficos de la Nación, 1965.

————. *Quinto censo de la población, 15 de mayo de 1930. Estado de Michoacán.* Mexico City: Talleres Gráficos de la Nación, 1935.

————. *Séptimo censo general de población, 6 de junio de 1950. Estado de Michoacán.* Mexico City: n.p., n.d.

————. *Sexto censo de la población, 1940. Michoacán.* Mexico City: Talleres Gráficos de la Nación, 1943.

Durán Ochoa, Julio. *Estructura económica y social de México: Población.* Mexico City: Fondo de Cultura Económica, 1955.

Fernández de Oviedo, Gonzalo. *Historia general y natural de las Indias, islas y tierra firme del Mar Océano.* 5 vols. Madrid: Biblioteca Autores Españoles, 1959.

Fernández de Recas, Guillermo S. *Mayorazgos de la Nueva España.* Mexico City: Biblioteca Nacional de México, 1965.

Figueroa Torres, J. Jesús. *Fray Juan de Larios, defensor de los indios y fundador de Coahuila, 1673–1676.* Mexico City: Editorial Jus, 1963.

Finberg, Herbert P. R. *Approaches to History: A Symposium.* Toronto: University of Toronto Press, 1962.

Florescano, Enrique. "El alza de los precios y la independencia de México. Las contradicciones de la estructura agrícola de la Nueva España (1720–1810)." *Revista de la Universidad de México* 22, no. 4 (December, 1967): 1–7.

————. "Las crisis agrícolas de la época colonial y sus consecuencias económicas (1720–1810)." *Cuadernos Americanos,* April–May, 1968, pp. 180–195.

Foster, George M. *Cultura y conquista: La herencia española en América.* Xalapa, Ver.: Universidad Veracruzana, 1962.

————. *Tzintzuntzan: Mexican Peasants in a Changing World.* Boston: Little, Brown and Co., 1967.

Gálvez Betancourt, Rubén. *Informe general sobre la exploración sanitaria de San José de Gracia, Michoacán.* Mexico City: Universidad Nacional Autónoma de México, 1946.

García Cubas, Antonio. *Diccionario geográfico, histórico y biográfico de los Estados Unidos Mexicanos.* 5 vols. Mexico City: Imp. de Murguía y Sría. de Fomento, 1888–1891.

García Urbizu, Francisco. *Páginas de Zamora y de Michoacán.* Zamora: Talleres Guía, 1965.

González, Luis. *El congreso de Anáhuac.* Mexico City: Cámara de Senadores, 1963.

―――. "Expansión de Nueva España en el Lejano Oriente." *Historia Mexicana* 14, no. 2 (October–December, 1964): 206–226.

―――, et al. *Fuentes de la historia contemporánea de México: Libros y folletos.* 3 vols. Mexico City: El Colegio de México, 1961–1962.

―――, ed. *Los presidentes de México ante la nación: Informes, manifiestos y documentos.* 5 vols. Mexico City: Cámara de Diputados, 1966.

González Godínez, Bernardo. "Industrialización de los subproductos lácteos regionales." Dissertation, Universidad Autónoma de Guadalajara, 1955.

González Navarro, Moisés. "El Porfiriato. La vida social." In *Historia moderna de México,* ed. Daniel Cosío Villegas. Vol. 4. Mexico City: Editorial Hermes, 1957.

Gram, Jorge. *Héctor: Novela histórica cristera.* Mexico City: Editorial Jus, 1953.

Henríquez Ureña, Pedro. *Historia de la cultura en la América Hispánica.* Mexico City: Fondo de Cultura Económica, 1959.

Hernández y Dávalos, Juan. *Colección de documentos para la historia de la guerra de independencia de México de 1808 a 1821.* 6 vols. Mexico City: J. M. Sandoval, 1877–1882.

Herrera y Tordesillas, Antonio de. *Historia general de los hechos de los castellanos en las islas y tierra firme del Mar Océano.* 10 vols. Asunción: Ed. Guarania, 1944–1947.

Huanimba. (Monthly.) Jiquilpan, Mich.

Jiménez Moreno, Wigberto. *Estudios de historia colonial.* Mexico City: Instituto Nacional de Antropología e Historia, 1958.

―――, and Alfonso García Ruiz. *Historia de México: Una síntesis.* Mexico City: Instituto Nacional de Antropología e Historia, 1962.

Junco, Alfonso. *Sangre de Hispania.* Buenos Aires: Espasa-Calpe Argentina, 1940.

Lebrón de Quiñones, Lorenzo. *Relación breve y sumaria de la visita hecha por el Lic. . . . , oidor del Nuevo Reino de Galicia por mandado de su alteza*. Guadalajara: Junta Auxiliar Jalisciense de la Sociedad Mexicana de Geografía y Estadística, 1952.

Lewis, Oscar. *Pedro Martínez*. Mexico City: Joaquín Mortiz, 1966.

———. *Tepoztlán: Village in Mexico*. New York: Holt, Rinehart, and Winston, 1967.

El libro de las tasaciones de pueblos de la Nueva España. Mexico City: Archivo General de la Nación, 1952.

Límites entre Michoacán y Jalisco: Colección de documentos oficiales. Morelia, Mich.: Tipografía de la Escuela I. M. Porfirio Díaz, 1898.

López Portillo y Rojas, José. *La parcela*. Mexico City: Editorial Porrúa, 1945.

López Portillo y Weber, José. *La conquista de la Nueva Galicia*. Mexico City: Talleres Gráficos de la Nación, 1935.

———. *La rebelión de la Nueva Galicia*. Tacubaya: Instituto Panamericano de Geografía e Historia, 1939.

López Velarde, Ramón. *El león y la virgen*. Mexico City: Universidad Nacional Autónoma de México, 1942.

Matesanz, José. "Introducción de la ganadería en Nueva España, 1521–1535." *Historia Mexicana* 14, no. 4 (April–June, 1965): 533–566.

Miranda, José. *España y Nueva España en la época de Felipe II*. Mexico City: Instituto de Historia, 1962.

———. *Humboldt y México*. Mexico City: Universidad Nacional Autónoma de México, Instituto de Historia, 1962.

———. *El tributo indígena en la Nueva España durante el siglo XVI*. Mexico City: El Colegio de México, 1952.

Mota y Escobar, Alonso de la. *Descripción geográfica de los reinos de Nueva Galicia, Nueva Vizcaya y Nuevo León*. Mexico City: Ed. Pedro Robredo, 1940.

Motolinía, Fray Toribio de. *Memoriales*. Mexico City: Luis García Pimentel, ed., 1903.

Muñoz, Fray Diego. *Crónica de la provincia de San Pedro y San Pablo de Michoacán, en la Nueva España*. Guadalajara: Ed. de la Junta Auxiliar Jalisciense de la Sociedad Mexicana de Geografía y Estadística, 1950.

Novo, Salvador. *La vida en México en el período presidencial de Lázaro Cárdenas*. Mexico City: Empresas Editoriales, 1964.

———. *La vida en México en el período presidencial de Manuel Ávila Camacho*. Mexico City: Empresas Editoriales, 1965.

———. *La vida en México en el período presidencial de Miguel Alemán*.

Mexico City: Empresas Editoriales, 1967.

Olivera Sedano, Alicia. *Aspectos del conflicto religioso de 1926 a 1929: Sus antecedentes y consecuencias.* Mexico City: Instituto Nacional de Antropología e Historia, 1966.

Orendain, Leopoldo I., and Salvador Reynoso. *Cartografía de la Nueva Galicia.* Guadalajara: Banco Industrial de Jalisco, 1961.

Ornelas Mendoza y Valdivia, Nicolás Antonio de. *Crónica de la provincia de Santiago de Xalisco.* Guadalajara: Instituto Jalisciense de Antropología e Historia, 1962.

Palacio, Fray Luis del Refugio del. *Santuario de Amacueca: Fuentes de su historia. Relato. Descripción.* Guadalajara: Et Caetera, 1952.

Papeles de la Nueva España. Relaciones geográficas de la diócesis de Michoacán. 1579–1580. 2 vols. Guadalajara: Col. siglo XVI, 1958.

Paso y Troncoso, Francisco del. *Epistolario de la Nueva España, 1505–1818.* 16 vols. Mexico City: Antigua Librería Robredo de J. Porrúa e Hijos, 1939–1942.

Pérez Hernández, José María. *Compendio geográfico del estado de Michoacán de Ocampo.* Mexico City: Imprenta del Comercio, 1872.

———. *Diccionario geográfico, estadístico, histórico y biográfico, de industria y comercio de la República Mexicana.* 4 vols. Mexico City: Imp. Cinco de Mayo, 1874–1876.

Pérez Verdía, Luis. *Apuntes históricos sobre la guerra de independencia en Jalisco.* Guadalajara: Ediciones I.T.G., 1953.

———. *Historia particular del estado de Jalisco desde los primeros tiempos de que hay noticia hasta nuestros días.* 3 vols. Guadalajara: Tipografía de la Escuela de Artes y Oficios, 1910.

Rea, Alonso de la. *Crónica de la orden de N. Seráfico P.S. Francisco, provincia de San Pedro y San Pablo de Mechoacán en la Nueva España.* Mexico City: Imp. de J. R. Barbedillo, 1882.

Redfield, Robert. *Peasant Society and Culture: An Anthropological Approach to Civilization.* Chicago: University of Chicago Press, 1956.

Relación breve y verdadera de algunas de las cosas que sucedieron al padre fray Alonso Ponce en las provincias de la Nueva España siendo comisario general de aquelas partes. 2 vols. Madrid: Imprenta de la viuda de Calero, 1873.

"Relación de las ceremonias y ritos y población y gobierno de los indios de la provincia de Mechuacán (1541)." Facsimile reproduction of the Manuscript c. IV.5 in El Escorial. Madrid: Aguilar, 1956.

Reyes, Alfonso. *Visión de Anáhuac*. Mexico City: El Colegio de México, 1952.

Rius Facius, Antonio. *Méjico cristero: Historia de la ACJM*. Mexico City: Editorial Patria, 1950.

Rodríguez Zetina, Arturo. *Zamora: Ensayo histórico y repertorio documental*. Mexico City: Editorial Jus, 1952.

Romero, José Guadalupe. *Noticias para formar la historia y la estadística del obispado del Michoacán*. Mexico City, 1862.

Romero, José Rubén. *Apuntes de un lugareño*. Mexico City: Populibros La Prensa, 1955.

Romero Flores, Jesús. *Diccionario michoacano de historia y geografía*. Morelia, Mich.: Ed. del Gobierno del Estado, 1960.

Romero Méndez, Salvador. *Ensayos y discursos*. N.p., [1968].

Rubio Lotvin, Boris. *El ejercicio de la medicina en la población de San José de Gracia, Michoacán*. Mexico City: Universidad Nacional Autónoma de México, Editorial Cultura, 1949.

Rulfo, Juan. *Pedro Páramo*. Mexico City: Fondo de Cultura Económica, 1966.

Russell, Bertrand. *Retratos de memoria y otros ensayos*. Buenos Aires: Aguilar, 1962.

Sánchez, Ramón. *Bosquejo estadístico e histórico del distrito de Jiquilpan de Juárez*. Morelia, Mich.: Imp. de E.I.M. Porfirio Díaz, 1896.

Sarmiento, Domingo Faustino. *Facundo: Civilización y barbarie*. Buenos Aires: Editorial Sopena Argentina, 1940.

Sierra, Justo. *Evolución política del pueblo mexicano*. Mexico City: Fondo de Cultura Económica, 1950.

Solórzano Márquez, Jorge. *Informe general sobre la exploración sanitaria de San José de Gracia, Michoacán*. Mexico City: Universidad Nacional Autónoma de México, 1945.

Tello, Fray Antonio. *Crónica miscelánea de la santa provincia de Xalisco*. Guadalajara: Font, 1942–1945.

Torres, Francisco Mariano de. *Crónica de la santa provincia de Xalisco*. Guadalajara: Col. siglo XVI, 1960.

Torres, Mariano de Jesús. *Historia civil y eclesiástica de Michoacán, desde los tiempos antiguos hasta nuestros días*. Morelia, Mich., 1905.

Varron, Marco Terencio. *De las cosas del campo*. With Introduction, Spanish version, and notes by Domingo Tirado Benedí. Mexico City: Universidad Nacional Autónoma de México, 1945.

Villar Villamil, Ignacio de. *Las casas de Villar y de Omaya en Asturias y el mayorazgo de Villar Villamil*. San Sebastián: Imp. y Enc. de J. Baraja e Hijos, 1910.

Villaseñor y Villaseñor, Alejandro. *Biografías de los héroes y caudillos de la independencia*. 2 vols. Mexico City: Editorial Jus, 1962.

Warman Gryg, Arturo. "La danza de moros y cristianos: Un estudio de aculturación." Dissertation, Instituto Nacional de Antropología e Historia, Mexico City, 1968.

Yáñez, Agustín. *Al filo del agua*. Mexico City: Editorial Porrúa, 1947.

Zarco, Francisco. *Historia del Congreso Constituyente, 1856–1857*. Mexico City: El Colegio de México, 1956.